Command at Sea

FOURTH EDITION

Command at Sea

By William P. Mack
Vice Admiral, U.S. Navy, Retired
and
Albert H. Konetzni, Jr.
Commander, U.S. Navy

Naval Institute Press   **Annapolis, Maryland**

Copyright © 1982
by the United States Naval Institute
Annapolis, Maryland

Library of Congress Cataloging in Publication Data
Mack, William P., 1915–
  Command at sea.
  Rev. ed. of: Command at sea / Harley F. Cope. 3d ed.
1967, c1966.
  Bibliography: p.
  Includes index.
  1. Leadership. 2. United States. Navy—Officers'
handbooks. I. Konetzni, Albert H., 1944–   .
II. Cope, Harley Francis, 1898–   . Command at sea.
3d ed. 1967, c1966. III. Title.
VB203.M34 1982   359'.002'02   81–85469
ISBN 0–87021–130–7

Printed in the United States of America

Contents

Acknowledgements

We would like to acknowledge the excellence of the original edition of *Command at Sea* authored by Rear Admiral Harley F. Cope, U.S. Navy, and the last (Third) edition written by Captain Howard Bucknell, III, U.S. Navy. Unfortunately, the passage of time since the publication of the Third Edition in 1966 and the dramatic and widespread changes in naval procedures, ships, equipment, aircraft, and weapons during that time have prevented us from using more than a few paragraphs from former editions. This book is, therefore, almost entirely new.

We would like to acknowledge the encouragement, expertise, and support of the staff of the Naval Institute Press. Acquisitions Editor Richard Hobbs and Press Director Tom Epley gave us a free hand and their confidence, and the Photographic and Art departments under Ms. Patty Maddocks provided many of the photos appearing in the book.

Mr. David Poyer, himself a successful author and book reviewer in Norfolk, Virginia, added the finishing editorial polish to the manuscript. Ms. Barbara Foster, our typist, turned our hand scribbles into clear typewritten copy.

We acknowledge the condensed wisdom of naval experts and philosophers from all ages and eras. We tried to preserve the thoughts of Sun Tzu, Wellington, Theodore Roosevelt, and many others from the past, and at the same time to present the contributions of the present generation. Where possible we have acknowledged quotations and advice from officers and enlisted men of the present, most of whom are still living. You will find advice from such diverse persons as Fleet Admiral Nimitz and Chief Yeoman Matthew Brady.

In most cases it is not practical to acknowledge in detail the contributions of each individual. Much of the philosophical discourse came from conversations, experiences, and statements of naval officers, senior and junior, who served from World War II to the present. This is entirely proper. John Paul Jones may have contributed much to the early American Navy, but it is not really feasible to compare the feats of a few isolated wooden warships with the accomplishments in World War II of the massive Pacific Fleet commanded by Admiral Nimitz. If we are to survive in the future, we must preserve the wisdom of the past, but we must also make use of the knowledge of the present to realize the full potential of the future.

We can list some who have contributed. There were personal conversations with Secretaries of the Navy Gates, Franke, Connally, Ignatius, Nitze, Korth, and Hidalgo; with Admirals Hart, Dennison, Nimitz, Halsey, Burke, Ricketts, and many others; and with other distinguished officers and petty officers of all ranks and grades.

The Oral History program of the Naval Institute, currently headed by Paul Stillwell, was a vast reservoir of naval wisdom.

From the current Navy establishment we were assisted by the Office of the Chief of Information, the staffs of the type commanders of the Atlantic Fleet, and the staffs of the schools for prospective commanding officers of the Atlantic Fleet. Persons in pertinent offices of the Naval Military Personnel Command and other Washington–based commands also gave invaluable assistance.

Finally, we acknowledge the support and patience of our wives and families.

Preface

The first edition of this book, *Command at Sea*, was written by then Captain Harley F. Cope, USN. Later revisions were made by Rear Admiral Cope and Captain Howard Bucknell, III, USN. These editions (the latest in 1966) were aimed at the commanding officer of the small ship, defined as "smaller than a destroyer." Appropriately, they dealt with the mechanics of command and made frequent and full reference to regulations and manuals. In the period in which they were written, ship equipment was relatively unsophisticated, and the requirements for well educated and trained officers and enlisted men much less.

The modern Navy has grown quite rapidly in unit size, complexity, and sophistication. There are fewer ships, but each is much larger than its 1960s' counterpart. The distinction between "small" ships and "large" ships has narrowed. Equipment has changed radically. Nuclear propulsion, high pressure steam plants, gas turbine propulsion, and sustained high speeds are now a way of life. Missiles are ubiquitous, and nuclear ammunition of various kinds can be carried by almost all ships. Communication systems now permit (and demand) instant interplay between the Washington command complex and ships on the far side of the earth.

This latest version is, therefore, not another edition of the original *Command at Sea*, but a new book, written for today's readership, and using an entirely different approach.

This book is intended as a discourse on the art of command; but it will also cover some of the mechanics. The elements of its philosophy have been gathered from acknowledged experts in the field. Some are quoted directly, where this is feasible; where it was not, the essence of their knowledge has been incorporated into the text. Every effort has been made to preserve the wisdom of the older generations of naval experts, but an equal effort was directed toward seeking out and bringing to the reader the opinions and philosophies of more recent commanders. As much as we revere John Paul Jones, he fought in only one war and some additional campaigns, in actions involving only a relative handful of ships and men; some of our modern-day admirals have served in three major wars involving hundreds of ships in both great oceans. Their contributions to the art of command at sea should be timely and important. We found it to be so.

We have assumed that the reader of this volume will have access to *Navy Regulations*, *Naval Military Personnel Command Manual*, and other official publications. The reader's library might also include the many superb Naval Institute Press books covering leadership, administration, and engineering, such as *Naval Shiphandling*, *Watch Officer's Guide*, *Division Officer's Guide*, *Engineering for the Officer of the Deck*, and the *Ops Officer's Manual*. A complete listing can be found in the bibliography. *Command at Sea* is so written that it can be read without these references at hand, but use of them will provide greater depth of understanding and more detailed information. Subjects are covered by referring briefly to the foregoing publications rather than by quoting them extensively. The reader will, therefore, be able to make easy reference to the basic publications.

Commanding officers of all sizes and types of ships should find this work useful. Executive officers and heads of departments should find it helpful in preparing for subsequent command. In addition, we hope all who have gone to sea, or hope to in the future, will find much of interest in it.

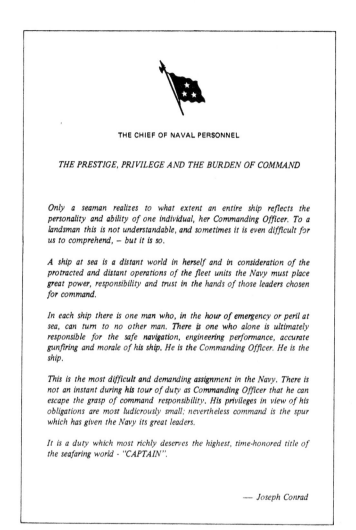

THE CHIEF OF NAVAL PERSONNEL

THE PRESTIGE, PRIVILEGE AND THE BURDEN OF COMMAND

Only a seaman realizes to what extent an entire ship reflects the personality and ability of one individual, her Commanding Officer. To a landsman this is not understandable, and sometimes it is even difficult for us to comprehend, – but it is so.

A ship at sea is a distant world in herself and in consideration of the protracted and distant operations of the fleet units the Navy must place great power, responsibility and trust in the hands of those leaders chosen for command.

In each ship there is one man who, in the hour of emergency or peril at sea, can turn to no other man. There is one who alone is ultimately responsible for the safe navigation, engineering performance, accurate gunfiring and morale of his ship. He is the Commanding Officer. He is the ship.

This is the most difficult and demanding assignment in the Navy. There is not an instant during his tour of duty as Commanding Officer that he can escape the grasp of command responsibility. His privileges in view of his obligations are most ludicrously small; nevertheless command is the spur which has given the Navy its great leaders.

It is a duty which most richly deserves the highest, time-honored title of the seafaring world - "CAPTAIN".

— *Joseph Conrad*

Several years ago a copy of this quotation from the works of Joseph Conrad was sent by the Chief of Naval Personnel to each newly ordered commanding officer. This custom is no longer followed, but the quotation is one which each officer prior to, during, and after command at sea will want to refer to.

Command at Sea

1

Taking Command

Many wonders there be, but naught more wondrous than man. Over the surging sea, with a whitening South wind wan, Through the foam of the firth he makes his perilous way.

—Sophocles, *Antigone*

The Rewards and Responsibilities of Command

The experience of command of a ship at sea is unforgettable; it is without parallel or equal. The responsibility is heavy, but its rewards are priceless. The captain of a United States ship of war stands at the end of a long line of predecessors, ranging from John Paul Jones to Chester Nimitz and Arleigh Burke, and he in turn will pass this mantle of command to the naval officers of future generations.

U.S. Navy Regulations, 1973, state that "the responsibility of the commanding officer for his command is absolute," and that "the authority of the commanding officer is commensurate with his responsibility." These are simple, clear, and binding statements. No amount of explanation can alter their placement of ultimate responsibility, whether for success or failure, squarely on the shoulders of the man in command.

In this respect, though the size of a ship may be important as a measure of her capability or durability, in terms of responsibility and reward the smallest minesweeper is equal to the largest aircraft carrier. The commanding officers of both are "captains," regardless of the number of stripes they wear on their sleeves. Each must assure the safety of his ship and the accomplishment of her missions. The

Figure 1-1. The size of a ship may be important as a measure of its capability or durability, but the commanding officers of the cruiser *Long Beach* and the experimental deep submergence submarine across the pier are both "Captains" regardless of the number of stripes on their sleeves.

penalties for failure and the glories of success bear with equal weight on all commanders, of whatever grade.

To achieve these goals, the commanding officer must work through those he leads; he can accomplish little alone, no matter how brilliant his individual talents. Admiral Chester Nimitz, on the occasion of a call by several of his captains, said, "Commanding a ship is the simplest task in the world, even if at times it seems complicated. A Captain has only to pick good courses of action and to stick to them no matter what. If he is good and generally makes good decisions, his crew will cover for him if he fails occasionally. If he is bad, this fact will soon be known, and he must be removed with the speed of light."

Again, the German general Erwin Rommel once commented that "The commander must try, above all, to establish personal and comradely contact with his men, but without giving away an inch of his authority."

The successful commanding officer, then, must learn to become as one with his wardroom and his crew; yet, at the same time, he must remain above and apart. This unique relationship has been the subject of study and story for centuries. It changes; yet it is timeless. It is a skill that must be mastered in turn by each commander if he is to carry out his task with success.

Two days prior to the Battle of Java Sea, in which HMS *Exeter* would be sunk, her commanding officer, Captain O.L. Gordon, Royal Navy, was having a late evening drink at a Surabaya hotel with a group of young British and American junior officers. One of the American officers asked him how he felt about going to sea the next morning to meet the approaching Japanese naval force. He knew that his ship would have little chance of surviving, but he smiled anyway as he said, "I would not trade all the Queen's jewels for the privilege of commanding *Exeter* tomorrow. I have the finest group of men ever to man a ship of war. They will not fail me, and they know I will not fail my Sovereign. We may not survive, but we will leave our mark." When the battle began, the gigantic battle ensign flown by the *Exeter* was an inspiration to the allied ships which accompanied her. They knew she would be commanded well, and therefore would fight well.

The Americans, the British, and the Germans are not alone in their attitudes toward command. The Soviets are rapidly approaching a similar feeling; the tradition of the sea is overcoming their decades-old policy of attaching a political commissar to each naval vessel to control the commanding officer. This new attitude was expressed by the commander in chief of the Soviet Navy, Admiral of the Fleet Sergei Gorshkov, in *Morsky Sbornik*, the Soviet Naval Digest:

> *The commanding officer of a ship*. Whoever is involved with service at sea knows with what pride and respect those words are re-

garded in the Fleet. This category of naval officers together with the billet are granted considerable rights and authority and are shown a high trust. For that reason the commanding officer of a ship bears a heavy responsibility to the party and to the nation for the warship entrusted to him and for its skillful employment, for the fate of the men under him, and for the armed defense of the freedom and independence of the Soviet homeland and her national interests on the sea.

The demands on the commanding officer of a ship increase with each year; the range of problems that he works out continuously expands; and yet the conditions for fulfilling his responsibilities are becoming more and more complex. In spite of that, every naval officer dreams of commanding a ship. This is due not only to the fact that an officer who has devoted his life to the Navy looks at the ship's bridge as a university for learning and developing organizational abilities and qualities, which make it possible to lead men and to put into practice skills and experience during the accomplishment of the primary missions in defending the interests of the homeland throughout the World Ocean, and as an essential step in filling the highest billets in the Navy.

. . . The extent of the commanding officer's influence on subordinates is determined by his personal merits. Officers, petty officers, and nonrated men carry out the orders and instructions of a commanding officer with diligence and eagerness if they observe in him unquestionable authority earned in the daily contacts with them. That authority lies primarily in the strength of his moral influence on each member of the crew, in his skill in organizing life according to regulations infused with the experience of many generations of Navymen, in his ability to arouse the interests of the individuals and through his personal example, to inspire them to actions, no matter how difficult they may be.

All seagoing nations, then, agree on the responsibilities inherent in command at sea. The rewards are less tangible. Officers of the United States Navy have traditionally sought command at sea to serve their country, with the greatest reward being the personal satisfaction of command.

The Accountability of Command

In navies in general, and in the United States Navy in particular, strict accountability is an integral part of command. Not even the profession of medicine embraces the absolute relationship found at sea. A doctor may lose a patient under trying circumstances and continue to practice; but a naval officer seldom has the opportunity to hazard a second ship.

The Soviets are beginning to understand accountability, as well as responsibility. Their Minister of Defense, Marshal of the Soviet Union Grechko, remarked recently:

> The commanding officer in our Army and Navy is in charge of everything. The success of the ship or unit, whether in peacetime or wartime, depends first and foremost upon him. Indeed, the commanding officer is the organizer of his men's training and education. He is responsible for their lives and their readiness to defend their homeland with dignity and honor. A commanding officer at times must make decisions on his own concerning very important and complex matters. He has an enormous responsibility on his shoulders. And he must use discretion, thoroughly analyze the situations as they develop, and resolutely struggle to accomplish the missions assigned to his ship.

Apparently the Soviets have discovered that the doctrine of accountability does not permit a political commissar to share responsibility and authority. They, too, now realize that the commanding officer must be the sole person accountable.

There have, at times, been those who question the strict and undeviating application of accountability in the Navy, but those who have been to sea have always closed ranks against the doubters. Even our land-dwelling brothers recognize the importance of accountability at sea. In 1952, for example, the destroyer *Hobson* collided with an aircraft carrier during night flight operations. Damage was extensive, and loss of life was heavy. There were extenuating circumstances, but the *Wall Street Journal* of May, 1952, in a frequently-quoted discussion of the disaster, concluded:

Figure 1-2. The ultimate arena of responsibility, collision at sea. The USS *John F. Kennedy*, shown here shortly after her collision with the USS *Belknap*, suffered relatively-little damage.

> On the sea there is a tradition older than the traditions of the country itself—it is the tradition that with responsibility goes authority and with them both goes accountability.
>
> It is cruel, this accountability of good and well intentioned men. But the choice is that or an end to responsibility and finally, as the cruel sea has taught, an end to the confidence and trust in the men who lead. For men will not long trust leaders who feel themselves beyond accountability for what they do.

The enormous burden of this responsibility and accountability for the lives and careers of other men and, often, the outcome of great issues is the reason for the liberality of orders to officers commanding ships of the United States Navy. The inexperienced officer may erroneously take this liberality to reflect vagueness or indecision on the part of superiors. Nothing could be further from the truth. It is

Figure 1-3. The *Belknap* in her collision with the USS *John F. Kennedy* suffered heavy damage and many casualties. Responsibility was found to rest with her commanding officer.

provided to give the commander the flexibility necessary to carry out his orders.

One incident in more recent years led to some speculation that the Navy had changed its attitude toward the doctrine of absolute accountability of command. The incident began with the collision of the USS *Belknap*(CG-29) and the USS *John F. Kennedy*(CV-67), in which the *Belknap* lost eight men and suffered $100,000,000 in damage. The tragic results of the collision are shown in the accompanying photographs.

The court-martial process which followed caused many naval officers to draw erroneous conclusions. To counteract this, the Chief of Naval Operations, Admiral J.L. Holloway III, issued a memorandum dated 2 October 1976. The entire text of this document, which sets forth the circumstances of the collision and of the consequent administrative and judicial processes, is included as Appendix X.

The essence of misunderstanding, according to this memorandum, was in two related areas. First, the charges against the officer of the deck included manslaughter, and the charges against the *Belknap*'s commanding officer, although not actually stating so, were interpreted by many to allege criminal action. These two supposed allegations seemed to indicate a new direction in court-martial proceedings in a collision case. Second, the commanding officer was acquitted, leading many to speculate that the doctrine of responsibility was being discounted. The CNO's memorandum pointed out that the court-martial proceedings were correct, that the acquittal of the *Belknap*'s captain was legal and proper, but that he was still fully responsible for the collision. He was otherwise punished, and thus the doctrine of responsibility remained (and remains) intact.

In view of the notoriety of this case and its subsequent misinterpretations, you may wish to review Appendix X and draw your own conclusions.

The Independence of the Commander

Traditionally, American commanding officers have been directed to accomplish missions without being told specifically *how* to do so. Occasionally they may be referred to doctrine or example about how their tasks might be performed, or how they have been carried out in the past. The choice of action, however, remains theirs to make; it is required only that their methods support intelligently the objectives of command.

In recent years, however, this traditional independence has been modified in practice. The issue today is not too much liberality, but rather a growing tendency of high command to exercise control in too great detail. There are two factors contributing to this trend. First, command in the present-day atmosphere of worldwide political unrest requires of each captain a detailed knowledge of international affairs, so that the objectives of our government can be effectively furthered. Inappropriate action, even by the smallest ship, can result in instant embarrassment to all, and today's press can be counted on to magnify any error. Second, our ships today are in almost instantaneous communication via satellite with the command structure at home, up to and including the Commander-in-Chief.

An excellent example of this narrowing of command prerogative is the "*Flying Arrow* incident." In the early 1950s, a shipping line magnate named Isbrandtsen decided to challenge the U.S. government's proscription of trade with mainland China. He began to send merchant ships, including the *Flying Arrow*, to Shanghai for cargo.

The United States countered by establishing a destroyer patrol in international waters off the mouth of the Yangtze, and the British did the same. Both patrols were given the mission of preventing the entry of U.S. and British ships into Shanghai. They stayed for several weeks, until Mr. Isbrandtsen decided to discontinue his efforts. One of the U.S. commanding officers later described the situation. As his ship neared the U.S. destroyer he was to relieve, a whaleboat met him containing a young naval officer, who carried two briefcases with four fat notebooks full of instructions and dispatches. The relieving CO read through these in somewhat less than four hours and then wearily sent the usual "I relieve you" message. His week on station passed without incident, other than that he added a fifth notebook full of lengthy advice and direction which poured in steadily all week via radio. Some weeks later, he encountered one of his British opposites in a Hong Kong hotel bar. After a drink or two, he recounted his consternation over the amount of direction he had received. His British friend commiserated. The American then asked him what kind of direction he had received. His commodore, the Briton said, had told him to proceed to the patrol area, relieve the other chap, and "protect the King's interest."

Perhaps someday the United States Navy will return to this idyllic state, but the odds are against it. Future commanding officers should expect explicit directions, and learn to live with them.

Notwithstanding these occasional hazards of command, the rewards make the exercise of it worthwhile. The facility of communications may have narrowed a captain's prerogatives somewhat, but no matter how much "help" he receives, it will be he, and he alone, who will make the final decision to fire or not to fire. If one succeeds in spite of this and other difficulties, he will be rewarded with further opportunities. If he experiences failure, he can still leave his ship with the knowledge that he sought out and undertook the ultimate challenge, command at sea.

Orders to Command

Orders to take command come in varied forms. They range from dispatch orders directing immediate relief to letter orders permitting attendance at various intermediate schools, visits, and briefings. Ideally, an overlap of ten to fourteen days is provided for, but emergencies may reduce this to zero. Nuclear surface ships, fast attack submarines, and the onboard crew of ballistic missile submarines will have the longest turnover periods, usually of thirty days, to permit the prospective commanding officer to observe the operation, maintenance, and readiness of the propulsion plant, as well as fulfilling other relieving requirements.

If time permits, the officer who is to be relieved should immediately inform his newly designated successor of the ship's operating schedule and upcoming locations. The oncoming officer should in turn inform him of the date he expects to report (unless the orders specify an exact reporting date). This exchange should enable both to determine the length of turnover, the relief date, and the employment of the ship during this period.

Once these matters have been settled, both officers can then begin preparations for the change of command.

Preparations for Change of Command

Navy Regulations, Article 0707, and appropriate type commander's instructions both provide guidance for the change of command process. *Navy Regulations* requires that both officers inspect the ship, exercise the crew at general quarters and general drills, discuss any defects that may be present, and transfer all unexecuted orders, official correspondence, and information concerning the command and its personnel. Specific requirements include a current audit of the post office, if any, the turnover of magazine and other keys, and an inventory and audit of registered publications. The officer being relieved must complete and sign fitness reports, logs, books, journals, and other required documents.

Each type commander requires some augmentation or variation in these basic procedures.

Generally, all of these requirements can be met on conventionally-powered vessels in from seven to ten days, regardless of the ship's employment. A busy schedule will make completion in four days difficult. Less than four days will require considerable cooperation and perhaps some rearrangement of priorities.

Ideally, the turnover period should be long enough to permit the new commander to determine the combat readiness of the ship, primarily by observing pertinent general drills. A ship whose crew performs well at general quarters and other drills related to her mission, which has the required number of specially-qualified personnel (such as air controllers and boiler tenders), and which has no equipment, material, or supply deficiencies, can be assumed to be combat-ready. In wartime, of course, this determination is vital and should be given first priority. In peacetime, other qualifications should take precedence, and the determination of combat readiness can be less thorough. In peacetime, give primary attention to determining that the ship can navigate safely and that, put simply, it will not burn, explode, or sink. If only a limited period is available for turnover, it should be used to determine that the ship has the charts, personnel, and equipment to navigate safely, that fire and collision bills are adequate, that qualified fire fighting and damage control personnel are on board and properly assigned, and that potential dangers such as ammunition, fuel oil, nuclear fuel, and nuclear munitions are stored, accounted for, and used safely. These areas must be brought under control immediately. Others can wait.

As the relieving officer, you should review carefully with the previous commanding officer the handling characteristics of the ship. Ask how she accelerates and handles in various sea states. If you are not familiar with the ship type from previous assignments, you will have to take much of this information on faith until you gain experience. It will be helpful, if you have some uncertainties, to review the appropriate sections of *Naval Shiphandling*, published by the Naval Institute Press.

Assuming that you have four days or longer for the turnover, however, these high-priority items can then be augmented. After ship's safety items, the next concern should be a thorough determination of combat readiness. Each type commander has requirements for numbers of specially qualified officers and petty officers for each class of ship. These should be checked, and noted as exceptions if necessary. All armament should be operable, or noted if not. Propulsion machinery should be capable of pushing the ship to its designed speed. Check the supply status carefully, especially in small ships without supply corps officers. Ammunition, spare parts, and consumable supplies should be present; discrepancies should be noted.

Once these essentials have been disposed of, any remaining time should be spent on the items listed below. These should be covered, if possible, before the change of command; if not, check into them as soon thereafter as you can.

1. Read the fleet, type, and unit commander's instructions.

2. Start the process for updating your security clearance, if this has not already been done.

3. Forward a photograph and a short biography to the Chief of Naval Information. This is in addition to the photo and biography required for the Naval Military Personnel Command by *NAVMILPERSMAN*, paragraph 5020140.

4. Review the last administrative inspection check list, the last material, supply, and medical inspection check lists, last operational readiness inspection check lists, naval technical proficiency inspection results, and, for nuclear-powered ships, the recent operational reactor safeguards examination results. Note trends in all these areas, as well as in radiological health comments, ship's own proficiency monitoring program comments, and quality assurance deficiencies.

5. Study the ship's organization, the ship's orders, and the type commander's orders and manuals.

6. Review financial areas other than the post office and commissary. Most ships have individual wardroom and other mess funds and other small accounts.

7. Review the ship's classified files and the prescribed methods of handling such correspondence.

8. Familiarize yourself with the current ship's maintenance program, shipalts, ordalts, and authorized minor alterations equivalent to repairs.

9. Review the status of the 3-M and personnel qualifications standards (PQS) programs.
10. Review the status of the ship's operating target (OPTAR) fund. Again, each type commander has a different method of handling this, and you should familiarize yourself with it.

Along with the keys referred to in *Navy Regulations*, various type commanders may require the commanding officer to assume personal custody of additional keys or safe combinations, such as reactor compartment keys, scram breaker keys, and weapon firing keys. On ships without permanently assigned medical officers, you or the XO may have custody of the supply of narcotics, alcohol, and other accountable drugs.

Finally, with all these "do's," one "don't:" *don't* read the fitness reports rendered by the outgoing commanding officer. Each of your officers deserves a fresh start. Instead, review the officers' qualification jackets, the chief petty officers' jackets, and as many of the records of the leading petty officers as time will permit. Look for qualifications rather than past performance. Review all career counselors' records, looking for effectiveness in complying with administrative policy.

Do not forget, in the welter of detail, that if convenient both commanding officers should call informally on your unit commander. You will be calling on him formally after taking command, but some unit commanders like to meet their new subordinate as soon as possible, and to be consulted regarding date and plans for the change of command.

The remarks above should provide sufficient guidance in most cases to conduct an efficient relief. There exist two special circumstances, however, which require deviation from normal procedure. First, a ship in a navy yard or repair facility obviously cannot meet the requirements for conducting general quarters and drills. In this case, the new commanding officer should concentrate on those drills (such as the fire drill) that will maintain the ship in a safe condition. The second circumstance is when an officer reports to relieve where there is no regularly detailed commanding officer present. Examples of this would be where the previous commander has been detached without relief, summarily relieved, or had died. In such cases the procedures prescribed by *Navy Regulations* should be followed as closely as possible.

Report of Transfer of Command

Navy Regulations, Article 0707, requires that a letter report of the routine change of command be prepared and signed by the officer relieved and endorsed by the man relieving him. This letter should be addressed to the immediate superior, with copies to the Chief of Naval Operations and others in the chain of command.

This letter report should be given careful attention. Be sure that all substantial deficiencies affecting the operational readiness and safety of the ship are listed. Note any propulsive and other machinery which is inoperative, armament which is not fully ready, and lack of full allowances of spare parts, munitions, or supplies. List all personnel shortages, whether in numbers, ratings, or special qualifications. It is not expected that all minor deficiencies will be listed; those chosen should be a matter of your professional judgment.

If the letter indicates the possible existence of unsatisfactory conditions, it should include both the opinion of the succeeding officer and an explanation by endorsement by the officer being relieved, if necessary.

The Change of Command Ceremony

Now that you have made all the required examinations and inspections, you are ready to take part in the tradition-laden ceremony of the change of command. For your part, you should prepare a copy of your orders with abbreviations and officialese removed or translated. Customarily, the relieving officer does not make a speech, so no further preparation is required.

Navy Regulations, Article 0707-1i, provides that at the time of turning over command all hands should be mustered, that the officer about to be relieved shall read his orders of detachment and formally turn over the command to his successor, and that this officer should then read his orders in turn and assume command.

This is a simple and straightforward requirement. Prior to World War II it was usually carried out strictly as set forth. Guests were seldom, if ever, invited, and usually only the unit commander attended. Since the war, however, it has become customary to invite numerous civilian guests, family members, the chain of command, and the commanding officers of all ships present. The arrangements are entirely the prerogative of the incumbent commanding officer. He schedules the ceremony, issues the invitations, and announces the time and place of the change of command to the SOPA and to all ships present. The oncoming commanding officer sends his invitation list to his predecessor.

In spite of this, you should at least be familiar with the procedure to be followed. The best overall reference is *Naval Ceremonies, Customs, and Traditions*, published by the U.S. Naval Institute Press. We will, however, touch on the salient points to be arranged.

The change of command ceremony should, if possible, be a full-dress affair, held in a dignified and ceremonious setting. It is important to emphasize that it is an all hands evolution; all members of the crew should attend. Also, the officers and men should be so informed and stationed (if possible) so that they and the two commanding officers are facing each other. The recent usage of inviting large numbers of guests has sometimes resulted in the guests occupying the front of the ceremonial area, with the officers and crew being stuffed in around the edges. This is not in keeping with the spirit of *Navy Regulations*. The ceremony itself was established so that the outgoing commander could bid farewell to *all* of his officers and men, and so that the new captain could see and be seen by all. Admiral Claude Ricketts, one of our finest administrators, felt strongly about this point. He always insisted that *all* officers and men face him directly whenever he took part in a change of command ceremony.

For official guests, of course, appropriate arrangements must be made for reception and seating. Usually, they will be received with proper honors at the quarterdeck and escorted to their seats. After the arrival of the senior guest, the official party (usually the master at arms, the chaplain, the two commanding officers, the unit commander, and guest speakers, if any) proceeds to the ceremonial area, where the executive officer will be waiting to act as a master of ceremonies.

The ceremony proper will proceed as follows. First, the chaplain will give his invocation. The outgoing captain then makes his remarks of farewell to the crew. At the conclusion of his remarks he reads his orders, turns to his successor, salutes, and says, "Sir, I am ready to be relieved."

The relieving officer returns his salute and then, either with or without an introduction by the executive officer, reads his orders. Upon finishing, he turns to his predecessor, salutes, and says, "I relieve you, Sir." If his next superior in command is present, he should then turn to him, salute once more, and say, "Sir, I report for duty." Traditionally the relieving commanding officer does not make a speech; you may say, however, "All orders of my predecessor remain in effect." It is also permissible to make brief remarks wishing your predecessor well and stating your pleasure at assuming command.

The ceremony proper then closes with a benediction, after which the executive officer announces the social arrangements. Officers and their guests usually take refreshments in the wardroom, the chief petty officers in their mess, and the remainder of the crew in the mess hall, recreation room, or other appropriate area. When this announcement is over, "attention on deck" is called to allow the official party to leave.

During the social activities following the ceremony, both commanding officers should try to visit all areas where guests are being entertained. This will be a busy period for you, since you will also have to be alert to tend the side for the departure of official guests, but it is a worthwhile way to begin to meet your crew.

The order and manner in which the change of command ceremony should be conducted, as well as a sketch of the ceremonial area, is contained in the sample order presented as Appendix I.

Courtesies Due a Relieved Commanding Officer

Remember that *Navy Regulations*, Article 0707–2, provides that the officer relieved, although without official authority after turning over his command, is entitled to all the ceremonies and distinctions accorded to him while he was captain. When departing, he should be given side honors appropriate to a commanding officer, and should be offered the use of the gig. Some ships use officers and CPOs as side boys, a remnant of times past, when officers rowed their old captain ashore.

The officer relieved should make every effort to depart promptly and completely. If possible, most or all of his baggage should be disembarked before the ceremony. If circumstances render it impossible for him to depart the area promptly, he should arrange for temporary accommodations ashore or on a tender.

Upon Taking Command

When the relieved commanding officer and the guests have departed, your real work begins at last. The first requirement, once again—as it will always be—is to ensure that the ship and her crew are in safe condition and able to perform as required. There are also administrative requirements to take care of. Ensure that a log entry has been made recording the change of commanding officers, the fact that the required inspections have been made, and the detachment of the former commander. Ensure that the personnel diaries have been changed accordingly. Finally, even though you may have announced at the ceremony that all orders and instructions of your predecessor remain in effect, you should also issue a written order saying this. Either endorse the old standing night orders or issue new ones.

The next item of business will be the making of calls. *Navy Regulations*, Article 1040, requires that an officer assuming command shall, at the first opportunity thereafter, make an official visit to the senior to whom he has reported for duty. Appropriate uniforms for the calling officer and his boat crew are prescribed. A return call can be expected within twenty-four hours, or as soon as possible.

Naval Ceremonies, Customs, and Traditions sets forth current Navy usage concerning official and unofficial calls in greater detail. As for unofficial (social) calls, if your ship is in home port for the relief, you and your wife should call on your unit commander and his wife as soon as possible.

This may also be a good time to let your executive officer know your own policy regarding calls, so that he in turn can inform your officers.

The senior officer present should be considered next. *Navy Regulations*, Article 0909, requires that all commanding officers keep themselves informed of his identity. They further provide that the commander of each unit shall inform him of the orders under which he is acting, to the extent permitted, and of the condition of his command. When circumstances permit, he should also call on him. This is usually interpreted, however, to require such action only in a foreign or isolated port. At a stateside base, with many ships constantly leaving and arriving, SOPA will usually declare that all calls are considered made and returned.

If your ship is in a navy yard, however, you should call upon the shipyard commander, and if alongside a tender you should call upon her captain as a matter of course.

Now that you have provided for the safety of your command, taken care of immediate administrative matters, and carried out the necessary social amenities, you can give thought to promulgating your philosophy of command.

Philosophy of Command

Throughout his long years of preparation for command, every naval officer studies leadership texts, observes his seniors, and gradually formulates certain thoughts and ideas concerning the proper way for him to lead.

You should now be eager to put these ideas to the test of practice. Your officers and men are waiting to find out what your policies are. How will you communicate your ideas to them?

The new commanding officer can do this in several ways. Some men have chosen the simple passage of time and events to reveal their philosophy of command. They never openly defined it. Many

Figure 1-4. The commanding officer should communicate with his crew in the manner best suited to his personality—closed circuit television, speeches, or personal exchanges with small groups.

successful commanders have taken this path, particularly those not skilled in making speeches.

Most commanding officers, however, have found it better to establish a quick rapport with their officers and men by addressing them directly and as soon as practicable. This initial address need not be long, formal, or all inclusive; but it should be carefully prepared, and it should include the most important elements of command.

What are these elements? Our first source for them is Article 5947, Title 10, *U.S. Code*. The Congress of the United States has stated very clearly in this law the basic elements of American command philosophy. According to the *Code*:

> Commanding officers and others in authority in the naval service are required to show in themselves a good example of virtue, honor, patriotism, and subordination. They will be vigilant in inspecting the conduct of all persons, they will guard against and suppress dissolute

and immoral practices. They will correct those practices according to regulations. They will take all necessary and proper measures under the laws, regulations, and customs to promote and safeguard the morale, physical wellbeing, and general welfare of the officers and enlisted personnel under their command.

These requirements are law. You must meet them all.

There are, however, additional elements of the philosophy of command which you should consider now, at the very beginning of your tenure. The elements and discussions which follow were carefully chosen from the writings on leadership listed in the bibliography, and from conversations with, and excerpts from the writings of, many naval leaders of recent years, including admirals Nimitz, Spruance, Burke, Dennison, Rickover, Ricketts, and many others. You may want to include some of their thoughts (in your own words) in your speeches or talks with your officers and men. Others may not fit your style of command; but you should think about them all.

The first element of command is to *know your ship*. This requirement is increasingly important. Fifty years ago an entire warship was less complicated than today's nuclear reactor or gun or missile mount.

You will most likely begin this effort with the general principles of engineering and science that you learned in your school days, backed up by your service education and training. You will have to apply these general principles to the specific equipment on your ship. As soon as you can, you must know as much as possible, preferably as much or more than any of your subordinates, about the workings of your ship. There will be manuals available and there will be many officers and enlisted men aboard whose brains you can pick. This can be done without "losing face." A chief petty officer doesn't expect you to know all his machinery the day you step aboard. He will tell you all he knows if you approach him correctly. Don't seem to be interested, *be* interested.

Whatever your leadership style, don't slight this requirement. Admiral Rickover has said on many occasions that the most important ingredient of leadership is *knowledge*.

Expect others to know the ship. If you have shown your own interest in a thorough knowledge of the ship, and made it plain to your officers and men that you expect the same from them, you will find that they will respond eagerly. This means hard work: arranging classes, making time available, and providing paths of advancement and qualification for all officers and men. But the rewards will be great, both for them and for you.

Theodore Roosevelt was an assistant secretary of the Navy before he became president, and an acknowledged naval expert of his times. In an address before the graduating class of the Naval Academy, in 1892, he reminded the new officers: "It cannot be too often repeated that in modern war, the chief factor in achieving triumph is what has been done in the way of thorough organization and training before the beginning of war." This truth is age-old; the Greek historian Thucydides wrote in his *History of the Peloponnesian Wars*, "They (the Athenians) had learned that true safety was to be found in long previous training and not in eloquent exhortations uttered when they were going into action."

Know your officers and men. There is a wealth of information about your officers and men in their various personnel records. You should review them; but even more important, you should meet and come to know personally as many of your crew as possible. This does not mean over-familiarity, however. Not only will that reduce your effectiveness, but your men won't like it, either.

Fleet Admiral Ernest J. King had a reputation as a rather crusty and unapproachable individual; yet his biography, Thomas B. Buell's *Master of Sea Power*, reveals him as a master at the art of relationships with his crew. King took great pains to know his officers and men. He found out their strengths and weaknesses. He helped them in every way possible when he was their commanding officer, and for years afterward as well. They responded to this care, disguised behind "crustiness" as it was, with loyal, dedicated performance.

Be loyal and honest. Let it be known that you expect to be honest in your dealings with higher authority, as well as with your subordinates. Never tolerate the covering up of unsavory facts. Require that all reports for transmission to higher authority be honest and thorough. In the other direction, give honest enlisted performance evaluations, and prepare officer fitness reports which recognize good performance but which also point out shortcomings. Failure to do the former stifles initiative. Failure to do the latter allows poor performers to discourage those who perform well.

Keep your crew informed. Any man will do his job better if he knows what is to be done and when it has to be finished. This can best be done by requiring your executive officer to give attention to the plan of the day. This is an excellent medium for informing the crew. Other commanders prefer to pass word down through the chain of command, in order to enhance the positions of those in the chain. Men feel better knowing that their immediate superiors know what is going on and are ready to pass "the word" on to him. The employment schedule is particularly important to morale; if security permits, publish it and pass any changes as soon as possible.

On smaller ships, information is readily passed in these traditional ways. On larger ships, the dissemination of word to the entire crew was once quite difficult. Now, however, all large ships and many smaller ones have internal television systems.

Use of this new medium is an ideal way for a commanding officer to reach the maximum number of his crew in a short time, while preserving a personal touch. It is ideal, that is, *if* you are a good speaker, *if* you have a personality that comes across well on camera, and *if* you don't over-use it. If you can meet these requirements, by all means use TV. There is no other way that the captain of an aircraft carrier can reach five thousand men, or that a cruiser captain at sea can take time out to talk to all of his officers and men. When preparing a television appearance, keep these hints in mind. Prepare your remarks carefully, memorize them, and then learn to speak without notes. Rehearse with the camera before going live. Try for a relaxed and natural stance, with your hands practically *anchored* somewhere. You'll become a better "actor" with experience; but above all, be natural, honest, sincere, and forthright. The American bluejacket will quickly spot any other attitude.

If you don't feel you're right for TV, you needn't appear that often. Delegate routine information-passing to someone who does it well. In any case, *don't* use television too much. Make the Captain's appearance an unusual and anticipated event, rather than a common and boring one.

The ship's internal communications (1MC) system is a secondary means of communication with the crew in large ships, and the main means in a smaller one. Use it when you need it, but the same ground rules apply as for television.

If you are simply a poor speaker (and, frankly, your upward mobility as a naval officer will be difficult if you are), perhaps you had best limit yourself to written messages in the plan of the day.

Personal demeanor. Next to knowing your ship and its crew, the most important aspect of command is the demeanor of the commanding officer. He should, of course, display all the personal characteristics of a naval officer, as John Paul Jones defined them; but he must go far beyond these minimums. He must in all that he does be confident, self-disciplined, and cheerful. All who observe him should draw the conclusion that he knows his business thoroughly and is prepared to carry it out. At the same time, he must show patience with others. He should never relax his standards, but he should react to violations of them by others in a constructive manner. Swearing and outbursts of temper are not acceptable methods of correction. Firm direction with early follow-up is better.

A good commanding officer must understand human nature and the motivation of men. He must be able to reconcile the differences between subordinates of strong character so that they cooperate rather than collide. His personal demeanor must radiate energy; he must appear to be strongly determined to achieve his goals. He must electrify his subordinates, but remain personally cool while doing so.

The tone of the ship. Even the smallest ship, undergoing the most demanding employment, can maintain an excellent tone. The first thing contributing to a good tone is appearance. Let your crew know that you want a combat-ready ship, clean at all times, and you will get it. Frequent and thorough sweepdowns will do more to keep up everyday appearances than excess painting and scrubbing, and will generate pride in those doing the work. Again, most Navymen know that a ship's boats and their crews indicate the tone of a ship. The competence, conduct, and appearance of the bridge and quarterdeck watches is another sure clue. Finally, a ship is also known by the appearance of its wardroom mess and the genial warmth displayed by its members to guests.

Admiral Raymond A. Spruance was a master at setting the tone of a ship. The early chapters of Buell's biography of him, *The Quiet Warrior*, describe the way he produced quiet confidence in his officers by showing them he trusted them. When a potentially dangerous situation began to develop underway, the then Captain Spruance would ask what the officer of the deck intended to do, rather than giving specific orders to solve the problem. His officers soon learned that he trusted them, that he would let them take the initiative when danger threatened, right up until the last minute, when he would take charge. The tone of this bridge and quarterdeck was one of quiet confidence and professional ability. The attitude belowdecks was the same, for Spruance insisted that his officers foster the same relationships with their juniors that he had demonstrated to them. His ships were superbly commanded, and they had superb tone as well.

Recreation and rest. There will never be a time when *something* will not demand your personal attention as commanding officer. The same can be said, though in lesser degree, of your officers and chiefs. Nevertheless, time must be provided for rest and recreation; team and individual athletic opportunities must be made available even at the occasional expense of other, normally more important duties. Again, you must set the example. A tired commanding officer can be a danger; so can an exhausted fireroom watch. Exhaustion in order to meet a one-time challenge or emergency is acceptable; chronic fatigue to compensate for poor planning is not.

The British are traditionally considered more reserved and less democratic than we Americans. However, we can sometimes learn from them in the area of relationships between officers and enlisted men. As Lord Moran, a noted British student of naval affairs, wrote, in his *Anatomy of Courage*:

Figure 1-5. Recreation and physical exercise at sea are a "must." They produce a happy ship and a healthy crew.

Team games, in which officers play with their men, have great value, as do aquatics such as pulling and sailing races. And the leader will find that he will get to know his men far better in the relaxed conditions provided by recreation rather than in the constricted circumstances of his ship or barracks. Nearly all young men have a desire to excel in some game or sport, and the leader should, therefore, go to great lengths to find out where each man's talent and interest lie. Then he must try to meet his needs——at any rate occasionally. The poor performer requires special encouragement to develop such skills as he does possess, or he will feel left out of all corporate activity

. . . The object always to be borne in mind is to make them feel that they *belong*.

Another great believer in athletics was Admiral Thomas C. Hart, who served with great distinction as commander in chief, U.S. Asiatic Fleet, in the years preceding the outbreak of World War II and until its dissolution in that conflict. Prior to Pearl Harbor, his ships spent many months patrolling and searching the Pacific in close to wartime conditions. Admiral Hart made every effort during this period to keep sports programs going in spite of the difficulties. On the occasion of awarding the Hart trophy to a destroyer division for winning the fleet championship in swimming, he remarked, "I am glad to see that this team is composed of both officers and enlisted men. There is no better way to learn to fight together than to play together. I want to see both individual and team athletics continued at a high tempo. This is the surest way of getting ready physically to go to war."

Boldness. Many of the tactical evolutions routinely performed by small, fast warships place them in what a merchant marine officer would recognize immediately as *in extremis*. The considered yet bold acceptance of this continual hazard must be an integral part of a small ship captain's makeup. He must train himself to make quick decisions at the conn, with the engineering plant, and with his weapons; and his reactions must be based on knowledge, so that they are sound and correct. Recklessness has no place at sea, but without boldness our small ships cannot realize their potential.

Boldness is not the property of a ship as a whole. It is an attitude of the commanding officer and the officers serving under him, and it must be fostered, tempered, and encouraged, never killed off because of occasional troublesome aspects.

Fleet Admiral William F. Halsey established a new high in naval tradition for aggressiveness. Long after he retired, he met with seven other officers to serve as pallbearers for a friend. The funeral service took place in a quiet old Maryland churchyard. While waiting for the family to gather, Halsey chatted quietly with the others, many of whom had served under him in the Pacific. One of them asked how he felt about his aggressive reputation. He replied, "Most of the strategists think I was a poor strategist, and maybe they were right, but I had to execute a lot of their strategic plans that wouldn't have worked if I hadn't pushed them boldly and aggressively."

During Admiral Arleigh Burke's unprecedented third term as Chief of Naval Operations, he made many trips by air to make appearances and speeches. Whenever possible, he took a small group of junior officers with him as observers. While enroute, he used the travel time to pass on his advice and wisdom to these future leaders. One of them once asked him how he felt about the attack. The question obviously hit him in a vital spot. "Son," he replied, "you decide how you want to make your attack, and be sure you have a sound and simple plan. Then you hit him with everything you have. Do it *fast*. If your ship can't make 31 knots, crank it up as fast as it will go. Then pound! pound! pound! You may think the enemy isn't yielding, but if you keep it up he'll weaken, and suddenly you'll break through."

Admirals Halsey and Burke were the equals of any tactical commanders of any era. Every commanding officer can learn from their sound and timeless advice.

It is sometimes hard to remember in peacetime service, but captains are, in fact, paid for their boldness. You should reflect on the fact that, in the ultimate contact with an enemy, it is you and your ship who will first bear this violence. Conversely, it is you and your ship who will first have the opportunity to inflict damage. In war, the first blow is worth ten others. Certainly planning, caution, and sagacity are demanded prior to the engagement; but upon contact with the enemy, the nation requires the utmost from its captains in calculated destructive effort. You must instill in your entire ship's company the desire to fight, for this is the ultimate reason for taking a naval vessel to sea.

Admiral Lord Louis Mountbatten, in a conversation about the necessity for boldness, said that he kept on his desk the same bit of poetic advice which he understood had also graced the desk of Admiral Cunningham. It was written by the Marquis of Montrose, and it should be remembered by every commanding officer:

> He either fears his fate too much
> or his deserts are small
> That dares not put it to the touch
> To gain or lose it all.

Appendix VII, a letter by Admiral Burke on the occasion of his retirement, may furnish more ideas for your own command philosophy.

Finally, having delved at length into the serious side of leadership, having considered the advice of the greatest naval experts, you will do well to look at the lighter side for a moment to regain your perspective. Vice Admiral Roland Smoot, one of the finest ship commanders of World War II and a veteran of the Bureau of Naval Personnel, often repeated his "four rules of life." He claimed no personal credit for these pearls of wisdom, however, stating that he had them from Rear Admiral Thomas Sprague, who in turn thought they had come from Ambassador Dwight Morrow. They may serve to lighten your first days in command.

1. Don't take yourself too seriously.
2. Don't take the other fellow too seriously.
3. Don't let the other fellow know that you know that he is a son of a bitch.
4. Don't ever get into a contest with a skunk.

If this doesn't relax you a little, procure and post over your mirror the rules of that ancient and wise man, Satchell Paige, the baseball pitcher. There are several wonderful bits of advice in them, but the last is the best: "Don't look back. Someone might be overtaking you."

Look ahead, don't take yourself too seriously, and resolve above all to enjoy every minute of *your* command tour. The day of your relief will come all too soon.

2

New Construction

And see! She stirs!
She starts—she moves—she seems to feel
The thrill of life along her keel,
And, spurning with her foot the ground,
With one exulting, joyous bound,
She leaps into the ocean's arms.

—Longfellow, *The Building of the Ship*

The significance of the commissioning process was aptly described by Fleet Admiral Chester Nimitz on a cold day in 1965. Retired, but in full uniform for the launching of USS *America*, he ran his ancient but still bright eyes over the great carrier, and remarked to the Secretary of the Navy, William B. Franke: "The birth of a ship really occurs at the point when the sponsor declares that she christens it . . . and the inert magnificent bulk of previously dead steel comes alive and moves increasingly rapidly toward its natural element, salt water."

Placing a new warship in commission, reactivating an old vessel, or recommissioning a modernized one—these are among the most challenging tasks a naval officer can undertake. Should you be assigned as a prospective commanding officer, you will have the job of forming a single fighting ship from millions of individual components, and of forming a crew from servicemen drawn from duty stations around the world. The degree of your success will be a func-

Figure 2-1. The fleet ballistic missile submarine *Ohio* is rolled out of her assembly building for final assembly and testing. Commissioning a new ship is a demanding test of the engineering abilities of her prospective commanding officer.

tion of your work, study, organization, and training during the long-drawn-out process of readying a ship for sea.

The PCO Represents the Fleet

From the very beginning of the construction process, you must remember that the task of the prospective commanding officer (PCO) can be described very simply. He is the representative of the forces afloat. As such, he must work with both shipyard and Navy representatives to ensure that his ship is the best product possible, delivered in a timely, safe, and cost-effective manner.

The duties of a PCO are clearly defined by *Navy Regulations,* headquarters instructions, and type commander's policies. By virtue of his assignment alone, he generally has no independent authority over the preparation of his ship for service until she is commissioned. However, he is still expected to set the standards under which the ship will be constructed and manned. His knowledge of the general arrangement, plans and specifications, his frequent inspections and progress monitoring, and his organization and preparation of his crew will determine whether the ship will be ready for sea after commissioning and ready for combat after refresher training.

These are heavy responsibilities. To accomplish them, you must work equally hard with your ship and with your crew. Both are equally important. We will deal first with the precommissioning crew, and proceed from them to the ship.

The Precommissioning Crew

Prior to commissioning, each ship should theoretically have her full complement of personnel necessary to fulfill her given mission. Recent shortages, however, have made it difficult to man each ship to her full complement. As a result, the unit will be assigned an allowance based on the current manning ability of the Navy. For this reason, it is vital that each PCO clearly understand the makeup, background, and level of training of the men he does have.

Because of these personnel constraints, crewmembers will usually report to a ship in two distinct groups. On conventional surface ships, these are known as the nucleus detail and the balance detail. The nucleus detail reports quite early, and consists of experienced personnel, who will assist in assembling the precommissioning outfit, monitoring work progress, and witnessing tests of machinery and equipment. They will be aided by the Fleet Introduction Team (FIT), which is permanently assigned at the building yard. This team of experienced operators can provide a wealth of knowledge to the commissioning crew in areas of quality control, crew organization, and equipment operation. The balance detail, the remaining crewmembers, generally report to the ship immediately prior to commissioning, after extensive enroute training.

In the case of nuclear-powered ships, the manning procedure is different. These crews are not split up. Instead, the PCO is designated "commanding officer" of the personnel assigned to the precommissioning unit. The first of these report three months prior to initial reactor plant testing in order to support the new construction reactor plant test program. This is done because, unlike conventional ship crews, nuclear crews are responsible for conducting the test program related to the propulsion plant.

Whether the propulsion be nuclear or conventional, however, the requirements for enlisted assignment to new construction duty are stringent. As a result, precom crews are generally stronger in individual performance and experience than their operating counterparts. However, this does not justify blind faith in them by the PCO. Many new construction volunteers are volunteers for new construction alone; they get "cold feet" as soon as the ship goes to sea. Submarines have been plagued with this problem, since their construction period is relatively long. Consequently, it behooves a PCO to distinguish between his permanent operators and those who will shirk their responsibilities to the Navy by requesting another new construction ship as commissioning nears. These latter must be identified as soon as possible by their actions or previous performance, and must be counseled early to avoid a manning problem later.

The increasing complication of propulsion, weapon, and digital ship systems may require significant additional training ashore and at sea for incoming personnel, even those who have been to sea before. As early as possible, the PCO must determine the ability of his personnel to operate the ship, and must take corrective training action if necessary.

The training sources available during the precommissioning period are varied. Many crewmembers can be routed to specialized "pipeline" training before arrival, while others can attend factory training, vendor presentations, lectures given by the building yard, or formal schooling. The FIT is prepared to render assistance, and personnel may even be sent to sea for temporary duty on previous ships of the class. Specific team training, such as damage control and firefighting, can be arranged through the type commander.

All of these types of training are valuable. An aggressive and organized precom unit will ensure that they are all scheduled. However, the heart and soul of your efforts to train your men safely and efficiently is the ship's onboard training and qualification program. This program must be aimed at producing a highly polished crew, one that can take the ship to sea and commence workup for combat. It must be based on thorough familiarity with the ship, strongly advanced by ship inspection, but organized to avoid interference with the work of the yard.

The first step in setting up this program is to assign system experts from among your most experienced personnel to instruct the remainder of the crew on their particular areas of expertise. They must be supplied with prints and diagrams of the ship; this helps qualify personnel, and has the additional advantage of catching system errors. Each newly reported man, in turn, should receive his own set of diagrams to assist him in qualifying himself.

This program is more demanding yet in nuclear-propelled ships. Here, one of the heaviest responsibilities the PCO faces is the qualification of an operating crew sufficiently in advance of the yard's construction process so that at each step he is ready to provide trained operators to test the plant. This program must be handled in a formal manner, with precise records on each officer and man. A building yard cannot maintain a team qualified for this, so the government provides this service. Thus, the PCO of a nuclear-powered ship will find himself acting, in a sense, as a test and trial-crew captain for the Sea Systems Command. Ultimately, after the examination and certification of the engineering department, this process provides trained teams of men to operate the reactor plant during the test program, and from there the transition to an operating three-section watch at sea is natural. The necessity of the PCO's personal involvement in the engineering details of the ship is obvious.

Whether your ship is nuclear or conventional, you will find that quite often, in hard-pressed construction programs, your precom detail will be called on to trace piping, locate valves, or review the locations of switchboards and junction boxes—in other words, conduct training—during odd hours, such as between shifts and on weekends. You must make the necessity for this obvious to your officers and men, and engender enthusiasm for it by your own example. This will be a test of your practical leadership capabilities, but the long-term results will be worth it.

The conclusion of this onboard training and qualification process will be the conduct of group training, such as sectional, departmental, general, and emergency drills and evolutions during the fast cruise. First, however, let us return to the PCO's function as the monitor of the physical construction of his ship.

Monitoring the Building Process

The inspecting and monitoring function of the PCO and his crew is essential to the success of the new construction period. Monitoring must in no way interfere with either the work of the builder or the quality control inspections conducted by the government. However, it must be consistent, persistent, and well-documented. It must be closely tied to crew training and, when the ship is nuclear-powered, to the provision of the builder with a test and trial crew.

Immediately on reporting, the PCO must set up a system for monitoring and recording progress on his ship. The key to success in this area is knowledge. The PCO and his organization must know the specifications in the same detail as the Supervisor of Shipbuilding (SUPSHIPS) ship superintendent. They must begin to study as soon as they report to the yard. Failure of the crew to understand "specs" will result in an inferior ship, since the SUPSHIPS organization alone cannot guarantee adequate quality control. After all, they won't be the ones to take her to sea. Late assimilation of building specifications may also result in not correcting many deficiencies because of the impact on ship delivery date.

In overseeing construction, the precommissioning detail must not only be alert for errors; they must also be well instructed in the need for practical damage control. Sea water and critical system valves must be accessible, not only for routine inspections, but also under emergency conditions. They must consider the damage control effects of such "niceties" as extra lockers and attractive false bulkheads that can conceal a smoldering fire or an incipient leak.

In addition to his monitoring system, the PCO must set up a procedure for notifying the builder of the deficiencies he finds. He must be able to place priorities on such shortcomings, since some items can be corrected at the ship superintendent level, while others require a PCO-to-SUPSHIPS contact. It is important that your men

Figure 2-2. Monitoring the building process of a large ship such as the *Forrestal* can be time consuming, but it is vital to the future of the ship and its prospective commanding officer.

understand that official comments and recommendations about the building of the ship will come only from you. Apart from preventing confusion and acrimony, this keeps official relations in the proper order. The PCO's handling of construction problems during shipyard conferences will insure that they are given proper attention. In addition, his status with the builder and SUPSHIPS will be enhanced. Brief yourself thoroughly before these meetings. Discuss critical issues with your key personnel, with SUPSHIPS, and with other technical agencies as appropriate prior to each conference. Your knowledge must include all deficiencies, an accurate picture of building progress, and a familiarity with the shift work manning on your ship.

In addition to a well-defined deficiency correction system, the PCO must also set up a formal agreement with the yard for space, major component, and ship's systems final inspection and transfer of responsibility. When the crew takes over the ship, the captain must know that what he has accepted responsibility for actually operates as designed.

In assessing construction progress, the PCO will have to weigh production department estimates, the contract administrator's estimates, and the results of his own inspections. Discrepancies must be noted and investigated carefully because the PCO is required by the Chief of Naval Operations to present his own estimate of delivery date, as well as to submit the reports that are required of him.

Reporting Progress and Readiness

In addition to his daily monitoring effort, the PCO must keep his seniors informed of progress. The basic source for progress reports is *Navy Regulations*. These reports are intended to forward timely narrative information in several areas of interest, providing early warning of possible need for changes or exceptions to plans and policy from the Navy Department level. They are not intended to by-pass the normal chain of command, nor do they supplant the normal function of those commands regularly engaged in monitoring progress or initiating corrective action. They are essentially informative. Because of this, when specific problems are encountered, the commanding officer will have to initiate separate correspondence up the chain, making each problem the subject of a separate letter.

Detailed reporting instructions are found in OPNAV Instruction 9030.2. This calls for "Progress and Readiness Reports" from the PCO, and stipulates that they cover the following items: the PCO's estimate of delivery; personnel manning comments; and comments on work status. This report should discuss deficiencies in construction and any other problems he feels may influence the progress or quality of work.

Type commanders and subordinate commanders charged with monitoring duties may also require periodic reports. Whether specifically required or not, it is both courteous and appropriate to send copies of the progress and readiness reports to the command responsible for the unit's shakedown, to the yard that will handle postshakedown availability, and to the organization to which the ship will eventually report for duty in the fleet.

When preparing these reports, and in all dealings with the yard and monitoring activities, you should bear one point in mind. When things go wrong (and they will), nothing is achieved by assessing the problem in a euphemistic way. Call a spade a spade, and a deficiency a deficiency! Subtleties in progress reports can often fail to move higher authority to action, while the activities responsible read them as insults. In some cases like this, the PCO has done nothing to improve his ship's position, but has simply acquired an enemy.

Be thorough, frank, and keep your seniors informed, and you will be doing your best for your ship, your crew, and for yourself.

Launching

The day your ship first takes the water will be one you will always remember. Nevertheless, take care; unless you understand the ceremonial distinction between launching and commissioning, you can embarrass yourself badly.

Launching is entirely the province of the builder. Any participation by the PCO and the precommissioning crew is strictly by invitation, though it has become customary. Since the Navy prefers to launch its ships "heavy" (i.e., as close to completion as possible) to take advantage of better working conditions on the ways, generally the precom crew will be present. This is especially true of nuclear-powered vessels, where the PCO and crew have been "aboard" for some considerable time. For this reason, the builder will normally invite the PCO and a specified number of the precommissioning detail to "ride the ship down."

This being so, all the arrangements for the ceremony will be made by the builders. You are in a sense a spectator, but you and your crew should participate to the utmost the builder will permit. You will also have to make a choice as to whether you will ride the ship down the ways or be present at the bow when the christening takes place.

One area in which your participation is especially fitting is in the invitations and arrangements for your ship's sponsor. By the time you arrive at the site, your ship will already have had a sponsor named for her by the Secretary of the Navy. Prior to 1966, ships' sponsors were usually the wives of Navy civilian officials and senior naval officers. After that date, the wives of congressmen and senior governmental officials were often named. In the case of destroyer types, which are named after deceased naval heroes, the sponsor will often be a female descendant of that family. You, the PCO, should take charge of the sponsor. You will issue the invitations, coordinate transportation and care with the builder, and handle the arrangements at the ceremony for the sponsor. This is not a passing task, and should be approached with care; you will be maintaining your relationship with your sponsor for many years, and will be expected to turn it over to your relief; it will last as long as the ship is in commission.

In-Service

A ship is "placed in service," according to *Navy Regulations*, when it is clean and ready. In the case of conventional ships, the ship may or may not be "placed in service," depending on circumstances leading to its commissioning. For nuclear-powered ships, however, the term has more complicated implications. Nuclear submarines are normally "placed in service" within the meaning of *Navy Regulations* several weeks before sea trials. At this point, the ship is essentially complete and habitable. At this time the PCO becomes an "officer in charge" (OIC). The responsibility for fissionable materials is then transferred to him from the supervisory authority. In addition, he then becomes responsible for the physical integrity of the ship,

Figure 2-3. Launching of a frigate, the USS *Lewis B. Puller* (FFG 23). General "Chesty" Puller was a "Marine's Marine," but also a favorite with his Navy shipmates. You, as a prospective commanding officer, will have to make a choice at the ceremony between riding your ship down the ways or being present at the christening ceremony at the bow.

the safety of personnel embarked, the physical protection of the reactor, and the security of the entire ship and its equipment.

For nuclear-powered surface ships, the term "provisional acceptance" has been used in lieu of "in service." The provisional acceptance period actually extends through to the preliminary acceptance of the ship (which occurs after preliminary acceptance trials). In a sequence roughly similar to that described for nuclear-powered submarines, the ship is "provisionally accepted" prior to placing of the reactor plant in operation, and the fissionable material is transferred to the custody of the officer in charge.

Once so designated, the OIC has the non-judicial disciplinary authority over enlisted personnel of the command as laid down for an "officer in charge" in Article 15 of the *Uniform Code of Military Justice.*

One word of warning is in order here. As with the provision in *Navy Regulations* concerning acceptance of the ship at commissioning, the PCO may, and should, refuse to accept the further responsibility for the ship implicit in such change of status unless he is actually satisfied with her condition and with that of his crew. *Navy Regulations* provides procedure for him to make this refusal, if necessary.

General experience is that there is no "backing out" once you accept "the load." Remember that you are responsible for the condition of the ship and crew; you can lose much of your leverage in getting deficiencies cleared up if you exhibit undue alacrity in "taking charge" when the ship is not actually at a satisfactory level of readiness.

Fitting Out

Fitting out is the placing on board of the material specified in a ship's allowance lists. This material is forwarded, under contract, to the fitting-out activity. The fitting-out activity for a given ship is designated by the CNO on the advice of the Commander, Naval Sea Systems Command, and is responsible for the procurement and delivery to the ship of allowance list items and general stores.

Although each ship's allowance list has been carefully researched, you would be wise to review and continually monitor the adequacy and appropriateness of the lists and receipts of spare parts. Unless you institute strong follow-up and expediting procedures, you are likely to end up without the items you need to have.

Before expediting procedures can be instituted, however, someone must assemble and inventory all ordered material. These are normally functions of the fitting-out activity, but the ship must conduct inventory also. To ensure the thoroughness of assembly and inventory, the PCO would be well advised to assign several repair parts petty officers to work along with the personnel of the fitting-out activity.

Any deficiencies in equipage and repair parts receipts, or questions on the appropriateness of the initial issue, must be brought to the supervising authority's attention as soon as they are noticed. Additionally, you should include such deficiencies in your progress and readiness reports. Shortages of repair parts can significantly affect the readiness of your ship for sea!

Dock Trials and Fast Cruise

The two final operational ship checks and crew training evolutions prior to going to sea are dock trials and the fast cruise. Dock trials should demonstrate that all equipment operates satisfactorily and that all fitting-out material is aboard. The fast cruise, meaning "fast" in a dock (you will actually be moored to a "pier;" a "dock" is the open space between piers), is the final check of the crew's ability to operate the ship safely under the conditions they will encounter at sea.

The keys to success in dock trials are planning and attention to detail. A detailed dock trials agenda is a necessity. Only strict adherence to a well-planned schedule of tests will insure that the ship is prepared to continue on to fast cruise. Divergence from the agenda only means that the ship was not ready for dock trials in the first place.

Type commander's instructions regarding fast cruise vary in re-

Figure 2-4. Testing of machinery and equipment during construction is mandatory. Here the USS *Robert E. Lee* fires a test slug from one of her Polaris missile tubes.

spect to what evolutions must be conducted. In all cases, however, the following rules apply:

1. Fast cruise must be conducted as if the ship were at sea.
2. No construction, testing, adjustment, or repair work will be allowed during the fast cruise.
3. There will be no communications with anyone external to the ship, unless emergencies (such as fire) arise.
4. A detailed list of discrepancies found must be compiled during the cruise. These must be corrected prior to sea trials.

Successful completion of the fast cruise is a prerequisite for sea trials. Any delay between completion of the fast cruise and the commencement of sea trials should be limited to the time necessary to rest the crew and embark the trial riders. Any requirement for equipment repairs or personnel retraining is evidence that the ship is unready to go to sea.

An excellent way to train for the sea trials is to set up the fast cruise agenda in a manner similar to that planned for going to sea. Use the fast cruise to "warm the crew up" for sea trials. Be sure they are exercised at such basic drills as reduced-visibility detail, casualty drills, and fire and collision drills. The builder may be anxious to get the ship out for engineering trials, but the responsibility for safety at sea rests with the captain, whether he is called the commanding officer, the officer in charge, or the builder's trial captain.

Sea Trials

There are basically two sets of sea trials for each new construction ship. Those conducted by, or for, the builder for his own purpose are called *builder's trials*. Those conducted for the government are called *acceptance trials*. NAVSEA Technical Manual contains an in-depth description of both kinds. The PCO and his key assistants should review this carefully in advance.

For conventional ships, the builder will normally operate the ship on builder's trials. The PCO will act only as an observer and as an advisor to the supervising authority. For submarines and nuclear-powered surface ships, however, the PCO will serve as the trial captain. In either case, you should review the trials agenda in detail to insure that it is in strict accordance with the specifications. Also, builder's trials—especially the first few, which are usually propulsion plant trials—provide an excellent opportunity to train your crew. You should make every effort to have your personnel observe (or, in the case of nuclear ships, operate) all equipment during builder's trials.

If you are to be the trial captain, bear in mind that you will be responsible for the ship's safety during the builder's trials. This is extremely important in the case of nuclear ships, or ships to be recommissioned. This was demonstrated during the Korean War, when the *Benevolence*, a hospital ship being recommissioned, was rammed and sunk in a fog off San Francisco while returning from sea trials. Her sad fate should be a reminder that your ship must be prepared, organized, and checked out for lifesaving prior to undertaking sea trials.

Following the successful completion of initial builder's trials, a succession of others may take place, depending on the ship type and the practice of the yard. Each trial has a specific purpose, and will be conducted according to an agreed-upon agenda. Depending on yard procedure, the ship may be docked between at-sea periods.

The acceptance trials begin following the builder's trials. They determine whether contract and authorized changes were satisfactorily fulfilled. The interval between the builder's trials and the acceptance trials is, practically speaking, the last opportunity you will have to ensure that any problems or deficiencies are corrected. Since the reputation of the builder largely rides on how his ships perform during these trials, he will display considerable willingness to correct any remaining discrepancies you identify. For this reason, you should have every deficiency clearly documented and explained prior to beginning the acceptance trials.

In documenting deficiencies, the PCO would be wise to factor in equipment usage and age. In many cases, the ship's pumps and electric motors have been operated for the yard's convenience well before the sea trials. As a result, unless you insist upon their repair or replacement, you risk the ship being delivered with important auxiliaries worn or abused.

The trial period is, properly speaking, not a training period, but a busy time made productive by the training already done. Nevertheless, the PCO should take every opportunity to train his crew in all areas of ship operation during this time. The habits formed during the initial trial period will be hard to break later.

Another fact to bear in mind during trials is that the reputation of the ship is formed during this period; and once formed, it is likely to stay with the ship for some time. Several simple points can help you start off on the right track:

1. Encourage forehandedness and smartness of performance by all hands, with particular attention to the establishment of routine.
2. Insist on silence during drills and general evolutions. Maintain rigid control of the general announcing system at all times.
3. Ensure that proper military phraseology is used in giving and replying to orders.
4. Demand strict adherence to proper procedures, and formality between officers and men in the conduct of operational business.
5. Encourage development in all departments of a "fix it now" attitude.

Delivery and Commissioning

Delivery and commissioning can occur simultaneously, or not, depending upon where fitting out is to take place. Delivery is purely a contractual matter. If need be, it can be deferred until the final requirements laid down by the government have been met. Commissioning, on the other hand, is a ceremonial function demanding long-range planning and extensive arrangements. *Naval Ceremonies, Customs, and Traditions* is probably the best in-depth guidance for planning the commissioning. However, in Appendix II of this book you will find a sample order for a commissioning ceremony. Note especially the division of responsibility between the commandant and the PCO, and the steps taken to coordinate them.

Shakedown and Guarantee Period

After builder's sea trials, for new construction ships, the INSURV Board will conduct a Combined Acceptance Trial (CAT) and a Preliminary Acceptance Trial (PAT) prior to delivery. Following delivery, the ship enters the shakedown period. The intent of shakedown is to identify remaining shipbuilder's deficiencies under operational conditions, while the guarantee period is still in effect. Following shakedown, the INSURV Board then conducts a Guarantee Material Inspection (GMI), as scheduled by the type commander, to identify further contractor-responsible deficiencies.

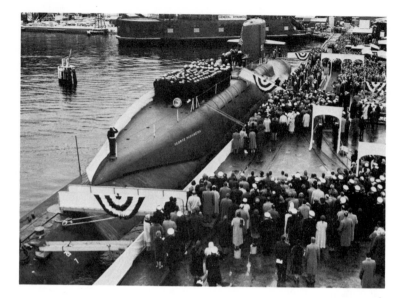

Figure 2-5. The commissioning ceremony for the submarine *George Washington*. Limited deck space required that guests be positioned on an adjacent pier.

The guarantee period, as its name implies, is the period of time specified in the ship's contract during which the contractor retains responsibility and financial liability for failures in performance, workmanship, or material quality. Its length, normally six months, is sufficient time to permit a reasonable operational evaluation. It is important that you properly log and report all deficiencies uncovered during this period, both for purposes of effective contract administration and, more importantly, for the orderly planning and scheduling of Post Shipyard Availability (PSA) work by the shipyard. *OP-NAVINST 4700.25*, *OPNAVINST 4700.7*, and *NAVSHIPS Technical Manual 9080* are the essential references for guarantee and shakedown period procedures.

Figure 2-6. A commissioning ceremony for a large ship, such as the *Nimitz*, requires close coordination between the delivering authority and the prospective commanding officer.

Post-Shakedown Availability

The PSA makes the ship available for the correction of such ship-builder-responsible deficiencies as may remain after shakedown. Most type commanders insist that only these deficiencies will be corrected during PSA. Alterations which are not essential to the safety of personnel, the primary mission of the ship, or of major importance to normal operations will not generally be recommended.

Generally five weeks is a desirable PSA length, with the last week reserved for dock trials, a fast cruise, and a sea trial.

If the PSA is scheduled before final acceptance trials, much of your efforts during this period will go into preparing the ship for presentation to the Board of Inspection and Survey.

Figure 2-7. Breaking the commissioning pennant marks the moment at which the USS *William H. Bates* joins the active fleet.

Final Acceptance Trials

As a rule, surface ships are scheduled for final acceptance trials at the end of the PSA period. During these trials, the commanding officer presents the ship to the Board of Inspection and Survey. How he does it, and how the board evaluates the ship, will reveal how well he has managed his maintenance and inspection program since commissioning.

However, this does not mean "papering over" any deficiency. Should the board not recommend the ship for final acceptance because of some defect in design or construction, you will not be subject to criticism. On the contrary, if you have documented all defects, and have taken the proper steps to correct them, you will be praised by the type commander, and will find favor in the eyes of Heaven.

Wartime New Construction

Thus far, we have treated the construction process as taking place under peacetime procedures. The chances are about one in one hundred that you as a commanding officer will ever be involved in a wartime construction program. Ships and submarines as designed today do not lend themselves to rapid construction. Further, the nature of conflict is now such that a prolonged full-scale war is improbable, and therefore a new construction program would never be started.

Nevertheless, one can envision a scenario where a limited war at sea might take place. Under these conditions, the United States might begin mass production of small antisubmarine warfare escorts, amphibious ships, and production or conversion of other service types. In view of this possibility, it may be worth while setting forth a few of the lessons drawn from our experience in World War II.

The normal procedure had each destroyer, for instance, assigned an experienced group of senior officers and petty officers, consisting of a commanding officer, chief engineer, gunnery officer, and a chief petty officer for each department. This nucleus crew "built the ship." The other ninety percent of the officers and crew, headed by the executive officer, attended various individual and team schools ashore. The two components merged aboard ship the day before commissioning. Many of the latter group of officers and men had never before been aboard ship, yet most were able to perform creditably as long as they stayed in their specialty.

Complications occurred, of course; one amphibious ship received a draft of thirty-eight seamen all named Williams, another triumph for a harried Bureau of Naval Personnel. The problem was quickly straightened out by the chief boatswain's mate, by assigning nicknames to each Williams, and more permanently by a pleading letter to BUPERS asking them to change their draft ordering system. In another case, a destroyer was assigned thirteen junior officers, all of whom had just graduated from law school. Courts-martial were a snap on this vessel, but other work suffered.

Any new construction programs of the future probably will not reach the rates sustained for three years in World War II, but it is worthwhile being prepared for a smaller and shorter version.

The construction and commissioning of a new ship of war is a busy and trying period. Assuming command of a ship that is not yet a ship, of men who are not yet a crew, and making a fighting unit out of them is a task that will try you to the limit. Yet someday, looking back, you may well remember this as the most rewarding period of your entire career.

Now that it is all over, though, the life of the ship, and of your command, has only begun. If you have organized and trained your crew; supervised your ship's construction; inspected thoroughly; won your skirmishes with yard personnel; programmed the weather, so that the sun shone on your commissioning ceremony; and been assigned an understanding and generous sponsor, you are now ready to begin preparing your ship for her service at sea.

3

Organization of the Ship

Ten thousand highly trained fighting men are but a milling mob when they are not organized. Proper organization should result in the transmission of the commander's will to each and every person in his command, both by indoctrination and by communication. So organized, a thousand men can conquer the unorganized ten thousand.

—General Holland "Howling Mad" Smith, USMC, during the landings on Kiska, 1943

The wooden sailing vessels that comprised the great navies of the nineteenth century were small, simple ships when compared with their modern counterparts. Most of the crew's efforts were put into manning the sails. Roughly half the men stood watch at all times when underway, ready to change or trim a huge area of canvas. Potential enemies came into sight slowly, giving the ship time to shift to its battle organization, which provided for manning the guns with approximately half the crew, while the remainder tended the wheel and sails. The ship either sailed, fought, or did both at once. There were no in-betweens, no aerial or subsurface enemies, and very few surprise encounters. The ship's organization could therefore be simple. There was a single watch, quarter, and station bill, a simple battle organization, no administrative boards except for an occasional court-martial, and only a few other bills, such as fire, collision, and prize crew.

Modern navies are very different. Only a small percentage of the crew is directly involved in propulsion. Guns, missiles, torpedoes, electronics, and communications equipment are extremely complex, requiring a large complement of well-trained men. During wartime, instant attack can be expected from the air, from the surface, and from the depths of the sea.

Reflecting these technological changes, the ship's organization has ballooned. The modern warship still has a watch, quarter, and station bill and a battle organization, but there are many other bills and boards as well, many of them quite complicated. Besides general quarters (condition I) and normal steaming (condition IV), there are two other principal watch conditions, and several minor ones. There is still a battle bill, but it can involve as many as five thousand men. Perhaps the best indication of the organizational proliferation of today's Navy is the fact that there are some fifty bills and twenty-eight boards and committees provided for in current instructions.

As ships become more complex, their organization must follow suit. There seems little likelihood of ever returning to the simplicity of the past. Today's commanding officer must learn to master this complexity, streamlining it and making it as efficient as possible in carrying out the age-old task of command.

General Principles of Organization

The *Standard Organization and Regulations of the U.S. Navy, OPNAVINST 3120.32A (SORN)*, describes some of the principles of organization in Chapters 3, 4, and 6. Commanding officers should read these chapters carefully. We will cover most of those same basic principles here, together with the personal opinions of many well-known naval officers who were acknowledged experts in organization.

The dictionary definition of the word *organize* is "to bring into systematic relation the parts of a whole." The *SORN*, in Chapter 1, defines *organization* as the orderly arrangement of materials and personnel by functions.

The *SORN* goes on to state that sound organization is essential for good administration, that organization must be designed to carry out the objectives of command, and that it should be based on division of activities and on the assignment of responsibilities and authority to individuals within the organization. Further, to insure optimum efficiency, all essential functions must be identified as specific responsibilities of a given unit or man. There must be a clear definition of individual duties, responsibilities, and authority.

Planning an Organization. To assist you in planning, the *SORN* defines several basic terms. We will list them here as well, since they will be used repeatedly throughout this chapter.

Accountability refers to the obligation of the individual to render an accounting of the proper discharge of his responsibilities. This accounting is made to the person to whom he reports. An individual assigned both responsibility and authority also accepts a commensurate accountability, which is the requirement that he answer to his superior(s) for his success or failure in the execution of his duties.

Authority is the right to make a decision in order to fulfill a responsibility, the right to require action of others, or the right to discharge particular obligations placed upon the individual himself.

Delegation is the right of a person in authority to send another to act or transact business in his name. Authority may be delegated, but responsibility may never be.

Duties are the tasks which the individual is required to perform.

Responsibility is accountability for the performance of duty.

There is nothing new about these definitions. They have been used and understood since the inception of the Navy, but they are not peculiar to it. You will find the same elements of organization discussed in Peter Drucker's authoritative books on business and management. Some of the terms may be different, but the concepts are the same.

Setting up an Organization. Chapter 1 of the *SORN* sets forth the steps in setting up an organization. Your ship, when you relieve, will already have an operating organization; or, if you commission a new unit, you will be required to use the type commander's version of the standard organization. Only if you commission the first ship of a new type, then, will you need to form a new organization by carrying out the following steps:

1. Prepare a statement of objectives or of missions and tasks.

Figure 3-1. The USS *Brooke* (FFG 1), first of her class, fires an ASROC weapon.Writing the Ship's Organization and Battle Bill for the lead vessel of a class is a difficult but interesting task.

2. Familiarize your planners with the principles of organization.
3. Group the ship's functions logically, so they can be assigned to appropriate segments of the organization.
4. Prepare manuals, charts, and functional guides.
5. Establish policies and procedures.
6. Indoctrinate key personnel concerning their individual and group responsibilities.
7. Set up control measures to ensure the achievement of your objectives.

The *SORN*, in Article 132, also sets forth these four principles of organization to serve as guidelines:

1. *Unity of Command*. Each person should report only to one superior. One person should have control over each segment of the organization. Lines of authority should be simple, clear-cut, and understood by all.
2. *Homogeneity of Assignment*. Functions should be grouped homogeneously, with individuals assigned to groups in accordance with their abilities.

3. *Span of Control.* A superior should be responsible for from three to seven individuals. The span of control should be varied according to the type of work, its complexity, the responsibility involved, and the superior's capabilities.

4. *Delegation of Authority and Assignment of Responsibility.* Authority delegated to a subordinate should be commensurate with his ability. Generally, authority should be delegated to the lowest level of competence in the command.

Organizational Authority. Chapter 6 describes in some detail the derivation of the authority of officers. Petty officers also derive that authority which comes from position in an organization. *Navy Regulations*, Articles 0812 and 0829, is the source of authority for both. The exact kinds and limits of authority exercised by each individual will be defined by ship, department, division, and other direction specific to the organization.

Organizational Directives. All ship organization is ultimately derived from *Navy Regulations.* Article 0704 provides that all commands will be organized and administered in accordance with law, *Navy Regulations*, and the orders of competent authority, and that all orders and instructions issued by a commanding officer will be in accordance with these directives.

Article 0750 goes on to state that the commanding officer should never leave his ship without an organized force sufficient to meet emergencies, and, consistent with requirements, capable of conducting operations. As a wise old chief used to say, "Never leave the old bucket so that it can be burned, sunk, damaged, or captured before you get back from liberty. Otherwise you won't have any place to sleep."

Article 0712 sets forth relations with military units and personnel embarked for passage, but not part of ship's company. Briefly, this article provides that such units will be subject to the orders of the ship's commanding officer, will comply with his uniform and other regulations, perform its share of mess and other common duties, but that it will otherwise be administered through its own organization.

When a unit is embarked for transportation only, its officer in command retains authority, subject only to the overriding authority of the commanding officer.

After *Navy Regulations*, the next level of guidance is the *SORN*. We have already covered some of its matter relating to organizational philosophy. Most of the *SORN*, however, is devoted to covering shipboard organization in detail. Chapter 1 covers basic organization; Chapter 2, standard unit organization; Chapter 3, the organization of departments, divisions, boards, and committees; Chapter 4, watch organizations; and Chapter 6, standard bills. The development of each subject is so complete that many sections can be adopted almost verbatim by any ship.

The next input to your organizational efforts will be your type commander. Many type commanders promulgate a standard organization and regulations manual for each type under their command. Some use the *SORN* as their basic organization, with modifying addenda at the back of the book. Others have kept their old standard organizations, modifying them to correspond to the standard. Some few have written completely new standard organizations. In any event, each type organization directive must conform to the standard directive.

The final level of detail is your own ship's organization. You may make it as simple or as complicated as you desire, but bear in mind that it must still conform to the standard organization set forth in the *SORN*. Note again that the italicized sections of the standard cannot be modified. Other sections may be changed in detail as you see fit, but not in principle.

After reviewing these directives, you are now ready, if commanding a new ship, to promulgate your own organizational instructions and standing orders. These will include a battle bill (with a condition watch system); a watch, quarter, and station bill; administrative, operational, and emergency bills; a safety program; a training program; and the necessary boards and committees. The *SORN* includes fifty bills and twenty-eight boards and committees. We can all be thankful not all of them are necessary on most ships.

If you are taking command of a ship already in commission, you will be spared the time-consuming task of organizing your ship. You will, however, want to spend some time determining what changes you want to make, and this will cover much of the same ground, though at a faster pace.

We will now cover briefly the major components of the task of organizing a ship. Again, most of the required reference material is in the *SORN* and in your type commander's addenda or standard manual.

Organization for Battle

A warship is built to fight, and your ship's allowance of officers and men has been tailored to that task. Any man without a battle station is not needed aboard. A man's place in the battle bill should be a source of pride to him; he should be honored to be assigned an important station. Many a ship's cook or barber has fought as a gun or mount captain, or as a vital member of a missile or torpedo crew. This feeling of pride should be encouraged, particularly since the technical requirements of today's weapons have made such qualification by non-technical personnel more difficult.

Battle Bill. The chief directive for the formulation of your battle bill is NWIP 50–1, *Battle Control.* This confidential publication describes shipboard battle organization and conditions of readiness, and should be used as your guide. It will be supplemented by a type commander's standard battle bill. You will probably have to adapt both bills somewhat for your ship, since today's rapid changes in weaponry and equipment are resulting in a variety of subclasses within each class. Although the references are confidential, we can discuss much of the philosophy and some of the specifics of battle organization here without violating security.

The battle bill assigns men to stations according to a) their qualifications and b) the requirements of the various weapons, equipment, and machinery of the ship. Where possible, divisions or parts of divisions should be assigned to related battle stations as a group; e.g., M division, to the engine and auxiliary spaces; first division, to mount 51. When this is impracticable, you should make every effort to assign men who work together administratively to battle stations where they can continue to work as a team.

Condition watch teams will be formed from the battle organization (condition I). They will man selected ship control, communications, weapons, and engineering stations. A few "idlers," or non-watchstanders, should be left over to man commissary stations, key administrative posts, and a few other billets.

If war should break out on your watch, you will initially be tempted to keep the crew at general quarters for long periods of time. As the newness of being at war wears off, however, you will have to deal with the fact that your officers and men still need rest and food, that a minimum of personal and ship cleanliness is still required, and, in general, that the work of the ship must continue even under conditions of high readiness for combat. Theoretically, condition 1E will allow the crew to take care of these necessities while still retaining all the offensive and defensive capabilities of condition I. You should anticipate the need, over long periods at GQ, for even further easements in certain aspects of readiness. Plan to have your cooks and messmen so distributed in the battle bill that they can be spared for food preparation and service even during GQ. While they are otherwise occupied, the ship should still be able to open fire, and they can quickly be summoned back to battle stations.

Another factor to plan for, either before the initiation of action or soon thereafter, is to make provision for the rotation of those personnel whose duties require close and continuous concentration. Examples of these are lookouts, radio watch personnel, radar operators, talkers, sonar operators, and throttlemen. The safety of the ship may depend on their alertness; assure that they stay fresh by providing reliefs.

Ship Manning Document. A new manning system, currently in effect only for certain classes, is described by the Ship Manning Document (SMD). This system approaches required manning by first calculating the number of man-hours required by the 3-M system. Each ship is then manned in accordance. This system divides manpower requirements into four categories: *operational manning*, which includes personnel required for condition watchstanding and battle; *maintenance*, including preventive, corrective, and ship's force overhaul; miscellaneous functions of *administration and support*; and *utility tasks* and *evolution* manning. Should your ship be covered by the SMD system, your basic reference will be the *Guide to the Preparation of Ship Manning Documents* (OPNAV 10P23).

Condition Watch Organization

According to NWIP 1, the condition watches to consider when making up your condition watch bill are:

Condition I:	General Quarters
Condition II:	Halfway between general quarters and normal watch (for large ships only).
Condition III:	Wartime cruising. Approximately one third of the crew will be on watch. Armament will be manned to match threat conditions. Some idlers.
Condition IV:	Normal peacetime cruising.
Condition V:	Peacetime watch in port. Enough personnel aboard to man emergency bills and to get underway.
Condition VI:	A variation of condition V permitting more relaxed readiness when ship is not able to get underway.
Condition IA:	Amphibious battle stations. Reduced armament readiness; boat launching and control stations fully manned.
Condition IAA:	Variation of condition I to meet AA threat.
Condition IAS:	Variation of condition I to meet ASW threat.
Condition IE:	Temporary relaxation of condition I to allow rest or messing of crew.
Condition IM:	Variation of condition I to meet mine threat.

In preparing bills for the above conditions, bear in mind that in

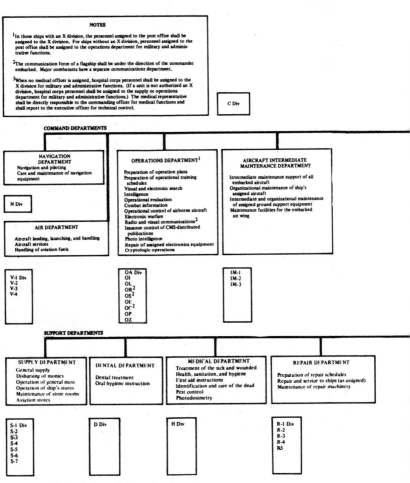

Figure 3-2. Shipboard Organization.

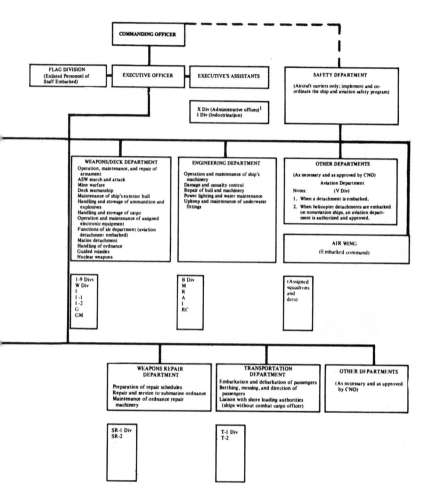

wartime (and that is what we are preparing for) condition watches, continued for hours on end, will soon "get old." Even in peacetime, after eight hours of daily watch not much is left of a man's productive time. In wartime, you should find yourself able to modify condition watches to allow some men to sleep on station or to work in the vicinity of their stations. For example, a mount crew might keep a talker and a trainer awake and on station, while the remainder of the crew sleeps, rests, or works in the same general area.

Watch Organization

The *SORN*, Chapter 4, covers in detail the watch organization of ships in general, both in port and underway. In making up your own watch bills, remember that those portions of the *SORN* in italics must be included as they are. The other parts of the chapter may be modified as you desire.

Development of a Watch Organization. You should, in developing your watch organization, start with the requirements of the *SORN*. Figures 3–2 and 3–3 show standard arrangements which should fit any type or size ship. Review them and the *SORN*, and deliberate on what you yourself will feel comfortable with. Delete those functions which do not apply to your own ship, add your own ideas, and the result should constitute your watch bill in chart form. You should then refine this, using the ideas of your heads of departments, and modifying your draft as necessary to suit the qualifications of your personnel. The last step is the writing and printing of written directives for your organization book. These should fully delineate the responsibilities and duties of each watchstander.

This would be a good time, also, to set up a training system, to make sure the personnel who will stand these watches will be properly qualified, and will in turn pass on their skills to others.

Establishment of Watches. Once your watch organization is in print, and a training system is in place, you are ready to implement the watch system. The *SORN* requires that the officer of the deck and the engineering officer of the watch watches be continuous. To fulfill this requirement, you may use any Navy line officer in your command for any watch for which you consider him qualified. Ma-

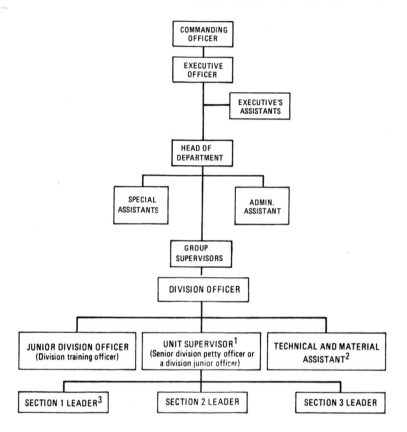

1. When a division has more than one function, such as deck and weapons responsibilities, it would have a supervisor for each of these functions.

2. Usually a warrant officer or limited duty officer assigned to supervise the maintenance and repair of certain material or equipment.

3. The number of sections in each division will depend on the number of watch sections in the individual unit

Figure 3-3. Department Organization.

rine officers below the grade of major may stand OOD watches in port and JOOD watches at sea. In smaller types, and in case of personnel shortage in others, petty officers and non-commissioned officers may be used as OODs in port in addition to your officers.

The general duties of watch officers are set forth in the *SORN*, Article 410. Subsequent articles cover orders to sentries, watch-standing principles, conditions for the firing of weapons, length of watches, performance of duty while on watch, setting and relieving the watch, and special watches. Your instructions, with the italicized portions of the *SORN* included, should be all your watchstanders need to read to stand a taut and knowledgeable watch. Additional information is available to them in the *Watch Officer's Guide*, published by the Naval Institute Press, and in several other similar publications listed in the bibliography.

Logs. The two main logs to be kept by your watches are the Deck Log and the Engineering Log. Other important records are the Magnetic Compass Record, the Bearing Book, the Engineer's Bell Book, and the CIC Log. Give your personal attention to the keeping of these documents. They are important historical records and also legal documents; there are a number of reasons they might be referred to in years to come.

Unit Bills

A unit bill sets forth the commanding officer's policy and directions for assigning personnel to duties or stations for specific purposes or functions. The *SORN* states that unit bills will include the following elements:

1. A preface, stating the purpose of the bill.
2. Assignment of responsibility for the bill's maintenance.
3. Information of a background, or guidance, nature.
4. Procedure, containing the information and policies necessary to interpret the material.
5. The special responsibilities of each man with regard to planning, organizing, directing, and controlling the functions and evolutions of the bill.

Chapter 6 of the *SORN* contains sample bills for every conceivable type of ship for every possible contingency or evolution. They are intended as a guide for type commanders and commanding officers. Your type commander will probably have modified the bills in the *SORN* to suit his desires and the types of ships he commands. You, in your turn, may modify further the bills which concern your particular ship.

Watch, Quarter, and Station Bill

The watch, quarter, and station bill is the division officer's summary of the assignment of his personnel for each of the other bills the ship uses. As its title states, it lists the watches, berthing assignments, and bill assignments for each officer and enlisted man. It is the working document for the division officer. It should reflect this importance by being kept up to date and neatly written, and should be posted for ready reference by all personnel. The supply system can furnish standard forms, replacements, and bulkhead-mounted holders, should these not be already available.

For ships under the SMD, that publication serves both as a battle organization manual and as a battle bill. However, the watch, quarter, and station bill should still be prepared as described by the *SORN* and as shown in sample form in the *Division Officer's Guide*.

Administrative (Unit) Organization

While the primary organization for a ship (and the reason for its existence) is the battle organization, it remains a fact that ninety-five percent of ship's time even in war is spent on administration. This requires an organization of its own, the ship's organization plan. We have already discussed the philosophy behind this plan and the directives governing it in the section of this chapter called "General Principles of Organization." Figure 3–4 shows a typical administrative organization of a large ship; yours might be much smaller. The normal progression of organization is from the commanding officer through the executive officer, heads of departments, division officers, and so down to the section leaders and non-rated men. Figure 3–5 shows the resulting lines of authority and responsibility. We will now proceed to discuss each level of organization in greater detail.

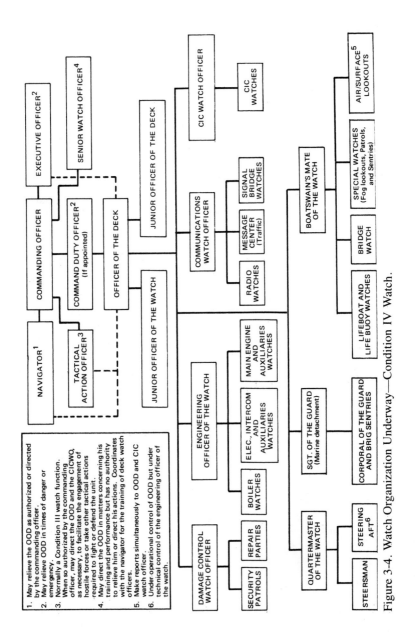

Figure 3-4. Watch Organization Underway—Condition IV Watch.

1. May relieve the OOD as authorized or directed by the commanding officer.
2. May relieve OOD in times of danger or emergency.
3. Normally a Condition III watch function. When so authorized by the commanding officer, may direct the OOD and the CICWO, as necessary, to facilitate the engagement of hostile forces or take other tactical actions required to fight or defend the unit.
4. May direct the OOD in matters concerning his training and performance but has no authority to relieve him or direct his actions. Coordinates with the navigator for the training of deck watch officers.
5. Make reports simultaneously to OOD and CIC watch officer.
6. Under operational control of OOD but under technical control of the engineering officer of the watch.

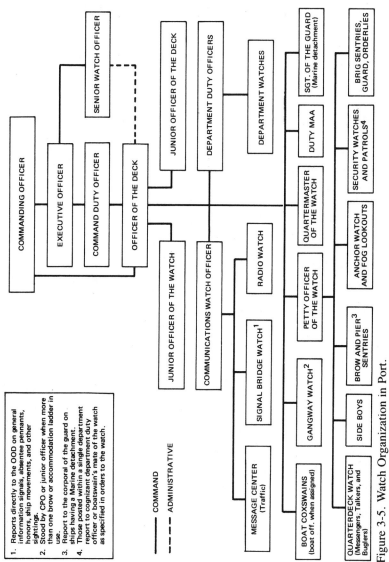

1. Reports directly to the OOD on general information signals, absentee pennants, honors, ship movements, and other sightings.
2. Stood by CPO or junior officer when more than one brow or accommodation ladder in use.
3. Report to the corporal of the guard on ships having a Marine detachment.
4. Those posted within a single department report to cognizant department duty officer or boatswain's mate of the watch as specified in orders to the watch.

———— COMMAND
- - - - ADMINISTRATIVE

COMMANDING OFFICER

EXECUTIVE OFFICER

SENIOR WATCH OFFICER

COMMAND DUTY OFFICER

OFFICER OF THE DECK

JUNIOR OFFICER OF THE DECK

DEPARTMENT DUTY OFFICERS

DEPARTMENT WATCHES

JUNIOR OFFICER OF THE WATCH

COMMUNICATIONS WATCH OFFICER

MESSAGE CENTER (Traffic)

SIGNAL BRIDGE WATCH[1]

RADIO WATCH

BOAT COXSWAINS (boat off. when assigned)

GANGWAY WATCH[2]

PETTY OFFICER OF THE WATCH

QUARTERMASTER OF THE WATCH

DUTY MAA

SGT. OF THE GUARD (Marine detachment)

QUARTERDECK WATCH (Messengers, Talkers, and Buglers)

SIDE BOYS

BROW AND PIER[3] SENTRIES

ANCHOR WATCH AND FOG LOOKOUTS

SECURITY WATCHES AND PATROLS[4]

BRIG SENTRIES, GUARD, ORDERLIES

Figure 3-5. Watch Organization in Port.

Heads of department. In addition to the specific duties and responsibilities assigned to a department head by his billet, each one also has certain general duties. First of all, he is the representative of the commanding officer in all matters pertaining to his department, and must conform to his policies and orders. All persons in his department are subordinate to him. He may confer directly with the captain concerning matters relating to his department, bypassing the executive officer, whenever he believes such action necessary for the good of his department or the ship. (Of course, he should use this right sparingly, and should inform the executive officer of his actions as soon as possible.) He must keep the commanding officer informed as to the general condition of his machinery and equipment, particularly in cases which might affect safety or operational readiness, and he must not disable machinery or equipment without permission.

The more specific responsibilities of each head of department are set forth in the *SORN*. You should read them carefully and insist that your heads of departments do likewise. Aside from his normal duties, additional specific requirements are laid on a department head during the precommissioning period, during fitting out, and during the period prior to his detachment. For example, before being relieved, he is required to inspect his department with his relief, submitting a joint report with him to the commanding officer. You should read this portion of the *SORN* carefully, and insist that your department heads do likewise.

Division Officers. Officers are assigned to command major divisions of each department. Their position in the organization of the command is shown in Figure 3–2. They are assisted by junior division officers, enlisted section leaders, and other leading petty officers.

The division officer occupies an essential place in the ship. He is the final officer link between you and your crew. His performance of duty is essential, since the enlisted men see him daily; they will react strongly to his leadership, good or bad. The *SORN* lists the division officer's specific duties, but a more detailed reference is *The Division Officer's Guide*, published by the Naval Institute Press. It is an excellent handbook, one you can well recommend to your junior officers for study.

Boards and Committees. A board, or committee, is a group of persons organized under a president, chairman, or senior member to evaluate problems in depth and to make recommendations to higher authorities for action. Many organizational functions in the Navy lend themselves to administration by these groups. Article 304 of the *SORN* describes the composition and purpose of the most common ones aboard ship. You will probably not need them all, but some will prove useful by undertaking long or detailed analysis of matters that do not require your immediate attention or decision. They are generally policy-setting groups, though you may choose to delegate executive functions to a few.

Ship's Regulations

Ship's regulations have traditionally been one of the most important elements in a ship's organization. Here, at least, is one thing that retains the flavor of tradition, many of its rules dating back to those days of wooden ships—though of course they have been brought thoroughly up to date where necessary.

Chapter 5 of the *SORN* contains a useful set of ship's regulations. This particular set may be obtained through the supply system printed on bulletin-board-sized posters.

You may be of the opinion, after a quick review, that they are too lengthy; too excessively detailed. Bear in mind, however, that they have evolved over many years, the product of the experiences of thousands of commanding officers facing the same problems you are facing now. Most of them, in fact, started as navy regulations, and were gradually downgraded to ship's regs.

The range of subjects covered is peculiar, granted. They start with "Alarm Bells" and end with "Unauthorized Entry." They cover such diverse subjects as swearing, swimming, grooming, hitchhiking, and a host of other odd activities. But before you decide to cut some out, remember that if one of your men conducts himself as you would not want him to, the court martial or non-judicial punishment hearing you convene will have to prove that he violated a law or regulation of some kind. The ship's regulations should, therefore, cover those rules of conduct that you want observed; and they must be *duly promulgated* to be legal. This means they must be *approved* by competent authority and *posted* in a place where the culprit could be expected to see them. Ship's regulations signed by you and posted on the man's division bulletin board in his living compartment constitute legal promulgation.

Bearing these considerations in mind, you will probably want to use the standard regulations as a *minimum* rather than as a *maximum*. Past commanding officers have found each one to be necessary, or it wouldn't be there.

Chief of the Boat Concept

One useful organizational concept not described in the *SORN* is the chief of the boat. This is a long-established post in the subsea force, and is in fact described in the two submarine type commanders' *Standard Submarine Organization and Regulation Manuals* (*SSORMS*). Not only has it been proven in submarine operations for years, but some smaller surface ships have also used it, also with good results. The Master Chief Petty Officer of the Navy and subsequent development of command chief petty officers are outgrowths of this idea.

The chief of the boat is that CPO chosen by the commanding officer as being the outstanding (and, it is to be hoped, senior) chief assigned to that submarine. In many instances, the billet is filled directly by the Naval Military Personnel Command. The chief of the boat has authority over all other enlisted men, and serves as the master-at-arms in addition to his other duties. Given his natural qualities of command, his position as MAA, and the very special prestige of his position, he can serve you well as a direct and somewhat informal link between you and the mass of your crew.

Organizational Communications

No matter how well it is set up on paper, no organization can function unless the will of the commander can be made known to those charged with carrying it out. Also, information must come up to him through the chain of command if he is to make sound decisions and communicate them back down for execution.

Today, ships are equipped with several methods of communication. The oldest and most reliable are the human voice and the written word. Normally, these simple methods are used to indoctrinate the crew, so that the policies of the commander are properly inculcated prior to action or emergency. They may still be used in time of battle or disaster, when newer, more complicated methods of communication fail. Many severely damaged ships have been steered out of danger by voice orders passed by men posted along the deck, and even today orders and reports from damage control parties are carried in written form by messengers.

In most normal operations, however, ships today can depend on several more advanced systems. The MC system, one of the most frequently used, serves specialized functions, such as ship control. "Squawk boxes" assure receipt of messages as long as someone is near them, but they have their disadvantages: they require the person answering to come to the vicinity of the transmitter; they depend upon electrical power for their operation; their effectiveness is degraded severely by the noise of battle. Other MC circuits, such as the 1MC, are one-way systems, and can cover large areas or even the entire ship at once. Other one-way announcing systems cover related areas such as engineering spaces or gun mounts. These, however, have the same limitations as the two-way systems (except for the answering requirements), as well as the added difficulty of ensuring that orders have been received.

Many larger vessels today also have a ship's service telephone system, linking many stations throughout the ship. Theoretically, this is an administrative communication system, but it can be used for passage of orders as well. It too suffers from its dependence on electrical power and its degradation by ambient noise.

Less complicated than either of these, and most reliable in battle and in emergency, is the sound-powered telephone system. It needs no external electrical power for its operation and therefore can be used under almost all conditions. Its parts are more rugged and it is less liable to casualty than the other systems. Headphones make it less subject to degradation by noise. There will be a number of sound-powered circuits installed, depending upon the ship type. Each circuit serves a major function, such as the Captain's Battle Center (JA) and the Battle Lookouts (JL). These circuits are usually manned for battle, condition watches, emergencies, and evolutions such as replenishment or anchoring. They can be cross-connected, giving them inherent flexibility and redundance. Talkers provide instant monitoring and answering. This is an advantage, but can also be a drawback in that the system is no better than its talkers. You will do well to have your officers insist on talker training and circuit discipline. It will pay dividends when seconds count.

Other, less flexible communications systems are the ship's alarms. Initiated from the quarterdeck or bridge by special switches, these simple, distinctive sound alarms assure the crew's prompt reaction to GQ, collision, chemical attack, flight crash, and other conditions requiring instant action.

Despite the wide variety of communication methods at your disposal, though, the one you will use most often is the 1MC. Not only is word passed over it; not only will your voice reach the crew by means of it; but a great deal of routine information can be passed over it as well—time checks, notification of upcoming events, boat information, notification of the arrival and departure of senior officers, meal calls, and much more.

Since it is used every day, you should give the use of the 1MC your personal attention. Used wisely and sparingly, it backs up your ship's administration. Used unwisely or too frequently, it will make your ship a noisy Bedlam. Your crew will hate it and in a nest your neighbors will detest you. Actually, if the ship is organized and administered well you will not need to use it much. To minimize passing word, insist that each division have an "office" or other fixed location where its leading petty officer can be found during working hours by message or telephone. He, in turn, should know the location of each man of his division at all times. When the "man with the keys to the paint locker" is absent, he should have left his keys or location with this leading petty officer. Allow word to be passed for an individual only in an emergency; then work on minimizing the "emergencies." Don't allow a long message to be passed telling a man where to go or what to do. Announcing his name should suffice; he should then call the quarterdeck in port or the navigation bridge underway for his message. For that word passing that *is* necessary, insist on standard phraseology as set forth in the *Watch Officer's Guide* or authoritative other source. Clamp down on the number of standard messages as well. Most events should be scheduled in the plan of the day. Pass the word when the plan of the day is changed, not to confirm it. When it says sweep-down is at 1130, expect the sweep-down to start at 1130, not when the word is passed. Don't accept the excuse that "no one passed the word."

Communications is one of the most vital elements of organization. A little attention to it, a lot of indoctrination in its proper use, and your ship can become a serene and efficient machine, running quietly and well.

Organization for Embarked Staff

Your chances are about one in six that you will carry a permanently embarked flag, and somewhat greater that you will at some time carry one temporarily. Your organization should take both possibilities into account.

The basic guidance for relations with an embarked commander and his staff is contained in *Navy Regulations*, Chapter 6. Articles 0607 and 0608 outline the organization of a staff and the authority and responsibilities of officers assigned to it. Article 0609 describes its administration and discipline. This article states that the staff of an embarked commander, along with the enlisted persons serving with them, are subject to the internal regulations and discipline of the ship. They will be assigned regular stations for battle and emergencies. Enlisted personnel are assigned to the ship for administration and discipline, usually as a flag division, under a flag division officer.

Additional details on accomodating an embarked staff are covered by the *SORN*. Basically, the organizational changes to take aboard a flag are relatively simple. The hard part is making them work. Chapter 11 of this book discusses this situation at greater length.

Organization: A Last Look

Now that your plans are complete, now that all of your officers and men understand their battle stations, administrative, and watch duties, you can now begin to think about the day-to-day running of the ship. But before you do, look back. Evaluate your organizational efforts one last time, using the following check list, taken from *Principles of Administration*, *Economics of National Security*, Volume IV:

1. Are all the functions provided that are necessary to accomplish the objective of the command?
2. Are any unnecessary functions provided that could be eliminated?
3. Are the functions, responsibilities, relationships, and authority of each unit of organization clearly defined?
4. Are the functions assigned to the proper unit, and are they grouped properly within that unit?
5. Is there duplication or overlapping of functions, responsibilities, or authority between units of the organization?
6. Is authority commensurate with responsibility?
7. Is the organizational structure in the simplest form capable of fulfilling the requirements of the command?
8. Is the organization properly balanced? Are too many units responsible to one individual?
9. Are the functions, duties, responsibilities, and authority delegated in such a manner that definite accountability for operating results can be established?
10. Does the organization lend itself to internal checks and control?
11. Are titles and other organizational nomenclature clearly descriptive? Are they used consistently?
12. Have individuals been selected to fit the organizational plan, or has the plan been made to fit the individuals?

In studying this chapter, you have probably been aware of its systematic, modern-looking approach to organizational mechanics. Yet neither the problems of organization nor their solutions are new.

They have existed since before the time of Moses (roughly 1250 B.C.). *Exodus 18*, for example, tells us that one day Jethro, Moses' father-in-law, found him seated on his bench of justice, and was surprised to see him surrounded from morning to night with a disorderly throng.

Seeking out his son, Jethro delivered himself of some sound organizational wisdom. He advised Moses to appoint capable men as leaders of small groups of people, and empower them to dispense justice within their groups. They should then bring the more difficult cases to Moses, who would either decide them himself or bring them to the attention of "Higher Authority." Further, through these leaders Moses should teach his people the statutes and laws and show them the right courses to follow.

Having delivered this advice, Jethro passes from the pages of history. Moses had the wisdom to take it, though, and after ordering his daily affairs he was able to pass on to more important work. He soon produced, in fact, a set of regulations covering all areas of human conduct, most of which have lasted to this day.

We too, having now mastered organization, are free to pass on to administration and regulations. We will do so without the advice of Jethro. Fortunately, however, more modern experts are available to us, and we will now proceed to their study.

4

Administration of the Ship

My Lord, if I attempted to answer the mass of futile correspondence that surrounds me, I should be debarred from all serious business of campaigning. I must remind your Lordship—for the last time—that so long as I retain an independent position, I shall see that no officer under my command is debarred, by attending to the futile driveling of mere quill-driving in your Lordship's office, from attending to his first duty—which is, and always has been, so to train the private men under his command that they may, without question, beat any force opposed to them in the field.

—Attributed to Wellington, 1810; possibly apocryphal

Any discussion of the administration of ships could cover a hundred subjects. In this chapter, we will limit our discussion to those which are universal to all types, and which are timeless in the sense that they must begin the day a ship is commissioned and continue to her last day in service. Ship's routine, correspondence, investigations, classified information, security, and public information are such subjects. Others, which might well be classified as administrative in some discussions, are covered best by having entire chapters devoted to them (the enlisted crew, logistics, and maintenance). Still others are dealt with in other chapters (training, drills, inspections, in the chapter on joining the fleet; officer administration, in the chapter on the ship's officers; and personnel administration, in the chapters on the enlisted crew and officers).

The subjects we will take up in this chapter are at best dull. If you carry out the responsibilities outlined well, you will get faint praise; but on the other hand, failure to do so will be costly. Try to master them all, to provide for their proper execution, and then to pass on to more exciting problems, with the knowledge that your rear is well secured.

Ship's Routine

Establishment of a formal routine is essential to the smooth operation of any large organization—including a ship. If a daily routine is lacking, vital functions such as training and qualification, maintenance, and even watchstanding will suffer as surely as night follows day. This is especially true of periods spent underway and deployed. Officers and men must then attend to their departmental and divisional duties as well as stand watches, but it is hard for even the best-organized, best-motivated man to stand watch on a one in three basis if the daily routine is slipshod. A stable schedule allows him to meet his personal requirements for food and sleep along with his assigned duties and watches.

The plan of the day (POD) is the document that formalizes the ship's routine. The *SORN* addresses the plan of the day in detail in Article 520.46. This article provides that a plan of the day, published daily by the executive officer or his authorized representative, will constitute the primary medium for the promulgation of such orders and directives as the executive officer, or the duty officer when he is absent, may issue. The plan of the day will be posted on all department and division bulletin boards, and will be read at quarters when the ship is in port. Each member of the crew is then responsible for obeying the orders it contains.

Your POD will prove most effective in administering the daily routine of the ship if it:

Is complete and addresses all shipwide major events;

Is understood to be inviolate, and never the subject of graffiti, negative comments, or additions placed thereon by readers;

Is published early (preferably the day before its execution) to allow departments to adjust to key events;

Is used to assist the ship's training program with training and qualification notes;

Is used to honor those men awarded recognition for superior performance, recent promotion, or reenlistment;

Includes topics of general interest to the crew, such as upcoming port calls and mail deliveries.

Correspondence

Correspondence Accounting System. It is essential that you have an absolutely reliable correspondence system. All incoming matter must be opened as soon as received, logged, and routed promptly through the executive officer and you to action and information personnel. The routing sheets can be filled out by anyone of your choosing, depending upon the size of the ship. Large ships usually use the ship's secretary for the captain's correspondence and the executive officer's yeoman for routine correspondence. Small ships usually task a yeoman with all correspondence. In any event, make sure all correspondence is promptly put in the hands of the person designated to take action, and that a deadline for writing a reply is designated.

Part of this system should be a tickler file, preferably kept by the executive officer's yeoman. Many commanding officers keep a small personal tickler file on selected important correspondence. Having ensured that each piece of correspondence will reach a person who will present a proposed answer to you within the required time, you can now turn your attention to the content of the letters.

Command Communications Content. As commanding officer, you should always be conscious of your choice of words in all conversation and writing. Poor communications skills will handicap you in whatever you attempt. On the other hand, your chances are enhanced by the use of plain, forceful words, correctly chosen and arranged into well-composed sentences and paragraphs, so as to convey your meaning directly, clearly, and unequivocally.

In addition to care in conversation and writing, you should always think at least one level above yourself. Try to imagine yourself as the senior officer who is receiving your request, answer, or statement. Is your case stated clearly? Will he understand the problem from what you have written, and have you made it easy for him to approve your request? Have you answered the questions of *HOW - WHEN - WHAT - WHERE - WHY?* Finally, if the written work is directed to an organization which may not understand shipboard terminology, have you completely explained or described the situation so that they can understand it? This last point is particularly important in communications involving investigations and fitness reports.

Tone. As commanding officer, you set the *tone* in which your command will speak. Your right to do so is obvious. Confusion and misunderstanding will occur, however, when you are unsure about the tone you desire or when your subordinates do not understand what you want. There are many examples of this. On one ship officers had letters constantly returned for rewriting until they learned that their captain did not like to see the word "however" in the middle of a sentence. On another, the executive officer would not sign letters of fewer than two paragraphs. Misunderstandings like these waste time and are hardly good for morale. If you seem to be returning a lot of correspondence for rewrite, the answer is to *make a list* of your pet words and expressions. Then circulate it for the wardroom to see. Such a list of fifteen or twenty desired and "forbidden" items can save much writing and rewriting.

Guidance. A substantial part of your job as commanding officer is the training of your officers. This training should include showing individual subordinates how to express themselves on paper. Many otherwise excellent young officers have failed to learn this aspect of their profession along the way, and have as a result been less effective at the executive officer level than they might have been.

If the "list" approach mentioned above does not result in acceptable correspondence, then you will have to devote more attention to this aspect of their training. Bear in mind, however, that harsh actions and words are rarely of value in teaching the art of corresponding and communicating. Stern discipline and quick censure may keep a man alert on a bridge or boiler room watch, but they are ineffective in stimulating him to think and write with enthusiasm and imagination.

Another approach to training young officers to write is the "sigh and sign it" system. It is best understood by reading the description of it by one destroyer commanding officer, who said, "Sure, the junior officers on my ship write some clumsy letters, but unless they are in error or could cause a misunderstanding, I let them go as written. The young officer gets a feeling of accomplishment out of seeing his letter go off the ship to carry out the ship's business. Next time he does it better because he has had more experience. However, if his work shows no improvement, then the executive officer or I talk to him and give him a few hints about what a good Navy letter should look like." You might keep this advice and this system in mind the next time you are tempted to "nitpick" a letter. Who will read it? What harm can it do if it is less than perfect? Is it really written badly, or is it just written differently from your style?

You will now have established a workable system for receiving, routing, and processing correspondence and for producing satisfactory answers. You can afford to pass on to solving some of the administrative problems that correspondence will bring you.

Investigations

From time to time, even in the best run ships, incidents will occur that require investigation. These may range from minor injuries to personnel or damage to equipment up to more serious matters. As commanding officer, you should familiarize yourself with the investigation process and be prepared to carry it out properly. A carefully conducted investigation is not to be feared, and in most cases may be to your advantage. If you give a senior all the information he needs he is more likely to make a decision in your favor, if he possibly can do so.

The *Manual of the Judge Advocate General* (*JAG Manual*) explains the three types of fact-finding bodies in the Navy: courts of inquiry, boards of investigation, and one-officer investigations. While investigations conducted by a court of inquiry are always "formal," those conducted by the other two fact-finding bodies may be either "formal" or "informal." The difference is that the "formal" investigation is convened by a written appointing order, testimony is taken under oath, and the proceedings are recorded verbatim.

Only an officer authorized under the *Uniform Code of Military Justice* to convene a general court-martial (or other person designated by the Secretary of the Navy for the purpose) may convene a court of inquiry. You, as a commanding officer, may convene either a board or a one-officer investigation. The informal one-officer investigation, convened either orally or in writing, is the type most frequently used in small ships.

Whenever a commanding officer has reason to believe that he himself may become a "party" (defined as a person whose conduct or performance of duty is "subject to inquiry" or who has a "direct interest" in the inquiry), he should ask his superior in command to order the investigation. This ensures objectivity and reduces the possibility of reinvestigation. Where reference to a superior is impracticable, however, or where the incident is of such minor nature that objectivity can be maintained in spite of an apparent personal interest of the convening authority, the *JAG Manual* states that the matter need not be referred to a superior in command, since one investigation does not preclude a subsequent investigation of the same subject by order of either the same or a superior commander.

Informal investigations are discussed in detail in the *JAG Manual*, which also includes required guides, forms, and checklists. You should be familiar with these provisions since most of your investigations will be of this type.

Classified Information

Some of your correspondence will be classified, and your handling of it will have to conform closely to the classified information handling regulations. Violations can lead to serious consequences, both for the violator and his commanding officer. Don't let this happen in your ship. Understand the appropriate regulations, school your administrative personnel, and give the subject command attention.

Navy Regulations, Article 1116, states in part that no person in the Department of the Navy shall convey or disclose by oral or written communications, publication, graphic (including photographic) or other means, any classified information, except as provided in the *Department of the Navy Information Security Program Regulations*.

Security of classified information should be an integral part of your command philosophy. It is wrong to assume that mere promulgation of the regulations will guarantee protection. Such regulations cannot meet every situation and cannot possibly cover all ship's equipment and the many classified details of operations and performance capabilities.

One of your primary concerns, then, is to ensure that classified information is not revealed to those without a need to know. This subject is also part of the larger subject of ship's security, which we will now discuss in detail.

Ship's Security

The security of the ship is another twenty-four-hour administrative concern of the commanding officer. In this case we are not talking about security in the sense of fire or flood prevention, but rather the protection of classified correspondence, materials, and equipment; unclassified but vital areas such as the engineering spaces; and other ship functions which might be the target of sabotage. This subject is so intermeshed with that of the preceding section that much of the information discussed will apply equally to both. Definitions of various levels of classification and some of the bills are the same for correspondence as for physical security.

Under the security program, your primary concern will be to develop several sub-programs, which will:

Control access to the ship and to specific areas within it by means of rules, alarm systems, locks, and guards.

Ensure that classified correspondence and objects are clearly marked, strictly accounted for, used only by authorized personnel, and securely stowed when not in use.

Ensure that all personnel are screened, instructed, and monitored to ensure their integrity, reliability, and understanding of the techniques for safeguarding classified information and nuclear weapons.

To accomplish the foregoing, you will need to establish certain regulations and bills.

Security Regulations. The *SORN* contains most of the information you will need to establish a strong security program. It prescribes the following bills for use afloat:

Security Bill, which describes and assigns responsibilities for the handling and safeguarding of classified material and information.

Ship's Official Correspondence and Classified Material Control Bill, which details procedures to be followed in handling classified correspondence.

Ship's Visitors' Bill, which specifies procedures and restrictions for control of visitors.

Ship's Repel Boarders and Sneak Attack Bill, which specifies procedures for defending the ship from external or internal attack.

Ship's Security from Unauthorized Visitors Bill, which promulgates instructions for dealing with unauthorized visitors when "repel boarders" action is not required.

Ship Destruction Bill, which outlines the procedures for destroying the ship.

Other sources, listed below, may be consulted for specific information regarding security of classified material:

Department of Defense (DOD) Regulations 5200.1-R (Information Security Program) and *OPNAVINST 5510.1* series (*Department of the Navy Supplement to the DOD Information Security Program Regulations*) provide detailed guidance for classifying, marking, handling, access to, and disclosure of classified information. *KAG-1* and *DNC-5* contain instructions regarding communications and cryptographic security.

OPNAVINST 5510.83 and *NAVMILPERSCOM 5510.11* contain information pertinent to the security and safeguarding of nuclear weapons (including personnel reliability).

The Security Officer. Chapter 3 of the *SORN* prescribes that a security officer be appointed to assist the commanding officer. This officer can legally be appointed only by him, or by a legally convened court-martial acting to safeguard security within the command.

An effective security officer or manager is vital to the success of the command security program. The officer you assign to this post should be well versed in all aspects of classified material control and security regulations.

Classification Categories. *OPNAVINST 5510.1* and the *SORN* describe the various categories of classifications and definition of terms used in security programs. All crew members should be instructed in the different classification categories, and should understand how they are handled. This means indoctrinating them in the meanings of the following terms:

Need to Know. The need for certain information by an individual in order to fulfill his duties. A security clearance does not in itself establish a "need to know."

Personal Security Clearance. An administrative determination by competent authority that an individual is eligible, from a security standpoint, for access to classified information up to and including the designated category.

Top Secret. Information the unauthorized disclosure of which could result in exceptionally grave damage to the nation.

Secret. Information the unauthorized disclosure of which could result in serious damage to the nation.

Confidential. Information the unauthorized disclosure of which could reasonably be expected to cause damage to the national security.

Restricted Data. All information concerning the design, manufacture, or utilization of atomic weapons, the production of special nuclear material, and the use of nuclear material in the production of energy.

For Official Use Only. Information not requiring safeguarding in the interest of national defense but still not considered releasable to the general public.

Access. The ability and opportunity to obtain knowledge or possession of classified information.

Security Areas. In certain ships, equipment and material of different classifications create the need for defining security areas on a graduated basis concerning the necessary restrictions on access, control of movement within the area, and type of protection required. Security areas are categorized in *OPNAVINST 5510.1* as:

Exclusion Area. An area containing classified information of such nature that access to it means, for all practical purposes, access to such information.

Limited Area. An area containing classified information such that uncontrolled movement by a visitor would permit access to it, but such that while within it access may be prevented by escort and other internal restrictions and controls.

Controlled Area. An area adjacent to or encompassing limited or exclusion areas, but such that uncontrolled movement by a visitor does not permit access to classified information.

Public Relations

Public relations is a very important responsibility. You must be aware of its pitfalls twenty-four hours a day. At the same time, you must be ready to take advantage of every opportunity to make a contribution to the Navy's overall PA program.

You will be assisted by your public affairs officer (PAO). Nevertheless, you must personally oversee the administration of the public affairs program. The PAO needs your command interest, and you, in turn, cannot afford a major error in administration. The duties of the public affairs officer are discussed in Chapter 6.

Much of your contact with the press and public will occur when you are on independent operations. Therefore, we have devoted a major section of Chapter 13 to public relations. Another section in that chapter covers the people-to-people program, and there is also a full discussion of the importance of the conduct of your officers and men ashore to public relations. On independent duty you will be conducting public relations on your own, with little help available. When operating as part of a fleet or when within the continental limits of the United States you will be able to get help from staff public affairs officers, larger ships, and shore commanders.

The following discussion of the administration of public affairs includes those aspects which apply both to independent operations and to periods when you are under another commander.

Shipboard public relations is essentially the advancement of the proper interests of the Navy by putting forward the ship's "best foot," with due regard for the requirements of good taste, honesty, and security.

Visitors. In a small ship, most of the commanding officer's "public relations" has to do with visitors. Visitors cannot be casually invited or lightly treated. Article 0714 of *Navy Regulations* makes you responsible for the control of visitors to your command. You must comply with the relevant provisions of the *Department of the Navy Security Manual for Classified Information* and other pertinent directives. *Navy Regulations* further requires that commanding officers take such measures and impose such restrictions on visitors as are necessary to safeguard the classified material under their jurisdiction. Finally, it requires that COs and other officially concerned personnel exercise reasonable care to safeguard the persons and property of visitors, as well as to take precautions to safeguard the property and persons within his command. The general visiting bill in the *SORN* describes visiting procedures in detail, and should be reviewed carefully prior to each "open house" or other visiting occasion.

When general visiting is permitted, encourage your officers and men to entertain visitors with such general information about the ship and the Navy as they can without disclosing classified data. In addition to security provisions, warn your men to be alert for pilferage, theft, and sabotage. Always conduct tours as if foreign agents might be among the visitors. Set up clearly marked routes so as to avoid crowding, confusion, and possible injury. Limit the number of people in any one space at a given time and have medical personnel available. Create a festive and welcoming air by arranging unclassified displays or exhibits with descriptive posters and by rehearsing escorts in the "patter" they can give while conducting groups around the ship. Courtesy, patience, and tact are the keys to success during these tours.

Unclassified, controlled visits of foreign nationals, within the capacity of the ship to handle them, may be authorized by the commanding officer, subject to local restrictions. Classified visits must be authorized by the Chief of Naval Operations in accordance with the *Security Manual*.

Dealers, Tradesmen, and Agents. Navy Regulations, Article 0715, prescribes that, in general, dealers or tradesmen or their agents shall not be admitted within a command. You may grant exceptions to this to conduct public business, to transact private business with individuals at the request of the latter, or to furnish services and supplies which would otherwise not be sufficiently available to the ship's personnel. Personal commercial solicitation and the conduct of commercial transactions are governed by separately promulgated policies of the Department of Defense.

We address this subject under "public relations" because salesmen so often cause headaches for commanding officers. Although you should encourage your crew to make financial and insurance provisions for their dependents, you should never allow solicitation of them by a specific company. The purchase of insurance, mutual funds, and financial plans is the private business of the individual and must be dealt with as such. Unfortunately, salespeople are inclined to take advantage of various service connections and demand the crew's time for a "presentation," which sooner or later becomes a sales pitch. You have firm grounds for refusing any such request. The *NMPC Manual* expressly prohibits commercial companies from soliciting participation in life insurance, mutual funds, and other investment plans, commodities, or services at any naval installation, with or without compensation. It also prohibits personal commercial solicitation and sale to military personnel who are junior in grade and rank. The intent is to eliminate any and all instances where it would appear that coercion, intimidation, or pressure was used because of rank, grade, or position.

Figure 4-1. An informal visit by the commanding officer to his engineering spaces will demonstrate his command interest to his engineering department.

Press Relations. The duties of the ship's public affairs officer, and the commanding officer's public affairs responsibilities, are discussed in Chapters 6 and 12; but a discussion of the generalities of relations with the press is in order here. Press personnel and correspondents occupy an unique place in our society. They are quite conscious of this position and of what they hold to be their prerogatives. Their need to produce interesting news and your requirements regarding security can conflict on occasion. This makes relations with the press a ticklish business for the average commanding officer.

Generally, press releases are not made directly to the press by ships, but there may be emergencies or special occasions where you will be authorized or even directed to make a press release locally.

Figure 4-2. A pleasant and happy wardroom atmosphere is the result of command interest.

Ask for help from your type commander if you need it. If not, be sure you comply with the provisions of the *Public Affairs Manual*. You may originate hometown news releases, but these should be sent to the Home Town News Release Center for screening and release.

When direct contact with the press is authorized or directed by higher authority, you should review with your PAO the questions which he thinks the press will ask and the areas of possible inquiry. Write down the details of the situation you are preparing to discuss and be sure of your numbers. Rehearse your answers if time permits.

If your ship does not have a public affairs officer of sufficient experience, ask help from the type commander or any nearby shore commander.

When you meet the press, try to be honest and forthright. If you feel you cannot furnish an answer for some reason, tell the press why. If you do not know the answer, say so and offer to provide it as soon as possible. Although journalists may strike you as "pushy" or lacking in respect, most are thorough professionals. They are required by their editors to ask embarrassing questions, and they don't always expect an answer.

The *U.S. Navy Public Affairs Regulations Manual* (*NAVSO P-1035*) provides all the guidance you and your PAO should need. In the administration of public affairs, though, keep in mind the inescapable fact that it is *your* responsibility.

Command Interest

To quote an old plantation saying, "There is no fertilizer like the master's footprints." There are many details in administering a ship, and this chapter has touched on only a few. Many others are covered at appropriate places in other chapters. Certainly the administration of your ship is primarily the executive officer's function, but never delude yourself that you can afford to neglect it. As in all areas of command, as soon as you fail to manifest interest in administration, it will become of less interest to your officers and crew. Show an appropriate interest, and your officers and men will do the rest, while you, with this "futile driveling" attended to, can concentrate on being another Wellington, and training your men to beat any force opposed to them.

5

The Executive Officer

As executive officer, I try to organize the work of my ship so that at the end of the day I have worked each officer and man productively and to his limit—but also so that all officers and men have worked equally.

—Commander Todd Nicholson, USN
(former executive officer)

Status, Authority, and Responsibilities

Title 10, United States Code, Article 5953, states that the Secretary of the Navy may detail a line officer of the Navy as executive officer of a vessel. When practicable, the *Code* goes on, he shall be next in rank to the commanding officer. While executing the orders of the commanding officer, he takes precedence over all other officers attached or assigned, and the orders he gives are to be considered as coming from the CO. The *Code* points out, however, that the executive officer has no *independent* authority. Any officer of a staff corps who is senior to the executive officer has the right to communicate directly with the commanding officer.

Prior to 1973, *Navy Regulations* amplified these provisions of the *U.S. Code* with a great many details. The 1973 revision, however, is much less specific about the position of the executive officer. Article 0843–1 states only that he shall be an officer eligible to succeed to command, and who, when practicable, will be next in rank to the CO. When the officer so assigned is absent or incapable of performing his duties, the commanding officer shall detail the senior line officer under his command to succeed him. Article 0805 states only that the executive officer, while in the execution of his duties as such, will take precedence over all other persons under the command of the CO.

It is in the *SORN*, OPNAVINST 3120.32A, that we begin to find details—lots of them. According to this reference, the executive officer is to be the direct representative of the commanding officer. All orders he issues as XO will have the same force and effect as though uttered by the captain, and must be obeyed accordingly by all persons within the command. He will be primarily responsible to the CO for the organization, performance of duty, and the good order and discipline of the entire ship. He will recognize the right of a department head to confer directly with the CO on matters relating specifically to his department. It is clear, however, that his most important duties lie in the conforming to and carrying out of the policies of the commander and in keeping him informed of all significant matters relating to the ship and crew.

Concerning the acting executive officer, the *SORN* states that he will have the same authority and responsibility as the assigned executive officer, but that he will not make changes in organization or routine and will endeavor to carry out affairs in the usual manner.

Specific Duties

Prior to the 1973 revision, *Navy Regulations* contained a detailed list of the executive officer's duties. Since then this has been omitted, apparently on the assumption that a partial listing was worse than none. Under the current regulations the duties of the executive officer are, simply, such duties as the commanding officer assigns him. If the CO is a good administrator, he will require his executive officer to be responsible for *all* aspects of his command, and therefore the listing function has been shifted downward.

The detailed list is now part of the *SORN*, Chapter 3; but this should be taken with a grain of salt. The *SORN* tries to include every conceivable duty that might exist on every type of ship, resulting in a long, labored discussion that may not be entirely relevant to your vessel. Remembering that the content of this instruction set in plain

Figure 5-1. The USS *Whale* (SSN 638) surfaces at the North Pole. Did the executive officer remember to order commemorative certificates for the crew?

type is for guidance only may help. Nevertheless, a thorough review of this chapter is in order for both you and your XO. It not only prescribes his duties, but those of all other officers in the ship's organization.

Despite the exhaustiveness of his listed duties, the executive officer cannot literally "do everything." He, like the commanding officer, must delegate many of them to his subordinates (in this case, the department heads); but like him also, even though he delegates, he is still responsible. The wise commander will insist on this delegation and will support the results, good or bad. Further, he should encourage the executive officer to use the ship's organization, requiring that his heads of departments delegate their authority downward in turn. The exec must use the abilities of all, coordinating their activities and correlating their purposes. If he does not, if he tries to run the whole ship himself, he dooms himself, his commanding officer, and his ship to failure.

One example should suffice. The executive officer must be the ship's planner, but he must subordinate to this function the larger everyday role of administrator and expediter. Administration and planning are important, but only when they implement larger goals. Delegation operates here when the executive officer originates the *overall* plan and requires that his subordinates make *dependent* plans.

Remember at all times that being executive officer is no piece of cake. He must compose conflicts, establish unity of purpose, and mold the spirit of the ship. He must assure that these duties are carried out within the policies you set forth, and everything he does must reflect your personality, rather than his own. This is a tall order, particularly for a relatively senior officer, one who has formed his own opinions and is preparing himself for his own eventual command. A wise CO will consider these facts in dealing with him, and will attempt to ease the burden with understanding rather than recrimination.

Relationship with the Commanding Officer

Field Marshal Paul Von Hindenberg, in commenting on the relationship between a general and his chief of staff, once remarked: "If the relations between the general and his chief of staff are what they ought to be, the boundaries are easily adjusted by soldierly and personal tact and the qualities of mind on both sides."

This German Army philosophy applies equally well to a naval commanding officer and his executive officer.

Official directives make plain what the relationship should be. *Navy Regulations*, Article 0706, provides that the commanding officer shall keep the executive officer informed of his policies, and normally shall issue all orders relative to the duties of that command through him. Accordingly, the CO will normally require that all communications of an official nature from subordinates be forwarded through the executive officer. The two exceptions to this, already mentioned, are the department heads, when necessary, and those senior to the executive officer (usually medical or dental officers). Even these officers, however, must keep the XO informed on matters related to the functions of the command.

Obviously, the executive officer must use the nicest sense of judgment in carrying out your policies. Equally obviously, you, as the commanding officer, must preside wisely. While you must require that your exec carry out the spirit and letter of the regulations, there will be times when you can learn from him, if you encourage his initiative and ask for his opinions and advice. This is particularly true if he has served in your ship type before.

There are ways you can help him to function more effectively. For instance, with regard to those provisions of the regulations which use the word "normally" when discussing communications "around" the XO, most senior officers counsel against permitting department heads too much latitude. Require them to communicate via the executive officer unless a real emergency exists.

Again, it is unwise to take upon yourself the executive officer's duties. This will be a specially inviting pitfall for you as a new commanding officer if you were XO in your last sea tour. In fact, it is doubly wrong. It occupies your attention uselessly and at the same time it deprives you of your executive officer's best efforts.

Finally, keep your executive officer informed at all times of your changes of policy and schedule. He is only as good as the last information he has.

The commanding officer must ask himself throughout his tour—*how do I use my executive officer*? Is he an administrator, a policy-setter, or both? Is he really the assistant commanding officer? Do I have to lean on him to make him perform? Does he follow me or go his own way? How is our rapport? How much do we talk each day, and where? Is he strong or weak? What is my evaluation of his potential for command?

The answers to these questions provide a basis for judging whether or not your relationship is healthy and providing the results you want as far as proper administration of your ship is concerned,

Figure 5-2. The executive officer at personnel inspection. He can take your place on some Saturdays and can be of great assistance on all days. Learn to use your executive officer's ability whenever you can.

as well as whether you are giving him an adequate opportunity to demonstrate and extend his abilities.

In the last analysis, the XO's performance will depend on yours. The successful commanding officer will develop in his executive officer the ability to manage his own and the crew's time and effort to do the most for the ship. He will instill in his executive officer the most efficient methods of keeping him informed of every aspect of the ship's administration and operation. He will delve into details when necessary to assure that correct action is being taken, but will not preempt responsibility or seem to run a one-man show. It is imperative that the commanding officer grant sufficient authority to his executive to enable him to carry out his responsibilities. He must set and make known his priorities. There is never enough time or money to do everything; the executive officer must know what you want done first. A continuous appraisal of "What have we accomplished? What do we intend to do next?" with him will insure that you are both running on the same track. All these are things *you* must do to make *him* more effective.

One exception to this principle is punishment. Punishment is the prerogative and duty of the commanding officer, and cannot be delegated. Establish early with your executive officer what you consider punishment and what is only "completing a prescribed duty satisfactorily." Never tolerate unofficial extra duty, but do support his judgment of when required work has been completed so that liberty can begin. (On a small and busy ship duty often can seem like punishment.) Avoid like the plague any form of mass punishment. Either find the culprit or make known your displeasure in some other manner.

Try to find ways to break free time for your XO to work. As soon as you can establish his competence in ship- and linehandling, shift your training effort in these fields to more junior officers. You should do so not only to train them, but also to free him for other duties about the ship. He can observe and train other special sea detail areas and can get an early start on paper work.

In fact, it is a good idea to look for ways to reduce the paperwork load not only on your executive officer but on all your officers. As suggested above, on surface ships you can start by giving your executive officer some extra time while you are getting underway and standing down the channel. You will have a large amount of correspondence that he has to read, route, and designate for action or reply. Have it all routed to you first, but unless you like being bogged down, let it pass through you with minimal or no comment on the routing slip. Let your young action addressees develop their initiative. If you have phobias or idiosyncrasies about writing letters, do your best to curb them; or, if this is not practicable, get out a list of do's and don'ts (as suggested in the previous chapter) as soon as possible. Don't accept sloppy typing or English, but do accept neat erasures or corrections, especially on routine correspondence and forms where the addressee is impersonal. A good tickler system run by your executive officer is invaluable. Keep a selective tickler file for very important items for your own use.

Finally, even though your executive officer's only function is to be your *alter ego*, try to make more of him. Make him feel that he is part of your team, that you want and will use his suggestions and opinions. Use some of them now and then even though you may not like them all that much.

See that he has a share in the success of your command.

Training for Command

Navy Regulations, Article 0728c, states that the commanding officer shall afford frequent opportunities to the executive officer, and to other officers of the ship as practicable, to improve their skill in shiphandling.

Most type commanders require notations in monthly ship's rosters regarding prospective date of qualification of the executive officer for command, and many require detailed determination of command qualifications by examination by, and demonstration before, special boards. Regardless of requirements and method of qualification for command, you have a special responsibility to the Navy, your type commander, and your executive officer to pay particular and continuing attention to his progress.

The first and most important aspect of qualification for command is shiphandling. There are many good books on the subject. The best is *Naval Shiphandling*, published by the Naval Institute Press. Require that your executive officer demonstrate theoretical knowledge of the kind contained in *Naval Shiphandling* before letting him handle the ship. The next step (assuming he is new to your type) is to have him observe your shiphandling under a wide variety of conditions and maneuvers. Then allow him to take the conn under your supervision. Finally, place him on his own, with corrections given by you only to avoid damage.

Admiral Robert Dennison was known throughout the Asiatic Fleet for his method of teaching shiphandling. Although he had been a competent shiphandler while commanding a submarine, when he reported to a destroyer as a lieutenant-commander he had never handled one. After taking command, he handled the ship continuously for a period of about two months, until he had demonstrated to himself and to his officers that he had mastered his ship completely. He then retired to his bridge chair and ordered his executive officer to go through the same procedure. After he had also qualified, he then required the officers of the deck to handle the ship on a rotating basis. Never once during this period did he raise his voice or countermand an order. His officers had learned so much from his demonstrations that they needed little additional instruction. They knew that he would not correct them unless actual danger was imminent, and with this confidence they learned rapidly to be bold, efficient shiphandlers. Not only did Lieutenant Commander Dennison train *all* of his officers in shiphandling, he also demonstrated one of the most important aspects of successful command at sea.

The second important requirement for training of your executive officer for command is preparation for battle. Every general quarters drill, every emergency drill, and all exercises involving the ship's armament, engines, and equipment are opportunities to impart to him, and of course to the rest of your crew, your philosophy of fighting a ship.

With these two essentials in hand, all that remains is your assessment of his overall character and potential command ability, and your efforts to correct any faults you might perceive in these areas. This task can be simplified by asking yourself, "What (in addition to professional competence) are the characteristics of a good commanding officer?" For your assistance, the following qualities are mentioned almost without fail when senior officers discuss this subject:

Common sense (political maturity)
Integrity
Enthusiasm (industriousness and a positive attitude)
Command presence
Composure
Managerial ability

A similar listing made a century ago might be somewhat different, leaning perhaps to physical courage, tenacity, and endurance. These qualities are still needed today, but emphasis has shifted over the years to the mental side. Very few men are born with all the attributes of an outstanding naval officer, and your executive officer will probably lack some of them. He must learn this from your example and from his discussions with you. You must help him to explore himself, judge himself, and then take advantage of his capabilities and compensate for his deficiencies.

The qualities of common sense (political maturity) and integrity are probably the most important of those listed. If a man is to take actions that can affect the entire Navy or even the country, he must realize that help is available if he asks for it, but he must also be prepared to stand on his own. Similarly, when a problem arises, it must not be covered up. An officer of integrity will bring it out in the open, try to solve it, and report to higher authority if he can't, without fear of the consequences.

Command presence may be one quality an officer is born with, but it can be enhanced by careful attention to personal detail. Uniforms should be kept clean and neat and worn with pride. The appearance, conduct, and language of the commanding and executive officers should be the standard for the ship. Your XO will have many occasions throughout the day to address small groups of officers and men. Encourage him to take a few minutes before each one to organize his thoughts so that his communications will be coherent and firmly and clearly delivered. The industry, enthusiasm, and dedication which you demonstrate throughout the day, as well as in your contacts with your executive officer, will encourage him to display the same qualities he sees in you. If you are unenthusiastic and unprofessional, you will hardly convince your executive officer that command is the best job in the Navy.

Composure is generally defined as a state of mind in which an individual remains calm and efficient in spite of adversity. Most executive officers have many opportunities during an average day to show composure, or lack of it. When the 0730 boat is late returning with the liberty party, when the OOD drops his binoculars over the side while leaning over to reprimand the coxswain, and when the commodore wants to know why the colors were hoisted five minutes late, the executive officer's composure will be severely tested. If he can hear the stories of the individuals involved, resolve differences, and take appropriate disciplinary action, all without raising his voice or showing undue dissatisfaction, he has sufficient composure to meet almost any situation.

The modern ship's executive officer, like his shore-based counterpart, must have managerial ability. The technical complexities of machinery and equipment, the large amounts of funds required for maintenance, supplies, and the general running of ships, and the massive amount of administrative matters generated by higher command need a firm managerial hand. Make sure your executive officer demonstrates that he can manage those assigned to solve these problems and does not attempt to take them on himself.

An impatient or intolerant commanding officer will often have such an uneasy and uncomfortable relationship with his executive officer that it detracts not only from his daily performance of duty but also from his efforts to prepare him for command. The wise commanding officer corrects and criticizes his executive officer in private and commends him in public, and requires, of course, the same behavior from him in relation to his own juniors.

If you can train your executive officer in this careful way, and end his tour by giving him good marks, you have helped produce a fine potential commanding officer. You may have improved your own style of command, too. Enjoy his performance while you can, before he goes off to his own ship. When he leaves, you will find your own task temporarily harder, but you will have made an important contribution to the Navy. The instruction and qualification of future commanding officers is, next to command itself, the most important task a senior naval officer has.

The Executive Staff

The function of the executive staff is to assist the executive officer in the discharge of his administrative responsibilities. The duties of staff members are set forth in the *SORN*, Chapter 3. It is important, however, to work for a good *spirit* in the staff, as well as towards professional competence. One of the finest executive officer's yeomen who ever sharpened a pencil, Chief Matt Brady, once said,

"Every man who comes to my office with a problem should leave satisfied—or understanding why he can't be." This attitude of service should pervade the executive staff.

The size of your XO's staff will depend on the size of your ship. In a large vessel you will have officers assigned to each billet in the standard organization illustrated in Figure 5–3. In smaller ships, a single officer may fill more than one of them. In very small ships either some of them will be left vacant completely or they will be filled by petty officers. Your own desires will also determine how many of your personnel can be assigned full or part time. In general, the executive officer's office will include his administrative assistant (usually a junior officer or chief yeoman), the ship's secretary (an ensign or rated yeoman), and a personnel officer (an ensign or rated personnelman). Exact ranks and rates will depend on the size of the ship.

Other officers shown on the organization chart, if assigned, will usually have small offices, or will operate from their staterooms.

The master-at-arms force is also part of the XO's staff. In a large ship it can be quite extensive, including a chief MAA, a mate in each division, and brig guards. In smaller ships the force will be reduced accordingly; in a submarine, it may consist only of the chief of the boat. In all vessels, the chief master-at-arms (or chief of the boat) should be a leader of impeccable record and outstanding capabilities. He should be duly honored and accorded precedence over all other enlisted personnel.

The public affairs assistant is shown in Figure 5–3 as being directly under the executive officer. You should make sure, however, that it is understood between you, the XO, and the public affairs assistant that he is to have *direct* and *instant* access to you on public affairs matters. (He should, of course, fill in the executive officer as soon as possible after he has found it necessary to contact you directly.) If you do *not* make this arrangement, your public affairs assistant, with a reporter in tow who has an important question and a deadline to meet, will cool his heels outside the executive officer's cabin someday. If the impatient reporter has to leave without an answer to his question, an unnecessarily adverse story may appear in

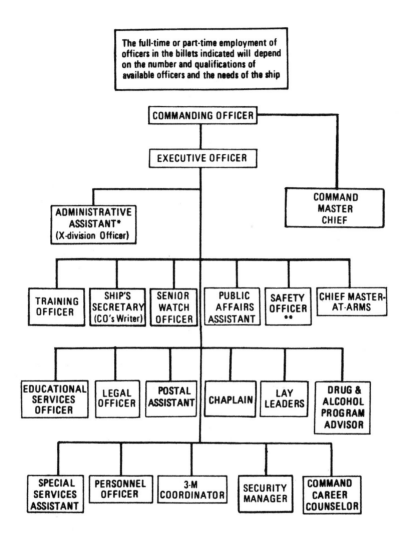

The full-time or part-time employment of officers in the billets indicated will depend on the number and qualifications of available officers and the needs of the ship

COMMANDING OFFICER

EXECUTIVE OFFICER

ADMINISTRATIVE ASSISTANT* (X-division Officer)

COMMAND MASTER CHIEF

TRAINING OFFICER

SHIP'S SECRETARY (CO's Writer)

SENIOR WATCH OFFICER

PUBLIC AFFAIRS ASSISTANT

SAFETY OFFICER **

CHIEF MASTER-AT-ARMS

EDUCATIONAL SERVICES OFFICER

LEGAL OFFICER

POSTAL ASSISTANT

CHAPLAIN

LAY LEADERS

DRUG & ALCOHOL PROGRAM ADVISOR

SPECIAL SERVICES ASSISTANT

PERSONNEL OFFICER

3-M COORDINATOR

SECURITY MANAGER

COMMAND CAREER COUNSELOR

* If approved by higher authority, the administrative assistant may be a department head and selected executive officer's assistants will report to him.

**In aircraft carriers, the safety officer heads the safety department and shall be listed on the ship's organizational chart with the other departments.

Figure 5-3. The executive assistants. These officers serve under the executive officer and carry out many of the ship's administrative functions.

the paper the next morning. *Public affairs will not wait on protocol.* It is your *personal* responsibility, and *no one* in your organization should be allowed to slow down the process, even inadvertently.

Chaplains, when assigned, are placed directly under the executive officer, as are combat cargo officers on amphibious ships. Enlisted medical personnel, when no medical officer is assigned, are part of the executive staff.

The senior watch officer on large ships is sometimes assigned under the navigator, but usually he is assigned under the executive officer. The senior watch officer is the senior man standing deck watches. His job is to make up the watch list for officers at sea and the duty list in port. In large ships, the command duty list is handled by the executive officer or senior head of department. You should make the senior watch officer responsible for instruction of watch officers and recording of qualifications and practical factors for watchstanders. This arrangement not only reduces the executive officer's work load, but gives the senior watch officer good experience in conducting and administering.

In submarines, the chief of the boat is considered the senior enlisted man on board. (The chief of the boat concept is also now being used by many small surface ship commanding officers, and where possible in larger surface ships.) As such, he is your principal enlisted advisor. He is responsible for keeping you aware of existing or potential situations, procedures, or practices which could affect the welfare, morale, job satisfaction, and efficiency of enlisted personnel. The *Standard Submarine Organization and Regulations Manual* (*SSORM*) addresses his duties in detail. In dealing with the chief of the boat, you and your executive officer must insure that he is looked upon with respect and given the latitude, authority, and responsibility he needs to perform. A good rapport with him will go a long way toward improving the effectiveness of your chain of command.

The 3-M coordinator, an officer or senior enlisted performing collateral duty, is the XO's assistant for matters pertaining to the Preventive Maintenance System and the Maintenance Data Collection

System. On a submarine, however, he will work more closely with and for the department heads. The leading yeoman is also uniquely important in the submarine force. He assists the executive officer in all clerical and personnel matters, though he must also be available to other officers. His exact duties are set forth in the *SSORM*.

Temporary Succession to Command

Navy Regulations, Article 0857, provides that in the event of the incapacity, death, relief from duty, or absence of the commanding officer, the executive officer shall succeed to command until relieved by competent authority or until the regular CO returns. If he is unable to take over, others then succeed to command by rank if attached to the ship and eligible for command at sea.

Article 0817 states that an officer who succeeds to command due to incapacity, death, departure on leave, detachment without relief, or absence due to orders from competent authority of the officer detailed to command has the same authority and responsibility as the officer he succeeded. However, his position is limited in that he is prohibited from making any changes in the existing organization, and he is required to carry out the routine and other affairs of the command in the usual manner. This is pointed up by the requirement that correspondence signed by this officer must carry the word "acting" below his signature.

Relieving Commanding Officer in Extenuating Circumstances

Occasionally an executive officer may have to relieve his commanding officer in extenuating circumstances. This should be done only after extremely careful consideration. *Navy Regulations*, Article 0867, covers the subject completely and should be studied thoroughly before contemplating such a step. It is rare these days that a ship is not in radio communication with the Chief of Naval Personnel or the fleet type commander, but it is possible in the case of a forward-deployed submarine that such communications could not be made because of intelligence reasons. In any event, the provisions of Article 0867 must be strictly followed. The executive officer who relieves under this article must make sure that his case is documented and witnessed in such a fashion that it will stand up in a military court.

A good executive officer makes your job easy by getting the most out of your officers. He will indeed work them to their limit, but if he assigns work fairly, supervises well, and praises appropriately, they will produce beyond their expected capabilities. In the next chapter we will examine their assignments and responsibilities.

6

The Ship's Officers

In my officers I look for quickness of perception, accuracy of judgement, and rapidity of decision, followed by strong and instant action—tenaciously pursued to an ultimate conclusion.

—Admiral Claude Ricketts, USN, 1960

The officers of a ship are the driveshaft between the commanding officer, with his supreme authority and responsibility, and the enlisted men, who man the watches, the weapons, and the equipment that give her life, mobility, and power. Without officers, a ship would be a static piece of machinery without a transmission; with them, she can become a smoothly functioning weapon of war, capable of accomplishing as much as the captain can command and inspire.

Unfortunately, good officers do not come completely trained and ready to fit into the organization. You will have to take those ordered to your command and place them so that you get the maximum benefit from their abilities. Analyzing their potential is not an easy task, but you should work hard at it.

Wellington, in his General Order of 15 May 1811, said:

> That quality which I wish to see the officers possess who are at the head of troops, is a cool, discriminating judgement when in action, which will enable them to decide with promptitude how far they can go and ought to go with propriety; and to convey their orders, and act with such vigor and decision, that the soldiers will look up to them with confidence in the moment of action, and obey them with alacrity.

When you have finished studying your officers' professional and physical qualifications, and are ready to assign them, remember also the less apparent qualities of leadership every good officer must have. Sometimes character and intensity can overcome a lack of qualification. Robert E. Lee, in a letter to Jefferson Davis, said, "No matter what the ability of the officer, if he loses the confidence of his troops, disaster must sooner or later ensue."

It is important to look for confidence-inspiring qualities in your officers. Such men will *avert* disaster.

The selection and placement of your officers in the ship's organization is only the first step in their efficient use.

In this chapter we will review and examine the command authority given to your officers by *Navy Regulations* and other directives; the limits on their authority; their ordering and assignment; career patterns and broadening; the responsibilities and qualifications of officers for various positions in the ship's organization; additional responsibilities of department heads, division officers, and watchstanders; leadership training; social usage; and fitness reports.

Basic Authority and Responsibilities of Officers

Basic Authority. The authority and responsibility of a naval officer begins the day he accepts his commission or warrant. Its very wording, "Know ye that, reposing special trust and confidence in the patriotism, fidelity, and abilities. . ." of the person commissioned, is an inspiration to the new officer. This is followed by an equally moving occasion, when he takes the oath of office, swearing to support and defend the Constitution of the United States against all enemies, foreign and domestic; to bear true faith and allegiance to same; to take the obligation freely and without any mental reservation or purpose of evasion; and to "well and faithfully" discharge the duties of the office on which he is about to enter. This is indeed an oath not entered into lightly.

Thus, the day he accepts his commission or warrant and takes his oath, he takes on certain basic responsibilities by virtue of these actions. At this time, and later, other responsibilities and the authority to carry them out are given him by *Navy Regulations* and other directives. These sources should be examined carefully by all of your officers so that they will know the extent and limits of their authority, and by you as a commanding officer, so that you can instruct and guide them.

Authority and Responsibilities under *Navy Regulations*

General Authority. Navy Regulations is quite general in its regulations concerning officers. These are found in Chapter 11, titled "Rights and Responsibilities of Persons in the Department of the Navy." Article 1101 gives the duties of officers with regard to laws, orders, and regulations, and states that every officer in the naval service shall acquaint himself with, obey, and, so far as his authority extends, enforce the laws, regulations, and orders relating to the Department of the Navy. He must faithfully and truthfully discharge the duties of his office to the best of his ability, in conformance with existing orders and regulations and his oath of office. In the absence of instructions, he shall act in conformity with the policies and customs of the service to protect the public interest. This requirement is very broad and covers a multitude of possible circumstances where an officer can, and should, take action. Every officer, then, upon acceptance of his commission or warrant, and upon taking his oath, accepts these general duties of all officers.

Required Conduct. Article 1103, "Conduct of Persons in the Naval Service," goes on to require all persons (including officers) in the naval service to show in themselves good examples of subordination, courage, zeal, sobriety, neatness, and attention to duty. All persons are to act to the utmost of their ability and the extent of their authority in maintaining good order and discipline, as well as in other matters concerned with the efficiency of the command. The next article following, 1104, requires all persons in the naval service to obey readily and strictly, and to execute promptly, the lawful orders of superiors.

Exercise of Authority. Article 0811, "Exercise of Authority," states that all persons in the naval service are at all times subject to naval authority. This article is somewhat convoluted, but in essence it provides that any officer, unless on the sick list, under custody or arrest, suspended from duty, under confinement, or otherwise incapable of discharging his duties, *may* exercise authority over all persons who are subordinate to him. A person on leave *may* exercise authority, as *may* a person in a ship or aircraft when placed on duty by the commanding officer or the aircraft commander. A person in the naval service *may* exercise authority when in a ship or aircraft of the armed forces other than the Navy when a commanding officer of naval personnel is embarked or when he is placed on duty by the commanding officer of that ship or aircraft. You *may*, if you are the senior officer at the scene of a riot or other emergency, or placed in such duty by another officer who is the senior officer, exercise authority there.

The underlining in the previous paragraph of the word "may" is not in the text of Article 0811. We inserted it to point out that any senior officer reviewing an officer's conduct under this article would take a very jaundiced view if that officer said he understood that he *might* exercise authority at the scene of a riot, but had decided not to do so. The general position of senior officers is that officers not only *may* exercise authority when necessary, but they *must* exercise it. Such action is a duty, not a right. If, when on leave between assignments, an officer observes misconduct by a member of the naval service, he is *bound* to take corrective action, if not strictly by naval regulation, then by naval custom.

Amplifying Directives Concerning Authority and Responsibilities

Authority from Organizational Position. While the basic authority for all officers stems from *Navy Regulations*, as discussed above, additional authority and responsibility come from the officer's organizational position, as set forth in the *SORN*.

The *SORN*, Article 150, in discussing authority and responsibility, states that authority is not absolute and cannot be applied in an indiscriminate manner. The article goes on to make the point that authority is tied directly to duties and responsibilities; that it is only to fulfill assigned duties and responsibilities that authority within the Navy is granted to individuals, and that the exercise of authority is inseparable from an acceptance of responsibility. This article states that authority falls into two classes or categories; *general authority*, which is necessary to carry out duties and responsibilities held by all officers by virtue of their position in the Navy organization (repeating the requirement that an officer correct the misconduct of naval personnel even when he is not attached to their command); and *organizational authority*, which is necessary to fulfill duties and responsibilities of the officer by virtue of his assignment to a specific billet in an organization.

The final fixing of responsibility has been a topic of interest in the military profession for thousands of years. One of the best discourses on the subject, however, is a recent one, by Admiral Hyman G. Rickover. Responsibility, he said, is

> . . . a unique concept. It can only reside and inhere in a single individual. You may share it with others, but your portion is not diminished. You may delegate it, but it is still with you. You may disdain it, but you cannot divest yourself of it. Even if you do not recognize it or admit its presence, you cannot escape it. If responsibility is rightfully yours, no evasion, or ignorance, no passing the blame, can shift the burden to some one else. Unless you can point your finger at the man who is responsible when something goes wrong, then you never really had anyone responsible.

These are strong but true words, and they amplify that portion of Chapter 1 on responsibility. The concept is a strong and almost sacred one in our Navy.

The *SORN*, in Article 150a(1), next cites Article 1103 of *Navy Regulations* (described above) as the authority for the fulfillment of general duties by all officers.

Organizational Authority. Article 150a(2) explains that organizational authority of an officer comes from his assigned billet within an organization. The command structure to which he is assigned is based upon guidance from this instruction as promulgated by command, department, division, and other instructions. The organizational structure sets forth the positions, duties, and responsibilities of all persons in the structure, and invests authority accordingly.

Limits on Authority; Lawful Orders

Injurious or Capricious Conduct. Notwithstanding the almost unlimited authority and responsibility of a naval officer, there are limits. They must be well known by you and your officers and carefully observed. *Only lawful orders must be given and obeyed.*

Most naval officers are familiar with the semi-fictitious examples of Captain Queeg of *The Caine Mutiny* and Lieutenant Roberts of *Mister Roberts*. These so-called stories drew upon true events. Other examples from history are difficult to bring to the attention of the reader and do not illustrate the point as well as the semi-fictional examples. Read both books; they will illustrate the points in question better than fact.

Navy Regulations, Article 0814, prohibits persons in authority from injuring their subordinates by tyrannical or capricious conduct, or by abusive language.

Limits on Organizational Authority. The *SORN*, Article 150a (3), in discussing limitation of authority, points out that since it is given only to fulfill duties and responsibilities, only so much as may be considered necessary to fulfill responsibilities need be delegated beyond the lowest level of competence. This is limitation of authority by command. It is a vague and not often encountered concept, but it should be noted.

Contradictory Orders. *Navy Regulations*, Article 0815, covers contradictory and conflicting orders. If an officer contradicts orders given to another by a common superior, he must immediately report that fact to the superior whose orders he contravened, preferably in writing.

If an officer receives such a contradictory order he shall immediately exhibit his previous orders, unless instructed not to do so, and represent the facts in writing to the officer who has given him the latest order. If that officer insists upon the execution of his new order, it shall be obeyed and the circumstances reported to the officer issuing the original order.

Article 0824 prohibits an officer from placing himself on duty by virtue of his commission or warrant alone.

Unlawful Imposition of Non-Judicial Punishment. The giving of only lawful orders must be carefully understood by all officers. Most instances where there might be doubt as to the legality of orders occur in the area of non-judicial punishment. The *SORN* spells this out in detail in Articles 150a (4), and Article 150b (1), (2), and (3). You and your officers should be intimately familiar with them. Article 150a (4) states that no order may be given that imposes punishment outside of the *Uniform Code of Military Justice (UCMJ)*. It further states that the administration of *UCMJ* non-judicial punishment is carefully reserved to certain commanders, commanding officers, and officers-in-charge. This is generally well understood. What is *not* well understood, according to this article, is what measures may be taken by officers and petty officers to correct minor deficiencies not meriting *UCMJ* punishment, to correct a subordinate in a phase of military duty in which he may be deficient, or to direct completion of work assignments which may extend beyond normal working hours.

Extra Military Instruction. In an effort to clear up the foregoing uncertainty, Article 150b establishes policy guidance for extra military instruction. This is a much-needed step. More letters have been written to commanding officers by parents, congressmen, and concerned citizens on this subject than on all others put together. Making sure your officers, leading petty officers, and enlisted men understand this subject will cut your administrative and letter-writing load drastically.

Article 150b(1)a defines "extra military instruction" (EMI) as instruction in a phase of military duty in which an individual is deficient. The article states that this instruction is sanctioned by paragraph 128c, *Manual for Courts-Martial*, 1969 (Revised) as a training device to improve the efficiency of a command or unit. It therefore must be used for this purpose and not for punitive action which should have been taken under *UCMJ*. Article 150b(1)b then describes how to implement this form of instruction and states that it will not be assigned for more than two hours a day, may be assigned at a reasonable time outside of working hours, will be no longer than necessary to correct the deficiency, and will not be assigned on the man's

Sabbath. Further, a man who is otherwise entitled to liberty may commence liberty upon completion of EMI.

EMI assignment during normal working hours may be made by any officer or petty officer as part of his inherent authority. EMI after working hours should be assigned by the commanding officer but may be delegated to officers and petty officers. If it is so delegated, the commanding officer must monitor the process. Commanding officers are advised that they *may* delegate authority to chief petty officers, and in some cases where trustworthy leading petty officers are filling organizational billets normally filled by chief petty officers, they *may* delegate authority to such petty officers.

Withholding of Privileges. Certain privileges may be withheld temporarily and this act is sanctioned by paragraphs 128c and 129, *MCM*, 1969 (Rev.). This procedure may be used to correct infractions of military regulations or performance deficiencies of a minor nature where stronger action is not required. Examples of privileges which may be withheld are special liberty, exchange of duty, special pay, special command programs, movies, libraries, and off-ship events on base. The authority to use this procedure rests with the individual empowered to grant the privileges. Withholding of privileges of personnel in a liberty status is the prerogative of the commanding officer. This authority may be delegated, but it must not result in deprivation of liberty itself.

Additional Work Assignments. Article 150b (3) is an important article and is usually the cause of most of the misunderstanding as to lawful or unlawful deprivation of liberty. It states that deprivation of liberty as punishment, except under *UCMJ*, is illegal, and therefore no officer or petty officer may deny liberty as a punishment for any offense or malperformance of duty. This is clear enough. The next part of the article then goes on to state that since it is necessary to the efficiency of the naval service that certain functions be performed and that certain work be accomplished in a timely manner, it is therefore not a punishment when certain men are required to remain on board and perform work assignments *that should have been completed*, for *additional essential work*, or *to meet the currently required level of operational readiness.* This is the crux of the problem and is so recognized by the *SORN*, which then goes on to suggest that good leadership and management practices will cure any resultant problems. This means extending working hours for all hands or for certain selected men *only when absolutely necessary.* When you do, or when your officers recommend that you do, you should make every effort to insure that your crew understands the necessity for such action. If they understand it, they will carry it out readily and well; if not, you can expect some additional mail.

The American bluejacket performs best when he knows *why* he is being called upon to make a sacrifice. In 1960, when Admiral Robert Dennison was Commander in Chief of the Atlantic Fleet and Supreme Commander Atlantic, he discussed this subject with his British counterpart when they were formulating a plan for a joint NATO exercise. The question concerned how much detail to put in the preamble to the operation order. The British admiral wanted to hold it to a minimum. Admiral Dennison, however, remarked that he felt a fuller explanation should be included so the participants would have a better idea of why the exercise was being carried out. Their difference of opinion, he then said, really stemmed from the fundamental differences between British and American sailors. British sailors, Dennison said, had always been conditioned to receive orders without explanation as to their purpose, and had in general carried them out well throughout history. American sailors, on the other hand, were different, perhaps because their ancestors came to this country to find greater independence, and consequently they did better when at least some explanation was given. Presented with a *good* reason why an important task must be carried out, they would respond with a correspondingly greater effort.

Admiral Dennison won his argument.

If these areas of questionable authority are clear in your mind, they will give you little trouble. If your officers understand the limits of *your* and *their* authority, they will perform more efficiently and with greater confidence, and your ship will benefit accordingly.

Assuming that you are prepared to evaluate and assign your officers to their proper billets when they arrive, and ready to supervise their use of their authority, it is now time to discuss their ordering and assignment.

Ordering and Assignment of Officers

Officer Distribution. The Commander, Naval Military Personnel Command has the responsibility for assigning qualified officers to authorized billets. He has also the parallel responsibility of assigning each officer opportunities for the development of his professional and personal capabilities. The officer distribution system, in implementing these twin responsibilities, assigns men according to the requirements of the service, the professional needs of the individual, his record and qualifications, and, where possible, his preference as to billet, ship type, and location.

The Officer Distribution System. The officer distribution system is organized under the Commander, Naval Military Personnel Command, as follows. A group of "placement officers" monitors ships and other organizations by types. Another group of officers monitors ranks. These officers are called "detailers." The placement officer posts his requirements for billets with the appropriate rank detailers, giving dates of expected rotation and qualifications. The rank detailer tries to fill the billet with a man of appropriate rank and qualifications who is due to rotate at the proper time. The two officers then get together to work out details of orders to be issued. The placement officer usually informs the ship commanding officer of the results, and the rank detailer writes to the officer to be ordered, giving him advance notice.

Program and policy personnel assigned to the Chief of Naval Operation's staff determine each ship's allowance list, which is a listing of numbers and kinds of billets in the ship's organization. Theoretically, all of the Navy's allowances are then added together, numbers added for those in transit, schools, and hospitals, and officers are then procured in the proper numbers and ranks to fill these requirements.

Actually, this never quite happens, or at least hasn't since before

World War II. In recent years the Navy has had difficulty retaining officers beyond their obligated service. Consequently there has been a shortage of lieutenants and lieutenant commanders. This shortage has been made up by procuring additional numbers of ensigns. Therefore, many billets must be filled by officers more junior than the billet calls for. The officer allowance section and the officer distribution section together determine what ranks of officers will be used to fill the various billets. The resultant compromise is known as the "manning level." Consequently, since the allowance list itself does not change, your ship will probably be short of lieutenant commanders and lieutenants and be over in lieutenants junior grade and ensigns, but you will have the correct number of bodies, anyway.

Officer Distribution Control Report (ODCR). The greatest help you can give the officer distribution system (other than patience and understanding) is to keep submitting up-to-date inputs for your *ODCR*. This document is used by the placement officer to monitor your present status and future needs. The most important entries on it are those indicating the billets for which each officer is in training and his qualifications to fill them.

Since this report is a summation of inputs from many agencies, you may become frustrated at the slowness with which it is updated. Should this happen, you should know that the central controlling activity for corrections to your *ODCR* is OP-16, under the Commander Naval Military Personnel Command. A telephone call or letter to this office will often correct longstanding deficiencies in your *ODCR* after other efforts have failed.

Communications with Detailers. A commanding officer should communicate freely with his placement officer. He in turn will write to you whenever necessary, giving you as much advance information as he can. Encourage your officers to take care in submitting their preference cards. The rank detailer will follow their wishes if at all possible.

As commanding officer, your inputs to your officers' detailers can play a large part in retaining them in the Navy and furthering their professional development. For one thing, your involvement in the detailing process clearly displays your concern for your men. It also tends to ameliorate the detailer-constituent disagreements that so often occur when requirements outnumber assets.

Assignment to Specific Billets. Only a few officers are assigned to specific billets. The commanding officer and executive officer are always assigned specifically. The reactor and engineer officers of nuclear-powered ships and certain narrowly qualified officers in air departments are assigned by name. Supply, medical, dental, and legal officers and chaplains are not assigned specifically, but their qualifications leave no doubt as to their intended billets. In larger ships officers with particular qualifications are ordered with the understanding that they will then be assigned by the commanding officer to the billet for which the detailer feels they are best qualified; but this is not mandatory. For instance, the detailer will try to see that each ship has one qualified officer assigned for each department head billet. If your *ODCR* shows that you have an officer in training for this billet, and his qualification date occurs a significant time before the end of his tour, the detailer will probably order another officer to your ship with lesser qualifications in the same department and detach the present head of department. The newly qualified man will then move up, if this meets with your approval. In any case, the detailer will work with you to assure that your ship is adequately manned.

Nuclear-powered warships are one exception to the above rule. They usually have the correct number of officers assigned of the correct ranks in the reactor and engineering departments. The remainder of the ship will be manned at manning level for its type.

You may, then, assign any officer to any billet, other than those ordered specifically by name. Generally, your assignments should be made so that your ship has the best qualified officers in each billet. Exceptions can be made where you can afford to do so by virtue of having a sufficient number of qualified officers.

Career Patterns and Broadening

If you can do so without decreasing readiness, you should do all within your power to increase the professional competence of your officers by giving them opportunities to broaden their assignments and experience.

Career Patterns. Before you take any specific action, analyze the career patterns to date of each of your officers. Study their officer qualification jackets and past assignments and then call them in one by one and find out where each one thinks he is heading professionally. He may not know. If so, you will have to be his counselor. There are various books, documents, and directives bearing on the subject; unfortunately, they relate to the past, while you need to predict the future.

You will probably find that you know more about career counseling than any one else aboard, simply by virtue of your experience. Read the directives concerning the subspecialist program. Read the latest letters of instruction (usually published in *Navy Times*) of the Secretary of the Navy to the presidents of the flag and other selection boards. These documents will indicate trends which will probably be valid for at least ten years. This information will be of value to your lieutenants. For your more junior officers, you and they will have to make educated guesses as to what experience and qualifications will be needed for promotion to captain and flag rank when they will become eligible.

Importance of Command at Sea. Notwithstanding the pace of progress, there are certain essentials which will never change. Command at sea will always be vital for promotion to senior ranks. An officer may reach senior rank by other paths, but command at sea will always be the route by which the majority of officers reach it. Any officer aspiring to command at sea should begin by learning all he can about his ship. This is best accomplished by serving in the three basic departments, operations, weapons, and engineering. It also means that if an officer wants to command our Navy's biggest and best ships he must try to qualify in nuclear power. Without this qualification he is limited. It can be argued that an officer can achieve high command by entering the submarine service early and remaining there indefinitely. This has been done, but with difficulty, and such an officer is handicapped in later years. It is true that the original selection system for entry into nuclear power was limited to the best qualified officers available, but in subsequent years the increasing numbers needed have required that selectivity be lowered to around the fifty percentile level. This means that selection to higher rank in future years will not be nearly as automatic for nuclear-power-qualified officers. They, like lesser-qualified officers, will have to meet the broad requirements for selection to senior rank.

Major efforts are now being made by naval leaders to increase accessions into the naval nuclear power program and to increase retention of these highly-trained officers. These increased numbers should permit greater broadening of these officers during their early years of service.

Counseling. With these factors in mind, you can counsel your officers easily. You will not need to be an expert at this time about the details of the subspecialist program, for your officers will not have to face this until subsequent shore duty assignments. However, if you do have expertise, experience, or opinions in this area, it will be of help to your officers in making out their preference cards for future shore assignments.

Your most important role in their career advancement will be to assign them to as broad a span of billets as possible. Advise them to qualify in a second or third major departmental area. They may resist, since obviously they may perform less well in an unfamiliar billet. It will take a good officer with a long-range outlook to agree if he thinks he will have to accept lesser fitness report marks in exchange for a "broadening experience." You can help by promising to mark his fitness report indicating the efficiency of his performance considering his lack of previous qualification rather than his absolute performance.

Self-Improvement. Even though not assigned to a "broadening" billet, your officers can broaden themselves, especially with your encouragement. A destroyer gunnery officer *does* have time to take the engineering officer's course if he will work at it. A cruiser weapons officer *can* qualify in communications, cryptography, and a number of other areas if he is willing to expend the effort. A selection board looks for these efforts, and you should make them more visible by including them in your fitness report remarks. More than one avia-

Figure 6-1. Take advantage of every opportunity to let your watch officers handle the ship in radical maneuvers. Here the *Enterprise*, *Long Beach*, and *Bainbridge* are maneuvered by their officers of the deck.

tion captain has been selected as a carrier commanding officer because he took the trouble to qualify as an officer of the deck underway when serving in an embarked squadron. Give all of your officers a chance to handle your ship, including radical maneuvers.

With these comments concerning billet assignments in mind, let us now review the qualifications required to fill various billets. Since we are talking about all kinds and sizes of ships, you will find many positions described which do not apply to the ship you are commanding at the present time. We will discuss them by major departments. The following discussion summarizes and comments on them; the *SORN* describes them in more detail in Chapter 3.

The Executive Officer and his Assistants

The duties and responsibilities of the executive officer are discussed at some length in Chapter 5, "The Executive Officer." Also discussed there are your responsibilities with regard to training him for command. The executive officer's assistants have also been listed before, but their duties and qualifications were not described at length. That will now be done in this chapter. The following billets on the executive officer's staff will all be assigned to single officers on large ships. On medium-sized ships some of these duties will be performed collaterally by various junior officers, and in a small ship petty officers will carry out most of them.

Administrative Assistant. The administrative assistant is an aide to the executive officer. He observes and reports to him on the effectiveness of the administrative policies, procedures, and regulations of the command. He carries out those duties assigned him by the executive officer, which may include screening and routing of incoming correspondence, assignment of responsibility for replies, maintenance of a tickler file, review of outgoing correspondence, and preparation of the plan of the day. He may also act as budget officer for the executive (X) division, supervise the print shop, and act as the X division officer.

You will be fortunate if you have an LDO or warrant officer aboard who is an ex-yeoman or ex-personnelman. He will make an excellent administrative assistant. Otherwise an alert, intelligent OCS graduate can be trained to do the job.

Chaplain. The chaplain is responsible for the performance of all religious activities, as well as such other appropriate duties as may be assigned to him. He may conduct worship according to the manner and form of his own church, but must do everything possible to provide for the other denominations, either by presiding himself, using lay leaders, or by arranging for visiting chaplains. He should make himself available for counsel on all matters and should be your liaison with the Navy Relief Society and the American Red Cross.

Command Career Counselor. The command career counselor is responsible for establishing a program to disseminate career information and furnish career counseling. Large ships may have an officer assigned full time to this billet. Others may assign an enlisted man. A limited duty officer with previous experience as a yeoman or personnelman is ideal. No matter who is assigned, he must be positively motivated, be thought of highly by the crew, and be a good administrator.

Drug and Alcohol Program Advisor. This officer's responsibility is to advise you on the establishment of a drug and alcohol abuse program, and then to establish and administer it.

Large ships may have a junior line officer assigned to this program full time. This is a line and not a medical function, although the medical department should be called upon for expertise and lecturing. Small ships will have to make this a collateral function. Junior officers from the Naval Academy, NROTC, and OCS will have had some grounding in this area, but may need further instruction if they are to do a satisfactory job.

Educational Services Officer. The educational services officer administers educational programs. He also acts as a member of the training board and assists the training officer. He may be assigned other duties in the educational and training area, and he usually administers examining boards and examinations.

Only very large ships can afford to fill this billet on a full-time basis. An officer from any source can be used, but he will require instruction.

Legal Officer. The legal officer is the staff assistant to the commanding officer and executive officer on all matters concerning the interpretation and application of *UCMJ* and other laws and regulations in the maintenance of discipline and the administration of justice. He should also make himself available to the personnel of the command for rendering legal advice.

On large ships a member of the Judge Advocate General's Corps is usually assigned to this billet. If one is not available, a graduate of the Military Justice School should be assigned, or a junior officer sent to this school prior to reporting.

On small ships the executive officer usually has to assume these responsibilities, unless the ship can spare an officer to attend school.

Personnel Officer. The personnel officer is responsible for the placement of enlisted personnel in accordance with the personnel assignment bill, and for the administration and custody of enlisted records. As with officer personnel, you will not receive enlisted personnel in the exact number of rates your ship's allowance calls for. Your personnel officer will have the same task you face with officers in fitting those men he actually receives into the listed billets.

On large ships a personnel officer is usually full time. On smaller ships a personnelman performs the job. You will be fortunate if you have a limited duty officer who was a personnelman.

Postal Officer. This officer supervises the postal functions of the command. It is an important billet in that accountability for postal funds is a sensitive matter. Obviously receipt of mail is important to the morale of your command. However, these duties cannot occupy an officer full time, and even on a large ship this duty is usually assigned collaterally. No particular schooling or qualification is required.

Public Affairs Assistant. The public affairs assistant is charged with carrying out the public affairs program of the command. This billet is a sleeper and is more important than you may think when first considering it. As noted in the previous chapter, *you*, as commanding officer, are responsible for the public affairs program of your ship, and you cannot afford to delegate the function so completely that you lose control of it. You must employ the talents and capabilities of the public affairs assistant to the utmost, but he cannot assume your final responsibility, nor can the executive officer, under whom he nominally operates. It is important that you establish the fact that you are available to him at *all* times.

Large ships may have a full time public affairs assistant, but small ships assign the duty collaterally.

Naval Academy graduates will have had a short course in public affairs and can fill the billet. Officers from other sources should be able to write and speak well. Common sense and social ease are also important qualifications.

Safety Officer. On ships other than aircraft carriers a safety officer is assigned the responsibility for the ship's safety program. He distributes safety information, maintains safety records, and carries out and monitors the safety program. On large ships other than aircraft carriers, this is usually a full-time billet. On small ships it is a collateral duty. In aircraft carriers, it is a head-of-department billet.

Any officer, preferably engineering-oriented, can be assigned. Chapter 9, "Safety at Sea," addresses the safety officer billet in depth.

Ship's Secretary. The ship's secretary is responsible for the administration of ship's correspondence and directives, for the administration and custody of officer personnel records, for the preparation of the commanding officer's personal correspondence, for the supervision of preparation of officers' fitness reports, and for the ship's non-classified reference library.

In large ships the ship's secretary is an officer assigned full time. On small ships a rated yeoman performs the job. An outstanding junior officer is usually assigned as ship's secretary. No specific qualifications are necessary, though the ability to handle English well is desirable.

Special Services Officer. The special services officer carries out the ship's special services program. This includes athletics, recreational programs, and entertainment. He is the custodian of the recreation fund and all special services equipment. Large ships have a full-time special services officer. Others assign it as a collateral duty. No special qualifications are required, but an ex-athlete usually gets the job.

Training Officer. The training officer is an advisor and assistant to the executive officer for training matters. He is a member of the training planning board, and prepares and monitors training plans and schedules.

On large ships a senior officer is assigned to this billet. On small ships the executive officer may assume it and assign a junior officer as his assistant, or assign it as a collateral duty.

3M Coordinator. This officer is responsible for administering the ship's Maintenance, Material, and Management (3M) system.

On large ships a fairly senior officer will be assigned to this billet. On small ships a junior officer or senior enlisted man will be assigned, usually full time. Whoever is assigned, he should have completed formal schooling in administration and operation of the shipboard 3M system or have had appropriate PQS qualification in the 3M system.

Security Manager. The security manager is responsible for all matters concerning security of classified information. He prepares destruction bills, security procedures, clearance requests, and declassification plans.

No specific qualification is required.

Collateral Duties. There are several other duties assigned as collateral duties to officers and sometimes to leading petty officers. A completely up to date list is probably impossible. However, they include:

> *Senior Watch Officer*
> *Athletic Officer*
> *Chief Censor*
> *Communications Security Material Custodian*
> *Brig Officer*
> *Crypto Security Officer*
> *Library Officer*
> *Mess Treasurer*
> *Mess Caterer*
> *Movie Officer*
> *Naval Warfare Publications Control Officer*
> *Nuclear Handling Supervisor*
> *Nuclear Safety Officer*
> *Photographic Officer*
> *Radiation Health Officer*
> *Recreation Fund Custodian*
> *Security Officer*
> *Top Secret Control Officer*
> *Witnessing Officer* (for Custodians)

Officers of the Operations Department

Operations Officer. In addition to carrying out the duties of a head of department, the "ops officer" is responsible for the collection, evaluation, and dissemination of the combat and operational information required by the missions of the ship. This includes air, surface, and sub-surface search; control of aircraft; collection, display, analysis, and dissemination of intelligence; preparation of operating plans and schedules; meteorological information; and repair of electronics equipment.

The operations officer on all ships is a relatively senior officer and should be well qualified both by previous duties and by having completed as many applicable schools as possible. You will be assigned a qualified or nearly qualified officer of appropriate rank to fill this billet, unless your roster shows a man now assigned to you who is about to be declared qualified.

The following officers report to the operations officer (on large ships they may, where indicated, be separate department heads). On small ships, unless indicated otherwise, they will be part of the operations department.

Administration and Training Assistant

Air Intelligence Officer (supplied by the appropriate type commander)

Carrier Air Traffic Control Officer (supplied by the appropriate type commander)

Combat Information Center (CIC) Officer

Communications Officer (when not a department head)

Electronics Material Officer (EMO) (except when the ship has a separate combat systems department)

Electronics Warfare (EW) Officer

Intelligence Officer

Meteorological Officer

Photographic Officer

Strike Operations Officer (supplied by appropriate type commander)

Computer Programmer

First Lieutenant (when the ship has a combat systems department but not a deck department)

Cryptologic Officer (on those ships which have a CESM capability)

You will do well to review the responsibilities and duties of your operations officer, and his relations with you. He will be close to you many hours of the day. A good source of information on this subject is *The Ops Officer's Manual*, published by the Naval Institute Press. It is also a good publication for the CIC bookshelf, and should be recommended to all officers of the operations department.

Officers of the Navigation Department

Navigator. The navigator is the head of the navigation department. He is responsible under the commanding officer for the safe navigation and piloting of the ship. His detailed duties are outlined in the *SORN*, Article 323.

The custom of ordering officers by name as navigator of large ships is no longer followed. The commanding officer may choose his own navigator, but he should be a senior and well-qualified man, preferably senior to all watch and division officers. In small ships this is not always possible.

The assistant navigator, if assigned, reports to the navigator. The engineering officer reports to the navigator concerning steering matters.

The navigator's relationship with the commanding officer is, like that of the executive officer, close. For this reason they bear examination. You should select as navigator an officer whom you trust personally, one who will tell you promptly and honestly when he doesn't know where he is, one who will make accurate and frank recommendations. After choosing him, do not bother with the details of *how* and by what *method* he navigates as long as he produces results. His methods are probably newer and better than the ones you grew up with.

Encourage him, however, to check all chart corrections entered by his quartermasters, and to keep clean and neat navigation workbooks and bearing books. These are official and important records, and if they are ever needed at an investigation, their neatness and correctness will pay dividends. He should in turn require the watch officers to write proper logs.

Officers of the Communications Department

Communications Officer. In ships with a communications department, the communications officer acts as its head. He is responsible
for visual and electronic exterior communications systems and the
administration of the interior systems supporting them.

Assistants to the communications officer include the *Radio Officer*, the *Signal Officer*, the *Custodian of CMS distributed material*,
the *Crypto-security Officer*, and the *Communication Watch Officers*.

You will have to train your own communications officer. You will
be fortunate if you have an officer of appropriate rank with some
communications experience.

Communications, like navigation, is very much a part of your
everyday affairs. You should make every effort to master it. It is just
as important in port as underway. The success of all your efforts
depends upon knowing *what* your ship is to do and *when* it is to do
it; thus, you can succeed only if communications with your seniors
are fast and reliable. There is nothing that makes an officer in tactical
command unhappier than a ship with bumbling communications.
You may have the best ship in the unit, but if the OTC can't get the
word to you, you are useless to him.

Efficient communications can be achieved. Success starts with
knowing your equipment. Both you and your communications officer should know the location, characteristics, capabilities, and limitations of every transmitter, receiver, and transceiver on your ship.
Know the effective range, frequency range, power, tuning capabilities, and frequency shifting speeds of your equipment. Send for the
manuals and study them. Ask questions. You will find out what your
subordinates know about the equipment and what they *don't* know.
Require frequent and accurate tuning and the use of the most efficient internal transmission and switching set-ups. If you display such
interest and knowledge, your communications officer will try to
equal or excel you, and your enlisted men will love it. When you go
to a pre-sail conference for an exercise or deployment be prepared
to make sensible and informed decisions about the communications
plan to be used. If you know your equipment you won't be trapped

into agreeing to guard more circuits than you have equipment or watchstanders . . . which is always embarrassing.

When your equipment is working at maximum efficiency you can turn your attention to other matters. The "word" is no good if it arrives on your ship and you never hear it. Consequently, you must assure that the communications department has a rapid and accurate system of writing up incoming messages, routing them, and filing them for future use. The same is true for the outgoing system. Insist on strict compliance with *U.S. Naval Communications Instructions*, *DNC 5*, in drafting messages. Good drafting is a matter of knowledge ingrained by habit. Make sure your messages are concise, clear, and free from "overkill." Obviously precedence, classification, and need-to-send-at-all should be considered.

Have your communications officer read the fleet broadcast schedule. Sometimes the best watch can miss a call decode.

A ship's most obvious interfaces with higher authorities (and other ships) are its voice radio circuits and its visual communications. Visual communications are relatively easy to set in order. Sharp lookouts for incoming calls, willingness to relay, and prompt to-blocking of flag hoists all contribute to your ship's reputation. The more difficult task is to excel at voice communications. This is the one most critical indication of the success of your communications department and even of the overall competence of your ship. *You and your communications officer must work at it continuously*. We have already emphasized the careful and frequent tuning of your equipment. (UHF and VHF equipment can wander off optimum tuning in less than thirty minutes, even though crystal-controlled.) Next, be sure you, as commanding officer, know and observe circuit discipline, proper procedure, correct vocabulary, and authentication and numeral coding procedures. If you demonstrate expertise and concern, your watch officers and enlisted operators will try to rise to your level. Insist on clear diction, prompt responses, correct phraseology, confident tones of voice, and avoidance of slang or redundancy. Monitor your ship's air control circuits from time to time; they are the most frequent sources of violations.

In essence, after safe navigation, communications is probably the most important area for your personal concern. The communications officer and other officers of this department should be carefully chosen and schooled.

Officers of the Weapons Department

Weapons Officer. In ships with a weapons department, the weapons officer is the department head. He is responsible for the ordnance equipment and for all equipment associated with deck seamanship (except for that specifically assigned to another department). On those classes with a combat systems department he will be called the "combat systems officer," but will have the same duties.

Large ships will not receive an officer specifically assigned for this billet, but the detailer will usually assign at least one senior officer with the necessary qualifications.

Assistants to the weapons officer, if assigned, are:

First Lieutenant
ASW Officer
Missile Officer
Gunnery Officer
Nuclear Weapons Officer
Ordnance Officer
Marine Detachment Officer
Fire Control Officer

The detailer will usually route the ASW, missile, gunnery, and nuclear weapons officers to appropriate schools prior to reporting. Correspond with him to assure that he helps you meet your needs.

Before the last reorganization of the standard ship's organization took place, there was much conflict among the gunnery officer, first lieutenant, and damage control officer, all of whom were equal heads of departments. They had differing responsibilities, but were forced to use many of the same personnel to carry them out. For instance, the gunnery officer would insist on long and frequent gunnery drills, while the first lieutenant champed at the bit waiting to use the gun crews to clean and preserve the ship. At the same time, the damage control officer's DC fittings and equipment remained untended. The result was the frequent whip-sawing of hard-working division officers, petty officers, and enlisted men.

The present organization is much better. You will notice, when you study the preceding officer billet assignment of a weapons department, and the succeeding organization of the officer billets of a combat systems department and a deck department, that the respective organizations are designed for ships where the main mission is weapons, combat systems, or deck. In each case, the department head represents the dominant mission area of the ship. His subordinates are responsible for their specialties. However, the department head has total responsibility for dominant as well as non-dominant specialties, and he can now decide when and how much of the crew's time and effort must be devoted to each. Life for the division officers is now much easier!

Officers of the Combat Systems Department

Combat Systems Officer. Ships having a combat systems department will have a combat systems officer serving as its head. He will be responsible for the supervision and direction of the ship's combat systems, including ordnance equipment. Figure 6–2 shows the organization of the combat systems department of a large ship.

No specific officer will be assigned by name to this billet, but the detailer will attempt to supply one with the necessary background and qualifications. You may have to help by ordering him to school enroute.

Under the combat systems officer, if assigned, are the following assistants:

Department Administrative Assistant
ASW Officer
Missile Officer
Battery Control Officer
Fire Control Officer
Ordnance Officer
Gunnery Officer
Electronics Readiness Officer

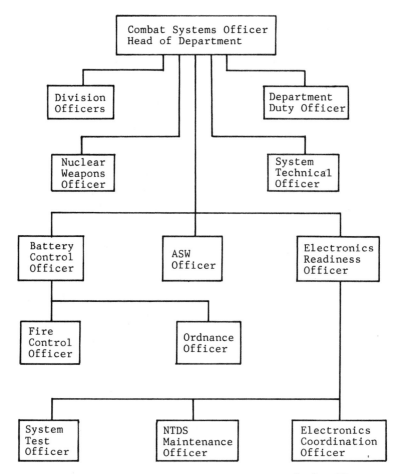

Figure 6-2. Sample Combat Systems Department organization. The exact organization of each ship will depend upon its size, type, and installed equipment, and will be based upon its allowance of officers and enlisted men as set by the Commander Naval Military Personnel Command.

Computer (NTDS) Maintenance Officer
Nuclear Weapons Officer
System Test Officer

Most of these officers will be partially qualified. Ask your detailer to order them to additional schools enroute, or send them yourself at the next opportunity.

Officers of the Air Department

Air Officer. On ships with an air department, the air officer is assigned as its head. He is responsible for the supervision and direction of launching and landing operations and for the servicing and handling of aircraft. He is also responsible for salvage, firefighting, aviation fuels, aviation lubricants, and safety precautions.

He will not be ordered to the billet by name, but there will be only one such qualified officer sent to your ship.

His assistants will include the *Assistant Air Officer*, the *Catapult Officer*, the *Arresting Gear Officer*, the *Aviation Fuels Officer*, and the *Training Assistant (Air)*. Most of these officers will be qualified by schooling or previous experience before their arrival aboard.

Helicopter Capability. In ships without air departments, where a Navy helicopter detachment is embarked, an aviation department should be organized with an aviation officer as its head. He should have under him a qualified *Helicopter Control Officer.*

Officers of the Embarked Air Wing

The air wing commander of an embarked squadron has the status of a department head. He is responsible for the tactical training and indoctrination of the air wing and for the coordination and supervision of its various squadrons and detachments.

He will be ordered to this billet by name.

Officers of the Deck Department

First Lieutenant. In ships with a deck department, the first lieutenant will be the department head. He is responsible for the supervision and direction of the employment of the equipment associated with deck seamanship and, in ships not having a weapons or combat systems department, of the ordnance equipment.

He will not be ordered by name. Most likely, there will be a senior officer ordered to your ship with previous experience in your type whom you can assign.

The following are his assistants, if billets exist: *Gunnery Officer*, *Cargo Officer*, *Ship's Boatswain*, and *Boat Group Commander*.

Officers of the Repair Department

Repair Officer. In ships with a repair department, the repair officer will be its head. He is responsible for the accomplishment of repairs and alterations in those ships and aircraft assigned to the repair ship.

Although not ordered by name, there will be an officer ordered to your ship whose experience will indicate he is meant to be your repair officer.

The repair officer will have as assistants the *Assistant Repair Officer*, the *Electrical Assistant*, the *Hull Assistant*, and the *Machinery Assistant*, as well as other assistants, depending upon the class of repair ship or tender.

Officers of the Engineering Department

Engineering Officer. The engineering officer heads the engineering department. He is responsible for the operation, care, and maintenance of all propulsion and auxiliary machinery, the control of damage, and, upon request of the head of department concerned, those repairs beyond the capacity of other departments.

The chief engineer is a very important officer in your organization. He will have great influence over the other officers in his department in building their approach toward good engineering practices and procedures. In small ships this influence is at a maximum, since the officers under him usually will have had no other exposure to engineering. Other officers not in his department will also be influenced. You should do everything possible to encourage officers in other departments to learn all they can about engineering. Have your executive officer and chief engineer set up tours of the plant, lectures, and opportunities to examine machinery when open for inspection or overhaul. In small ships, and even in large ones, officers who really want to broaden themselves can do so by volunteering to stand instruction watches in engineering spaces, taking qualifying courses, and otherwise trying to qualify for engineering. Make notes in the fitness reports of such officers, including their attitudes, accomplishments, and status of qualification. It will help them later. Such entries have been significant in selection for promotion in the past.

In his Oral History, recorded for the Naval Institute's oral history program, Vice Admiral William R. Smedberg, USN (Ret.), commented on the ability of some officers. He said:

> I noticed that the best of my young officers showed tremendous initiative and willingness to accept responsibility. I think that is the thing I always look for in my young officers, their willingness to accept responsibility, and then I watch them to see how well they carried it out. Did they slough it off? Did they carry it off well? The officer I liked best was one who would come to me and say, "Captain, I've got this job you gave me, but frankly I can't crack it. I need a little more help." Sometimes you'd find an officer who couldn't do it but he'd give up without saying anything to anybody about it. Of course, that's the fellow you really have to watch out for.
>
> I think the officer with initiative and ability makes his own opportunities and it begins to come to the attention of senior people that he is a spark plug. Once you find a spark plug, you load more and more onto him and the good officer gets better and better the more work you load onto him.

Admiral Smedberg was an outstanding Chief of Naval Personnel as well as a distinguished and experienced officer. His comments on officers in general apply particularly to the engineering area.

Keep abreast of proceedings in the engineering department through your engineering officer. Require that he know *Engineering Administration (NAVPERS 10858B)* thoroughly. An engineering night order book is not required by higher authority, but you will do well to require one yourself and approve it personally. *Engineering Administration* has samples of engineering night orders. This is a sound practice from an administrative point of view, and provides for continuity of control in the absence of the engineering officer. Having such a night order book is also a help in indoctrinating young officers in proper engineering procedures.

The advent of nuclear power has required many changes in ship organization. If a nuclear-powered warship does not have a separate reactor department, the chief engineer will be detailed as the reactor officer. Under this arrangement, the duties of the reactor and mechanical assistants devolve upon the main propulsion assistant, and an additional billet for reactor control officer is provided. The *Standard Submarine Organization and Regulations Manual* (*SSORM*) for SSN/SSBNs amplifies this organization.

The following are assistants to the engineering officer, where billets are assigned: *Main Propulsion Assistant, Reactor Control Assistant, Damage Control Assistant, Electrical Officer*, and other assistants as provided in nuclear-powered ships.

In a conventional ship the chief engineer will not be detailed by name, but the detailer will provide an officer of proper qualifications either from your organization or from an outside source. In a nuclear-powered ship the chief engineer will be ordered by name.

Submarine Ship's Diving Officer. In submarines a ship's diving officer is assigned under provisions of the *SSORM*. This function may be a collateral duty handled by the chief engineer personally, or by his damage control assistant, if so qualified.

The diving officer is listed here with officers of the engineering department, but he is not a part of that department. He reports directly to you in matters concerning the safe submerged operations of the ship, and to the executive officer concerning the administration and training of personnel. He keeps the engineering officer informed of technical matters concerning submerged operation, but is not otherwise under his control.

Officers of the Reactor Department

Reactor Officer. In ships with a reactor department, the reactor officer is the head of department. He will be ordered by name, and will be senior to all engineering watch officers and engineering and reactor division officers. He will be responsible for the operation, care, maintenance, and safety of the reactor plants and their auxiliaries. He will receive all orders concerning these responsibilities directly from the commanding officer and will make all corresponding reports directly to him. He reports to you for reactor matters and acts as your technical assistant. He reports to the executive officer for administrative matters.

The special nature of a nuclear plant requires that the reactor officer and the engineer officer cooperate very closely. The reactor officer and his assistants are responsible for some duties (as prescribed by their specific duties) normally prescribed for the engineer officer and his assistants on non-nuclear-powered ships not having separate departments.

Assistants to the reactor officer are the *Reactor Control Assistant*, the *Reactor Mechanical Assistant*, and the *Reactor Watch Officers*. The reactor officer and his principal assistants will be qualified before arrival aboard.

The reactor officer will be ordered by name to that billet. Specific responsibilities of the reactor control assistant and the reactor mechanical assistant are described in the *SORN*, Article 325.

Officers of the Research and Deep Submergence Departments

Research Officer. In ships having research as their mission a research officer is assigned as head of department, and carries out responsibilities regarding research.

Deep Submergence Officer. In ships having deep submergence as their mission a deep submergence officer serves as head of department and carries out appropriate responsibilities.

Officers of the Supply Department

Supply Officer. In ships having a supply department, its head is designated as the supply officer. He is responsible for procuring, receiving, storing, issuing, transferring, selling, accounting for, and, while in his custody, maintaining, all stores and equipment of the unit.

On large ships and most medium-sized ships an officer of the Supply Corps is ordered as supply officer. On very small ships the commanding officer must designate a line officer as supply officer.

The supply officer of a large ship will have as assistants a commissary officer and a disbursing officer.

Officers of the Medical and Dental Departments

Medical Officer. The senior medical officer is the head of the medical department. He is responsible for maintaining the health of all personnel, making appropriate inspections, and advising the commanding officer on hygiene and sanitation.

Almost all ships will have a medical officer ordered. Small ships without them will have a hospital corpsman qualified for independent duty, who will function under the executive officer.

Some words of advice may be useful here. Medical officers sail to a different wind than line types. Most have undergone years of study and preparation as interns and residents, all at relatively low pay. When they come to you they will have what may seem overly high rank in relation to their military qualifications and time in service. They will receive high pay by virtue of a generous special bonus. You and your line officers may resent all this, but if you keep an open mind and carry out some indoctrination, you will find that your young medical officer will contribute much to the efficiency of your ship and a good deal to the education and tone of the wardroom. The more senior and navy-experienced medical officers you receive will have been through this indoctrination process and will probably have adapted to navy ways.

Medical treatment of your crew comes first among the duties of your medical officer. After this is assured, he can delve into his other duties: hygiene, food preparation, sanitation, cleanliness, and venereal disease control. Some young officers prefer to concentrate on pure medicine and must be pushed to perform their other duties.

Young medical officers also sometimes neglect the keeping of adequate medical records. Military need in this area parallels the malpractice aspects of civilian medicine. This argument can be used to point out the necessity of giving this area their attention. In the military, of course, such records are necessary for future evaluation in retirement and disability cases, and in some instances for the determination of line-of-duty status.

First aid instruction is an important duty of medical officers. In battle, damage control requirements for closed doors and restricted access will result in many isolated areas. Prompt first aid until the wounded can be moved to battle dressing stations can save many lives.

Dental Officer. The dental officer is the head of the dental department. He is responsible for preventing and controlling dental disease and for supervising dental hygiene.

Small ships without a dental officer have their dental affairs overseen by the leading hospitalman, who arranges periodic dental checkups and other care at nearby facilities.

Department Heads

The duties of officers assigned as heads of departments in various ship organizations have been outlined in previous pages. Those who are so designated have certain other duties by virtue of that designation.

As stated before, heads of departments may confer directly with the commanding officer concerning matters within their department if they believe such action to be necessary for the good of their department or the naval service. This right should be used carefully, and in any event the executive officer should be brought up to date as soon as possible.

The head of department is responsible for organizing and training his department for battle, for preparing and writing bills and orders for his department, and for assigning and administering all of its personnel.

A detailed description of all his responsibilities and duties is contained in the *SORN*, Article 310.

The head of department on a large ship may have an assistant department head and an administrative assistant. On almost all ships he will have a department training officer and division officers.

Division Officers

Division officers are assigned to major groups of personnel within each ship's organization. They train, supervise, and administer all personnel assigned to their division, and are responsible for their total performance. They assign division personnel to watches, battle bills, other bills, and non-recurring assignments. Their detailed responsibilities are outlined in the *SORN*, Article 350. Division officers usually have other duties assigned collaterally, and have assignments in the battle and other bills.

Division officer billets are filled by junior officers ordered to you without specific qualifications. Naval Academy graduates will have about four times the professional training of NROTC graduates, who will in turn have about twice that of OCS graduates. If you want them to be schooled, you will have to make arrangements with the placement officer for them to be ordered to specific schools enroute. Alternately, you may send them on temporary additional duty at first opportunity after they have reported, when you can spare them.

Division officers are your direct contact with the enlisted men of your command. Time spent in observing, training, and encouraging them, done in concert, of course, with their department head, will be time well spent.

The detailed duties of the division officer are outlined in the *SORN*. The *Division Officer's Guide*, published by the Naval Institute Press, is a bookshelf must for all division officers. It merits your reading also. It translates the cold listing of duties into chapters and paragraphs that tell the division officer *how* to carry them out.

Watchstanding

The preceding paragraphs have set forth the duties of officers with regard to specific billet assignments and the administering organization. However, your ship won't move far or accomplish much without a watch organization.

Senior Watch Officer. A watch organization begins with a senior watch officer. The senior watch officer, under the executive officer, is responsible for the assignment and general supervision of all deck watch officers and enlisted watchstanders in port and underway. He maintains records concerning the qualifications of all deck watchstanders, coordinates their training, and prepares appropriate bills.

Deck Watchstanding. The *Watch Officer's Guide*, published by the

Naval Institute Press, is a good source of information on deck watch-standing. It covers the deck watch in general, log writing, shiphandling, rules of the road, and other safety at sea problems. It also covers the duties of the officer of the deck in port.

CIC Watchstanding. The duties, responsibilities, and requirements of the CIC watch officer and his subordinates are set forth in *The Ops Officer's Manual*, also published by the Naval Institute Press. CIC is a vital part of a ship's operations. A commanding officer should delve deeply into the details of CIC and its watches. Familiarity will pay dividends.

Engineering Watch. The chief engineer is responsible to you for preparing and administering the engineering watch bill and for qualifying all watchstanders. Assure that he is strict in his qualifying procedures and that he maintains adequate records of those qualified.

Cooperation between your officers of the deck and your engineer officers of the watch is essential. In order to be sure that your OODs understand the problems below decks, insist that they be familiar with *Engineering for the Officer of the Deck*, published by the Naval Institute Press. This publication, in easily readable form, describes "what happens below" and why.

Communications Watch. As stated above, you should keep a close eye on your communications watch. *With* a good one, you will be informed rapidly of the requirements of your superiors, and can make correspondingly rapid responses and reports. You will live a satisfying and relaxed life. *Without* one, you will run scared, never sure that you're up to speed. Work with your communications officer, his coding board, his communications watch officers, and your signal officer and his gang. Again, it will pay dividends.

Leadership Training

After your officers are placed in their proper billets, qualified and trained for their primary responsibilities, and integrated into a viable watch bill, your ship should be properly officered.

It is time now to turn to improving your officers as individuals.

This starts with leadership training. You, as commanding officer, must lead in this effort. You can get help from your executive officer and your heads of departments in organizing and carrying out a leadership training program, but you need to spark this effort with your own personal interest and drive. Even if you are blessed with these personal qualities, you will need external help. There are many fine texts that you can use. One good one is *Naval Leadership*, compiled by a group of officers at the Naval Academy and published by the Naval Institute Press. If you need additional lesson plans or materials, the Superintendent of the Naval Academy will be glad to furnish them. All USNA graduates have had an extensive grounding in leadership and can be used as instructors.

The discussion of leadership training for officers falls into seven easily identifiable categories: personal characteristics, moral leadership, gentlemanly conduct, personal relations with seniors, personal relations with juniors, techniques of counseling and communication, and the role of the officer in training. Let us examine each of these aspects of leadership in more detail.

Personal Characteristics. First, an officer must *want* to be a naval officer. If he doesn't want to go to sea, command, fight, and lead, he ought to seek another profession. This does not mean being over-aggressive personally. Some of our greatest naval officers have been quiet men who preferred peaceful solutions if possible, but who fought hard and aggressively when necessary.

Moral Leadership. Moral leadership has always been important in our navy. Americans have long felt that the first essential for a leader is confidence in himself, a strong moral position, and a sense of self-worth. In this area "moral" means what is *right*, considering integrity, sense of duty, and obligation to one's country. Flowing from a sense of self-worth is the attribution of equal worth to others. Any person with this attitude cannot be bigoted, partial, or unfair towards other people.

There is nothing new about moral leadership. Confucius, in his *Analects*, as far back as 500 B.C., said, "Respect yourself, and others will respect you." Bronson Alcott, in *Table Talk*, said in 1880,

"First find the man in yourself if you will inspire manliness in others." If *you* are moral, your followers will be moral.

Gentlemanly Conduct. Any officer with a strong moral position is probably also a gentleman, for the characteristics are quite similar. There are hundreds of definitions of a gentleman. By the dictionary, a "gentleman" is a well-bred and honorable man. In more common parlance, a gentleman is a man of absolute integrity and honesty, who applies some form of the Golden Rule to every contact he has with others. General Robert E. Lee was a gentleman, but so was the rougher General Grant. John Paul Jones was a gentleman, as was Admiral Nimitz, and so were a host of junior officers and enlisted men. In our country, rank, birth, and social position are not requirements. The final determinant is in the head and heart of the individual.

Personal Relations with Seniors. No officer can be an effective leader if he cannot first be a good follower. Simply put, this means being loyal to seniors, but not blindly loyal. Encourage your juniors to question in their own minds your decisions and the decisions of all seniors. They need not be outspoken about their disagreement, or contentious, or overly aggressive. In most cases only the mental process needs to be followed and no expression of it is necessary. In those cases where there is definite disagreement, a junior is duty bound to express his honest opinion to his seniors. Explain carefully to your officers the classic procedure of military dissent: if one disagrees with an order or decision of a senior he should say so, privately if possible, but promptly, frankly, and fully. Once the decision is explained to him or reaffirmed, he must, then, immediately and loyally proceed to carry it out. If you find a young officer who is inept in his relations with seniors, counsel, instruct, and correct him.

Personal Relations with Juniors. Once a junior officer learns to follow, he is ready to learn to lead. His own personal characteristics are the basis of this ability. He must also learn to communicate, for no man can know what his leader wants him to do if he does not receive a lucid and correct order. Communication means the ability to speak (and write) clearly, logically, plainly, and promptly. It means giving orders impersonally, yet leaving no doubt that they are to be obeyed. It means talking before small and large groups, both extemporaneously or from a prepared text, using proper, simple language, free from slang, idiom, and obscenity.

Other characteristics will help a senior lead well. A senior must learn not to be tolerant of small deficiencies, but to correct them patiently and in a low key, and not to accept large deficiencies at all. He must plan ahead to insure that his men do not do useless work that foresight could have avoided. He should know all of his men, but should avoid using first names, nicknames, or taking other familiarities. He must be considerate, fair, and tactful, but still firm and exacting. Above all, if he knows his job, his machinery and equipment and tactics, he will be respected by his men and they will probably forgive or tolerate other deficiencies.

Technique of Counseling. A leader must gain the confidence of his men to be able to counsel them. This means finding out as much as possible about their families and relationships in order to analyze their problems and provide help. He can begin this by examining their service records. After this grounding, discreet questioning can add to knowledge without invading privacy. If each division officer has a basic knowledge of the record and personal situation of each of his men, he will recognize when a man appears to be troubled, and will be able to help with problems beyond his capability to handle alone. The Navy Relief Society, the American Red Cross, and various legal aid societies can be called upon for assistance. After learning as much as he can about his men, an officer will find, however, that most problems can be solved by cultivating the art of listening and by learning to analyze character.

The Role of the Officer in Training. Most of an officer's career is spent in training. No sooner is a man, a gun crew, or a CIC team trained adequately than ends of enlistments, transfers, or illnesses start the training cycle all over again. An officer must recognize that training is both never-ending and important. Men must first be trained to fill the ship's billets. Next they must learn the administrative duties of their rates, and then they must know the duties of their battle stations, emergency and other bills, and their watchstanding duties. In addition, they must be trained for advancement in rating and to further their general education.

For the officer this means formulating a plan, procuring manuals, training aids, course books, and other materials, and then preparing lectures, on-the-job training sessions, discussions, and examinations. This is an endless task, but a satisfying one if done well. Make sure your officers do it well, and encourage them by your example.

Leadership, then, is a continuing effort. It has been the subject of hundreds of books and thousands of lectures and articles, yet every naval officer fancies himself an expert on the subject. Few are. Admiral Rickover said this well in a letter to the U. S. Naval Institute *Proceedings*, published in January, 1981. He wrote:

> The Naval Institute for many years has been publishing articles on leadership, many written by young, inexperienced officers. The fact that the Institute has found it necessary to publish articles on this very same subject for many years causes one to wonder what good these articles do.
>
> Leadership is an esoteric concept which cannot be defined—particularly by young and immature officers. The principles of leadership are the same in the military service as they are in business, in the church, and elsewhere:
>
> a. Learn your job. (This involves study and hard work.)
> b. Work hard at your job.
> c. Train your people.
> d. Inspect frequently to see that the job is being done properly.
>
> I recommend that the Naval Institute call a hiatus on leadership articles for a decade or so. No harm will be done to the U. S. Navy or to the commonwealth. In fact, some good may ensue. Readers of the *Proceedings* will not be faced with more of the same sophomoric drivel.

His point may be slightly overstated, but it is a good one. What we *don't* need is more words. What we *do* need is more of Admiral Rickover's four principles.

Other Characteristics. There are many other necessary personal characteristics of a leader than those seven we have discussed above.

Some are: loyalty to country, command, and associates, both senior and junior; courage, both physical and moral; honesty; sense of humor; modesty of mind and demeanor; self-confidence; common sense; judgment; enthusiasm and a cheerful demeanor; tact; self-control; and consideration of others. You can't teach these qualities, nor any of the others; but you can recognize them, provide an example of them, encourage them, and provide a climate in which they can flourish.

Professional Competence

In the context we are using it in, professional competence starts with general education and includes qualifications to fill billets, other technical qualifications (such as air controller), watchstanding qualifications, and general professional capabilities.

When an officer reports for duty his general education may be well advanced, but it is *never* completed. Officers should be encouraged to take university extension courses, to read in disciplines other than their educational majors, to read widely in the liberal arts, and to prepare for future postgraduate formal education. You can help by encouraging them, by making time available, and by overseeing the stocking of the ship's library.

Each officer must be required to master his billet. This can be done by reading manuals and publications, taking on- and off-ship qualification courses, asking questions, and receiving instruction from seniors. When their services can be spared, officers should be sent to shore-based schools to increase their knowledge and prepare them for more important and demanding billets.

Cross-training should be accomplished whenever the ship can afford it. In most cases junior officers can be rotated without impairing the efficiency of the ship too much. Where this cannot be done, encourage your officers to complete courses of instruction in other departments, to stand qualification watches, and to examine equipment and machinery when it is opened for overhaul or repairs. Follow up with entries in fitness reports to reflect the initiative of the officer and the status of his progress.

Qualification in such specialties as air control, catapult operation, and other areas not primary duties should be encouraged. When possible, officers should be sent to school in excess of the numbers you require. This gives you flexibility in future assignments and broadens the professional competence of the officers involved.

Watchstanding should be made to seem a privilege rather than an onerous chore. To do so you will have to set the tone. Good watchstanders should receive your approbation in public and your private acknowledgment in the form of good fitness report entries. Encourage junior officers to qualify in other areas, such as deck watchstanders qualifying in engineering and vice versa. This broadens professional competence.

Finally, encourage your officers to prepare for eventual attendance at war college by taking correspondence courses in strategy and tactics, and in other useful subjects such as naval justice.

Your involvement, example, and encouragement will help your officers to enlarge their areas of professional competence. If you find an officer who is not interested in doing so, counsel him, for otherwise he has little future in the Navy.

Social Usage

As commanding officer, you also have the responsibility of guiding the social development and conduct of your officers, and by example and advice of influencing the involvement of their wives.

The first essential of social presence for an officer is that of being a gentleman. We have already discussed briefly the definition of this word. In the present context this does not necessarily mean being a master of social customs and pleasantries. Rather, it means being considerate of others. This single, simple quality is the basis for correct social usage. With this quality in hand, the mechanics of proper social behavior can be learned; they are not difficult.

General Social Conduct. Naval Ceremonies, Customs, and Traditions, published by the Naval Institute Press, covers the general conduct expected of officers in the wardroom, ashore, and in the messes of other navies. Some of the history behind these customs is included, and the explanations of their origin help the young officer to understand them.

Social Usage and Protocol, OPNAVINST 1710.7, is the Navy's official and very adequate guide for invitations, seating, dining, receptions, calls, ceremonies, and almost any social event which would involve your ship or any of your officers. Any officer, armed with a sense of consideration for others, and with the contents of these two publications under his belt, can move in any social circle in the world with confidence and success.

Wardroom. Your wardroom (and other messes on a larger ship) is the center of social usage for your ship and should receive your personal attention. If you command a large ship and have your own mess, you will have to depend on your executive officer to set the tone of the wardroom mess. Correct social usage begins here. Make sure it is clean, well run, correct in all respects but not stuffy, and that it is a place where your officers will be proud to bring their guests.

Help the wardroom to extend its social presence ashore by making it easy to have wardroom-sponsored social affairs.

The subject of social calls and visits is fully covered in *Naval Ceremonies, Customs, and Traditions*.

Wives. There are many opinions regarding the influence of a spouse on an officer's career. One extreme holds that a wife's social activities are essential. The other thinks the wife has little or no influence on the career of an officer.

During the deliberation of one selection board, it is said, one Commander Jones' record contained fitness report after fitness report with entries such as "Mrs. Jones is very active socially" and "Mrs. Jones gives wonderful parties." As the records were flashed on the projection screens and briefed, there was little comment by the board members. Finally one said, "Too bad we aren't voting on *Mrs. Jones.*"

The truth is somewhere between the extremes. Use your own judgment and act accordingly. Long experience and the consensus of many senior officers indicates that a wife cannot lift her husband beyond the position to which his capabilities entitle him. Yet, a wife who is overly loud, who habitually drinks too much, who fails to control and provide for their children properly, can hurt a husband's

Figure 6-3. This fine-looking wardroom is the first requirement for a satisfactory onboard social life for the officers of this ship, but to make it a home will require the courtesy, hospitality, and friendliness of all the members of the mess.

position in the Navy, or in any community. In essence, a "good Navy wife" should concentrate on looking after her husband and children and providing a supportive atmosphere and home for them. She will almost always be judged on this factor alone. If, in addition, she can participate in the social life of the ship, so much the better, but this should not be required of her.

In later years and in certain billets, such as being the wife of a naval attaché, more will be required of her, but not unless she and her husband are volunteers for the billet.

Fitness Reports

One of the most important aspects of the administration of officers is the writing of their fitness reports. *Navy Regulations*, Article 1152, gives brief and general guidance on the subject of fitness reports by stating that records will be maintained reflecting officers' fitness for the service and performance of duties, and that promotion and assignment of duty is determined by an individual's record, of which the report of fitness is an essential part. This article goes on to state that the fitness and performance report is decisive in the service career of the individual officer, and has an important influence on the efficiency of the entire Department of the Navy. The preparation of these reports should be regarded by superiors and commanding officers as one of their most important and responsible duties. The importance you should place on the preparation of this report could not be stated better or more plainly ordered.

You may have some difficulty in determining just what guidance to follow in the detailed filling out of fitness report forms. There is lots of it, but it is rarely current, because, like our economy, inflation eats away at it each year. This year's "superior" marks are next year's "excellent," and so on down the line. We will return to this later, for it is a major problem in our reporting system.

In preparation for the final decisions, review the supporting directives. *NAVMILPERS MANUAL*, Article 3410115, essentially repeats *Navy Regulations*, and then adds a paragraph stating that detailed instructions regarding the preparation of fitness reports are promulgated by NAVMILPERS series 1611 directives. They are, but they change so frequently that it is useless discussing here any specific fitness report form or the instructions for its use. A little history of their evolution and the changing philosophy of their use will be of more value to you.

Over many years the fitness report form has had at least two distinct sections, one for arithmetical marks in personal qualities and attributes, and another for a written summary of the performance of the officer. Changes and additions over the years have turned numerical marks into percentages and boxes to be checked, and have added comparative systems and classes of recommendations for promotions.

The basic reason given for these changes has been that they improve the ability of the reporting officers to make an accurate and meaningful report. They do, but the driving force behind the changes has always been the failure of the previous system to differentiate between officers sufficiently to permit selection boards to make correct promotions. After each form was introduced, reporting seniors soon found that accurate and honest marking hurt the persons so marked since other less conscientious seniors tended to give higher marks to protect their officers. When the process reached the stops, 90% of all officers were being reported in the top 10%. Selection boards then had to read between the lines of the written summaries in order to make selections. Complaints by the boards soon reached the Commander, Naval Military Personnel Command, who then tightened the marking requirements or modified the forms with various devices. Perhaps the Navy has reached the ultimate in objectivity with the present forms, where officers of each category must be ranked within that group as to performance and promotability, but don't count on it. This form too may eventually be degraded.

The only way to write a *fair* fitness report is to *be* fair. Start by telling each officer (through the administrative chain, of course) what you expect of him. Some commanding officers like to require a short memorandum of each officer, stating what he thinks he has accomplished during the reporting period. Use your own system, but do something to draw each officer's attention to his performance *before* the reporting period ends and he realizes that he could have done better if he had only known what was expected of him.

Some officers in the past have given very junior officers low marks under the theory that they were inexperienced, didn't know much, and therefore couldn't perform well. This, of course, is a mistake. Mark each officer according to his performance within his group. An oustanding first-year ensign *can* get a 4.0.

Once you are satisfied that the attributes, promotion potential, and ranking sections of your reports accurately portray your assessments, spend some time on the written section. In large ships and on some small ones commanding officers have those in the chain of command fill out fitness reports in the rough on their juniors. This is an excellent approach. It gives you a starting point for the report, and it trains your younger officers in implementing the fitness report process. Don't forget to correct them if they go too far astray in their assessments or marks.

Remember also that lukewarm comments are the kiss of death in later selection for promotion. If you mean it that way, fine; if you don't, rephrase the comment.

There is a well-defined process for removing an unsatisfactory officer from your command, and it is outlined in NAVMILPERS Instruction 1611 series. Follow it carefully and preferably make your request by dispatch. If you decide to have an officer removed, speed is essential; otherwise the wound festers.

Finally, make sure your fitness reports on each officer relate to your former reports on him in the way you intend. Selection boards look for trends. If his marks improve each period, they will conclude that the officer reported on is making satisfactory progress. If his marks decline they will try to determine if the officer really declined in performance or whether you were just careless in your marking. *You* are the best-qualified authority to assess the performance of your officers and their promotion potential. If you shirk this responsibility by submitting meaningless or careless reports, you shift it to an overworked selection board which will have to make a selection without your recommendation. The validity of the system depends on *you*. Keep the faith.

7

The Enlisted Crew

You cannot fool the American bluejacket, and I advise you not to try. You can, however, readily gain his loyalty and respect. You will then have something money can't buy.

—Fleet Admiral Ernest J. King, USN

The Nature of the Crew

In a discussion on the enlisted crewman of World War II, Admiral James Fife, Commander Submarine Force Atlantic Fleet, once stated:

> I believe the attitude of the Captain is reflected in the wardroom and the attitude of the wardroom is reflected throughout the ship. The thinking and behavior of our personnel ashore is indicative of and reflects their thinking and behavior on board ship. If it is sound in one place it is good in the other.

This comment is still true today. Admiral Fife has pointed out one of the foremost challenges of command—that of *molding the attitude of the crew to best support the ship's mission.*

This indoctrination of the crew is no easy task. Most of the men you will take command of will be young and inexperienced. Worse, you will find that to varying degrees they suffer from the permissiveness which permeates today's society. You will also find, however, that your crew is better educated than in previous years, and more willing to get a job done properly if well motivated. Our ships are meeting more commitments than ever before, and their weapons,

Figure 7-1. This composite picture of the American Bluejacket shows but a few of the types of men who will be members of your crew. Each will be different, but they can be molded into a single unit by a capable commanding officer.

communications, and engineering systems require a high degree of skill even to maintain them adequately. The fact that our enlisted men can operate these systems in a highly professional manner is a credit to them and to their superiors.

Your job as commanding officer will be to instill pride and professionalism in each and every crewmember. This will depend in large

Figure 7-2. Storekeeper First Class Robin Marsh, Pacific Fleet Sailor of the Year, of the USS *Greyback*, is a fine example of Navy personnel. His professionalism exemplifies the many CNO messages on the subject promulgated by Admiral Hayward in the early 1980s.

measure on the personal attributes you bring to command, and the degree to which you give your subordinates responsibility and require that they perform.

In the Chief of Naval Operations *Situation Report* for 1980, Admiral Thomas B. Hayward, USN, clearly defined the nature of the crew, as well as Navy plans to combat the permissiveness tolerated in the past few years under the guise of individualism. In his report, he stated that the performance of Navy crews today has been "absolutely tremendous." He continued: "Fighting professionals that they are, the people in today's Navy must strive to become even better warriors. They must be able to use their excellent ships and planes in a still more professional, military manner." Although satisfied with current progress, the Chief of Naval Operations made it clear that in the area of military professionalism there was much room for improvement. "It's clear to me," he said, "that now is the time to redirect more of our efforts toward revitalizing our leadership skills—upgrading military standards and the quality of good order and discipline throughout the Navy." To do this he stressed his desire to "move toward re-establishing a firmer, more effective chain of command by tightening up on leadership principles and putting them into daily practice."

Noting that some may complain about the emphasis on the hard, professional life during peacetime, the CNO said:

> Don't be fooled by the fact that we are technically at peace. We are operating at a very high tempo. I see nothing downstream that promises significant relief from the commitments we are now experiencing around the globe. The world is going to continue to be an increasingly turbulent place. The Russians are willing to employ every resource at their disposal—including their globally mobile forces—to achieve their expansionist ambitions. We must work hard to maintain a credible Navy to counter theirs. We should not be lulled into thinking that the job will be any easier because we are operating in a peacetime environment. Some of our people might say you're taking away individualism. Society is different today. That's not the way I look at it and I know that's not how professionals in the Navy look at it.
>
> I think there has been an unfortunate—not an intentional—migration of the permissiveness of our American society that has sprung up over the last ten or fifteen years into the military in general and, clearly, into the Navy. Our standards must be more than a mirror of society's. Civilian members of our society have not taken solemn oaths; we in the Navy have. We must not take our obligations lightly. Our standards must be visibly higher than those of the society around us. Everything I have been able to learn about the subject tells me that young people come into the Navy expecting it to be tough; expecting it to demand higher standards of personal and professional behavior from them than civilian society does. If they don't find it

Figure 7-3. This man knows what rate he is striking for, and his pride shows.

that way, as is too often the case, they are disappointed and that's when disciplinary problems develop and performance drops off. Crews which already consider themselves top drawer may see little need for improvement; after all, there is no higher state than perfection. Other crews, however, will recognize that they have genuine room for improvement—for fine tuning. These crews can achieve success and professional perfection. It's the approach of the commanding officer that counts.

The commanding officer thus must assure that his crew seeks success, that it desires to be a winner. No sailor in the Navy would leave a hardnosed winner to serve with a permissive loser. *Your crew will serve at the level you demand.* If your demands are less than standard, your organization's performance will be less than the standard.

Command Inputs and the Nature of the Crew. The command atmosphere you set will determine the nature of your crew's efforts. Integrity, especially, is a quality which you must demonstrate. The crew has opportunities each day to measure it, and they will set their standards by those you show in your own behavior. Your impartiality, a component of integrity, is a necessity in building a good crew. The old expression "a taut ship is a happy ship" is true largely because in such a ship there is impartiality of treatment, fairness, and thus justice; each crew member knows where he stands and what is expected of him.

Another factor involving command integrity is loyalty. The commanding officer has every right to expect his crew to be loyal to the ship—and to him personally because he represents the ship. Loyalty, however, must be worked for; it does not come automatically. Along with being solicitous of the well-being of his officers and men, the captain inspires their loyalty by exhibiting his own, not in words, but in deeds. As commanding officer they expect him to be loyal to the chain of command, to "make the best of what you have", as Admiral King phrased it in his famous *Order to the Atlantic Fleet* of 24 March 1941. When—as sometimes happens—the "best you have" is not good enough for readiness, or where the process of achieving readiness works real hardship on your men, you must do what you can to alleviate their problems while making suggestions for bettering the situation up the chain of command.

A crew considers a captain loyal to them when he stands up for his men. The seaman who brags about his ship is beyond price, but he does not come to think of his ship as a "good ship" simply by being told it. Integrity, impartiality, and loyalty of command bind the captain, wardroom, and the crew into an effective fighting unit!

The Command Chief

Function. The command chief, or chief of the boat on submarines, is the principal enlisted advisor to the commanding officer. He keeps him aware of existing or potential situations, procedures, and practices which affect the welfare, morale, job satisfaction, and effective employment of crew members. The command chief reports directly to the commanding officer.

Duties, Responsibilities, and Authority. The command chief will take precedence over all other members of equal or subordinate pay grades within the command during the tenure of his assignment. The

SORN assigns the command chief the following duties and responsibilities:

He acts at all times to maintain and promote the effectiveness of the chain of command.

He advises the commanding officer in the formulation of and changes in policy pertaining to enlisted members.

He ensures that established policies are adequately explained, understood, and carried out, by inspiring subordinates to develop and use basic leadership principles. He encourages other enlisted members to maintain the highest standards of conduct and appearance through effective middle management.

He routinely attends department head staff meetings, and, when invited, participates in wardroom discussions in order to promote communications between the officer and enlisted communities.

He assists in the preparation for, and participates in, ceremonies concerning enlisted members.

When appropriate, he represents or accompanies the commanding officer at official functions, inspections, and conferences.

He participates in the reception and hosting of official enlisted visitors to the command.

Upon invitation, he represents the command and the Navy by participating in community and civic functions.

He acts as a member of, or functions in close coordination with, the following boards, committees, and other groups:

Command Retention Team
Career Counselor
Quality Control and Retention Board
Awards Board
Striker Board
Sailor of the Quarter Board
Human Relations Council
Enlisted Advisory Council
Welfare and Recreation Committee
Commissary, Navy Exchange, and BEQ Advisory Boards
CPO, PO, and EM Club Advisory Boards
Navy Wives' Club and Ombudsman.

Importance of the Command Chief. To a large degree, the morale of your crew and therefore the success of your command will depend on the effectiveness of the command chief. As the *key* link between the commanding officer and the crew, he expedites the execution of command policy and advises you when that policy requires redirection. If he doesn't carry out these important functions, command communication will be slowed, resulting in a ship less able to fulfill its assigned missions. He does *not*, however, take the place of the normal command system; he assists its functioning, as we will point out later.

A good command chief will make it his responsibility to know what is going on in the command. On smaller ships he should be aware of all personnel problems and should ensure that proper action is being taken to correct them. For example, if your drug abuse program fails to the point that the ship experiences a major "drug bust," you should consider carefully the effectiveness of your command chief. It is his responsibility to sense and ferret out those indicators which normally precede such personnel problems.

Your relationship with the command chief must be one of total openness and frankness. It does little good for morale for him to become a "yes man" and a "rubber stamp" for all command policy. Yet, when policy is set he must support it thoroughly and ensure that his subordinates do so as well. He must carefully consider the comments of the crew regarding policy and forward them up to you when appropriate.

Command Chief and the Chain of Command. The command chief position was created to strengthen the chain of command, *not* to replace it! As commanding officer, you must therefore ensure that the role is used as a command strengthening mechanism. It is not a vehicle for bypassing the chain of command with petty gripes and complaints. You must ensure that all hands understand the command chief's role as that of principal enlisted advisor to the commanding officer.

As an example of a proper use of this position, consider one situation from our own experience. Master Chief Torpedoman Edwin F. "Bud" Atkins, USN, embodied all of the attributes desired in a command chief. Reporting to a ship that suffered from feelings of indifference and apprehension among the chiefs and senior petty officers, he set out to improve the cohesiveness of the chiefs and open communications up and down the chain of command.

A physically and mentally large man, he used *every* means to influence his contemporaries to take charge of their divisions. He did away with the "leading first class" and "leading second class" syndrome, which had permitted several divisional chiefs to retire to the chiefs' quarters while still on active duty. He insisted that they tour their spaces frequently and regain control of all divisional functions. Throughout his early months onboard he stressed delegating authority to the lowest competent level while demanding full accountability from his subordinates for their actions. He did this while maintaining an infectious sense of humor. He made operating the ship fun and instilled a new sense of pride and professionalism in the crew. His efforts contributed to the ship winning the Battle Efficiency "E" less than eighteen months after his arrival onboard. Certainly there were other factors which helped, but Master Chief Atkins served as the catalyst in making his ship a more effective military organization.

As commanding officer, you must foster the same desire in your command chief. If you can, your tour will be considerably more enjoyable. If you fail to do so, it will only result in a less efficient command and more heartache for you.

Chief Petty Officers

Backbone of the Fleet. Throughout our Navy's history, the chief petty officer has occupied a position as "a man apart." Over the years the wisdom and success of this policy has been amply demonstrated. The Navy chief petty officer continues to occupy a position of general respect unmatched by comparable ratings in the other services. This distinction is fundamental to the way our ships operate at sea. It is your business to recognize the importance of the chiefs, to protect and enhance their prestige, and to use all your authority to ensure that their ranks include only well-qualified men.

The importance of the chief has never been greater than today. Under the division officer, he is responsible for young, inexperienced personnel who must operate equipment of increasing complexity. Realizing this, it is no surprise that in early 1981 the then CNO, Admiral Thomas B. Hayward, called for renewed emphasis on middle-management professionalism in these words:

> I'm looking for things like delegation of authority down through the chain of command to the lowest competent level. I'm looking for junior officers and division officers who will employ the chain of command to perfection; challenging senior petty officers to assume an increased leadership role within the division and giving them the authority to do so. In particular I'm looking for the chief petty officer to take the initiative in shouldering a major part of the division leadership. I'm looking for seniors who establish high standards for themselves and then demand similar performance from their juniors. I'm looking for seniors who will not tolerate laxity, slackness, in discipline or unmilitary behavior by the relatively few who just can't seem to conform. If what I have been hearing from the chief petty officers and career officers is right, I have no doubt that they want to see me demand more of us all in the way of military professionalism, good order and discipline. They want the Navy run in a manner consistent with the highest standards of military performance—those standards which make us all proud to be Navy professionals.

These words are not a departure from any past Navy policy, even though there have been periods of apparent regression. On your ship the chain of command, used properly, is the best means of bringing about the improvements mentioned by the CNO. The pivotal point of the chain of command is the individual chief. He must be made a *participating* member of your chain of command. He must clearly understand his authority as well as his responsibilities to you.

The commanding officer should quickly put to rest any chief's concern regarding authority. This concern often appears as complaints about the "diminishing authority" of senior POs. For example, a recent brain-storming session between the chief petty officers of a frigate and their commanding officer resulted in a list of those *authority* areas in which they considered their present involvement inadequate. It covered three typewritten pages. Among them were:

Scheduling of maintenance activity for their divisions
Assignment of enlisted evaluation grades
Issuance of extra military instruction
Scheduling of divisional training
Preparation and approval of personnel for advancement in rate
Use of the non-judicial punishment system
Award recommendations
Supervision of maintenance
Supervision of cleanliness and preservation
Senior supervisory watchstanding

At the end of the meeting, after the CO had made it clear that they would participate more fully in these activities in the future, he stated, "Now you all know more regarding your *authority*. It is *your responsibility* to see that each item is carried out to the best of your ability. It is *my responsibility* to see that you do."

Retention

Command Retention Team. Retention, the stated number one objective of the Chief of Naval Operations, will be one of your prime responsibilities in command. The CNO clearly defined his retention policy in the foreword to the *Retention Team Manual*, published in April 1980. As commanding officer, you should be thoroughly familiar with its contents—including this cover letter:

To The Command Retention Team,

Never in our nation's history has it been more important to have a strong Navy to protect our national interest. The prime ingredients of a strong and ready Navy are competent, well trained and disciplined personnel.

The most effective way we can improve our Navy's readiness is to retain the high quality, trained personnel already on active duty. Thus our retention effort is directly related to readiness improvement, and the Command Retention Team is a key element in making it happen. With the dedicated efforts of every officer, chief petty officer, and petty officer in the Navy we can improve retention to provide sufficient personnel to meet our pressing needs. This retention team manual provides the guidance and administrative requirements for the individual command to establish and provide maximum support to its retention team.

Retention is my number one objective. You have my strongest support, and I count heavily on you to carry to each Navy man and woman the message: "We want and need you to stay!"

T. B. Hayward, Admiral, USN

The retention team concept was initiated to foster a career "satisfaction environment" within all commands and to develop a means of strengthening policy and programs designed to increase retention. The command retention team on each ship is organized as follows:

Commanding Officer. Serves as the senior career counselor aboard.

Executive Officer. Serves as retention team coordinator.

Command Career Counselor. Works directly for the commanding officer, serving as his principal advisor on policies and regulations related to Navy career planning matters. The command career counselor serves as a primary technical assistant in support of the command's retention team and maintains an awareness of revisions and innovations in retention programs through his access to directives, reference materials, experience, and training.

Command Chief. Works in close association with the career counselor to support the command's retention team efforts. Works with senior petty officers to enhance the retention and counseling effort, and to motivate the Navy's number one asset—the senior petty officer.

Department Head. Serves as retention team coordinator for his department.

Division Officer. Serves as retention team coordinator for his division.

Service-Oriented Divisions/Departments. Personnel, disbursing, medical, and dental departments support the retention team as required, and provide personalized services to enhance the climate in support of retention.

As the senior career counselor, the commanding officer's specific responsibilities are to:

Pursue a vigorous retention program utilizing the retention team concept.

Frequently measure command retention effectiveness.

Insure that the command career counselor is properly trained.

Actively involve every level of the command structure in the unit retention program. An effective retention program requires the support and active participation of all levels of supervision.

Ensure that the proficiency and motivation of the team members is maintained at a high level.

Accord appropriate ceremony and attention to reenlistments, advancements, awards, and other ceremonies and special occasions.

In establishing or updating your own retention program, beware of blindly following retention program policies. The overall Navy program was designed to give latitude to each command in formulating its own program. Each ship will face a unique situation, because of its own home port, deployment schedule, facilities available, and other factors. Your initial objective should be to identify those areas that adversely affect retention so that you can deal with them. Each person counseled will reveal problem areas. Once you identify them, you can begin to eliminate these problem areas. For example, the command's first-term retention may be excellent, but the second and third term reenlistments can be down. In this case, your program should place increased emphasis on second and third term personnel.

Keep in mind always that *all* retention areas must be considered. It's easy for one facet of the program to absorb your attention when other problem areas may be as bad or worse. To meet the needs of the command as a whole, the system you establish must "police" itself through appropriate control or feedback designed to ensure that *all* elements of the problem receive the necessary attention.

Specific Aids to Retention

Advancement. Advancement is one of the primary reasons enlisted men stay in the service. Moving up the ladder, making more money, having more responsibility, and having more benefits are things that everyone seeks as measures of a successful career. Without the command's use of available service schools and correspondence courses, however, advancement becomes difficult for your men. Approval of travel to service schools and provision of assisted study hours and on-the-job training will assist a man's quest for advancement and thus improve his dedication to a career. It will also help those of your crew who desire specific training for striker designation and change of rating. Another useful technique is the publication of lists of personnel who are eligible and ineligible for advancement-in-rate examinations. This can help motivate both groups.

After advancement results are published, hold individual or group ceremonies, with the entire department or crew attending, depending on the size of the group and the desires of the individual. Such ceremonies will not only give recognition to those advanced, but may "light off" those who have previously lacked motivation.

Education. Although not a written rule, men generally assume that higher education will provide better career opportunities. Although benefits change with the years, there will always be *some* educational program available to your enlisted personnel. The *Retention Team Manual* describes the current programs in detail. By providing flexible hours and command recognition of the importance of the various educational programs available, you will generate interest and involvement—and enhance your retention climate.

Dependents' Organizations. The welfare and happiness of your crew's dependents is an important element of morale. You can reach dependents in many ways, but one of the best is through dependents' organizations. The following programs can be presented to the ship's wives' club and other dependents' organizations for consideration:

Figure 7-4. The welfare of the dependents of your crew is very important to their morale, and will occupy much of your time. This wives' club group is appearing on a ship's television program on the USS *Nimitz*. The commanding officer, officers, enlisted men, and their dependents will now understand the ship's problems better.

Welcome aboard packages

Designated sponsor (if a member's sponsor is unmarried)

Ensuring that the wives' club president and ombudsperson contact all newly reporting families

Luncheons for new families and departing families

During deployments, the organization of potluck suppers, picnics, card games, bazaars, swimming parties, sightseeing tours, bowling leagues, and other recreational activities

Welcome home parties for the command, using Navy clubs and facilities

A list of educational institutions available in the area with points of contact so dependents can continue their education.

Reenlistment. There is no guarantee that your command retention efforts will produce "Golden Anchor" results. However, by having an effective retention program, by providing an atmosphere of genuine interest in each individual's desires, and by command concern for the family unit, you can strengthen your reenlistment program significantly.

At set intervals have personnel office staff provide the other retention team members with a list of personnel who do not meet the professional growth requirements for reenlistment. They can then contact each ineligible member and encourage and help him to meet them.

Finally, if the reenlistee is agreeable, hold a reenlistment ceremony with all hands present. This serves a fourfold purpose:

It provides recognition to the reenlistee
It displays the results of the retention team and command efforts
It may encourage others to reenlist or to work on eligibility
It reemphasizes the solemnity of the "Oath of Enlistment" to all hands.

Though not all-inclusive, the following is a list of additional benefits you may want to provide the reenlistee:

Photograph of the ceremony
Letter of congratulation to wife or parents
Reenlistment day liberty
Reenlistment leave
Command plaque with name and date of reenlistment
Head of line privileges for a given period of time.

Request Mast. When an individual submits a special request form (chit) through the chain of command, *it will be the most important thing on his mind until he gets an answer.* Resentment sets in rapidly if the chit is slowly or sloppily handled, or disappears in someone's pocket or "in-basket." Few things say so clearly to a man that he isn't very important as a badly handled request chit. Remember, that chit is his own, personal, *formal* test of your personnel management standards. It isn't a "yes" answer that is important, it is that the command cares enough to give him *some answer quickly!*

Welcome Aboard/Sponsors. This is an area where many commands fail in their retention efforts. Some years ago, a young second class petty officer assigned to a fast attack submarine stopped to chat with the commanding officer prior to his discharge. The captain asked him if there was anything he personally would recommend to improve the retention climate onboard. The petty officer replied, "I'm grateful for the education and I liked my shipmates, but I knew the

Figure 7-5. Dependents living overseas will help the morale of your officers and men, but you will have to be concerned with their welfare. This family is arriving in Greece to be with their husband and father.

day I reported that I'd leave at the completion of my obligated service." When questioned further he said, "When I reported aboard I got absolutely no assistance in settling into my new job. When I asked the chief of the boat about a place to sleep, he assigned me to a temporary bunk in the torpedo room next to a torpedo, and I was never assigned a personal locker. From that first day I knew that if the system cared that little for me I did not want to be part of it." The CO learned from this unfortunate episode, but the Navy lost a fine young petty officer. Ensure that your welcome aboard practices are formalized and *always* carried out. Sponsors should be intelligently chosen and should contact the new man before his arrival in the area. Send spouse-to-spouse notes when this is possible. Publishing a "welcome aboard" note in the plan of the day, introducing the crew to each newly reporting individual, can also prove highly beneficial.

The Family. Family happiness is vital to a man's continued career satisfaction. There is no way a command can solve all family problems, but concern for them can go far in easing the difficulties of service life and can certainly improve your retention program. Some thoughts in improving your practices in this area are to encourage spouses to come aboard often, both for ceremonies and formal counseling and presentations on Navy Career Benefits. Make the spouse a "co-star" in award, advancement and reenlistment ceremonies. Scheduling a few minutes for coffee with the commanding officer can often turn a wife into a real booster of the command and its programs.

Striker Selection Board. Establishment of a Striker Selection Board can provide significant motivation for the non-designated community. Recognition for professional achievements and initiative through designation as a striker can be decisive in a future reenlistment decision. This is not to imply that all non-designated personnel should be designated through this process. Only those who have shown a sincere desire and personal initiative in preparing for a particular rating should be designated.

Recognition. This is the most important ingredient in a successful retention program. Recognition is a measure of the command's care, concern, and appreciation for the efforts of an individual. The use of "all hands" quarters to recognize individual and group achievements is very important. "Positive strokes," when deserved, are a proven method of improving the morale of a crew.

There are other levels in the command, such as in work centers or divisions, where recognition ceremonies can also be carried out. The act of recognition is more important than the level of recognition.

Discipline

Aboard ship, discipline means a prompt, willing responsiveness to commands. The best discipline is self-discipline; the individual doing the right thing because he *wants* to do it. You can create it in your command by building willingness, enthusiasm, and co-operation. It will then exist not only while men are under the eyes of their superiors, but while they are off duty as well.

Admiral Arleigh Burke wrote: "A well disciplined organization is one whose members work with enthusiasm, willingness, and zest as individuals and as a group to fulfill the mission of the organization with expectation of success. Lack of discipline results in loss of smooth, determined operating action and combat efficiency."

In striving for a high level of discipline, remember that men admire an individual who lives in accordance with the code he enforces. They will resent a commanding officer who demands behavior from his followers he doesn't exhibit himself. The captain who expects unflinching obedience and cooperation from his men will do well to give the same obedience and cooperation to his own seniors. If he combines this with ability and a genuine interest in his men's well-being, he will eliminate many of his disciplinary problems.

Positive Discipline. Naval Leadership, published by the Naval Institute Press, discusses positive discipline as follows:

> Positive discipline is the development of that state of mind in which individuals endeavor to do the right thing, with or without specific instructions. In order for positive discipline to operate most effectively, it is necessary that personnel *know* their jobs thoroughly. Training, therefore, is one of the basic factors involved in this type of discipline. The commanding officer must strive constantly to train his men to perform their duties in such a way as not to break regulations. In this way he is disciplining them just as surely as by punishing them after an infraction, but in a much more productive manner.

The following actions on your part will assist in the achievement of positive discipline. You must:

Maintain a general attitude of approval of the crew. A feeling of distrust on your part is soon transmitted to the men, and causes a general sense of insecurity.

Let your crew know what is expected of them. This can be done by formal written directives and by clear verbal instructions.

Keep the crew informed of their mission. A sailor works better when he fully understands the relationship of what he does and how he does it to the whole task of the ship.

Let your men know that their officers are behind them as long as they perform their duties to the best of their abilities.

Keep your crew informed of their progress. This is equally important whether their work is good or bad.

Keep your crew informed, within security restrictions, of any changes which will affect their future.

Assure the crew by your actions that each will receive fair and impartial treatment.

Improve your own professional ability. Enlisted men have been asked what they think makes a good leader. They say they like and respect professional competence more than any other single attribute.

Delegate authority, with corresponding responsibility, as far down in the organization as competence exists.

Punishment. Punishment, like positive discipline, which it is intended to uphold, is your personal responsibility. It cannot be delegated, since it can legally be awarded only by you or by a legally convened court-martial acting in accordance with the *Uniform Code of Military Justice.* No officer except the commanding officer has any authority to inflict punishment on any person he is assigned to control. Your subordinates must be careful not to assume this authority under the assumption that they will save time for you, or that the accused will get a fairer deal from them than from you, or for any other reason. You must ensure that your officers and chiefs understand they can only exercise *positive* discipline in guiding the offender's future actions. That failing, they must place them on report for you to deal with. Insist that all infractions are fully investigated before this is done. The mast process aboard ship should be a tribunal feared and respected by all crew members.

Military Justice. Present day command qualification requires training and examination in military justice. It is essential that you review the *Manual for Court Martial* and *Judge Advocate General*

Manual frequently, especially prior to any legal proceeding. The captain who relies on his past experience to conduct mast is being unfair to his crew and may find himself on the wrong side of the military justice system.

The American military justice system is designed as the last resort in enforcing standards of behavior and discipline in the services. It is governed by the *Uniform Code of Military Justice (UCMJ)*, which came into effect in 1951.

The *UCMJ* is a compromise between the necessities of military discipline and the need to guarantee that this discipline does not hinge simply on the wishes of the commanding officer. As an added safeguard, an all-civilian Court of Military Appeals, insulated from military control, reviews the records of military trials to ensure due process.

The following constitutes a brief overview of the system, as an aid to you in explaining it to the crew.

The military justice system provides for three kinds of courts-martial. The most formal is the general court-martial. This court can impose any punishment up to and including death, subject to the limitations described in the *UCMJ*'s Table of Maximum Punishments.

The second type is the special court-martial. It requires no trained lawyer to serve as "judge," and is less formal than a general court. A special court-martial is convened for less serious offenses, and can impose up to six months' confinement and a bad conduct discharge.

The summary court-martial, now seldom used, is the third kind of court-martial. It is similar to a civilian police court: a one-person court, usually consisting of a field-grade officer. The maximum sentence it can impose is thirty days' confinement.

In addition to the three kinds of courts-martial, service members may be subject to nonjudicial punishments, called Article 15's, after the article of the *UCMJ* that governs nonjudicial punishment. All service members may be subject to Article 15 actions, but some types of punishments are applicable only to certain ranks.

Article 15 permits the commanding officer to impose such punishments as:

Restriction to the ship

Withholding of privileges

Extra duty

Reduction to the next lower grade, if the grade from which the accused would be reduced is within the promotion authority of the commanding officer

Forfeiture of pay

Correctional custody

Confinement for not more than three consecutive days on bread and water.

The accused may submit matters in extenuation and mitigation to the commander, and may have counsel present when appealing. Further, the officer who imposes the punishment, or his superior, can suspend the punishment, set it aside, or remit any part of it. Any appeal or suspension of punishment does not affect the question of guilt or innocence, however.

Procedures of general or special courts-martial are somewhat different from civilian courts. For instance, the number of court members usually is smaller—at least three in a special and five in a general court-martial. The members of the court will be officers, unless the accused is enlisted and requests trial by an "enlisted court." In that case, at least one-third of the court must be enlisted men.

After an evidence-gathering investigation, the first step in the court-martial process is a so-called "Article 32" hearing. This is similar to a civil preliminary hearing or grand jury hearing. However, in contrast to civilian procedure, a defendant must hear the charges against him and may question witnesses at this time.

The results of the Article 32 hearing are then submitted to the "convening authority"—the officer in the chain of command with the power to convene the court. In another departure from civil law, the convening authority then appoints the court's members.

As the judge does in civil courts, the law officer of a general court-martial gives detailed instructions of law for the court members to apply to the evidence before them. This "jury," in addition to determining guilt or innocence, imposes sentence.

The accused has the right to request that the military judge, or law officer, act as a jury. The accused may also request that the government produce witnesses he thinks essential, but the defense has no subpoena power.

The conduct of the court-martial is similar to that of a civil court, with the prosecution presenting evidence first, followed by the defense. If a guilty verdict is reached, evidence is presented before sentencing concerning the accused's general military record. The accused may give other evidence in extenuation and mitigation—for instance, proof of good character. If the court has several members, the law officer will then advise them as to the maximum penalty permitted.

Court members vote on sentencing. In most cases, two-thirds of the court must concur with the sentence, although three-fourths must concur if it calls for more than ten years confinement. A sentence of death must be affirmed by unanimous decision.

The military justice system also has an automatic appellate review. In lesser cases, this is done by the convening authority and his staff judge advocate. The convening authority may reject a conviction or reduce a sentence, but he cannot impose a harsher punishment.

In more serious cases, the Court of Military Review reviews the case. After this, the accused may appeal a case to the Court of Military Appeals, the three-person civilian court. Final appeal of a court-martial case is to the U. S. Supreme Court.

Passing and Getting the Word

It is worth your attention to determine how well the word is passed in your ship. It is often a shock for a commanding officer in talking to one of his younger sailors to find out that the man does not know what the ship's operating schedule is, what exercises the ship is engaged in, or, for that matter, the name of his division officer, the executive officer, or the captain!

Making a habit of passing the word on policy and future expectations and inculcating the same habit in his officers and petty officers are two of the most important contributions a captain can make toward a successful command tour and a well-integrated crew. Various ways and means of communicating have been discussed in this chapter and elsewhere. Nothing is more destructive to a man's morale than not to know what is going on.

A corollary to "passing the word" is the commanding officer's "getting the word" about the policies and objectives of his superior in command. "Getting the word" in a timely manner allows you to efficiently implement policy from above. Failure to promulgate current policy changes and directives can result in a disorderly implementation, which displays to the crew the fact that the commanding officer is not running the ship efficiently.

Minority Affairs

Naval Regulations, Article 1163, states that equal opportunity and treatment shall be accorded all persons in the Department of the Navy irrespective of their race, color, religion, sex, or national origin, consistent with requirements for physical capabilities.

The subject is covered in greater detail in the *Navy Equal Opportunity Manual* (*OPNAVIST 534.1*) and *Navy Race Relations Education* (*OPNAVINST 1500.42*) and should be well understood by all officers in command. The policy of equal opportunity has its roots in the Constitution, which all service personnel are sworn "to support and defend," and in the moral concept of human dignity. As commanding officer, you must instruct all those under your supervision in the concept of equal opportunity, and you must implement the equal opportunity program on your ship through the Command Action Plan (CAP).

The problem of race relations is an offshoot of intercultural prejudices, stemming from widespread misconceptions regarding the capabilities, dignity, and worth of individuals of different races, creeds, or national origins. These prejudices have pervaded our society at many levels since well before 1776. The most notable abuses have been in black-white relationships. However, yellow-white, red-white, and even white minority group clashes have been present throughout our history. It is hard indeed to change the way men think, but if you fail to ensure the equality of treatment of all both morally and under the law, you will make a farce both of the Constitution and of the naval profession.

As commanding officer, you must ensure that every person meets the same minimums of performance for advancement. Similarly, each person appearing before you at mast must be judged solely on the merits of his case. Ethnic background, religious belief, and political persuasion must be separated from qualification and performance standards.

The racial incident in the early 1970's on the USS *Constellation* shows the danger of failing to treat all men equally. From the viewpoint of many experienced commanding officers, it is difficult to visualize some 130 white sailors refusing to report for duty, and then being treated as gently as those on the *Constellation* were treated. Whatever the complaints of the dissidents, there was little question regarding their direct disobedience of lawful orders, and for this the penalties they were given were unusually lenient. Such apparently preferential treatment, seemingly based on racial considerations, does not alleviate racial tensions; it exacerbates them. This is the flaw and tragedy of *unequal* treatment in the pursuit of racial peace. By the same token, never think that you are obligated to compensate for previous racial injustices by using reverse discrimination. Rather, strive for *real* equality in all aspects of your command.

Families and Dependents

The welfare of dependents has been partially treated under retention. However, there are other aspects of this problem which you should consider.

The importance of the family as a unit of the Navy team has been well established over the years. Morale, job performance, retention, and unit readiness are directly linked to the well-being of the families of those you command. The key to success here is *concern*. This concern must be displayed by the commanding officer in his daily actions involving personal problems and hardships, and by his command's earnest efforts to inform dependents of their privileges and the services available to them.

Common Navy programs and dependent privileges and services are described in such publications as the *Retention Team Manual*, *Sea Legs*, *A Handbook for the Navy Family* (*NAVMILPERS 15309A*), and the *Navy Times' Handbook for Military Families*, which is published annually. These publications should be made available to spouses of your crew members by means of seminars, welcome-aboard packages, and individual counselor interviews.

The Enlisted Performance Evaluation

Enlisted evaluations are vitally important for a person's promotion and for selection for special billets. The commanding officer is responsible for insuring that they are submitted on time and that they give a fair assessment of an individual's performance. In preparing these important documents comments should be succinct, objective, and consistent with the marks assigned. Outstanding crewmembers should receive marks and written evaluations that reflect their contribution to the command. Special accomplishments should be highlighted. Unique or difficult watch qualifications, performance as leading petty officer, assignment as command chief, contribution to a Ney award, etc., are accomplishments which each leading petty officer and division officer should include in evaluations. You must insist that your chain of command fully understands the importance of the enlisted evaluation system as defined in *NAVMILPERSMAN* Article 3410150, including the use of evaluations as described below:

To determine eligibility of a member for reenlistment, for honorable discharge, and for good conduct awards

To permit the commanding officer to accelerate the advancement of outstanding members and to reduce those who show themselves incompetent

To inform the various selection boards which select members for advancement, appointment to commissioned status, assignment to special duties, and for special education programs

Adequate performance evaluations are essential for all the above reasons. Failure to objectively appraise a person's performance is a grave failure to meet a public trust, and could constitute an injustice not only to him but to his peers as well

As commanding officer, you must insure that the preparation of enlisted evaluations is not lost in the welter of other required reports, inspections, and the other calamities that occur from time to time. It is no understatement to say that fitness reports and evaluations are the most important documents processed on your ship!

Performance Evaluation Hints. The comments and hints that follow were taken from recent senior and master chief petty officer selection board remarks regarding evaluation preparation and wording. They are, however, applicable to all evaluation reports. Study them and pass them along. They can help upgrade your enlisted evaluation system.

Once an individual is selected as a senior enlisted petty officer (E-6 through E-10), department heads and commanding officers should endeavor to give him a variety of assignments to evaluate his potential for further advancement. These can be made in such a way that they do not prevent him from demonstrating his ability to carry out his primary responsibility. Too many CPO's are content to remain within the confines of their work centers. In this capacity, however, they cannot be judged on their ability to function satisfactorily on department and command levels, as they will have to as E-8 and E-9 leaders.

Many candidates were content to "homestead" in a particular assignment rather than maintain a rotation of assignments which could be beneficial to them and to the Navy. These candidates should not be surprised when they are not selected.

The detailers sometimes have to fill the more difficult (less desirable) assignments with qualified personnel. This possibility should be considered and commented upon.

Don't waste narrative comments in describing how well the ship did on deployment, inspection, etc. Tell exactly *what* jobs the individual had and *how well* they were performed.

Eliminate flowery adjectives and get to the point in plain English.

Place your emphasis on the individual's ability, potential, and willingness to accept positions of leadership and management. Indicate *why* he should be advanced.

Take care to list all collateral duties, awards, education, and qualifications.

If all CPOs and other similar rates are marked in the top 1% or 5%, indicate in the narrative where the individual fits in relation to his peers.

If an individual is marked higher or lower than his peers, explain the reason clearly in the narrative.

Don't recommend an individual for advancement just because he meets the time in service requirements.

School commands should not mark students. Their evaluations should read simply, "student under instruction."

Proofread the evaluation. Many blocks were left blank. Do not leave the selection board to reconstruct the record.

Don't type over any of the block labels. This interferes with form-reading equipment.

Write succinctly, in organized paragraphs.

If your command is not composed of "highly selected" or "specially chosen" individuals, don't say that it is. The board will know better and your efforts will be discounted accordingly.

Fill in blocks on duties completely and specifically. Don't assume that board members know what duties specific billets in your unit entail.

Establish an evaluation review board or some other method of ensuring that correct evaluations are submitted.

Your enlisted personnel make your ship. Don't shortchange them!

8

Maintenance of the Ship

Combat readiness—this is the condition which determines the degree of preparedness of a ship for accomplishing the combat missions which it has been assigned. It includes a whole series of components which, like the links in a single chain, are closely interconnected and objectively depend upon one another. It has to do with keeping at full strength the availability of the necessary material, and maintaining the ship, weapons, and equipment in good working order.

—Fleet Admiral Sergei Gorshkov,
Commander-in-Chief, Soviet Navy

Philosophy of Maintenance

Navy Regulations, Article 0768, "Care of Ships, Aircraft, Vehicles and their Equipment," states that the commanding officer shall cause such inspections and tests to be made and procedures carried out as are prescribed by competent authority, together with such others as he deems necessary to ensure the proper preservation, repair, maintenance, and operation of any ship, aircraft, vehicle, and equipment assigned to his command.

OPNAVINST 3120.32A, the *SORN*, further establishes policies for the assignment of personnel to duties involving maintenance, preservation, and cleanliness of a ship.

These regulations and policies regarding maintenance are not unique to the service. Civilian engineers and industrial managers have emphasized sound maintenance procedures for years.

Let's open our discussion of maintenance, then, with the recent remark of one civilian quality control manager. "Americans," he said, "are carefully conditioned by education, religion, and ethics to believe that they are not perfect and will make mistakes. By adulthood, when they are ready to enter the industrial field, they are fully convinced that people are human and that human beings make mistakes. For most people, to feel that one will *not* make mistakes would seem rather immodest."

Acceptance of this philosophy allows people to make mistakes and to feel that this is normal. As a result, they don't become upset when they or others make mistakes, and they feel little need to improve the situation. They may even feel that some mistakes *must* be made, and that if they aren't, something is wrong. They may even expect to make the same percentage of mistakes in everything they do, at work, at home, and at play!

Obviously, this attitude can be a disaster in the workplace. The solution is to develop a dual attitude. A person may feel that he *cannot* make a mistake in his bank balance or his income tax (punishment awaits of a personal nature); but he (being human) can be expected to make a certain number of mistakes in his maintenance duties. He accepts the principle of zero defects at home, but not at work. All of his supervisory maintenance personnel must work to break this attitude. Knowledge, training, and indoctrination can bring to each man the concept that a zero defects situation *can* and *should* be reached.

This must be done on your ship.

Many senior engineering officers feel that mistakes are caused by a *lack of knowledge* on the part of maintenance personnel and by a *lack of attention* to the task at hand. The first condition can be corrected by testing personnel to determine that each has the necessary knowledge to perform his tasks and stand his watches. The second condition, lack of attention, is a state of mind which can be changed. The supervisor must observe the man's mental habits. Is he mentally lazy? Uninterested? Over-qualified, and thus bored? If he is none of these, there is hope. He needs to be reminded that he must watch each detail, that he must maintain an orderly "scan" or examination of each indicator of success or failure of that responsibility, and that, if he concentrates, he can reach *his* goal (and *yours*) of zero defects in *all* things and at *all* times. You, as commanding officer, may have to accept some slowing down as your men get used to more thorough performance, but attainment of habit and development of confidence will soon bring them back to near their previous speed. Lack of defects will more than improve the overall performance.

While each man must eventually decide for himself that he wants to become a zero defects worker, your policy, example, encouragement, and patience will help him to make the commitment. The feeling is catching; demonstration that it can be done will bring many more converts. Comment frequently to your men on the importance of a zero defect plan, and recognize its importance by rewarding those who achieve it. These rewards should go beyond the personal satisfaction each man feels when he sees the results of his work.

One way of starting such a program is to offer it as a challenge to a group, so that they will want to excel individually and at the same time be part of a team with the same goals. Peer pressure and team spirit are powerful stimuli. After a prolonged demonstration that such a program is possible, men will develop the feeling that zero defects is an accepted way of life, indeed the only way. In addition to their personal satisfaction, your personnel will suddenly notice the secondary rewards: less time spent at work, no glowering commanding officer, no impatient executive officer, no unhappy engineering officer, and no irascible and unkind petty officers. Their gains will be substantial and readily apparent. The only thing they have to lose is their mistakes.

Once you have converted a group or team to the zero defects philosophy, and they see for themselves the rewards, it will automatically spread to other parts of your ship. Obvious candidates outside the engineering department are the weapons, combat systems, and deck departments. There is no reason, either, why this philosophy cannot be applied to such areas as clerical work, mess management, and communications.

Figure 8-1. If these men have committed themselves to a zero defects philosophy, they will keep the missile tube they are about to enter in commission at all times.

Having converted your ship to this philosophy, you, as commanding officer, must also raise your own personal and command standards so that you make it clear you will accept nothing *less* than zero defects. Good men will rise to any challenge. If your standards are high, and they are shown how to meet them, they will.

Your insistence on accountability for maintenance performed and strict adherence to maintenance and operating procedures form an essential part of the ship's general philosophy concerning the safe and proper operation of all equipment.

Emphasis on Maintenance and Repair Afloat

Realize this from the first: you will have to stress material readiness throughout your tour. Today's fleet consists of complex and highly capable ships. Any single casualty or material failure, if quickly corrected, will seldom detract from the ship's readiness for war. Those which are not quickly corrected, however, will usually precipitate an avalanche of problems which, once started, is very difficult to reverse. This snowball effect can result in a significant degradation of the ship's readiness, as well as an extraordinary amount of work. Careful attention to detail on the part of all hands is a necessity for all ships large or small. Demand uniform *formality* with respect to the definition, reporting, logging, and clearing of material deficiencies, whether large or small. Insist that identified deficiencies be pursued aggressively in accordance with the priorities you have established, and train your personnel not to learn to "live with" deficiencies. Similarly, you must attack your ship's established corrective and preventive maintenance routines with vigor and care. An unenthusiastic or careless attitude toward scheduled PM will result in the certain degradation and failure of mechanical, electrical, and electronic equipment. These failures will affect operating time and cause the expenditure of large amounts of effort and money to repair.

The fleet can ill afford expenditures of time, money, and manpower correcting damage from improperly performed maintenance. Keep in mind that the improper maintenance your men perform today may have twenty or thirty years to catch up with your ship. You won't be there to see the result; but the Navy will suffer.

Training of Junior Officers. Most maintenance errors can be prevented by conscientious planning and by supervision by officers and senior petty officers. Personnel reporting to a ship for the first time generally have little practical training in maintenance and test procedures. They can only gain competence through conscientious training aboard ship, by supervised on-the-job experience. It is false economy to assign inexperienced men to independent maintenance jobs without at least spot supervision.

To assure that this supervision is effective, you must provide your

Figure 8-2.These machinists will maintain and repair their ship well, if proper maintenance procedures are followed and supervised by her officers.

junior officers proper training in maintenance management and the need for material readiness afloat. Among the many duties of a commanding officer, there are few that have more lasting importance than the responsibility for the proper employment and development of junior officers. The influence and impact of your policies on the eventual development of these young men cannot be overemphasized.

Your division officers should not be confined solely to routine administrative functions and repetitive training tasks. They must be taught how to perform their divisional responsibilities, and then they must be *used* as division officers. They must know that they are held directly responsible for the repairs, maintenance, and equipment assigned to their division. All too frequently, when a problem occurs, the department head will bypass his division officers or usurp their authority. You should prevent this. The division officer must be required to work on these problems, at least initially, by himself. He should recognize that, as a matter of command policy, he will be

Figure 8-3. Maintenance on this flight deck, supervised by capable leading petty officers and their officers, will pay dividends in the future.

consulted concerning, and held accountable for, all the material matters of his division.

In an effort to increase this awareness among their junior officers, some CO's have instituted a policy of having a junior officer accompany them on at least one of their daily tours through the ship. They then discuss with him each of the discrepancies noted on the tour. As a result of these tours, these commanding officers have noted a significant increase in awareness of conditions and responsibility for material readiness.

Material Readiness

Good Engineering Practice. "Good engineering practice" means the safe and proper operation of engineering plants. It is a philosophy based on a respect for, and an understanding of, the equipment being operated. It applies not only to shipboard propulsion plant operation, but to everyday operations and maintenance routine on all other shipboard systems as well. Good engineering practice begins with each watchstander. It means such things as feeling pipes and equipment for abnormal temperatures, listening to equipment for unusual noises, fixing minor discrepancies such as drips, packing leaks before they become more serious, keeping the bilges pumped down, and double-checking logs and records.

Good engineering practice recognizes that there is a "right way" and a "wrong way" to perform maintenance. Although written instructions and procedures usually specify the "right way" to maintain a piece of equipment, there are many instances for which specific guidance is not given. It is then necessary for the operator to use his judgment, his experience, and his knowledge of his equipment to determine the action he will take—in short, to exercise good engineering practice.

The exercise of good engineering practice is the essence of material readiness. The commanding officer will improve the engineering practice of his command if he insists on the involvement of his subordinates (in particular, his officers) in the material management of the command.

Officer Involvement. Obviously officers are not trained as technicians, nor should they be so employed. As managers and trainers, however, junior officers must learn the practical aspects of their division's responsibilities. This includes the ability to recognize when proper tools and instruments are being utilized and when and how various tasks are performed by his division. This may require an officer to perform certain tasks himself to learn the required knowledge. It definitely requires his periodic, routine verification that his division is properly performing assigned maintenance functions, by his thorough review of required documentation.

Proper officer involvement in the technical supervision of a division requires a thorough theoretical and practical technical knowledge of appropriate operating and maintenance procedures. He acquires this by study of applicable documentation and by sufficient "on the job" practice and observation for him to understand the correct methods of operating and conducting maintenance procedures. For example, the division officer responsible for a diesel engine should understand thoroughly each step in the diesel lineup and operating procedure. He must have the practical knowledge to recognize if the procedure is being conducted properly when he monitors the personnel actually performing the lineup and operation. He should know what inspections are required and how they are conducted.

He must direct actively the planning of division work to ensure that required maintenance is completed at necessary frequencies and in the required sequences, as set forth by PMS instructions.

He must review maintenance, alignment, and operational data to ensure that they are within allowed specifications, that trends are analyzed, and that they correctly reflect the readiness of the systems and equipment under his charge. He must have a thorough enough knowledge of the correct specifications to readily recognize abnormalities.

He must examine completed work and maintenance records and other data to ensure that they are maintained in accordance with applicable directives, that the operation or maintenance action has achieved the desired goal, and that the records reflect this.

He must establish and use "check points" to ensure that complicated or lengthy work proceeds satisfactorily. "Check points" are a technique of requiring periodic reports to determine that work is proceeding as planned. Prudent choice of check points in a procedure or maintenance task keeps an officer informed about what is going on without the close degree of supervision implied by monitoring.

He must insist that his senior subordinates actively involve themselves in planning, supervision, and execution of all divisional maintenance, training, and operational responsibilities.

Application of good engineering practices will enhance the professional development of the officer, improve the performance of the division, and result in increased material readiness of the entire ship.

Preventive Maintenance

The 3-M System. The Navy ships' 3-M (Maintenance and Material Management) system was created to help manage required mainte-

Figure 8-4. Preventive maintenance on this teletype system will assure that it will be ready when needed.

nance in an atmosphere of growing complexity of equipment, increased tempo of operations, and decline in available resources. The 3-M system is an integrated system to improve the management of maintenance and provide for the collection and dissemination of maintenance-related information for use in developing better management, engineering analysis, and techniques of equipment maintenance.

The ships' 3-M system, when properly used, provides for the orderly scheduling and accomplishment of maintenance and for reporting and disseminating maintenance-related information. It is comprised of two subsystems—the PMS (Planned Maintenance

Subsystem) and the MDCS (Maintenance Data Collection Subsystem).

The PMS pertains to the planning, scheduling, and management of resources (men, material, and time) to keep equipment running within its design characteristics. It defines uniform maintenance standards (based on engineering experience) and prescribes simplified procedures and techniques for the accomplishment of maintenance. The procedures and tools of the PMS are described in detail in *Planned Maintenance Subsystems*, *OPNAVINST 4790.4*.

When used properly, PMS improves maintenance practices and significantly upgrades equipment readiness. One of your most difficult challenges in command will be to utilize this vital system effectively. During the past few years, type commanders have investigated the way it is used in the fleet. They found considerable differences between procedures on maintenance requirement cards, (MRCs) and in equipment technical manuals; and, again, between the procedures on the MRCs and the actual performance of maintenance. In particular, they found that equipment guide lists were not always prepared properly, and that in several cases the preventive maintenance item they asked about had never been accomplished before. This was evident from failure to refer to technical manuals, the finding of errors in manuals and MRCs, the use of improper tools, identification of improper equipment wiring, identification of long term equipment misoperation, and general unfamiliarity of personnel with maintenance procedures. In some cases, the type commander inspections showed that no preventive maintenance procedures at all were in effect and that no one had even requested the MRCs and manuals that would have been needed to institute them.

Testing Effectiveness. The simplest test to use to measure your preventive maintenance effectiveness is to select a single maintenance action and audit its performance from start to finish. The commanding officer can do this by checking:

The preventive maintenance card against the technical manual and feedback reports

The use of correct tools

The identification and use of proper repair parts

The use of correct safety procedures, tag-outs, and internal ship command control procedures

The use of proper work procedures.

Corrective Maintenance

In the area of material management, you must strive to get deficiencies identified early, and develop a positive plan to correct them. The wise commanding officer will not tolerate the "it's always been that way" syndrome and will insist upon a strong corrective maintenance program. He must expect his men to attack every minor deficiency, before it becomes a major problem and results in a last-minute crisis before a deployment or other operational requirement.

Maintenance Training

In the area of maintenance training, the commanding officer must ensure that ship's force personnel understand what is expected of them and of repair or maintenance activities. Furthermore, the captain must build in each of his men a desire to determine and correct the "fundamental cause" of equipment malfunctions rather than merely treating its symptoms.

Training on individual equipment must include formal presentations on maintenance procedures, hands-on training sessions, and formal examinations to determine effectiveness of the program.

Shipboard Training Program. In a more general sense, the program should ensure that all personnel understand these rules:

For each work item to be accomplished, specific procedures that define the system and component to be worked on, the work to be accomplished, and the desired results, must be formulated and approved by proper authority. This is generally what has been done by the 3-M system.

Proper permission will be requested from higher authority prior to commencing maintenance work.

Systems will be tagged out properly prior to maintenance.

Figure 8-5. Your ship's sides are highly visible. These young sidecleaners labor long and hard to keep them looking shipshape. An occasional appreciative word from the captain will keep their morale and production up.

Watchstanders are responsible for monitoring work being performed by outside maintenance activities.

Watchstanders should report to duty officers any discrepancies they notice; for example, missing danger tags, or tags attached to the wrong components.

Safety precautions as outlined in the *SORN* will be strictly enforced.

Maintenance Records

CSMP. Over the past several years, type commanders have made significant progress in making the Current Ship's Maintenance Project (CSMP) a meaningful maintenance control document. The automated CSMP provides the depth of information necessary to evaluate and quantify the backlog and scope of work for ship's force, intermediate maintenance activity (IMA), or depot accomplishment, and to plan, schedule, and fund upkeeps, availabilities, and overhauls. As the Navy moves toward extended operating cycles between regular overhauls, with continuing reductions in overhaul funds, the automated CSMP becomes increasingly important as a controlling record at all levels of supervision. However, recent observations by type commanders indicated that the CSMP is not always maintained properly on all ships. Specifically, they identified these problems:

Junior officer and work center supervisors must develop a working knowledge of the CSMP.

The CSMP should be cleared promptly of deferred maintenance which is no longer required or has been completed.

Ships must identify deferred maintenance as it occurs and enter it into the CSMP.

Deferred maintenance documents must be prepared thoroughly to generate complete work requests.

Maintenance documents must be delivered to the designated CSMP maintenance activity on time.

CSMP accuracy, completeness, and management are important. If the ship's CSMP is not a valid assessment of material condition and maintenance requirements, you should examine internal handling of Maintenance Data Collection System documents, internal CSMP distribution and use, and junior officer/work center supervisor knowledge and understanding of the CSMP. Upkeep and availability work packages can be significantly improved through advanced planning from an improved CSMP.

Testing

After most repair and maintenance work, equipment must be tested to see that it is working properly. Where these tests are not properly organized and supervised, the expression "give her the smoke test" may be more than a joke.

The basic assumption in the testing of equipment should be that it will not respond as expected (else why the test?) and that the personnel involved are unfamiliar with the procedures to be followed (testing is seldom a routine operation). Where a series of large, expensive, or inherently dangerous components are involved in a system test of one sort or another, poor procedures may have very serious consequences indeed.

Testing Guidelines. For such systems it is good engineering practice to follow, as applicable, the following guidelines.

The test must be properly authorized. For many components or systems this involves the approval of higher authority and perhaps the material command concerned.

The test procedures must be approved by an authorized source and reviewed for accuracy on board by the head of department (and in some cases, commanding officer) concerned. In most cases it is mandatory to commit procedures to writing.

Brief all personnel involved about the purpose of the test, prerequisites (i.e., steps to be taken before the test begins), step-by-step procedures in sequence, communications, precautions, out-of-commission indications, expected readings and results of the various test stages, and possible casualties.

A test station bill, separate from the normal watch bill, should be drawn up, with specific assignments of qualified personnel by name where tests of any complexity are involved. This bill should provide for personnel relief if the test is to be of appreciable duration. The relief personnel should be given the same briefing as the original test gang.

The station bill should include the communications circuits to be manned.

Make up proper data forms, where applicable, before the briefing. Operating personnel should not normally be assigned data collecting duties. Data gathering communications circuits should be separate from operating circuits.

Valve and switch lineups following the written test procedures should be made independently by two persons prior to the test. Double-check any changes made during the test as well.

Plan for a rehearsal, or dry run, before complicated or potentially dangerous tests. The officer in charge should check each station and each communications channel before the rehearsal and the actual test.

Testing is not comparable in urgency to operating. If anything "goes sour," the test should come to "all stop" and the equipment put in the safest condition possible while the difficulty is resolved.

Quality Assurance

All type commanders have issued detailed instructions regarding quality assurance. It is good engineering practice for the ship to have a strong quality assurance program in order to check maintenance and recertify repaired systems.

Importance of Inspection. Perhaps of even greater importance is inspection by the ship when outside activities conduct repair work. One of the weaknesses of our Navy repair and overhaul system is that the quality assurance system within the repair organization generally reports to the repair or production officer rather than directly to the commanding officer of the repair facility. This means that even with the best inspectors available, originally objective reports on quality are often considered subjectively if they might influence completion dates. Needless to say, it is up to you to look hard and long at the thoroughness and quality of the work completed by repair or maintenance activities.

Material Inspections

One of the characteristics of a good commanding officer is his ability to inspect. Whether material, personnel, or administrative, no inspection can be properly performed unless the inspector knows what to look for. This ability is not born in a man, but comes through years of experience spent mostly on the receiving end of inspections.

If a captain really knows how to inspect, good things will happen in short order. A sense of pride will develop within the ship when previously unnoticed discrepancies are now noticed and quickly corrected. The commanding officer who knows how to conduct a material inspection will soon discover fewer items to comment upon unfavorably, as material readiness improves.

Use of Inspection Forms. In preparing yourself to do effective material inspections, you would be well advised to review the annual summaries of shipboard deficiencies noted by the Board of Inspection and Survey, by the Type Commander Operational Readiness Examinations, and the Fleet Operational Reactor Safeguards Examinations. These summaries are provided to applicable ships and form a useful general index of where trouble can be anticipated. Appendix XIII provides some guidance on conducting material inspections. You can use this appendix to help junior officers gain the experience necessary to become good inspectors in the material area.

Your Ship as Others See Her

The captain who serves his ship well is one who can stand back occasionally and see her as others do. This is not easy.

To start with, take physical appearance. The conduct of morning quarters on deck is the business of the executive officer; but you are in unfortunate straits if you are the only officer in the squadron who does not know that quarters on your ship is referred to in the flag mess as the "0800 mob scene." The military appearance of your formations, the smartness of your deck watches, the proper handling of colors, anchor lights, and absentee pennants, the cleanliness of your quarterdeck and topside areas—all these are taken by the rest of the fleet as outward signs of your ship's inward state; and more than likely, they are right.

Without deluding yourself that dressy show can long conceal less pleasant realities belowdecks, you will do well to make first-hand, periodic checks on how these outward symbols look from the flag bridge, as well as to check on the details of watchkeeping and maintenance below decks.

Since this chapter deals primarily with the subject of maintenance, it is also appropriate to consider at this point how a maintenance activity views your ship.

In the eyes of any maintenance activity, the best customers are those who solve problems during availabilities at the lowest possible level. You can do this by encouraging communications at every level in both chains of command. This occurs naturally once good relations have been established and ship's force and maintenance activity people know each other.

Maintenance activity CO's appreciate the ship captain who keeps them informed. They will work closely with him to improve this type of relationship. The other end of the spectrum here is the commanding officer who cries "wolf" at every difficulty to the next senior in command (i.e., the commodore).

Ships that perform well during availabilities make use of the ship superintendent. They let him know what they need and keep him cut in on ship conditions which might preclude specific maintenance or testing.

Maintenance activities appreciate ships that react quickly to emergent work by rapid submittal of necessary work requests. Delay in this will only cause problems downstream, when many work items are simultaneously scheduled for completion. In this regard, maintenance activities also feel positively about the ship that does required testing right after repairs rather than waiting until the end of the maintenance period.

Maintenance activity commanding officers feel secure when they work with a ship CO who is safety-conscious. They are particularly sensitive to diver safety and the fact that refit poses many hazards to men and machinery. The alert commanding officer will concentrate his efforts on general safety, with particular emphasis on hull integrity and personnel safety.

Finally, maintenance activity sailors appreciate praise. This praise, where warranted, can inspire them to increase the quality of the refit or upkeep period.

By keeping this advice in mind, you can better the chances that your ship will receive a good availability.

Availability Planning

An "availability" is the period assigned a ship for the uninterrupted accomplishment of work which requires services of a repair activity ashore or afloat.

The key to success in availability or upkeep/refit planning is early and complete preparation. This starts by educating all work center supervisors in the proper preparation of work requests. This training must include the mechanics of filling out work requests but must, in addition, insure that the following items will be clear to the maintenance activity when you submit the work package:

Accurate identification of the problem, including just what assistance is required

Inclusion of all necessary equipment name plate data, reference publications, drawings, and repair procedures

Inclusion of equipment location

Identification of knowledgeable shipboard contact men

Assignment of correct level of maintenance assistance; intermediate maintenance activity (IMA), depot, or drydock

Identity of key events

Special controls identified, if applicable

Commanding Officer or designated representative signature.

Once the work center supervisors are well versed in work request preparation, the commanding officer must insure that his departments identify *all* work necessary prior to submission of the work package to the repair activity. Late submittal of known work items will degrade the effectiveness of the availability, and also will create ill-will between the maintenance activity and the ship.

At present, most maintenance activities also perform certain routine work items during an availability. These include lagging, sail loft work, and fuel and lubricant analysis, as examples. The well-prepared ship will insure that work requiring lists, such as lagging, are properly prepared, indicating the problem and exact location.

Another significant input to availability planning is the CSMP. The end product of the CSMP is a listing of all ship's work items yet to be accomplished, including responsibility, status, and complete description. Ships with good maintenance programs work to keep the CSMP updated at all times. This provides the maintenance activity with a complete status of current work and allows them to plan most of the availability well before your work package arrives. The results are obvious. The better the planning input, the better the resulting work period.

Once the work package is complete, the next milestone in a successful availability is the arrival conference. The arrival conference permits the ship, the immediate superior in command, and the maintenance activity to discuss the work package in detail and to factor in controlling work items.

The commanding officer can help his ship and his reputation by being prepared to discuss all work items in detail. He must have the facts regarding all work items in order to be able to make recommendations on management decisions. Furthermore, he must leave the conference with a clear understanding of the various actions taken on work requests, and must get this information to his crew. Since the arrival conference sets the tone for the availability, the commanding officer and his availability coordinator (usually the engineering officer) must attend. If possible, division officers and leading petty officers should be invited as well. They can learn from the experience and will be able to transfer firsthand information on the conference to their subordinates.

Most maintenance activities conduct periodic management or work review meetings throughout the availability. Generally, only the commanding officer and his availability coordinator are invited. These meetings track work items with a view toward maximizing maintenance activity effectiveness. It is during these meetings that supply effectiveness is measured, emergent work is reviewed, and the critical flow points are checked for validity.

To be effective at management meetings, the commanding officer must be well briefed on the status of all work items on the ship. He must do his homework and have the facts prior to the meeting. Some successful commanding officers have used a technique whereby they discuss each pertinent work item with the respective department head in the presence of the ship's superintendent just prior to the meeting. This gives them the up-to-date job status as seen by the ship and the maintenance activity.

During the management meeting try hard to avoid placing others in an adversary position, particularly if you don't have all the facts. Likewise, if you feel it necessary to introduce a big issue at the meeting, it is wise to "grease the skids" with the maintenance activity and administrative seniors prior to it.

In summary, the success or lack of success which attends upkeep, availabilities, and overhauls depends greatly upon the relations established between the ship and the maintenance activity, whether afloat or ashore. Sources of friction often encountered are the lack of understanding on the part of the ship's officers and men of the organization of the repair activity and the lack of knowledge about the differing responsibilities of the ship and the maintenance activity.

When going alongside a tender for upkeep or into a yard for availability, it is good practice to obtain an organization chart of the activity. Study it and promulgate its contents to the leading personnel in your ship. It can usually be assumed that the tender or yard knows what gear comes under this or that shipboard department, but a good many stumbles, fumbles, and grumbles come about from the ship's company thinking that one shop or office in the yard or on board the tender is taking care of something when actually it is the concern of another. Availability or refit period success is enhanced when ship managers know who in the maintenance activity hierarchy they interface with on repair management issues. Figure 8–6 shows proper corresponding levels of repair management during a tender availability.

The communications network set up by the ship is all-important in establishing the proper rapport with the maintenance activity.

As to jurisdictional questions, there are some key articles in *Navy Regulations* which apply.

Article 0750 states:

> Except in matters coming within the policy or regulations of the ship, the commanding officer shall exercise no control over the officers or employees of a naval shipyard or station where his ship is moored, unless with the permission of the commander of the naval shipyard or station.

Article 0751:

> 1. No ship or craft shall be moved or undergo dock trials during its stay at a naval station, except by direction or with the approval of the commanding officer of such station.
>
> 2. Ships arriving at, or departing from a naval station shall be furnished such assistance, including tugs when available, as, in the

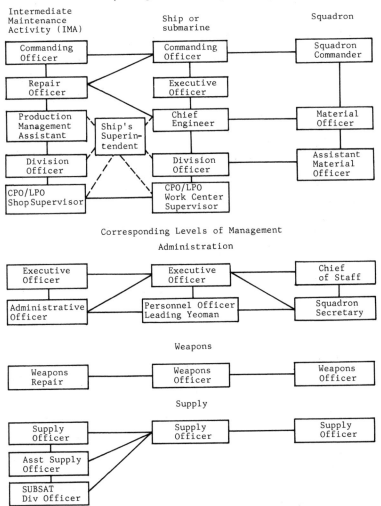

Figure 8-6. Corresponding levels of repair management. The person to see to help solve your repair problems is directly across from you in the diagram.

opinion of the commanding officer, may be necessary for their safe handling.

Article 0752:

1. (a) The commanding officer of a naval station shall be responsible for the care and safety of all ships and craft at such station not under a commanding officer or assigned to another authority and for any damage that may be done by or to them.

(b) It shall be the responsibility of the commanding officer of a ship in commission which is undergoing overhaul or which is otherwise immobilized at a naval station or shipyard to request such services as are necessary to ensure the safe berthing of his ship. The commanding officer of the naval station or shipyard shall be responsible for providing the requested services in a timely and adequate manner.

2. When a ship or craft not under her own power is being moved by direction of the commanding officer of a naval station, that officer shall be responsible for any damage that may result therefrom; the pilot or other person designated for the purpose shall be in direct charge of such movement, and all persons on board shall cooperate with and assist him as necessary.

The same policy outlined above for Navy yards pertains to tenders. It is good practice for the ship alongside a tender to enquire about her uniform regulations and ship's orders and to brief its own crew accordingly to avoid friction.

Tenders normally coordinate the water and garbage barge needs of ships alongside, and early conformance with the procedures laid down helps to keep day-to-day relationships on an even keel.

Drydocking

Normal drydocking is scheduled during the regular overhaul period. Drydocking may also be accomplished between regular overhauls (interim drydocking) for routine maintenance or to repair propellers, replace propellers, repair shafting, sonar, or other underwater damage, or to examine the bottom for possible damage or deterioration.

Drydocking is accomplished in a navy yard or naval repair facility, or at a commercial yard under contract to the Navy. When docking at a commercial yard, arrangements will be made for the proceedings by an industrial manager.

Prior to docking, a conference should be held between the commanding officer and the docking officer or commercial dockmaster to arrange for time of docking, tugs and pilots, the condition of the ship when entering, and the housekeeping arrangements for the visit. These consist of the brows to be furnished, utility services to be provided, sanitary services needed, garbage and waste removal arrangements, and other necessary services. Reactor safety provisions should be discussed for nuclear-powered ships.

At this same conference, provide the yard with any information about the last docking, the ship's docking plan, if not already held, and make arrangements regarding working and linehandling parties.

A similar conference is held near the end of work to set time and date of undocking and other events leading to it, such as flooding of the dock. Weight shifts must be reported and arrangements made for berthing.

Responsibility for Ship During Drydocking. Article 0752–4 of *Navy Regulations* prescribes that when a ship operating under her own power is being drydocked the commanding officer is fully responsible until the extremity of the ship first to enter the dock crosses the sill and the ship is pointed fair. The docking officer then assumes responsibility, and retains it until the dock is pumped dry. In undocking, the docking officer assumes responsibility when flooding commences and returns it to the commanding officer when the last extremity of the ship crosses the sill and the ship is pointed fair. In a commercial drydock the responsibilities are the same, with the supervisor of shipbuilding being responsible for ensuring that the contractor performs satisfactorily.

Safety in Drydock. In drydock, the commanding officer is responsible for assuring closure when unattended of all valves and openings in the ship's bottom on which no work is being done by the repair facility. The CO of the repair facility is responsible for closing at the end of working hours all valves and openings in the ship's bottom being worked on by the repair facility. Prior to undocking, the commanding officer of the ship shall report to the docking officer

Figure 8-7. The responsibility for the safety of a ship in drydock is divided between the docking officer and the commanding officer, but in the final analysis the commanding officer is responsible for the overall safety of the ship.

any material changes in the amount and location of weights on board made by the ship's force and that all sea valves and other openings in the ship's bottom are closed. Flooding will not commence until he has made this report.

Preparation for Regular Overhaul

Experience with ship overhauls indicates that their success depends in large measure on the preparations made by the ship's CO during the pre-overhaul period. During the overhaul, heavy demands are placed on the crew for auxiliary and propulsion plant operations, preventive maintenance, ship's force overhaul work, monitoring of shipyard work, and training. Ships which have prepared for these demands during the pre-overhaul period have more time during the overhaul to meet them.

In order to assist you in preparing for your next overhaul, we will now discuss the areas requiring special attention before overhaul begins.

Pre-overhaul Testing. Since the results of pre-overhaul tests are used in determining the scope of work required, accurate recording of data and expeditious completion of these tests are important.

Overhaul Work Package Planning. One of the key elements in the successful accomplishment of shipyard overhaul is planning. Years before the overhaul or conversion starts, representatives of the fleet, shipyards, and technical commands work together to define the desired work package. As a result of approved alterations, deferred maintenance actions, and improved repair techniques, this package is periodically refined. Ideally, as the shipyard period begins, overhaul planning is complete, and a workable schedule exists for the accomplishment of the required package. Realistically, this is not a totally achievable goal. Additional work will result from arrival inspections, open and inspect deficiencies, and equipment breakdowns during the overhaul. Aside from this, though, any other major deviations from the initial work package will confuse orderly planning and can eventually destroy even the best schedule. In this case much shipyard effort is wasted and delays become inevitable, with a resultant rise in total costs.

Ship's force can significantly affect the impact of "new work" on planning efforts. It is your responsibility to prepare thoroughly for the shipyard overhaul. This is accomplished by reviewing the proposed work package and by submitting work requests for *all* necessary items not included.

The earlier you identify this work, the more easily it can be assimilated into the package and thus minimize disruption. Recent reviews of supplemental work packages submitted after overhaul commencement have shown that pre-overhaul preparation was inadequate. In addition, a shipyard can refuse to do new work identified after the overhaul starts, based on their total workload. This rejection leaves only two options for the ship's type commander: (1) designation of the work as mandatory and acceptance of a schedule slip, or (2) disapproval of the work.

Review of Operating Procedures and Instructions. While they are doing pre-overhaul and overhaul tests, the ship's force will be exposed to infrequently used operating procedures and instructions. Ships must utilize the period prior to overhaul to familiarize themselves with these procedures and instructions.

Preventive Maintenance. Preventive maintenance must be kept current before and during the overhaul. Numerous delays in post-overhaul test programs can be avoided if equipment is properly maintained during the overhaul.

Watchstanding and Surveillance of Shipyard Work. During overhaul, the combination of abnormal shipboard conditions and the presence of shipyard workers not familiar with the ship make it imperative that ship's force maintain close surveillance to ensure safety. The crew must be indoctrinated well before the overhaul in the following areas:

The necessity to tag out systems in accordance with shipyard procedures prior to the commencement of work.

The necessity and procedures involved in providing adequate support for fire protection and keeping the number of fire hazards to a minimum.

Maintenance of proper standards of system and component cleanliness.

Contacts with the Overhaul Shipyard Prior to Overhaul. During upkeeps prior to overhaul, shipyard personnel may visit the ship to check alteration plans to verify that all interferences have been identified. This can save a great deal of wasted time. The yard may also ask to review shipboard records to aid their planning and material procurement. You can use these contacts with the shipyard to obtain documents to familiarize the crew with shipyard administrative procedures, such as rip-out control, tag-out of systems, and verification of valve line-ups prior to the start of overhaul.

In summary, know your job, work hard, and conduct good fol-low-up inspections, and you can get as effective and efficient over-haul in these days of complex equipment as was common years ago. The conduct of proper overhaul preparation and the overhaul itself are not new to the Navy.

In early 1940 the ancient four-stack destroyer *John D. Ford* en-tered the Navy Yard at Cavite, Philippine Islands, for an annual over-haul. The World War I-built ship had served in the Asiatic Fleet for twenty years, and had deteriorated increasingly every year in the tropic heat and humidity. Nevertheless, her commanding officer was determined to bring her out of her overhaul as an effective fighting ship. He could see that war in the Pacific was inevitable, and that every ship would be needed. He arranged with his ship's supervisor to conduct a thorough and extensive overhaul of the *Ford's* engineer-ing plant and weapons systems. The crew was worked overtime, at first with some resentment, but later with increasing enthusiasm as they realized the commanding officer's engineering knowledge and dedication. The ship's supervisor worked his yard crew equally hard and insisted on careful quality assurance inspections. After her 1940 overhaul the *Ford* operated for eighteen months without ever missing an assignment or an engineering bell.

When the Japanese attacked Pearl Harbor, she was anchored off Cavite, ready to enter the yard for her next overhaul. A flight of fifty-four Japanese bombers quickly rearranged that schedule, and the crew put all equipment and machinery back in full operating condition. From that day until June 1942, the *Ford* took part in every major battle of the Asiatic campaign, finally returning to Pearl Har-bor via Australia in time to join a back-up torpedo attack force for the Battle of Midway. Her commanding officer was awarded three Navy Crosses and the *Ford* received the Presidential Unit Citation. She had carried out every assignment given to her, and never missed an engineering requirement or had so much as a misfire. Her ma-chinery and weapons performed superbly despite her age and lack of recent overhaul. Her performance was a tribute to her commanding officer and ship's supervisor at the time of her 1940 overhaul. Both believed that the key to a good overhaul was knowing their jobs, working hard, and following up. Their names? The commanding officer was Lieutenant Commander Robert L. Dennison. The ship's supervisor was Lieutenant Commander Hyman G. Rickover.

9

Afloat Logistics

Logistics is that branch of military science having to do with moving and supplying forces. A ship's engines must be fueled, her equipment maintained, her crew fed, and her weapons munitioned. With proper logistics a warship can fight anywhere anytime; without, it might as well stay in port.

—William B. Franke, former Secretary of the Navy

The science of logistics has for many years been an important part of our mobility-conscious armed forces. Ashore, at headquarters, it means determining the needs of all elements of our Navy and then procuring and supplying these requirements world-wide. Solving these complicated problems requires the best talent the Navy has.

Afloat, logistics is the determination of what individual ships need to carry out their projected tasks, and the supply of these items and services both before they leave port and on a continuing basis by replenishment underway.

Afloat logistics is carried out on the individual ship level by the commanding officer and his supply department. In large ships, the commanding officer will be assisted by a well-qualified Supply Corps officer. In small ships, he may have either a newly commissioned and schooled officer of the Supply Corps or a line officer. This chapter is intended to help the commanding officer with the demanding task of running a small ship with an inexperienced supply or junior line officer. It will also be of assistance to the captain of a large ship in monitoring the performance of his supply system.

The supply officer of a small ship has one of the most difficult jobs the Navy can offer a young man. This officer is responsible, often singlehandedly, for administering all ship's supplies and equipage, coordinating a budget of well over one million dollars, and providing food and personal services for the entire wardroom and crew. The billet appears even more difficult when one considers that the average supply officer assigned to such a ship has had little or no prior experience in supply matters and that his seniors, the commanding officer and executive officer, can often provide only cursory direction in the daily management of his department.

Ship Supply Officer's Responsibilities

OPNAVINST 3120.32A, the *SORN*, states that in addition to his duties as head of department, the supply officer is responsible for procuring, receiving, storing, issuing, shipping, transferring, selling, accounting for, and while in his custody, maintaining all stores and equipment of the command.

Specifically, depending on the size and organization of the ship, he is responsible for the following:

The operation of the general mess, including the preparation and service of food

The wardroom mess, on those ships where a billet has been established for a supply officer to be wardroom mess officer, or where the wardroom dines on food prepared by the general mess

The ship's store and the subsidiary activities and services thereof

Disbursing government funds; although where there is an assistant for disbursing, the supply officer will be relieved by that officer for responsibility for the procurement, custody, transfer, issue of, and accounting for funds. In such case the supply officer will exercise general supervision over and inspect the accounts of the assistant for disbursing.

When there is an assistant for food service afloat or for the ship's store, that officer may relieve the supply officer from personal financial accountability and responsibility for food service or ship's store material. The supply officer must request such relief in writing, and

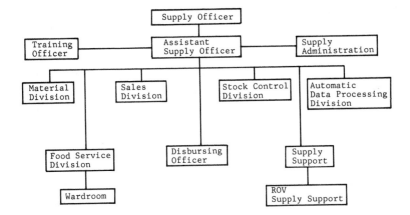

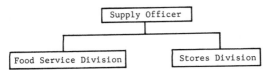

Shipboard supply organizations can be as large as that shown above for a tender and as small as that shown below for a submarine. Each, in its own way, performs a vital logistics function in support of its ship.

Figure 9-1. Typical Supply Department organization.

it must be approved by the commanding officer. It is terminated upon relief or detachment of the supply officer or his assistant. In any case, he will continue to be responsible to the commanding officer for the overall administration of the supply department.

Supply Department Personnel

The Supply Officer. On a large ship the supply officer will undoubtedly be an officer of many years' experience in all aspects of logistics. On the other hand, the supply officer on a frigate or submarine is likely to be a young ensign directly out of the Naval Supply Corps School at Athens, Georgia. This chapter, as we stated earlier, is directed *specifically* to the small ship with a first toured or junior supply officer.

Your young supply officer was specifically chosen for his assignment as an independent duty department head as a result of his outstanding performance at supply school. He reports aboard technically qualified as supply department head, but with no previous experience whatever. In order to make up for this he will need strong support and counseling from you and your executive officer. He may also require some help in establishing himself in the wardroom with his contemporaries, who often tend to be overly critical of the "chop" and his apparent inability to meet their divisional supply needs and their culinary desires. Problems such as these can make life uncomfortable for your supply officer, reduce his effectiveness, and make his resignation certain at the end of his obligated service.

Supply Department Enlisted Personnel. Your young supply officer's lack of experience would be a minor liability were his subordinates well-qualified. Today, however, more than ever before, the Navy suffers from severe shortages of senior storekeeper personnel and mid-grade mess management specialists. These shortages only complicate his problems. In order to adjust for this you will have to insure that he establishes an adequate training program. This is difficult to accomplish aboard a small ship, and it behooves you to take advantage of the excellent tender and shore establishment training programs established for storekeepers and mess management personnel. The monthly training schedule is usually published in advance by the tender, and ship personnel are always invited to participate. Use of this convenient formal training will not only help the ship, but will also help your enlisted personnel in their advancement.

Mess Management Specialist Chief Raymond Bennett was especially successful in providing such training to his subordinates. During his three year tour on USS *Kamehameha* (SSBN-642), he trained all of his subordinates in food service administration and safety as well as the more esoteric fields of cake decorating, ice carving, and French cuisine and baking. As a result of his efforts his personnel felt like, and were, professionals; his division enjoyed exceptional retention and *Kamehameha* personnel enjoyed delicious meals. The moral of this story is that you can bring your supply organization up to your expectations by providing training and support to compensate for lack of experience.

Repair Parts and Material Management

Coordinated Shipboard Allowance Lists (COSAL). The COSAL shows the repair parts, special tools, and other material required on board to support installed equipment. All of your onboard parts are based on the COSAL. Over the past decade it has become a highly effective repair parts management tool.

Your COSAL was designed using a .25 fleet logistics support improvement program criterion. In simple words, this added a repair part to your COSAL if the installed part failed once every four years. Obviously this has many loopholes, and as a result the Navy is presently developing a .1 criterion; that is, your equipment will be spare part supported if the part fails once over a ten year period. In addition to this new failure criterion, plans have been developed to fully support critical equipment such as digital combat systems regardless of the experienced failure rate. This type of system has been effective in supporting our strategic underseas missile fleet for years and should work as well for the rest of the Navy.

Your ship's COSAL is complete at initial outfitting and is checked at every supply overhaul, but an active COSAL maintenance program is necessary to maintain supply efficiency while the ship is operating. Maintenance actions regarding the COSAL occur when equipment is added to or deleted from the ship. Parts for most new equipment changes are funded by the Naval Sea Systems Command COSAL allotment, so the ship is not charged. Failure to update the COSAL can only result in out of commission time for critical equipments, failure of your ship to meet its commitments, and unhappy unit and type commanders.

Inventory Maintenance. Your onboard repair parts are determined by your allowance (COSAL) and are adjusted by demand (usage). When discussing usage the term "selected item" (SIM) is often used.

A selected item is one which is required twice or more within a six-month period. The idea here is to spotlight such material in regard to its inventory, control, and need to be reordered. A SIM item is inventoried semiannually and, it is recommended, also before deployment. Stock items which are not designated as SIM will be completely inventoried only at the time of the ship's supply overhaul.

You can upgrade your inventory control system by tasking the supply department to spot inventory a designated number of parts each week. However, many ships have been lulled into a false sense of security by spot inventorying from stock records rather than actually locating the parts. A more effective method is to insist on actual location using stock record inventories. In addition, this is a good way to find and identify parts your crew may have hidden in lockers without stock records.

On the other hand, your inventory control system will lose effectiveness if you *permit* or are *perceived to condone* "deployment" spares. The supply system has come a long way in recent years. The use of "deployment" spares breaks the system's feedback link, hides the need for greater repair part support for certain equipment, and will frustrate your efforts to improve inventory control. Your attitude toward deployment spares should be: *if we really need it, submit an allowance change request.* You will find that your older petty officers will be hard to break of their habits of foraging for spares. You will have to curb their ship loyalty and individual initiative by promising to call upon their "talents" if needed, but at the same time explaining why you want to use the regular allowance system.

Repair Parts Maintenance. Many a ship has been forced to interrupt scheduled operations because a normally carried critical spare was not onboard. This tale becomes tragic when investigation shows that ship's force realized the problem but failed to take proper action to correct it. There are different versions to the story, but in almost every case the error was a lack of management of repair parts.

Each head of department is responsible for maintaining a full allowance of repair parts, and for requesting the supply officer to replace damaged, worn out, or missing items. Depending on ship size, the commanding officer can require either the heads of departments or the supply officer to maintain stock records. In either case, repair part petty officers must be assigned from each division to assist in the work. Repair part availability is directly proportional to the degree of strictness of accounting for each part.

To make things simpler, on small ships storekeepers should be required, except in genuine emergencies, to make *all* issues of onboard repair parts at sea, and while in port to make *all* issues during normal working hours. Time and time again, supply inspection teams report that "generally those ships that allow division repair parts petty officers to draw parts from the individual repair parts lockers are those ships with poor stock record validity." Ships without a full allowance of storekeepers should leave the assigned storekeepers off the underway watch bill. In addition, specific procedures requiring the command duty officer's approval should be adopted for issues of repair parts in port after normal working hours. On larger ships, where it would be difficult for a storekeeper to make each and every issue, the command must insure that the repair parts petty officers are thoroughly trained in stock record keeping, allowance lists, and location of material, and that *they alone* have access to the lockers for their divisional parts.

Regardless of whether the ship is large or small, the commanding officer must train his supply personnel to take rapid replacement action on every repair part issued from stock. The supply officer should take follow-up action on all requisitions more than three months old. If there is no record of a requisition on the tender, and your ship has no "status cards" on the item, there is a strong possibility that your requisition has been lost!

Cannibalizations. There will be times when the ship will need to "cannibalize," or take a critical part or component directly from the physical plant of another vessel. (Note here that stock transfers from one ship to another are not cannibalizations.) The commanding officer must submit requests through his commodore for both inter- and intra-squadron cannibalizations. It is wise to keep in mind that fleet commanders are generally opposed to cannibalization, and have controlled such material transfers very closely. When considering whether cannibalization is warranted, keep in mind that only mission-essential transfers will be approved, and that if your request is not backed up by a CASREP you are probably over-reacting. In any case, review your type commander's directives to understand fully his policy on cannibalization.

Consumables. In small ships, consumable material is not controlled by detailed stock records but rather in a running account on stock tally cards. Most smaller ships have found that the "commodity manager" concept for consumables is sound. Under this concept, one division or department is responsible for providing a particular commodity to the entire ship. This system precludes wholesale duplication of stock where space is in short supply and also improves consumable financial management. Where the commodity manager concept is used, it is essential that the ship devise consumable load lists from actual usage. These load lists should be refined often to support actual usage of an item through a deployment. Periodic informal reports from commodity managers to the CO or XO may prevent a minor disaster during independent operations. There have been several classic consumable problems over the years; the ship on independent operations which reaches the low level alarm on toilet paper, or the ship which runs out of machinery-wiping rags with six weeks of independent steaming to go, are among the most notorious. These problems impact on ship's operations, crew morale, and your *congeniality*. They are problems that you don't need, and won't have if your system is set up properly.

Controlled Equipage. Controlled equipage is given extra management control afloat because of high unit cost, vulnerability to pilferage, and importance to the ship's mission. Over the years the number of required controlled equipage items has been reduced to make management simpler. You should review additions carefully so as not to dilute the system's effectiveness. Modern power tools and portable test equipment are two categories that should definitely be included, though. In maintaining your controlled equipage inventory, require that all *signature required* material be accounted for. Most ships have found that the use of custody cards is the best way to maintain the system. Remember that if culpability is suspected for a controlled equipage item, you must require a formal survey.

Requisition Management. The commanding officer must imbue his officers with a strong sense of responsibility regarding requisition prioritization. The priority of any requisition must be carefully determined, for the shore supply system can act only on the priorities ships assign it. Improper priorities are like false fire alarms; abuses only erode prompt and proper operation of the system.

Many operational commanders use "hot" or critical list systems to highlight command concern for certain items. These lists, if used efficiently by minimizing their length, can guide the supply officer in his efforts to obtain critical spares. In order to make such a system effective, the ship will have to coordinate parts status closely with the parent tender or Intermediate Maintenance Activity (IMA). This is made easier by keeping onboard status records up to date through a reconciliation process with the IMA. The supply officer should reconcile his outstanding requisitions and financial status with the tender at least weekly. Deployed ships should mail error lists to the tender so that support personnel stateside have a proper picture of their requisition and financial accounting status for spare parts. This reconciliation process, plus constant monitoring of requisitions, will also identify over-age requisitions. This is important since some old, unfilled requisitions are probably no longer needed and should be cancelled. The present fleet commander Material Obligation Validation (MOV) program strives for a goal of 98% validity of all outstanding requisitions. 100% is a reasonable goal; less than 80% is UNSATISFACTORY on an annual supply inspection.

Financial Management. Budget planning for spare parts and supplies is a valuable tool for all ships, and promotes foresight among the different shipboard departments. Your financial account for spare parts and supplies is termed your Operating Target (OPTAR). On a small ship, your commodore maintains the account and you do the spending. On a large ship you will maintain your own. You can avert embarrassing situations if you observe your budget, make your personnel aware of constraints, and insist upon frequent reconciliation of your account with the squadron and tender. You will find that your parent squadron or type commander will invite inputs on your needs, but be ready to back up your requests with facts. Most commanding

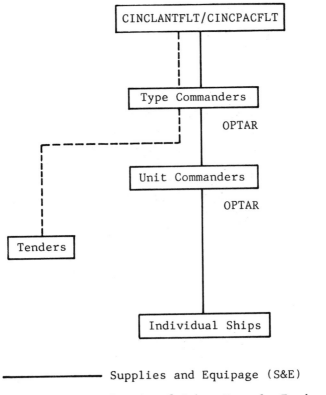

Figure 9-2. Flow of funds in the fleet. Keep within your target if you can. Additional funding is possible, but difficult to justify.

officers have maintained control of OPTAR by personally reviewing requisitions above a particular threshold value. A $100—$200 threshold value is widely used.

Figure 9–2 shows a simplified flow-path of OPTAR funds. The Repair of Other Vessels (ROV) fund also is often controlled by the commodore or type commander. This fund is managed by the tender and used to support tender repairs on your ship. Procurement of parts using ROV funds for ship's force is not authorized; however, use of ROV funds for justifiable "IMA assist" procurement is usually all right.

Supply Readiness Monitoring and Supply Assistance

Readiness Monitoring. There are several methods for a commanding officer to monitor his ship's supply readiness. The most obvious is to learn the details of the supply system and ask your supply officer the *right* questions. All too often, line officers take on a supply system problem without adequate knowledge of basic inventory control, financing, and prioritization. Several years ago, a young supply officer in the process of being relieved for his displayed inability to operate his department described his problems to his commodore. He said that he couldn't dine in the wardroom for fear of being ridiculed by his peers and the commanding officer. He described how his critical list of needed repair parts had grown to well over one hundred and that he had not had time to perform COSAL maintenance in over six months. The lesson here is obvious. Your young supply officer needs the same support (and probably more) that you give your other junior officers. His responsibilities must be clearly defined and given priorities. You can never accept substandard performance, but you must be alert to see that your supply officer is not placed in a "reaction mode" and that he doesn't react to every comment, request, and gripe from the wardroom and crew. A proven way to build your young supply officer's confidence and performance is to insure that the executive officer supports him, much like a "sea daddy" would help a young enlisted man, until he is clearly capable of taking charge.

Another help in monitoring your supply readiness is the Supply Edit Audit SIM System (SEAS) Report. This monitoring system uses a copy of each requisition to provide a measure of consumption rate versus obligation rate, providing a measure of ship's supply effectiveness.

Supply Inspections also provide an excellent assessment of the ship's internal supply management. These inspections, normally conducted at eighteen- to twenty-month intervals, will bring out any major deficiencies. The wise commanding officer will review the inspection report with a critical eye toward *trends*, as well as absolute grades, and will set up a continuing program to solve identified deficiencies.

In addition to the above, there are a few critical figures that provide you a good overall picture of your ship's supply status. Appendix XI provides an example of a report using these figures that can be used readily by the commanding officer as a "snap shot" of his supply status. Most type commanders use such a system and you would be wise to review his instructions in this area. All the data to prepare the report is readily available from routine supply records. The supply officer should be able to complete it in thirty minutes. The design of the report format permits trend analysis as well as weekly situational analysis. You may require additional data; Appendix XI contains the minimum that should be of continuing interest to you.

Supply Overhaul

Background. Supply overhauls are designed to upgrade supply effectiveness by establishing proper repair parts support for the ship's current configuration. A successful supply overhaul requires the combined efforts of shore-based support activities, fleet staffs, and ship's force. Normally, supply overhauls are conducted in conjunction with shipyard overhauls. In view of the number of activities involved, they are generally not conducted without prior approval and planning of your type commander. Since 1979, supply overhauls have been called "Integrated Logistics Overhauls," because since then they have encompassed a complete audit and update of not only the ship's supply package, but also the preventive maintenance support system and all technical manuals, and have also provided training to all hands in COSAL maintenance. Thus far this new system has proven worthwhile, improving the coordination of preventive maintenance requirements, technical manual support, and the COSAL.

Supply Overhaul Events. A schedule of milestones for your supply overhaul is generally promulgated about a year prior to the scheduled start. To establish an accurate configuration baseline and effective COSAL, a validation baseline of all shipboard equipment must be completed well before the overhaul starts. The *NAVSUP Supply Operations Assistance Program (SOAP) Manual (NAVSUP-INST 4441.21)*, and the type commander instructions comprise the basic guidance necessary for successful completion of a supply overhaul. They should be required reading for your supply officer.

During your overhaul, the initial allowance of onboard repair parts for newly installed equipment and components and new items appearing in the COSAL as a result of Allowance Parts List (APL) revisions will be provided, using Commander Naval Sea Systems Command (COMNAVSEASYSCOM) funds as set forth in *NAVSEAINST 7323.1*. Funding for deficiencies other than these is the responsibility of your type commander. As you can see, failure to record consumed spare parts prior to overhaul to conserve OPTAR funds will only catch up later when the type commander has to pick up the tab for needed spares. This situation is embarrassing and unnecessary. Don't get caught in it!

During your overhaul, numerous configuration changes will be made to the ship. *NAVSEAINST 4441.3* tasks the Naval Supervising Activity (NSA) with responsibility for all COSAL changes during overhaul. You and the SOAP team are responsible for forwarding COSAL change data to the NSA for all configuration changes made by the ship's force and by special assistance teams outside the shipyard overhaul effort. Your supply officer must be alert to identify these and to provide the information to the allowance section of the shipyard. Continuous liaison with the allowance section, and careful review of alterations conducted by your crew, are required throughout the overhaul to ensure that your COSAL reflects the final configuration of the ship.

In conclusion, then, to ensure that complete equipment support is achieved during your supply overhaul, you must carry out the following responsibilities:

Sufficient enlisted personnel must be assigned to support the supply overhaul.

Applicable instructions and procedures must be fully understood by ship's supply support personnel.

Written procedures must be established to coordinate the issue, control, accounting, and replacement of allowance list material withdrawn during the course of overhaul work. Issue of material from your ship should be made only in cases of urgent need and where the material is not readily available from other sources. Such issues should require the approval of the supply officer as a minimum.

You must insure that prompt follow-up action is taken for all shortages. Prior to departing the shipyard, you must ensure that your current status is provided to the parent tender for continued monitoring and expediting.

Alterations and Improvements

Background. We have discussed the necessity of maintaining your ship's COSAL up to date. This section provides a summary of the Navy's Alteration and Improvement Program, to enable you to understand better the forces behind equipment modifications on your ship.

Definitions. It is hard to understand the Alteration and Improvement Program without some knowledge of the terms used in it.

Military Improvement of Ships. Changes to military or operational characteristics, qualities and features which increase the capabilities of ships to perform their approved missions and tasks. These are approved by the CNO.

Technical Improvement of Ships. Changes to improve safety of personnel and equipment, increase the effectiveness of equipment, improve system performance, and increase reliability and maintainability.

Alteration Equivalent to a Repair (AER). An alteration which meets one or more of the following conditions:

(1) The substitution, without change in design, of different materials which have prior approval of the cognizant systems command for similar use and which are available from standard stock.

(2) The replacement of worn-out or damaged parts, assemblies, or equipments with those of later and more efficient design previously approved by the cognizant systems command.

(3) The strengthening of parts which require repair or replacement in order to improve reliability, provided no other change in design is involved.

(4) Minor modifications involving no significant changes in design or functioning of equipment, but considered essential to eliminate recurrence of unsatisfactory conditions.

Ship Alteration (SHIPALT) Categories. Alterations on Navy ships are assigned the following categories:

(1) Title A. Title A is assigned to alterations requested for certain ships under construction, in which authorization is anticipated during the obligation period under construction funds. Title A ship alterations are funded under Ship Construction Navy (SCN) funding. On expiration of these funds, Title A alterations may be classified as Title K alterations, discussed below.

(2) Title D. Title D is assigned to alteration equivalent to a repair. These are authorized by type commanders and funded under Other Procurement Navy (OPN) funds as operating expenses.

(3) Title F. Title F is assigned to alterations that can be accomplished by forces afloat. They are authorized by type commanders and require no industrial assistance.

(4) Title K. Title K is assigned to all other type ship alterations authorized by NAVSEA as specified within the Fleet Modernization Program (FMP) and funded under OPN.

     (5) Title K-P or Title D-P are assigned to those alterations designated for inclusion in the SHIPALT Package Program of the FMP.
     (6) Type Commander Alterations and Improvements (A&I). Used by some type commanders for the following reasons:
       (a) To authorize accomplishment of alterations equivalent to repairs.
       (b) To authorize accomplishment of interim corrective action for recognized problems prior to the issuance of a ship alteration.
       (c) To maintain accountability for various required inspections, tests and modifications.

Alteration and Improvement Programs. Each type commander administers an alteration and improvement program. This lists the various approved alterations, field changes, and AERs that apply to ships of the type. Your type commander's program is based on the Navy's Fleet Modernization Program (FMP). The FMP is an integrated program which combines ship alterations of a technical and military improvement nature and lists them based on scheduled ship overhauls. The Navy's FMP consists of all alterations applicable to specific ships on a yearly basis within a five-year period. The current year program then becomes the schedule for implementing presently funded ship alterations. Future year programs form the basis for annual Navy budget submissions. Based on the FMP, material managers budget and procure supporting material and identify COSAL support as needed.

NAVSEAINST 4720.2 outlines policies and procedures for the development, administration, and execution of the Navy's program for alteration and improvement of ships and equipment. Your officers should be familiar with this instruction, as well as with type commander guidelines governing the submission of alteration requests and the accomplishment of those approved.

In support of the shipboard alteration program, the commanding officer must ensure that his department heads keep abreast of infor-

Figure 9-3. Food service is an important task for any supply officer. This large carrier mess must serve hundreds of meals around the clock during operations.

mation on package alteration kits which are, or will become, available for the ship. He must ensure that package alterations are installed expeditiously after receipt and that proper COSAL maintenance is conducted to support the change. Finally, he must ensure that completed installations are reported in a timely manner and that feedback is provided to Navy technical agencies when difficulty is experienced in completing any alteration.

Food Service

Food Service Officer. Although you may assign a separate food service officer, the more common practice in smaller ships is to have the supply officer carry out this function. In most such ships the wardroom eats from the general mess, and no provision is necessary for a separate wardroom mess. The young supply officer will probably have little or no experience in the management of messes. Thus, it behooves you to keep a close eye on his operation of both the general and wardroom messes. You should review the menu carefully before approving it and should insist that deviations be approved by you in writing. Make it clear to the food service officer that you expect a high level of performance from each man assigned food service responsibilities. If a meal is not prepared palatably, find out why. You should not sit in the wardroom and eat poorly prepared food. If it doesn't taste good to you, it doesn't to the crew. As commanding officer you should strive for the reputation of being the best feeder in the Navy. Getting this reputation does not take as much money as it does attention.

An important corollary to rejecting substandard performance in the food service area is to recognize outstanding work. On the mess decks, the junior mess cook is of equal importance to the leading mess management specialist. These men and those who work with them should be publicly recognized for superior work. This type of recognition pays dividends. Recognition is directly related to morale, job satisfaction, and retention. Additionally, it sets the tone for all food service operations, and will result in improved relations between the mess management specialists and the rest of the crew.

Food Service Personnel and Service. At the present time, a shortage of experienced mess management specialists exists in the fleet. Improved retention of food service personnel will, in time, raise experience levels in this vital area. In the meantime, the commanding officer should strive to improve the food service skills of his personnel. In doing so he must work to improve both management and the personal desire for excellence of his subordinates.

An example of improved food service management is in the area of menu planning. Many ships continue to require the leading mess management specialist to write a menu from scratch each week rather than using a five- or six-week cycle menu. He can save significant time on this job if your ship adopts a cycle menu. Each week the cycle menu is reviewed to reflect special events and seasonal fruits and vegetables, but the basic foods are fixed. A cycle menu will not hurt quality or variety if properly managed.

In the area of personal desire, the commanding officer must use technical training and his own support to strengthen his food service organization's morale. Your food service division will respond in a positive manner to frequent sanitation inspections and insistence on attention to detail. Obviously, these rules apply to wardroom service as well as to the enlisted dining facility. The key to success in food service throughout your tour will be consistent *attention to detail* and *prevention of deterioration of service* afforded your officers and men.

Accountability. NAVSUP Pub 486 sets forth stringent requirements regarding financial accountability files. Improper accounting and procedural control in the food service area can ruin a career. As commanding officer, you must involve yourself in food service accounting to the degree necessary to insure *its* effectiveness and *your* peace of mind.

It is not necessary that you become a *full-time* food service or commissary officer to monitor properly the food service operation of your ship. It does take some knowledge, however, to ask the proper questions and conduct necessary audits. More importantly, it takes some of your time and interest to get the point across to food service personnel that you will accept nothing less than strict adherence to food service accounting.

The following simple audit items and questions, used periodically, will provide you a clear picture of your food service effectiveness. In asking questions or reviewing logs listed below, remember that a well-run general mess will consistently be able to provide crisp, unambiguous responses without delay. Long waits for answers or records are cause for concern and should be pursued.

> Review the accountability file. It should be in the supply officer's sole custody, locked in his safe. Contents of the file are listed in Appendix 1 of *NAVSUP 486*. Key documents are the original inventory and a copy of all receipt or transfer papers. The file should be orderly and well-organized. A stack of unkempt papers is as unacceptable in this as in any area of ship's administration.
> Compare the accountability file with the requisition log (NAVSUP Form 1336). Every document should be listed for control.
> An adding-machine tape of receipt papers in the accountability

file should agree with the value of receipts as indicated on the receipt/expenditure log (NAVSUP 367).

Look at the receipt and expenditure log. Does it reflect recent known stores receipts? Is it up to date?

An inspection of reefers, storerooms, and food service areas should show them to be clean and sufficiently full to meet type commander endurance requirements.

NAVSUP Form 338 is the ration control record. This determines how much can be spent during the quarter for food, and shows a daily accounting of over- and under-issue status. You can make the following checks on this record:

(1) Daily report of ration status. This shows the cost of feeding for one day and the current issue condition. A daily report also keeps records up to date.

(2) Sometime during the quarter, insist on an inventory and trial closing of records. This will produce a "stores consumed" NAVSUP Form 1059, which should agree to within two percent with the stores consumed figure on the NAVSUP Form 338 (ration control record).

Periodic spot inventories of a number of food service items will also be helpful in determining record accuracy. Have the supply officer conduct these personally and compare the inventory quantity with the subsistence ledger (NAVSUP Form 335).

Review the breakout log periodically. All stores used that day should be entered on one page. This is later transcribed to an issue document (NAVSUP Form 1282) which is posted to records and maintained in the accountability file. The breakout log should completely record all food used that day. An incomplete record is indicative of problems with (1) inventory accuracy, (2) control of the "stores consumed" figure, and (3) accuracy of the ration control record.

Ask to see the subsistence ledger occasionally. These volumes show quantity and type of food on board. They should be up to date, maintained in ink, reflect high and low limits, and show the last receipt price for an item.

Ascertain who is signing requisitions. It should be the supply officer. The requisition log (NAVSUP Form 1336) should indicate ultimate resolution of all requisitions submitted for food.

Monthly Evolutions. In addition to periodic food service auditing or questioning, the command must ensure that the supply department submits the reports that procedures require.

Collections for officers' meals should be completed by the fifth of the month, and should never be in arrears. Check the NAVSUP 1046 meal record to determine if all payments have been made.

The ration and sales report (NAVSUP Form 1357) should be mailed out not later than the fifth of each month. The cash sales (Forms 1046 and 1357), number of rations (Forms 1046, 338 and 1357) and receipts with charge (Forms 367, 1336, and 1357) should all agree. The retained copy of the ration and sales report is part of the accountability file.

Quarterly Returns. Insist that the supply officer and his key food service assistants directly involve themselves in the inventory and recording process. The quarterly inventory establishes accountability for the past and future quarter, and no departures from the precise procedures of NAVSUP 486 are permitted.

You should insist on seeing the "inventory adjustment" or "differences" NAVSUP Form 1059, which reflects discrepancies between the subsistence ledger and the actual inventory. This document, required by NAVSUP 486, provides an indication of how accurately the mess has operated for the quarter. Differences of one thousand pounds of beef or five hundred pounds of sugar indicate a precarious situation. A total money value on this document of less than two percent of the "stores consumed" figure indicates good control through the accounting period.

Lastly, the commanding officer should review the commissary "price adjustment." This is an arbitrary adjustment computed on the record of receipts and expenditures (NAVSUP Form 367) to account for price differences on receipt of stores. Since a forced or arbitrary figure can contain errors, review an amount above five percent of the stores consumed figure with caution. A value above ten percent requires written justification.

Figure 9-4. The combat stores ship USS *Concord* (AFS 5) transfers cargo simultaneously using highline and H-46 Sea Knight helicopters.

Replenishment at Sea

Each ship should leave its base, tender, or port as fully provisioned and supplied as possible. Normal fleet operations provide for further replenishment, when needed, at sea. Each fleet unit must be ready to use the U.S. Navy's outstanding system of extending almost indefinitely the time and range of operations.

First, each ship must know how to communicate its requirements to replenishing ships. *Operational Reports* (*NWP-7*) requires that underway replenishment (UNREP) requirements should be submitted twelve to twenty-four hours in advance of the rendezvous. Complete instructions for submission of these reports is contained in *Replenishment at Sea* (*NWP-14*).

Secondly, each ship commander must be skilled at bringing his ship alongside promptly and accurately, and maintaining it there. His crew must be skilled in rigging replenishment systems and receiving and striking below provisions, ammunition, and fuel received by all means, including helicopters.

Figure 9-5. Replenishment at sea is performed by all types of ships. Here the fast combat support ship USS *Seattle* (AOE 5) refuels the aircraft carrier USS *America* (CVA 66) and the Coast Guard cutter *Sherman* (WHEC 720).

Figure 9-6. Ships of all sizes must be able to conduct underway replenishment. The ocean minesweeper USS *Endurance* (MSO 435) is refueling from the oiler USS *Mispillion* (AO 105).

Figure 9-7. Replenishing ammunition at sea is always a potentially danger-ous operation. The fact that millions of rounds have been handled safely in the past should not make you any less safety conscious in the present.

Submarines replenish at sea only in emergencies, and must be particularly careful to set out on patrol or on operations fully sup-plied.

Future Replenishment Developments. In years to come the Navy will make further strides in the art of underway replenishment. Rapid electronic communication will someday permit a ship's UN-REP request for spare parts to trigger instantaneously the manufac-ture and movement of replacements through the logistics system. This will mean quicker response at a much lower inventory. We can expect the increased use of helicopters, bringing modular spares and other critical replacements on short notice. Each commanding officer should be prepared to participate in this continuing development of logistics—the force that moves and supplies the fleet.

10

Safety

Nothing is more dangerous than for a seaman to be grudging in taking precautions lest they turn out to have been unnecessary. Safety at sea for a thousand years has depended on exactly the opposite philosophy.

—Fleet Admiral Chester W. Nimitz, USN

Historical Background. Prior to World War II, safety at sea was a relatively simple matter. All of shipboard safety could be treated under only three major categories. First, the ship had to sail safely, which meant avoiding grounding and collision by good navigation and proper shiphandling. Second, fireroom casualties, mainly boiler explosions and fires, had to be avoided by the observance of traditional precautions and the careful use of check lists. Third, ammunition had to be received, stored, moved, and fired safely. This task was the subject of elaborate, almost sacred safety precautions, which were observed to the letter. As for minor hazards, most ships had a paint locker, which occasionally produced a rousing fire (and a resultant flurry of corrective instruction), and a five-inch loading machine, which amputated at least one finger a year. Other than these small irritants, the safety program, then not yet dignified by a name, was simple, straightforward, and effective.

Today safety is a much more complex subject. Nuclear power, nuclear weapons, high pressure steam plants, exotic missile propellants, more powerful conventional explosives, aviation fuels, automatic gun and missile loading machinery, complex replenishment systems, the threat of biological and gas warfare, the possibility of nuclear contamination, and a host of other developments make a far-ranging, integrated, formal safety program necessary. The safety program now must cover almost every function of your ship, from the location of your brow to the storage of special weapons.

Many of the areas which require safety bills and programs are peculiar to each type of ship. Many are simple and require no discussion. These latter will be found in *OPNAVINST 3120.32A*, the *SORN*. Those general programs of the greatest importance, however, will be discussed in the following pages.

Accident Prevention Education

Responsibility. The *SORN* assigns the commanding officer the ultimate responsibility for all safety matters within his unit. To help him carry out his responsibilities in this area, he may appoint a safety officer to provide day-to-day staff assistance. The *SORN* also requires that a command safety program be built on policies and goals established by the captain. A typical safety organization is shown in Figure 10–1.

A good safety program must imbue the crew with the understanding that *safety is an all-hands responsibility*. Each man must develop an attitude which makes him stop and think before he makes, or allows another man to make, that one wrong move that can bring disaster. In light of current shipboard manning problems, and the declining level of supervisory experience in the fleet, you must aim for this attitude in every man, down to the rawest seaman recruit.

Safety Officer. You will have to use insight and judgement in appointing your safety officer. Assigning this program to the "boot ensign" will guarantee its failure. This officer will serve as your principal advisor on all internal safety matters, and his relationship with you, the executive officer, and the crew is the key to success.

A successful safety program does not have to mean extra work for the crew. The most successful programs, in fact, are those which have been incorporated in the ship's normal training and qualifica-

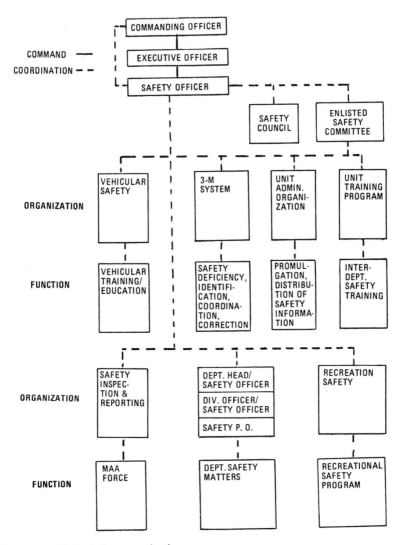

Figure 10-1. Safety organization.

tion procedures. This can be done by concentrating safety training efforts in areas that complement shipboard operational and administrative training.

As an example, accident prevention education can be presented as part of the ship's general military training. This can be done in a painless way by proper dissemination of pertinent safety bulletins. The Navy spends thousands of dollars annually publishing such fine periodicals as *Flash*, *Fathom*, and *Safety Notes*, as well as defective material reports, lessons learned, and many other items. The wise will learn by the mistakes of others; the foolish are destined to learn by their own bad experiences. Needless to say, these publications should also be routed and reviewed by all supervisory personnel.

Routine Inspections. Another safety-related training vehicle is the use of routine inspections to highlight safety hazard awareness, as well as material conditions. Daily inspections of spaces by division officers and leading petty officers should be directed to instill hazard awareness in their personnel. Your periodic inspections, and those by the other senior officers assigned, can emphasize the same points. In addition, selected monitoring of hazardous evolutions will tell you much about your ship's safety awareness.

Naval Safety Center. Your command accident prevention program can get off to a good start by inviting the Naval Safety Center inspection team aboard to perform a safety survey. Many ships fail to utilize properly these surveys because of a general fear of outside inspection teams. This was aptly voiced by Captain Larry G. Vogt, COMSUBLANT Prospective Commanding Officer (PCO) instructor, who once stated, "There is no such thing as a free inspection." This is probably true in every area *except* Safety Center Surveys.

Safety Center Surveys are completely informal. They are designed to provide the ship with the latest safety information, and to discuss hazard identification and safety management techniques with your key personnel. No preparation is required other than making time and personnel available.

Most surveys consist of several elements. First, an all hands accident briefing is generally presented, detailing current accident prevention methods. A wardroom briefing is conducted simultaneously with the all hands briefing. Next, the survey team conducts a hazard review. This passes the latest safety programs and accident prevention methods to each division. The team will, if you desire, also conduct a hazard identification walk-through with key personnel. This is carried out using a checklist derived from hazardous items identified by Board of Inspection and Survey inspections and through the SAFETYGRAM system.

Your ship's safety program should also be reflected in the watch station qualification program and in the formal certification of watchstanders. This can readily be done by promulgating standard procedures to cover all operational, maintenance, and repair evolutions, and by making use of these procedures mandatory.

Safety Investigations. Finally, your safety program should provide a way to analyze accidents afloat and to report them properly when necessary. Ensure that your safety officer is thoroughly versed in the conduct of investigations. Particularly, direct him to place his emphasis on determining *why* the accident happened. He should also be familiar with material damage and injury reports, the use of accident reports for accident analysis, and hazard reporting.

All this might seem like a large load for one junior officer. However, familiarity with the references below will provide him all the information necessary to do the job properly:

> *OPNAVINST 3120.32A, Standard Organization and Regulations of the U. S. Navy,* Chapter 7
> *OPNAVINST 5101.2, Accident Prevention Manual*
> *OPNAVINST 5102.1, Accident Investigating and Reporting*
> *OPNAVINST 5100.19, Navy Safety Precautions for Forces Afloat*
> *NAVSAFECEN 5102/29, Accident Investigating Handbook*
> *The Watch Officer's Guide,* published by the Naval Institute Press.

You can give your program another boost by sending your safety officer to the unit safety supervisor's course, taught at the fleet training centers on both coasts.

Figure 10-2. Careful navigation will bring a ship through tight places safely. Close coordination between commanding officer and navigator will be required.

Watch Officers and Safety

Watch Officer Responsibilities. A ship is administered departmentally, but her operation at sea is directed on a watch basis. Watch officers assigned directly assist the captain with the safe navigation and operation of his ship. The *SORN*, Chapter 4, authorizes you to establish such watches as are necessary for the safe and proper operation of the command. In addition, it directs that the watch of the officer of the deck and of the engineering officer of the watch be regular and continuous underway.

The remarks below amplify those watch officer responsibilities and relations provided by *Navy Regulations* and the *SORN*, especially as they relate to safety underway.

Officer of the Deck (OOD). The officer of the deck underway is that officer on watch designated by the commanding officer to be in charge of the ship. He is primarily responsible, under the captain, for the safe and proper operation of the ship and for the safety and performance of her personnel. The OOD must keep himself continually informed concerning the tactical situation and geographic factors which may affect the safe navigation of the ship, and must take appropriate action to avoid grounding or collision in accordance with tactical doctrine, the *Rules of the Road*, and the orders of the commanding officer or other proper authority.

The OOD reports directly to the commanding officer for the safe navigation and general operation of the ship; to the executive officer for carrying out the ship's routine; and to the navigator for sightings of navigation landmarks and course and speed changes.

Engineering Officer of the Watch (EOOW). The engineering officer of the watch is the officer or petty officer designated by the engineer officer to be in charge of the engineering department watch. He is responsible for the safe and proper performance of the engineering department watch, in accordance with the orders of the engineer, the commanding officer, and higher authority. The EOOW reports to the OOD for the speed and direction of rotation of the main engines and for direction as to standby power requirements and other services anticipated or ordered. He reports to the engineer officer for technical control and on matters affecting the administration of his watch.

Command Duty Officer (CDO). The *SORN* also provides for an inport watch organization, led by a command duty officer, to ensure the security and safety of the ship. The CDO is responsible for security, for the conduct of routine, and, in the absence of the regularly responsible officer, for the supervision of all ship's activities. He succeeds to the responsibilities and authority of command when all eligible ship's officers senior to him are absent or incapacitated.

As head of the inport watch organization, the duty officer must ensure that all hands are continuously alert to their responsibilities while in a duty status. Fire, flooding, sabotage, and enemy attack are always possibilities. Early detection will prevent or minimize damage. The CDO is your direct representative, and if he is the senior officer aboard, he is also the acting commanding officer. In either capacity, he has all the authority necessary to execute his duties.

Watchstanding Principles

Procedures. Procedures for safety at sea and in port are clearly defined in the *SORN*, Articles 630.13 and 700. In addition to the formal organizational requirements of this instruction, you must stress proven watchstanding principles to your subordinates as prerequisites to the safe and efficient operation of the ship and for its security from all hazards.

Each watchstander must clearly understand that his effectiveness is a function not only of his basic understanding of operations and equipment, but also of his watchstanding habits and regard for safety. Even the best operational and safety training program will only be as effective as the standards he keeps. The following paragraphs briefly describe those attributes required by the members of a watch section to enable them to maintain the ship in a safe manner.

Attention to Duty. Watchstanders must be vigilant and attentive to all details. The appearance of normal, steady state conditions should never be an excuse for relaxing attention. Watchstanders should never conduct business except as required by the duties of the watch.

Conduct While on Watch. Each man must stand his watch in a smart military manner. In doing so, loud conversation and unnecessary noise are never appropriate. Reading of any material not directly pertinent to the watch should never be allowed.

Physical Condition of Watchstanders. No man should be allowed to relieve the watch unless he is physically and mentally able to stand an alert, effective watch. Watchstanders whose abilities are impaired by sickness or exhaustion should inform their supervisors and request a relief.

Congestion. The conduct of any watch requires proper access to equipment and clearly defined duties and responsibilities. Spectators should never be permitted at any station or in any space where they might obstruct or distract the watch.

Communications. All watchstanders must conduct communications in strict accordance with the ship's interior communications bill.

Casualty Action. Each watchstander should read and understand all casualty procedures pertinent to his watch station. He should review these procedures periodically as necessary to ensure complete familiarity. While on watch, he should be encouraged to review mentally the actions he would take under various casualty conditions.

Log Keeping. The keeping of logs and data sheets, while important, must never be allowed to interfere with the effective and *safe* operation of the ship and its equipment. If it does, the watchstander should report it immediately to the next senior in the watch organization.

All watchstanders must understand the significance of log entries and trends evident therefrom. A review for trends at the time of recording hourly readings may indicate a system change which can be diagnosed and rectified before the situation deteriorates into a casualty.

Instrumentation. Experience with naval machinery and equipment has emphasized the importance of instrumentation and records. In general, it is best to proceed by assuming that all instruments are reading correctly, or operating on the safe side of the worst indication of the instrument. Never blame the instrument until investigation has proven it defective.

Relieving the Watch. Relieving the watch should be a controlled and precise procedure. The ability to handle casualties and tactical decisions is significantly reduced during the transition period between watches. Accordingly, observe the following procedures during watch relief:

1. The relieving watch should be on station sufficiently early to become familiar with equipment conditions and the overall situation and still relieve on time.
2. The relieving watch must make a thorough and complete inspection of all spaces and equipment under his cognizance *before* relieving the watch. This is particularly applicable to engineering and weapons areas, but is not limited to them.
3. Both the relieved and the relieving watch are responsible for ensuring that the relieving watch is completely aware of all

unusual conditions that exist. These include the tactical situation, equipment out of commission or being worked on, outstanding orders, deviations from normal "line up," forthcoming evolutions, and any other matters pertinent to the watch.

Underway Operational Safety

Underway Safety Directives. Navy Regulations, Article 0775, and the *SORN* both state that the commanding officer is responsible for the safe navigation of his ship or aircraft, except as prescribed otherwise for ships at a naval shipyard or station, in drydock, or in the Panama Canal. In time of war, or during exercises simulating war, the provisions of these references pertaining to the use of lights and electronic devices may be modified by competent authority.

The commanding officer of a ship and, as appropriate, of an aircraft, shall:

Keep himself informed of the error of all compasses and other devices available as aids to navigation.

Ensure that efficient devices for fixing the ship's position and for ascertaining the depth of water are employed when underway on soundings, entering or leaving port, or upon approaching an anchorage, shore, or rock, whether or not a pilot is aboard. If circumstances warrant, he must reduce speed to the extent necessary to permit these devices to be operated efficiently and accurately.

Observe every precaution prescribed by law to prevent collisions and other accidents on the high seas, inland waters, or in the air.

When underway in restricted waters or close inshore, and unless unusual circumstances prevent, steam at a speed which will not endanger other ships or craft, or property close to the shore.

Take special care that the lights required by law to prevent collisions at sea, in port, or in the air are kept in order and burning in all weathers from sunset to sunrise, and that means for promptly relighting or replacing such lights are available.

Piloting Errors. Failure to heed these regulations has resulted in disaster at sea as a result of collision or grounding. In the matter of grounding, a review of investigations over the past one hundred years has clearly pointed out that one or more of a group of common piloting errors have been found to be the cause of each disaster. Yet these errors still occur all too often. The wise commanding officer will review the below list often, asking himself *does my organization suffer in any of these areas?*

Failure to obtain or evaluate soundings.

Failure to identify aids to navigation.

Failure to use available navigational aids effectively.

Failure to correct charts.

Failure to adjust a magnetic compass or maintain an accurate table of corrections.

Failure to apply deviation, or error in its application.

Failure to apply variation, or to allow for change in variation.

Failure to check gyro against magnetic compass readings at frequent and regular intervals.

Failure to keep a dead reckoning plot.

Failure to plot information received.

Failure to properly evaluate information received.

Poor judgment.

Failure to do own navigating (following another vessel).

Failure to obtain and use information available on charts and in various publications.

Poor ship organization.

Failure to "keep ahead of the vessel."

In addition to reviewing your organization for these errors, you should ask yourself the following questions each time you review the navigation picture with the navigator or the OOD:

What is the reliability of the present indicated position? How was it obtained?

Does the OOD clearly understand his responsibility under *Navy*

Regulations to positively establish the ship's position and track as being safe?

Where do the greatest hazards lie on the track ahead?

What is the bottom contour along the track?

Will there be adequate warning of approaching danger?

What would the worst conditions of set, drift, and position mean?

Am I rushing the ship at the expense of safety?

Training OODs. The effective commanding officer will train his officers to ask themselves these same questions prior to relieving and while on watch as OOD or JOOD.

All too often, grounding investigations determine that the OOD did not clearly understand the burden on him regarding the safe navigation of the ship. The *SORN* clearly describes his obligations in regard to navigational safety. *The officer of the deck underway must keep himself continuously informed concerning the tactical situation and geographical factors which may affect the safe navigation of the ship, and must take appropriate action to avoid the danger of grounding or collision.*

Investigations have also shown that often the OOD took insufficient interest in navigation simply because the navigator or one of his assistants was on the bridge. Each OOD must understand that the navigator's position as the authoritative advisor on the safe navigation of the ship does not relieve him of any of his responsibilities.

Navigational Readiness. Procedures for checking your ship's navigational readiness are important, and proper use of them will pay you dividends. Appendix XVI provides a navigational evaluation guide that will give you some idea of how your ship stands in navigational safety.

Collisions. Thucydides, in the fifth century before Christ, said "A collision at sea can ruin your entire day." This witticism has been repeated in some form by each generation of seamen since. Analysis of collisions over many years has shown that one or more of the following mistakes caused each incident:

Failure to realize in time that there was risk of collision.

Failure to take timely avoiding action.

Failure of a darkened ship to turn on running lights in an emergency.

Failure of a watch officer to notify the commanding officer of a potentially dangerous situation.

Failure to check for steady bearing in a closing situation until too late.

Reliance on CIC to the exclusion of a common sense evaluation of the situation being made on the bridge.

Poor judgment in evaluating the effects of wind and tide.

Failure to understand the tactical characteristics of the ship.

Injudicious use of the power available in the ship.

Bridge and CIC radars both on long-range setting, thereby making the detection of close-in targets difficult, or bridge and CIC radars both on short-range setting, resulting in a failure to detect distant targets on a collision course until very close in.

Failure of bridge personnel to keep sharp visual lookout.

Failure of CIC and the bridge to ensure that the commanding officer understood tactical signals.

Making a radical change in course without informing ships in the vicinity.

Failure to use whistle signals.

Failure to make the required checks between gyro and magnetic compasses.

Failure of a ship in formation to broadcast a warning by voice radio when contacts are seen to be merging.

Failure of the bridge to check maneuvering board solutions provided by CIC, and vice versa.

Deck watch officer's lack of familiarity with the rules of the road and with accepted procedures for preventing collisions.

Failure to execute tactical signals correctly.

Most of the errors above are elementary, but still they are made all too often. In addition to training his officers in the academics of watchstanding, the commanding officer must imbue them with a general attitude of vigilance, a highly developed sense of responsibility, and the faculty of good judgment. He must stress the value of mental review of casualty actions while the watch is slow, and insist upon formal communications by watchstanders. Failure to use proper phraseology and to preserve strict formality of address among members of the watch is asking for trouble.

Underway Operational Safety. Safety at sea is enhanced by emphasis on all of the areas mentioned above. By such emphasis, safety becomes command philosophy and policy. You must avoid letting the routine performance of safety measures deteriorate into carelessness.

Many commanding officers tend to standardize the procedures they use to approach channel entrance ranges and make turns and speed changes in proceeding to or from their berth. This standardization can help the captain in the development of his supervisory ability on the bridge by shifting some of his concentration from decision-making to supervisory observation.

Supervisory ability is distinct from the ability to conn the ship or specifically to conduct any evolution personally. It involves keeping in mind what the OOD is doing, where the navigator wants to go, what lookouts are reporting, what signals are in the air, what is happening on the forecastle, who is at quarters aft, whose barge is passing down the side, and whether or not the ship ahead is turning early—*but without being directly involved.*

Cultivation of this faculty permits overall observation of the ship's performance, avoidance of dangers that more preoccupied personnel may miss, and, finally, the ability to handle the ship successfully in combat. When the captain's personal skill must be applied to the conn, or when he has to concentrate his attention on any other one facet of operations, he runs the risk of missing something vital. In contrast, the captain who insists on navigational and piloting briefs before entering restricted waters, who ensures that his subordinates plan and brief supervisory personnel prior to any non-standard or complicated evolution, will be prepared better to practice overall supervision. This is particularly true when the risk of overlooking something important is increased by several days of strain, lack of sleep, and physical "pounding."

Figure 10-3. The USS *Finback* (SSN 760) on the surface at high speed. Safety at sea begins with simple safety precautions.

A Pacific Fleet letter by Fleet Admiral Nimitz has a bearing on this:

> There are certain psychological factors which have fully as much to do with safety at sea as any of the more strictly technical ones. A large proportion of the disasters in tactics and maneuvers comes from concentrating too much on one objective or urgency, at the cost of not being sufficiently alert for others. Thus, absorption with enemy craft already under fire has led to being torpedoed by others not looked for or not given attention; while preoccupation with navigation, with carrying out the particular job in hand, or with avoiding some particular vessel or hazard, has resulted in collision with ships to whose presence we were temporarily oblivious. There is no rule that can cover this except the ancient one that eternal vigilance is the price of safety, no matter what the immediate distractions.
>
> No officer, whatever his rank and experience, should flatter himself that he is immune to the inexplicable lapses in judgment, calculation and memory, or to the slips of the tongue in giving orders, which throughout seagoing history have often brought disaster to men of the highest reputation and ability. Where a mistake in maneuvering or navigating can spell calamity, an officer shows rashness and conceit, rather than admirable self-confidence, in not checking his plan with someone else before starting it, *if time permits*. This is not yielding to another's judgment; it is merely making sure that one's own has not "blown a fuse" somewhere, as the best mental and mechanical equipment in the world has sometimes done.

Who Has the Conn?

Distinction between Conn and Deck. When underway, the commanding officer must ensure that the officer of the deck is thoroughly aware of the distinction between the conn, which is the actual control of the movements of the ship, and the deck, which is the supervisory authority of the watch as outlined in the *SORN*. When the conning officer is also OOD he has all the responsibilities imposed by the *SORN*, as well as those additional ones imposed by the directives of the commanding officer.

Changing the Conn. In order to insure that no confusion exists over "who has the conn?", a definite routine of taking it over and relinquishing it must be followed. The status of the conn must be clearly understood by the OOD, verbally acknowledged by him and, most important, loudly brought to the attention of all personnel who perform manually the orders given by the officer who has the conn. A considerable measure of responsibility for the ship's safety remains with the OOD even when he is relieved of the conn by the CO or other qualified officer.

Although there is no official set of rules about the conn, the following principles have been evolved through the experience of seamen. The commanding officer may at his discretion relieve the OOD of the conn at any time. In addition, he may instruct him how to proceed without assuming the conn. Any direct order to the wheel or engine order telegraph will, however, in itself constitute assumption of the responsibility for direction of the ship's movements—the *conn*. Under these conditions, in order to ensure efficient response and eliminate the possibility of conflicting orders, the OOD should announce to the bridge watch, "The captain (or other officer as appropriate) has the conn," and immediately thereafter report to that officer, "Sir, I have relinquished the conn."

Involuntary Relief of the Officer of the Deck. In the previous section it was pointed out that the commanding officer could relieve the OOD at any time. Over the years the authority of the executive officer and the navigator with regard to involuntary relief of the OOD has changed. Prior to 1973, the executive officer and the navigator could relieve at any time. At present, Article 323, *SORN*, states that the navigator may relieve the officer of the deck as authorized or directed by the commanding officer in writing.

The authority of the executive officer is less clear. The general authority of the executive officer delegated by the commanding officer would seem to cover the matter, but it is advisable, in order to avoid misunderstanding, to give the same authorization in writing to the executive officer to relieve the officer of the deck. Both officers should be instructed to inform the commanding officer as soon as practicable after relieving.

Good Sea Manners and Shiphandling Tips

Shiphandling Tips. Naval Shiphandling, by Captain R. S. Crenshaw, USN (Ret), published by the Naval Institute Press, should be read by every officer who goes to sea. In addition to a comprehensive explanation of the principles of shiphandling, this excellent book includes most of the information and advice which makes up its "folklore". These are little rules that are picked up as one's experience broadens at sea, and which in total are the wisdom that prevents one from repeating mistakes. They might be called the safety precautions or "good manners" of shiphandling.

In listing these tips, Captain Crenshaw made no attempt to record them in order of their importance. We reproduce them here to provoke thought for safety at sea.

Keep your ship's stern away from danger. If the propellers and rudders become damaged, you are crippled. If the stern is free to maneuver, though, you can usually work your ship out of trouble.

Don't take a chance. If you recognize it as a chance, it is probably too risky.

When ordering rudder, look in the direction you intend to turn. This is as wise at sea as in a vehicle ashore.

Check to make sure that the rudder moved in the direction you ordered. Watch the helmsman move the wheel if you can see him. Check the rudder position indicator to see what the rudder actually did. Check the compass for direction. On a surfaced submarine, check the rudder.

When ordering rudder, tell the helmsman your intended final course. You may be distracted during the turn, and the ship will continue to swing.

When swinging to a new course, bring the rudder amidships a number of degrees before reaching the new course equal to one-half the rudder angle being used. When using thirty degrees of rudder, order the rudder amidships when you have fifteen degrees yet to go. This works remarkably well for coming smartly to a new course.

Beware of a ship lying to. She is often moving imperceptibly.

Don't trust your sense of distance in a flat calm. This sense is undependable under any conditions, but is at its worst across a glassy sea.

Don't attempt precise maneuvers when going astern. Ships handle awkwardly when backing, and occasionally veer erratically.

Give buoys a wide berth. You can't see the cable to the buoy anchor from the surface. Many a screw has been damaged on a buoy that had been "cleared."

If you are confused, consider that the other ships in the formation are, too. When the situation seems confused, a normal maneuver by another ship may catch you by surprise.

When uncertain what to do, come to formation course and speed. This will give you time to clarify the situation.

During a complex formation maneuver, remember the direction towards open water. This is the avenue to safety; you may need it.

When collision is imminent and a safe course of action is not apparent, back emergency and turn toward the danger. The backing will delay the collision and reduce the impact. The turn toward the danger will reduce the target you present, and a ship can withstand impact better forward. A head-on collision will crumple the bow, but the ship can be cut in two if hit from the beam.

Never trust a compass or a chart. Keep checking the ship's heading by landmarks and auxiliary compass. A compass doesn't announce its departure when it goes out. And all charts have minor inaccuracies; some have major ones.

If blown against a ship or pier when going alongside, stay there until you have made complete preparations to get clear. The ship is normally quite safe resting there, but can sustain major damage trying to pull clear without assistance.

Never trust a mooring, check it. Anchor chains part, mooring shackles break, buoys break adrift, even bollards pull out of piers. Check the position regularly.

In low visibility, keep the radar tuned for short range. The power setting and tuning of the main control console should be selected for best coverage of the band 0–5,000 yards. Though you can expand the presentation by changing the scale setting on the remote scope on the bridge, you can't get optimum results unless the main console is properly adjusted. Remember, it is the contact at short range that presents the danger!

When sounding fog signals, shorten the interval once every few minutes. You may be synchronized with another ship and not hear her signal because of your own.

Sound the danger signal early. This is legal, and it declares that you do not understand the other ship's intentions. It will prompt her to commit herself and thus clarify the situation.

A ship on a steady bearing is on a collision course. Take precise bearings on approaching ships, and check the trend.

Avoid passing starboard-to-starboard close aboard. The other ship may evaluate the situation as being nearly head-on, and cause a collision situation by altering her course for a port-to-port passage. It's safer to alter course to starboard at an early stage and pass port-to-port.

Join other ships by coming up from astern. Relative speeds will be lower and the whole maneuver will be more comfortable for yourself and your formation mates.

The faster the ship is moving through the water, the better control you will have. Both rudder force and hull stability improve with speed, and wind and current are felt less.

When adjusting position alongside with the lines over, don't wait for the ship to begin moving before stopping the engines. The time lags are too long for this.

Steer your ship as you would a boat. Look ahead and steer where good sense indicates. Orient to the real world of landmarks, channels, buoys, ships, and obstructions. Keep your head up and your eyes open. Charts, maneuvering boards, and compasses are aids, not substitutes. If the navigator's recommended course doesn't look right, stop your ship and "let her soak" until you are sure that the course you are taking corresponds both with the indications of the chart and the physical situation you see.

When following a tortuous channel, or the movements of another ship, steer with rudder angles instead of ordering successive courses. You are fitting curves to curves and you must adjust as you move along the curved part.

When entering a narrow channel, try to adjust your heading to compensate for cross wind and cross current before getting into the narrow part.

When required to maneuver by the rules of the road, turn early and turn plenty. Make your intention completely clear to the other vessel; you can refine your course later.

When the bow goes to port, the stern goes to starboard; make sure to allow room for it. In a tight place, where even a small drift in the wrong direction spells trouble, leave a spring line secured to check a faulty movement until the ship is actually moving in the right direction.

If your ship loses power or steering, notify any other ships in the vicinity immediately so they can stand clear.

Keep the jackstaff up when maneuvering in port. It is a valuable aid in verifying the ship's head with respect to other ships and landmarks, and in judging the rate of swing of the bow in a turn.

Peacetime Incidents with Communist Bloc Ships

Incidents at sea with Soviet bloc ships continue to occur all too frequently. Often, this is because communist bloc ships habitually violate the provisions of the *International Regulations for Preventing Collisions at Sea* and the *Agreement between the United States of America and the Union of Soviet Socialist Republics for the Prevention of Incidents On and Over the High Seas*.

The U.S. Navy and the government of the United States of America consider these to be deliberate actions. In order to maintain his ship's safety under such deliberate acts of harassment, every commanding officer must clearly understand the international agreements cited and the international signals to be used to avoid harassment.

Should harassment occur, the commanding officer must avoid collision and document the incident to the best of his ability. Such documentation should clearly show the degree of harassment in order to provide supporting evidence when a formal complaint is lodged with the Soviet government. Use a camera if your ship has one. Even a privately owned camera operated by an amateur crew member will help.

Figure 10-4. A Soviet warship plays "chicken" with a U.S. carrier by cutting in front of her.

Weather

Shiphandling in Heavy Weather. Crenshaw's *Naval Shiphandling* provides excellent information on handling a ship in heavy weather. All members of your wardroom should be familiar with it.

It is one thing to pass the word "secure ship for heavy weather," and another to have it done effectively. You would be wise to order a thorough inspection each time the ship is preparing for a storm. Hatches, lifelines, storerooms, holds, and engineering spaces should get special attention. The more effort spent in preparing for heavy weather, the less damage the storm can cause.

As opportunity permits during bad (but not dangerous) weather, experiment to determine the best courses and speeds for the ship during rough seas. The average and extreme rolls of the ship on courses into and with the seas should be compared, and any tendency to pitch severely or to pound noted. Prove to yourself and to your crew the capabilities and limitations of your ship, so that when actually faced with a hurricane or typhoon you can have confidence in your ability to cope with it. Decide firmly the best method of handling the ship in a hurricane or typhoon and make sure that all conning officers are acquainted with this decision.

Figure 10-5. Carry out your heavy weather bill *before* the storm arrives.

Figure 10-6. This destroyer captain has decided that in the hurricane approaching he will be safer at sea than in Guantanamo Bay. You will be required to make such decisions when you are in command.

Safety at sea is a combination of learning well the lessons of the past, conceiving and implementing a sound safety program and organization, and then exercising firm but flexible command, tempered with good sense.

11

Joining the Fleet

One of the most satisfying moments in the life of a commanding officer occurs when, after a long and arduous preparation period, he is able to send to his Fleet Commander, "Reporting for duty."

—Admiral Robert L. Dennison, USN

In this chapter we will discuss the problems of transition from new construction or overhaul to becoming an active and productive member of the fleet. To make this transition smoothly, you will have to drill and exercise your crew as individuals and as ship's teams, prepare them for inspections, and, finally, train them in advanced intership exercises and operations. You must be able at an early date to communicate and deal with your administrative and operational commanders, make and receive proper calls, render honors, and conduct ceremonies. All of these activities are important, and we will discuss them in the approximate order you will have to carry them out.

Joining the Fleet

A newly constructed ship "joins the fleet" after it completes its post-shakedown availability and refresher training. In a sense, an older ship also "joins the fleet" after a major overhaul. Like its newer sister, it also undergoes shakedown, post-shakedown availability, and refresher training.

In the days before World War II, "shakedown" was the word used to describe a period of four to six months given to a newly commis-

Figure 11-1. A proud moment in the life of one commanding officer as his ship, the USS *Clifton Sprague* (FFG 16), steams up to "join the fleet."

sioned ship to make itself ready to join the fleet. Early in World War II, however, it became obvious that this independent workup would no longer serve, and that a permanent organization was needed to supervise the shakedowns of the hundreds of ships being constructed. Thus, the Training Command was formed, with a command in each major fleet, with its main task being the preparation of ships for active service.

After World War II, the training commands were reduced in size, but retained the mission of refresher training, along with the added one of providing shore-based training facilities. The word "shakedown" is now used to describe the very brief period after commissioning and before commencement of refresher training. Generally all that can be done in this period is alignment of weapon batteries, compensation of magnetic compasses, and other similar preparations.

The Training Cycle

After either means of joining the fleet (commissioning, shakedown, post-shakedown availability, refresher training; or major overhaul, shakedown, post-shakedown availability, refresher training), a ship commences her training cycle. This cycle takes place in the interval between regularly scheduled major overhauls. Its length varies with ship types, but averages about sixty months. During this time a ship will usually work up for and complete two deployments. In wartime the entire cycle may be spent deployed. In either event, and particularly in time of crisis, wide variations in employment and in deployment dates and lengths may be expected. The normal became the exception during the war in Vietnam, for example, with its lengthy deployments and rapidly changing overhaul schedules.

In this chapter we will cover the early preparations and actions required by the training cycle. We will describe deployments, preparation for deployment, independent operations, and combat operations in later chapters.

Admiral Chester Nimitz, in addition to being a superb wartime commander, was an expert on training. In a conversation with former Secretary of the Navy William Franke, he once made the following observation in describing the fundamentals of training: "First you *instruct* men, then you *drill* them repeatedly to make the use of this knowledge automatic, then you *exercise* them, singly and in teams, to extend their individual abilities ship-wide; then the authority one level above the person who trained them *inspects* to insure that the desired results have been achieved."

In a broad sense, this is what you must do. Early in the training cycle, you must form a *training organization*, prepare a *training program*, and under this program and using this organization, instruct your individuals and teams. When instruction is completed, *drills* are used to assure the thoroughness and quality of instruction and to instill automatic reactions. *Ship exercises* then extend the drilling of individuals to drilling ship's teams. These intra-ship exercises then progress to intership exercises to bring the unit up to fleet standards. Finally, administrative seniors make *inspections* to determine the state of training of each ship. Inspections can cover a wide range of administrative and operational areas. All of these areas of preparation will be described in subsequent sections; but before getting too involved in them, you should be in touch with your type commander.

Relationships with Administrative Commanders

As soon as possible after taking command, and as early as possible in the training cycle, try to establish a good working relationship with your type commander. His staff can be of great assistance as you form your training organization and program. They will help with drills, exercises, and inspections.

Your senior's personnel officer, for example, can keep your allowance filled according to your position in the training cycle (and can pull it down, too!). You can expect to be at par when commencing refresher training, through advanced training, and halfway through deployment. At this time emergency detachments and medical problems will begin to pull you down slowly, and he will be reluctant to replace these losses. You will come home increasingly short-handed and will remain so until filled up again just prior to your next deployment. Remember that allowances are ideal manning numbers. The actual makeup of rates in the Navy at any given time will not correspond to the total of allowances in the Navy. Therefore, you will probably receive your pro-rata share of each rate, with shortages made up from lower rates or from non-rated men.

Also, do your best to remain on good terms with those men of the type commander's staff who administer funds. Like the personnel staff, they will be generous early in your cycle and increasingly stringent as you head home.

Most type commanders have inspection teams of various kinds. Some are mandatory and some are "on call." Make inquiries as to their relative worth to you and find out their reputations. Use the good and valuable ones and avoid the others.

One of the type commander's chief functions is to assist you.

Keep him informed and get help when you need it. It will be helpful to review the responsibilities which *Navy Regulations* place upon him. Chapter Six sets forth the regulations regarding commanders-in-chief and other commanders, and will give you an understanding of the duties of your type commander. Article 0604, "Readiness," states that the commander (type and others) shall take all practicable steps to maintain his command in a state of readiness in conformity with the orders and policies of higher authority. The article then states, in summary, that he shall organize his forces, prepare plans for their employment, and make such inspections as are necessary to ensure the readiness, effectiveness, and efficiency of the components of his command. Administratively, your ship will always be "one of the components of his command," even when under the operational command of one of the fleet commanders or operating independently. Understanding the type commander's responsibilities will aid you in obtaining full assistance from him, and will also temper your anger when you think he and his staff are "interfering" in your operations or administration.

Routine Reports

The moment your ship leaves the building yard or overhaul facility, you will come up against the requirement to render routine reports. Any attempt to discuss *all* routine reports here would result in another volume as big as *NWP 7*, *Operational Reports*. We have chosen instead to summarize in this section those routine reports with which you should be most familiar, and which will plague you most if you do not make them correctly. Non-routine reports, such as SAR reports and reports of emergencies or international incidents, are covered wherever the general subject is discussed. We cover SAR reports, for instance, in the chapter on independent operations, because it is when in this status that you are most likely to render them.

Movement Report. The movement report (MOVREP) is the most important routine report you make. It is discussed in more detail in the chapter on independent operations, since, again, you will be most likely to make such a report when you are operating independently. When operating as part of a fleet unit you should be included in the unit's movement report. Review Chapters 9, 10, and 11 of *NWP 7* to make sure that your commander is including you properly.

Submarine Notice. A submarine notice (SUBNOTE) is a type of movement report peculiar to submarines. It should include all information required for a movement report. An original submarine notice serves as a departure report and should cover all intermediate points. Submarine transits to and from a patrol zone are never made the subject of the same submarine notice. A submarine makes arrival reports on arrival at any intermediate port and at her final destination, if the latter is a port, in any movement covered by a SUBNOTE. However, a unit operating under a submarine notice is not required to file arrival reports for intermediate points, including rendezvous, for a final destination which is not a port. A submarine operating under the submarine notice system is also accountable to the movement report system. For further details, see Chapter 12 of *NWP 7*.

Mail. Article 1003 of *NWP 7* reminds you that postal officials use MOVREP information to verify the forwarding information they have on file. However, MOVREPs do not relieve you of the responsibility for submitting separate mail routing instructions to the appropriate fleet commanders in accordance with either *CINCLANTFLT 5110.1* series or *COMNAVLOGPACINST 5112.1* series.

Casualty Report. The purpose of a casualty report (CASREP) is to provide seniors in the various chains of command and other interested agencies, such as shipyards, with early information concerning equipment, machinery, and hull damage which impairs the combat readiness of your ship. CASREPs are coded with readiness ratings of C-2, C-3, and C-4, which are assigned on the same basis as mission area M-ratings. Chapter 4, *NWP 7*, covers the casualty reporting system in detail. Get to know it *before* you have a casualty. If you submit a CASREP you must also submit a report under the Combat Readiness Reporting System (NAVFORSTAT). Note the requirement to submit followup reports when your casualty is being reduced and to submit a final report (CASCOR) when it is corrected.

Personnel Accidents and Incidents. Section 405, *NWP 7*, covers reports of accidental death or injuries of Navy personnel on or off duty. *OPNAVINST 5102.1* also applies.

Combat Readiness Reports. Section 410, *NWP 7*, covers the requirement to make combat readiness reports (NAVFORSTA). *OPNAVINST C3501.66* and fleet and type instructions cover details of categories of readiness and their application to various types.

Logistic Requirements Reports. Logistic requirements reports (LOGREQ) are covered in more detail in the chapter on independent operations. The LOGREQ system requires that each ship (or unit, if more than one ship) submit a logistics requirement report 48 hours in advance of arrival at a U.S., British, or Canadian port. If there is a national logistic support force commander in the port, address the message to him; otherwise, it should go to the base commander or other appropriate naval authority. Submarines are usually required to submit LOGREQs by speedletter (surface ships should do so where practicable), but in case of change submarines may *not* send change messages (surface ships may).

The LOGREQ is an important report. If you make it fully and properly you will be taken care of on arrival. Make it incompletely and you will be pacing the quarterdeck wondering what happened.

Other Reports. *NWP 7* describes many other reports, many of which you will never make either because they will never be required or they are only required of higher authority. Be aware, however, of their existence.

Official Calls

Another activity which will face you as soon as you leave the building yard or overhaul activity is that of official calls. They are not just "formalities." The way you make your calls can add to or detract from your reputation and that of your ship.

Navy Regulations covers in great detail the requirements for making and receiving calls. You must be meticulous in carrying them out. This includes calls to and from officers of the naval service, ashore and afloat; calls to and from officers of foreign navies; and calls to and from U.S. and foreign governmental officials ashore. Be sure that you and your crew understand quarterdeck procedures with regard to calls and that you and your boat crew are in proper uniform.

Your first calls will probably be on your unit commander, your type commander, and the head of the training command. These are all important, for these men will be close to you in one way or another for your entire tour in command. You need not bring up *all* of your problems on your first calls, but be prepared to answer questions. If asked about your needs, unburden yourself gracefully, showing confidence in your abilities and the potential of your ship and crew. You can go into the details later with members of the various staffs. If you don't get satisfactory answers and assurances, however, then return to the top.

Honors and Ceremonies

Another area meriting your close personal attention is that of rendering honors and courtesies promptly and correctly. Honors and courtesies at sea begin with visual approach to other ships. Make sure that your bridge force understands the proper procedure of exchanging visual call signs with U. S. and foreign men of war, and for answering dips from foreign and U. S. merchant vessels. Remember to request permission to proceed on duty assigned when falling in with seniors.

Your next exchange, as you approach port, will be of visual call signs with port authorities. *DNC 5, U. S. Naval Communication Instructions*, requires that you send the sign DE followed by the call of your embarked flag officer, if any, and your own international call. In daylight you must display calls at your yardarms as required, with yours to port and your unit commander's to starboard. Display speed lights and indicators when appropriate. As you pass other naval vessels be sure that your ship renders passing honors correctly and promptly. If in doubt as to distance away, render anyway.

After anchoring, your ship will be watched to see if you render morning and evening colors promptly and smartly. As you receive calls, you will be judged again by the smartness of your quarterdeck.

Finally, but not of least importance, the appearance and conduct of your boat crews will be noted.

Now that you have mastered the housekeeping details of relationships with your administrative commanders, official calls, and honors and ceremonies, you are ready to get on with the active training of your crew.

Shipboard Training Program

Mark Twain, in *Puddn'head Wilson's Calendar*, said: "Training is everything. The peach was once a bitter almond; cauliflower is nothing but cabbage with a college education." It is your task to make your men into "cauliflowers." If you prefer a more dignified assessment, Josephus (37–100 A.D.) said that "The Romans were sure of victory—for their exercises were battles without bloodshed, and their battles were bloody exercises."

The Importance of Training. The basic directive for shipboard training is Chapter 8, *Standard Organization and Regulations of the U.S. Navy, OPNAVINST 3120.32A* (the *SORN*). The *SORN* points out that the training of personnel to operate and maintain shipboard equipment and systems is one of the prime factors contributing to battle readiness. This training requires instruction of operator and maintenance personnel in the requirements of their rates, as well as the additional requirements of their Navy Enlisted Classifications (NEC).

The *SORN* further states that for purposes of orientation training can be characterized as follows:

1. Individual in-rate maintenance training, normally conducted at a shore facility as a prerequisite to assignment of personnel to a fleet unit
2. Individual in-rate operator basic training, traditionally accomplished ashore
3. Individual watch station qualification, normally accomplished in the command
4. Systems training for individual operators and teams which includes subsystem training (ASW, AAW, repair party, etc.) and

total integrated systems training (combat systems, damage control, etc.), traditionally ashore, with training to maintain efficiency accomplished in the fleet. Integrated systems training must necessarily be conducted at the unit. This unit training as discussed in the *SORN* concerns individual watch station qualification and operator and team proficiency in sub-systems and integrated systems.

Requirements for Effective Training. The *SORN* states that to be effective:

1. Instruction must be dynamic and progressive, with repetition avoided except for emphasis
2. Instruction must be regularly scheduled, daily if possible
3. The instructor's degree of preparation and method of presentation must reflect his deep interest in the subject
4. Persons in authority must show interest in the progress of individuals in self-education and in all other forms of education.

This last requirement is aimed directly at you as commanding officer. If you show interest and concern, all those under you in the training organization will follow your lead.

Formulating a Training Program. Training without a firm, sound program is wasted. Thucydides, as far back as 404 B.C., recognized this when he said, "The Persians' want of practice will make them unskillful, and their want of skill timid. Maritime skill, like skills of other kinds, is not to be cultivated by the way or at chance times." This is just as true today as it was 2400 years ago. Put your strongest efforts into the development of a training program.

Your shipboard training program, as we said in Chapter 2, should be created while your ship is still under construction or early in its yard overhaul, and it must be based on Chapter 8 of the *SORN*. This publication and the parallel supplements put out by each type commander should become your "bibles" for training.

The *SORN* covers training in detail. It gives general guidance for the establishment of a training program as follows.

1. Establish long range goals to cover the periods between overhauls and short range goals which recognize scheduled operational commitments. These should be expressed in terms of achieving and maintaining the highest possible readiness for each assigned mission area.
2. Develop resource requirements in terms of personnel/NECs, shore training site curricula, watch station qualifications, and subsystems and systems proficiency.
3. Identify deficiencies in resources and take action to correct them.
4. Identify factors in the unit's schedule that clearly will affect established shipboard training goals.
5. Establish a schedule for the conduct of unit training, including:
   a. Specific accomplishments.
   b. Means of conducting the training.
   c. Means of evaluating the training.

Your training program must include the formation of a shipboard training organization, the carefully considered appointment of a training officer, the constitution of a planning board for training, the formulation of a set of detailed training plans, and the creation of a comprehensive set of training records; and then, with these preliminary organizational steps accomplished, the use of these tools to instruct, drill, exercise, and inspect your crew. We will take up each of these steps in turn.

Forming a Training Organization. The backbone of your training program must be a strong and effective training organization. A typical organization is shown in Figure 11–2. Yours will vary somewhat according to your ideas and the numbers and qualifications of personnel assigned. *No* organization will work, however, unless the men assigned to it are instructed as to what is wanted and how you want them to carry out their missions. This means instructing the instructors, making sure adequate teaching materials are on hand, and ensuring that lesson plans are prepared and made available.

The key person in this organization is the training officer. Give

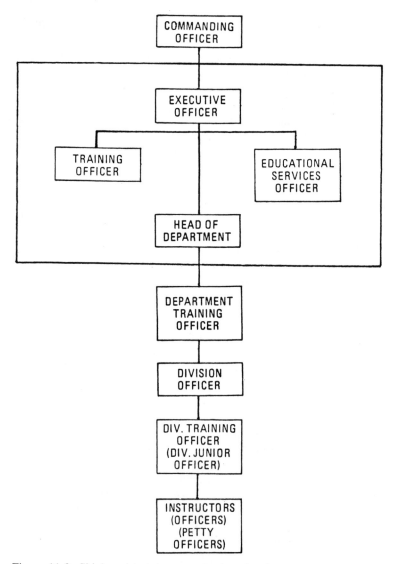

Figure 11-2. Shipboard training organization showing composition of the planning board for training.

careful consideration to choosing and assigning this individual and make sure he fits the organization you have formed.

Training Officer. Large ships can afford to assign as training officer a fairly senior man, who can exert a goodly amount of authority, but small ships must depend upon the executive officer. One course of action is to appoint him as training officer and to assign a junior officer to assist. Another is to assign the task to a junior officer and then direct the XO to oversee and support his efforts. A third is to assign the task to the operations officer. Of these choices, the soundest seems to be to assign the XO as training officer and to assign a junior officer as assistant training officer. In training, the full authority of the executive officer is needed, and his every action should take into account the training of the crew. The assignment of any other officer as training officer would sound an uncertain trumpet. You will remember the warning in First Corinthians: "If the trumpet give an uncertain sound, who shall prepare himself for battle?"

When the executive officer blows his horn, everybody listens.

Planning Board for Training. Regardless of your decision with regard to the training officer, it can be retrieved by your next action, which is to form a planning board for training, as required by Article 812 of the *SORN*. You must include on this board the executive officer as chairman, the heads of departments, the educational services officer, and the training officer. Figure 11–2 shows the relative position of the planning board for training in the ship training organization. If you have decided to appoint a JO as training officer, ensure that the executive officer applies firm direction as head of the board. His interest and direction can buttress the efforts of the junior training officer, counteracting the tendency of more senior department heads to put other activities ahead of training.

Training Plans. With a training organization in being, headed by a well-chosen officer, your next step is to develop a series of training plans. Article 0822 of the *SORN* describes the preparation and use of plans. These start with a long range training plan, which is the basic plan for all training and for keeping personnel informed of projected training aims and operating schedules. It should contain enough information to ensure that the training effort can be made effective. The quarterly and monthly training plans, which should go into more detail, can be formed from it. Minor details should not be included in the long range training plan.

This plan may be prepared on form OPNAV 3120/1A, and it should cover the battle efficiency competition cycle (if in effect) or other training cycle, such as between deployments. The form provided is good, but you may want to expand it. The *SORN* gives the following considerations you should use in preparing this plan:

1. *Training during overhaul.* For most ships, the overhaul period provides an opportunity for sending personnel to schools. However, shipyard overhaul periods also impose heavy workloads of repairs, tests, fire watches, and supervision of shipyard work. On-the-job training, inport fire drills, self-study courses, and drills by ratings must also be pursued during this period.

2. *Training during leave and upkeep periods* following deployment is usually limited to formal school attendance and onboard damage control drills.

3. *Coordinating training and maintenance* should be done by allotting the available work hours in accordance with the requirements for maintenance and training. Accordingly, major maintenance should be shown in the plan.

The *SORN* also gives these instructions for preparing the long range training plan:

1. Schedule fleet exercises, trials, inspections, and other major evolutions required by type or fleet commanders.

2. Schedule all required exercises in kind and frequency required by the type commander to maintain C-1 readiness.

3. Schedule other applicable unit exercises, keeping in mind the considerations above.

4. Schedule all unit training (damage control lectures, counterinsurgency, security orientation, boat crew training, telephone talker training, military training, etc.).

The quarterly training plan is extracted from the long range training plan. It can be prepared on a single sheet of paper and should be kept updated. It should contain more detail than the long range training plan.

The monthly training plan gives a daily schedule of training, evolutions, and operations for each month. Figure 11–3 shows a typical plan. It should be prepared by the training board, and should show all unit training, evolutions, and operations scheduled in the quarterly plan, expanded with necessary detail.

The *SORN* points out that no information classified higher than confidential should be included in these plans. The crew should be able to guard this level of classification, if properly instructed.

A plan should also be prepared summarizing the scheduling and completion of drills, exercises, and inspections required by the type commander. When the battle efficiency competition is in effect, one plan will probably suffice for both these purposes.

Each division officer should prepare a division officer's plan, and keep records of all operational drills, team training periods, and instructional periods in his division. The resulting division training schedule can be kept on both sides of an OPNAV 1500/32. The *SORN* contains detailed instructions for keeping it properly. Your training officer should require that all division officers keep these records. Proper instruction on the division level is the final payoff for your program. Without it, all the plans are just pieces of paper.

You must also plan for the training and indoctrination opportunities that do not occur as part of your planned program. This includes a variety of presentations for all hands, such as career benefits, minority affairs, drug and alcohol abuse, and safe driving.

Newly arrived personnel, particularly recruits and class "A" school graduates, will need special consideration and careful indoctrination. This is important, and it deserves the personal attention of the commanding and executive officers. Recruits are graduated in a state of mind that needs to be seen to be appreciated. They have been taught patriotism, respect for themselves and others, and exemplary conduct, and are eager to join their ship and become part of

JULY 1973

MONTHLY TRAINING PLAN

SUNDAY	MONDAY	TUESDAY	WEDNESDAY	THURSDAY	FRIDAY	SATURDAY
OPPORTUNE: Z-26-S(R) Z-28-S(O) Z-29-S Z-13-CC	1 G. Q. Z-10-D NBC Lecture Intelligence Briefing UNREP: 3 DER	2 DIVISIONAL SCHOOL J. O. School Crypto Drill UNREP: 2 MSO	3 DIVISIONAL SCHOOL J. O. School INREP: An Thoi	4 Hand grenade & small arms training all day for Deck and Ops	5 Field Day	6 G. Q. Battle Prob Z-6-D Z-11-S(R) Z-10-D Z-14-S Z-24-D Z-27-D Z-52-D Z-111-E(R)
Arrive Subic Z-27-D	8 Z-20-C (O) Z-27-D (Sec I)	9 GMT III DIVISIONAL SCHOOL J. O. School Crypto Drill Z-27-D (Sec II)	10 GMT III DIVISIONAL SCHOOL J. O. School Z-27-D (Sec III)	11 Lookouts lecture (Steaming Watches) Z-27-D (Sec I) PAY DAY	12 0500 Depart SUB G. Q. Gun Shoot Z-20-S Z-14-CC (R) Z-1-AA(R) Z-1-N(R) Z-3-AA(O) Z-5-N(O) Z-29-G (R) Z-110-E (R) Z-21-S (O) Z-1-E(R)	13 SF-1, 6-M (R) for all departments GQLT NBC Lecture Training Board Z-27-D (Night)
14	15 Mil/Lead Exams E-3 Exams	16 Arrive YOKO DIVISIONAL SCHOOL J. O. School Crypto Drill Z-27-D (Sec II)	17 DIVISIONAL SCHOOL J. O. School Blood Donations Z-27-D (Sec III)	18 Z-27-D (Sec I)	19 Field Day Z-27-D (Sec II)	20 DEPART YOKO C. O. Pers Insp. C. O. Zone Insp.
21	22 G. Q. Battle Prob. Z-6-D Z-10-D Z-24-D Z-27-D	23 DIVISIONAL SCHOOL J. O. School Crypto Drill	24 DIVISIONAL SCHOOL J. O. School	25 Telephone Talker Drill (GQ talkers) PAY DAY	26 Field Day SF-2, 5-M (R) for all departments	27 GQLT NBC Lecture Training Board Z-27-D (Night)
28 Arrive PEARL Z-27-D (Sec III)	29 COMSERVPAC visit G. Q. Z-10-D NBC Lecture Z-27-D (Sec I)	30 Depart PEARL DC Lectures DIVISIONAL SCHOOL J. O. School Crypto Drill	31 DC Lectures DIVISIONAL SCHOOL J. O. School	1 AUG Hand grenade & small arms training for Supply & Engineering	2 AUG Field Day	3 AUG C. O. Zone Insp. C. O. Pers Insp. 5 AUG Arrive SFRAN

Figure 11-3. Sample monthly training plan.

the active Navy. If they join a crew whose morals are suspect, whose love of their ship, navy, and country is low, and whose language and appearance mark them as poorly disciplined, the shock and disappointment can be devastating. These young recruits need not be pampered, but they must be encouraged to maintain their high standards.

Training Records

It is important that you set up a comprehensive recordkeeping system, one which will show at any instant the exact status of all phases of training. Article 0821 of the *SORN* sets forth the responsibilities for recordkeeping and states that the preparation and maintenance of schedules and records should be decentralized, so that no one officer or petty officer is unreasonably burdened. The training officer and department head might well keep the long range (annual and quarterly training plans), the monthly training plan, and the record of exercises, trials, and inspections required by the type commander. On small ships this might be done with one set of records, but on a larger one an overall record might be required, with additional records kept by heads of departments.

The senior watch officer should keep records of deck watchstanding officer and enlisted assignments and qualifications and deck watchstander's courses and training record. Similarly, the chief engineer should keep the same records for engineering watchstanders, and the communications officer should maintain records for the communications and coding watch. The division officer should keep a record of drills and instructions, formal school training, and a personnel record. The chief or leading petty officer of each rating should keep a record of practical factors completed, and a personnel qualification standards (PQS) progress chart.

The foregoing record program is only a minimum; you will find additional records desirable, depending upon your ship type. Record forms for most programs are available from your type commander. Others can be easily drawn up.

The *SORN* provides a simple and workable training record program that you can vary to suit your needs and preferences. It includes nine standard forms, as follows:

1. Long Range—Quarterly Plan
2. Monthly Training Plan
3. Type Commander's Required Training Exercises, Trials, and Inspections
4. Division Training Schedule
5. Group Record of Practical Factors
6. Record of Qualifications at Watch and Battle Stations
7. Personnel Qualification Standards
8. Formal School Training Records
9. Division Officer's Personnel Record Form.

A well-established system of training records will be of great value. For you, it will provide an instant overview of the state of training of your crew. For your officers and petty officers, it will be both a reminder of past accomplishments and a record of tasks still pending. It may seem at times like useless paperwork, but you will find in the end that your training program will be no better than its records.

Personnel Qualification Standards

In earlier days, junior officers and senior petty officers had ample time personally to train and qualify junior petty officers and nonrated men. In the past four decades, however, the steadily increasing sophistication of ships, submarines, and aircraft, and the ever more rigorous demands placed upon their personnel, have combined to require a new system of training for personnel.

This new system is known as Personnel Qualification Standards (PQS). It is now the heart of the training program, and we will, therefore, discuss it now in detail.

The PQS System. The PQS system is described and set forth in *OPNAVINST 3500.34C* and in *NAVEDTRA 43100–1, Handbook on Personnel Qualification Standards.* In essence, PQS is a listing of the knowledge and skills required for a man to qualify for each watch station, to maintain a specific equipment or system, or to perform as a member of a given team. It is a qualification guide, one which asks the questions a trainee must answer to prove his readiness to perform a given task. It also provides a record of progress and final certification. PQS is an *individualized* learning process. The trainee has the complete program in his hands. The supervisor serves both as a source of assistance to the trainee and as a quality control over the learning process by certifying the completion of each step.

Standard lesson plans are provided by bureaus and offices, training commands, and type commanders. They provide a detailed, step-by-step breakdown of the requirements of each task and watch.

The PQS system does not completely replace normal division training. Rather, it is a key element of that program.

PQS Handbook. Every commanding officer should be familiar with the *PQS Handbook*. It begins with an introduction to the theory, format, and organization of the system. A glossary defines PQS words, phrases, and terms. The main portion of the *Handbook* discusses theory, system, watchstanders, and qualification cards.

PQS Progress Charts. The PQS progress chart shows which persons are in training for each watch and major task, their progress toward qualification, and the watch on which each person is qualified, together with the date of qualification. The *SORN* has a good sample chart which you can use.

PQS Qualification Card. The PQS qualification card is carried by each learner. It is a record of the completion of each item required for qualification for that task. The card is given to each trainee to be used by him to train himself with minimum supervision.

A typical card contains these items:

A *final qualification page*, identifying the long term goal. Final commanding officer certification is placed on this page.

A *qualification summary*, giving the subordinate qualifications necessary to achieve total qualification within the specialty.

A *theory and systems summary*, which is a record of completion of the various theory and system requirements for qualification. Many of the systems are required to be completed for more than one watch station. If so, they are summarized on these pages, so that only one signature is necessary.

A *watch station checkoff* section, giving all the various duties that a trainee must complete to achieve qualification.

PQS standards in existence are listed in *CNET Notice 3500*. Additional standards are being produced as the need for them becomes apparent.

Properly administered and used, the PQS system is a valuable adjunct to your training system. Let your crew know that you support it, demand progress, and they will produce corresponding results.

Leadership and Management Education and Training

Leadership and Management Education and Training (LMET) is a relatively new program. It originated in the years 1973 to 1975, in programs begun at the Naval Academy and other activities. It was designed to train Navy personnel to specific minimum standards of professional competence in leadership and management. In 1976 this new program was officially established as "LMET."

Those to be Trained. At present, commanding officers, executive officers, department heads, division officers, chief petty officers, and petty officers of grades E-5 and E-6 are being trained under LMET. These personnel are either in the fleet or enroute to it. In fiscal year 1981 and thereafter, this instruction will be extended to officers and petty officers of all ranks and levels and eventually to reserves and civilian employees. Instruction will be repeated at higher levels as men are promoted.

Course Curriculum. In analyzing the total area of training required, the Navy determined that the LMET curriculum should include sixteen characteristics and behaviors (called "competencies"), which could be classified for instructional purposes into five major skill areas. These are:

1. Concern for Efficiency and Effectiveness
   a. Sets Goals and Performance Standards
   b. Takes Initiative

2. Management Control
    a. Plans and Organizes
    b. Optimizes Use of Resources
    c. Delegates
    d. Monitors Results
    e. Rewards
    f. Disciplines
3. Skillful Use of Influence
    a. Influences
    b. Team Builds
    c. Develops Subordinates (Coaches)
    d. Self-control
4. Advising and Counseling
    a. Postive Expectations
    b. Realistic Expectations
    c. Understands
5. Conceptual Thinking
    a. Conceptualizes; Applies Concepts to a Job Situation.

Training Sites. Training sites are located at Bangor, Pearl Harbor, Treasure Island, Coronado, San Diego, New London, Newport, Little Creek, Charleston, Mayport, Pensacola, and Rota. Not all levels of courses are available at all locations.

Changes. The LMET program is developing rapidly and changing frequently. As a new commanding officer, you will probably be sent to school enroute. If you are already in command, consult the relevant instructions for locations, convening dates, quotas, and the methods for obtaining travel funds.

With a training organization formed, a training officer designated, a planning board for training established, appropriate training plans in being, a PQS system operating, and a recordkeeping system set up, your ship is now ready for active training, which begins with refresher training.

Preparation for Refresher Training

Refresher training is an intense, concentrated period designed to take a ship which is materially ready, fully manned, and fully supplied, and in about two months turn it into a ship capable of performing any individual function required of its type.

Refresher Training Group. Refresher training is accomplished under the supervision of the Refresher Training Group of the Training Command. The Atlantic group is located in Guantanamo, Cuba, and the majority of its training is accomplished in operating areas off Guantanamo. The Pacific group is located in San Diego, and its training is mostly accomplished in the operating areas nearby.

The underway training period is preceded by an assessment inspection by the training staff. This visit determines whether the ship is reasonably ready for refresher training. You, as commanding officer, should already have anticipated this rather corrosive event by your liaison with the type commander's staff, so that your ship is at prescribed manning level, all its machinery and equipment is in working order, and its allowance of spares is complete. Woe unto you if you have not, for the training command staff will be thorough and pitiless.

Another way to prepare is to spend some of your overhaul or availability time visiting the training command. Ask for the initial inspection check lists. A little extra work will help you to pass the arrival inspection and get off to a good start. More work will assure that your watch, quarter, and station bills are up to date, and you may even be able to schedule a few simple drills to make sure that all hands know their assignments and how to get about the ship using the proper routes.

Any time allotted to you as a shakedown period, however, will be brief and busy. Don't expect sufficient time for all preparations for refresher training. Anticipate this by using some of your construction or yard overhaul time.

Indeed, the best way to prepare for refresher training (and for your whole cycle) is to devote the necessary time during your building or overhaul period. After your visits to the type commander and the commander of the training command, you will know approximately what numbers and kinds of personnel you will have aboard on entering refresher training. You can then determine from these sources and their staffs what personnel you will need to man the ship, stand watches, and perform the required exercises and evolutions. The next step is to request quotas and travel money to school the requisite personnel. For instance, your ship will need a certain number of qualified air controllers. You will need that number on board when you start REFTRA. It will take your best efforts, however, to obtain the necessary quotas for schooling and to make candidates available to fill them. You will have the same problems in other qualification areas, but your future will hinge on solving them. Vigorous and aggressive use of the PQS system will produce the required number of watchstanders. Other sources of training, such as firefighting school, gas mask indoctrination school, emergency shiphandling school, and damage control school, must be located and used. All of this will cut into the time available for ship's force work in the yard, but it will be worth it. Do it adequately and you will enter refresher training as prepared as possible. Slight it, and you will never catch up.

Refresher Training

The refresher training period begins with a series of lessons, inspections, exercises, drills, and battle problems of increasing complexity and difficulty. These culminate in an advanced battle problem designed to test every facet of the ship's machinery, equipment, and armament, and all of her officers and men, first as individuals and second as members of various teams and parties.

An average day under refresher training will find a group of instructors and observers from the refresher training group boarding at dawn. You then proceed to the operating area, where you conduct a series of exercises and inspections in rapid succession, and return to port late that evening. The routine will be demanding, since you and your crew have to prepare for the exercises, conduct them, and then hold post-exercise critiques to try to benefit from each day's efforts before preparing for the next.

There is no magic formula for success in REFTRA. Foresight, diligence, ability to delegate, and stamina in equal parts will produce the maximum benefits, though.

After about five weeks of action-packed days and nights, you should be ready for the final days of advanced exercises and inspections and a graduation battle problem designed to push your ship and its crew to the utmost. Again, there is no magic formula for assuring a passing grade. The harder you work the better you will be.

If you should fail any of the earlier exercises, they will be repeated until you pass them. Obviously, a failed exercise means that assessment of the causes and corrective action must be sandwiched somehow into your already crowded day. Failure of the graduation battle problem is more serious. If you have to repeat it, not only will you lose precious recreation time and availability, you will enter the type commander's arena under a cloud and a week late. What you need to do to pass a second problem depends entirely on why you failed the first, although there have been instances of a ship failing a second battle problem for entirely different reasons. Hold a critique, call upon the advice of the training group staff, and do your best to correct your problem areas.

If you have done well in refresher training, your ship should emerge ready in every respect for advanced training in preparation for deployment.

Routine Drills

You may think that after completing REFTRA you can forget drills and exercises for a while. Unfortunately, this is not the case. Drills must be as much a part of your ship's daily routine as instruction, exercises, and inspections. Refresher training just gets you into the swing of things.

Drills are conducted to prepare a ship's crew to meet any conceivable requirement or contingency. The basis of drilling is ship's bills, each of which is designed to meet one of these contingencies. Your ship's bills, as we have said before, must stem from the basic bills in the *SORN*. This publication contains sample bills in four categories: adminstrative, operational, emergency, and special. Type commanders augment these with additional and modified bills peculiar to their types.

Those bills requiring action by the crew also require *drill*. Drill allows those in authority to determine that qualified personnel are

Figure 11-4. Frequent and thorough damage control drills will prepare your crew for any eventuality—collision, fire, or war damage.

assigned, that requirements of bills are correct, and that equipment is in working order and on hand. Once this is established, repeated drills produce a set of automatic responses that will carry over under the most stressful conditions. Each person should be able to perform his part even though wounded, in the dark, or if gas or nuclear fallout is present.

Once individual teams, such as damage control teams or gun crews, are organized and drilled, you may shift emphasis to larger groups such as gun batteries, boat loading teams, or missile firing teams, culminating in exercising the ship as a whole. Drills must be repetitive, thorough, and short. Obviously drilling of a prize crew can be done infrequently, but the fire party must be drilled often and thoroughly, and it is important that this be done for each section.

This is of special importance during overhaul, when daytime de-

Figure 11-5. Don't overlook the value of shore-based training facilities such as the one shown here in keeping your officers and crew up on the latest tactics and technology.

bris and welding sparks may be smoldering at night in spite of the best efforts of your fire watches. You will sleep better if you require the CDO to report to you each day when under overhaul that he has mustered and instructed the fire party.

General quarters is the most important underway drill. If you make GQ frequent, interesting, and as short as possible, it will then be most productive. A good procedure is to plan a short battle problem for each drill, followed by imposed damages which will require the execution of various bills such as nuclear attack or collision.

In all your drills, remember that modern ships depend on internal communications systems. If you have a real collision, however, you may find a ship's bow in the middle of your IC panel with no means of communications left to you except word of mouth and messenger. Condition your crew to this and other unpleasant eventualities. In World War II some ships steered in battle at night by chains of messengers. Try it. You may have to be even more inventive. Make repetition work for you, not against you. Simple repetition induces boredom, but repetition tempered with imagination produces both rapid response and the ability to react to the unusual.

Exercises

By dictionary definition, drilling is "instructing thoroughly by repetition" and exercising is "training by practice." These terms are frequently used interchangeably, but in this discussion we will adhere to the proper meanings.

Exercises, then, are used to put the knowledge given by instruction and ingrained by drilling to a more practical use. A telephone talker is *instructed* as to how to use a battle telephone, *drilled* in its use by transmitting and receiving many made-up messages, and then *exercised* in its use by manning and using his telephone when his gun battery conducts a firing exercise.

Exercise Direction. Major exercise programs are set forth in the FXP series of fleet tactical publications and the AXP series of allied tactical publications. Both series are classified, so we will have to limit the amount of detail given in this section. There are eight publications in these series:

FXP 1, *Submarine and Antisubmarine Exercises*.

Establishes tactics and procedures for conducting submarine and antisubmarine exercises, with criteria for evaluating results.

FXP 2, *Air and Antiair Exercises*.

Presents procedures and tactics for conducting aircraft exercises, as well as criteria for evaluation.

FXP 3, *Ship Exercises*.

Provides exercises for all types of surface ships and guidance for observers in evaluating them.

AXP 1, *Allied Submarine and Antisubmarine Exercise Manual*.

Establishes tactics and procedures for conducting Allied antisubmarine exercises with criteria for evaluation.

AXP 2, *Allied Tactical Exercises Manual*.

Contains standard seamanship, gunnery, torpedo, and miscellaneous exercises for use by NATO navies in training their forces for participation in Allied operations.

AXP 3, *Allied Naval Communication Exercises*.

Presents standard instructions for the conduct of communication exercises by the Allied navies.

AXP 4, *Allied Naval CIC/AIO and Radar Calibration Exercises*.

Presents general instructions for the conduct of Allied naval exercises to prepare the CIC/action-information organization for performing its functions. An appendix provides guidance for evaluating the results of the exercises.

AXP 5, *NATO Experimental Tactics and Amplifying Tactical Instructions*.

Provides a means of testing new naval and maritime/air tactics and exercises developed by a NATO nation, group of nations, or NATO Commander. AXP 5 has a mine warfare supplement and a secret supplement.

Type Commander's Supplements. Each type commander issues his own exercise publication modifying or supplementing the FXP series. Where FXP 3, for instance, sets forth the goals, scoring, observation requirements, and reporting for a surface ship gunnery exercise in general terms, he describes these criteria in exact terms for each type and subtype of surface ship.

Exercise Designation System. A self-translating, short-titling system is used to designate exercises for ease in communications. A typical title is Z-24-G. "Z" means an exercise for surface ships, "24" is a particular exercise, and "G" means it is a gunnery exercise.

Advanced and Inter-type Exercises. Advanced and inter-type exercises are usually conducted by unit commanders using a written operation order or a letter of instruction (LOI). The operation order is used for more complicated exercises and can be quite lengthy. The LOI system is used when the unit has a standard operation order already in existence or when the exercise is relatively simple. The LOI can be nothing more than a schedule of exercises.

Advanced exercises are usually given self-descriptive titles, such as ASW Hunter-Killer Exercise (ASWEX), Air Defense Exercise (ADEX), Amphibious Landing Exercise (LANDEX), Amphibious Fire Support Exercise (FIREX), Composite Training Unit Exercise (COMPTUEX), and Fleet Readiness Exercise (READEX).

An ASWEX may last up to three weeks. Forces will include an ASW carrier, if available, a land-based patrol squadron, a destroyer squadron, other ASW surface ships, shore-based surveillance systems, and several submarines. The operating area may cover thousands of square miles.

An ADEX may last up to two weeks and may include two or more carriers, several cruisers, a destroyer squadron, and shore-based aircraft. Again, operating areas may be quite large.

A LANDEX may last for a month and may include an amphibious group or smaller unit, a destroyer squadron, a minesweeping unit, embarked Marines, and miscellaneous units. The exercise usually includes an opposed transit, opposition in the objective area, a landing, and a withdrawal. LANDEXES are limited to areas where landings may be made.

A FIREX is a shorter exercise designed to exercise ship and air portions of the fire support system of an amphibious force. Exercises are limited to areas where firing and bombing may be done.

A COMPTUEX may last one or two weeks. This is a relatively simple exercise arranged to combine available forces due for training so as to use them most efficiently. A unit commander usually operates under an LOI and schedules exercises using areas and services available.

A READEX is a fleet problem type of exercise in which available forces are split in two and exercised against each other. Forces involved can be quite large, often including all those available and due for advanced training or deployment. They usually include units of all types. Extensive advanced planning is required, and pre-sail and post-exercise critiques are always held.

Larger fleet exercises are occasionally scheduled. Each of these is different, and their planning, preparation, and execution can run into months.

It is Navy policy to include underway replenishment (UNREP) in each of the above exercises, using whatever replenishment units are available. UNREP is such an integral and important part of our operations that unit commanders and commanding officers should make every effort to keep ship skills at a high level. If Service Force units are not available, replenishment and other alongside maneuvers should be scheduled using other units of the exercise force.

Inspections

Inspections are a means of ascertaining the state of battle readiness, administration, preservation, and training of your ship and its crew.

Inspections can be divided into two categories: those which you make, or cause to be made, under your authority as commanding officer (internal inspections); and those imposed on you and conducted by higher authority (external inspections). We will treat internal inspections first.

Internal Inspections. The longest-established inspection in the Navy is the weekly captain's inspection. Article 0708–2, *Navy Regulations*, prescribes that the commanding officer hold periodic Saturday personnel inspections. Except for reservists undergoing weekend training, other weekend inspections are prohibited. Article

0708–1 directs the commanding officer to hold periodic inspections of the material of his command to determine deficiencies and cleanliness. If the command is large, he is permitted to designate zones and delegate assistants to inspect them, alternating the one he inspects so that he covers the entire command at minimum intervals. This has become known as "lower decks inspection," or "zone inspection," and is generally held on Friday afternoon. The same zoning system is used to inspect upper deck areas following personnel inspection. This has become known as "upper decks inspection." Many type commanders insist on a literal interpretation of this regulation, and require an inspection every Saturday without exception. A wise CO takes care of this by scheduling Saturday inspections and having them performed in his absence by the acting commanding officer. On some occasions only the duty section might be present for inspection. Even such a reduced inspection, however, can train junior officers and petty officers in inspection procedures.

Weekly inspections offer you an excellent opportunity to impress your policies on the crew. Tell the men when you inspect what you want, what is wrong, and, more importantly, what is right. If they know what you want, then they will give it to you. It is also wise to require your XO to make a daily topside and living space inspection to see that proper cleanliness and maintenance plans and techniques are being used. The surest incentive for daily work is the knowledge by those doing it that it will be seen *every* day. Be circumspect about making daily inspections yourself, though, for too much "presence" can undermine the confidence and authority of your division and petty officers. They expect the executive officer, but they don't expect you. When you *do* inspect during the week consider confining your efforts to trouble areas or special projects. This is a time to show interest, to bestow praise if warranted, but not to find too much fault. If you do find errors have the XO correct them privately later. You must presume that he, the division officer, or the leading petty officers would have found the fault in due time if you had not preempted them.

There are other internal inspections which you can make by

means of boards. You can form a board or group to inspect any aspect of your administration. However, the *SORN* requires you to form certain boards which, in effect, make inspections even though they may be called "audits." The most important are:

Communications Security Material Board. Conducts audits, or inspections, of the records of the communications security material custodian.

Hull Board. Inspects the hull, tanks, free flood spaces, outboard fittings, valves, and appendages at times of drydocking and prior to undocking.

Flight Order Audit Board. Inspects and audits to ensure that all requirements concerning hazardous duty pay are met as per instructions.

Mess Audit Board. Audits the various messes on a monthly basis to ensure that they are correctly administered.

Monies Audit Board. Inspects to determine that all government properties and monies are present and accounted for, are properly protected and disposed of, and are otherwise properly administered. Audits disbursing cash verification, post office funds, imprest funds, and recreation funds.

Naval Commercial Traffic Funds Audit Board. Audits the account of the naval commercial traffic fund.

Personnel Reliability Board. Screens and continuously evaluates personnel assigned to duty with nuclear weapons.

Precious Metals Audit Board. Audits precious metals in the custody of the dental officer.

Ship Silencing Board. Assists the commanding officer in the development and execution of long range plans for reducing the acoustic signature of the ship.

Inspections by Higher Authority. Over the years, higher authorities have formulated and imposed more and more outside inspections. This started in World War II, when the Training Command was created and refresher training was established. The large number of ships being commissioned, the relative inexperience of many commanding officers, and the preoccupation of type commanders with wartime operations made a system of outside inspection necessary. After World War II the use of formal inspections remained high as administrators sought a substitute for wartime motivation. They felt that competition, in combination with graded inspections, would be an incentive to superior performance.

The crux of this system of inspections and the centerpiece of the annual competitions is the operational readiness inspection (ORI).

Operational Readiness Inspection. The ORI tests the ability of the ship to operate in wartime conditions and in battle. A period of twenty-four hours is set aside for this inspection. The unit commander is usually the chief inspector. His party comes from another ship of the unit, sometimes augmented by specialists from the type commander's staff or from the training command. Most of the inspection is conducted with the ship underway at either battle stations or with condition watches set.

The central part of the ORI is a lengthy and realistic battle problem with the crew at GQ. Where possible, the ship will actually fire her weapons. Amphibious and submarine types have exercises that test their particular capabilities. The battle problem usually progresses through a series of imposed contingencies which test all the capabilities of the ship, usually including defense against nuclear attack, use of gun, missile and torpedo batteries, defense against all other forms of attack, damage control, collision, towing, and finally abandon ship. Engineering capabilities and casualty procedures are tested both as part of the battle problem and in additional special drills.

The type commander places heavy emphasis on the operational readiness inspection, and you should make every effort to prepare for it. There are no short cuts. *All* of your bills must be up to date, and *all* of your personnel must be trained individually and as members of their various weapon and drill teams. The ORI will be a realistic assessment of your success in preparing your ship for battle. As we pointed out earlier, you will do well to emulate the Romans, whose exercises were battles without bloodshed and whose battles were bloody exercises.

In the event that you fail all or part of your ORI, you will need to sit down with your planning board for training and plot a course to "get well." Failing one exercise usually just drags down your grade in the overall inspection. Failure or adverse comment on some aspects of your training or abilities is more serious. A failing grade on the whole inspection is, of course, extremely serious. The type commander will take the nature of your failure into account when deciding your fate. You may have to repeat the whole ORI, or just parts of it. If you are badly needed for operations you may be given a reprieve and enjoined to correct your deficiencies. In any event, you will want to bring your ship up to higher performance as soon as possible. You, the planning board for training, and your entire crew will be busy for some time.

Administrative Inspection. The next most important inspection is the administrative inspection. Some type commanders give it annually, while others give it twice a year, once on a scheduled basis and once by surprise. It is generally given in port over a twenty-four-hour period. The unit commander is usually the chief inspector, augmented by an inspection team from another ship. The inspection starts with a formal personnel and upper decks inspection, sometimes in a variety of uniforms. Some lower decks and machinery spaces are inspected. A standard type inspection form is used to record the results.

You would be wise to procure this form at an early opportunity and organize and administer your ship to pass a surprise administrative inspection at any time. The checklist requirements are not that difficult, though there will always be differences of opinion as to interpretation. The biggest problem, mostly found on small ships, is that in time of busy employment, or when shorthanded, personnel tend to let required records and procedures lag. You will have to make it clear that just the reverse should happen, even if you have to arrange temporary help. The records setup and administrative procedures are designed to keep people (and your ship) *out* of trouble, not *in* it. A properly administered ship can pass an "admin" at any time.

Should you fail an administrative inspection, sit down in the wardroom with your administrative personnel and test the advice given above against the record. Ninety percent of the time you will just have to start doing what you should have been doing all the time. The other ten percent of failures probably will fit within Murphy's law or some variation thereof. The ever-ingenious bluejacket can find a hundred ways to avoid paperwork. It is up to you and your executive officer to keep his marvelous energies directed where *you* want them. Do so before the inspection and you will pass; do so after a failure, and you will quickly become satisfactory.

Medical Inspection. The unit commander will make a comprehensive inspection of the medical department either at or near the same time as an administrative inspection. This inspection determines the qualifications and state of training of personnel, the adequacy of medical procedures, both peacetime and wartime, and the completeness of medical material allowances.

Supply Inspection. This is done to determine whether the ship's supply department is performing in accordance with directives and is supporting you in the supply, disbursing, and messing areas. A supply inspection is thorough and worthwhile. If your supply department does not pass, your ship is being shortchanged. The chapter on logistics gives you adequate guidance for determining whether it is operating properly. Apply this guidance and you should get a satisfactory grade.

Supply inspections are sometimes carried out as part of an administrative inspection, and sometimes separately.

Propulsion Examination Board Inspection. In recent years the Navy has converted to high pressure steam plants (600 and 1200 psi) and gas turbine installations. These plants require a higher degree of care and expertise than did the older low pressure steam plants. This situation has been recognized by the establishment of the propulsion examination board (PEB) for conventionally powered ships.

The PEB is described in *OPNAVINST 3540.4c* and in corresponding supporting instructions issued by the Commanders-in-Chief of the Atlantic and Pacific Fleets. You and your officers should read and understand these instructions thoroughly in order to be prepared for your examination.

The mission of the PEB, as set forth in *OPNAVINST 3540.4c*, is to assist the fleet commanders-in-chief in verifying that steam and gas turbine propulsion plants in certain conventionally-powered ships are safe to operate. The fleet commanders also use it to promote improved engineering training and readiness within the fleets. This includes coordination of program evaluation, drill criteria, and standardization of procedures among the various training and inspecting commands.

The PEB has the following responsibilities:

1. Examine propulsion engineering personnel to determine their state of training and qualification. The appropriate engineering personnel qualification standards (PQS) are used to evaluate the level of qualification of all propulsion plant personnel.
2. Witness and evaluate the conduct of propulsion plant drills and evolutions, employing the installed engineering operational sequencing system (EOSS) as a guide.
3. Inspect the material condition of the propulsion plant to ascertain its state of readiness, preservation, and cleanliness.
4. Review and evaluate the administration of the ship's engineering department and the completeness and accuracy of all ship's records relating to propulsion.

All 1200 psi ships are inspected by the PEB. Those classes of 600 psi ships and gas turbine powered ships to be inspected are listed in *OPNAVINST 3540.4c*.

The Atlantic and Pacific Fleets both have boards of twenty officers. Each officer is well qualified and schooled in at least one of the three types of installations. Inspections are conducted by sub-boards of varying numbers of members depending upon the size of the ship inspected.

The PEB conducts two main types of inspections. The first is the *light-off examination* (LOE), conducted prior to lighting off the first fire in any boiler (or first light-off of a main or auxiliary gas turbine) during a regular overhaul (ROH), major conversion, fitting out availability, or restricted availability (RAV) in excess of four months in length. In the case of new construction ships, the LOE will be conducted following delivery and prior to initial light-off by ship's company. The second class of inspection is the *operational propulsion plant examination* (OPPE). This is conducted no more than six months after the completion of an evolution for which an LOE was required, and at periodic intervals thereafter, within the ship's operating cycle, but not to exceed eighteen months between examinations. Subsequent to the post-ROH OPPE, all ships will be subject to unscheduled examinations. The CINCLANT PEB conducts this inspection on ships homeported in Europe. Examination of forward-deployed ships, and those under the administrative cognizance of the Commander, U.S. Naval Forces Europe, will be coordinated with the operational commander. Similar arrangements exist in the Pacific area.

The LOE can be divided into three parts. First, the PEB verifies that the propulsion plant is in a material condition which supports safe operation. Associated auxiliaries are included in the examination; i.e., ship's service and emergency electrical plants, air compressors supporting propulsion plant operation, and any other equipment located in the propulsion spaces and/or normally operated by propulsion personnel.

The PEB also determines the adequacy of the administrative/operating procedures directly related to the propulsion plant, and the capability of shipboard personnel to safely operate and maintain equipment, systems, and spaces; e.g., logs and records, liquid programs, hearing and heat stress programs, equipment tag-out procedures, and training.

Lastly, it determines whether engineering personnel have the knowledge to operate the plant safely. For a satisfactory finding, the ship must present at least two qualified watch sections with the proficiency to support safe auxiliary steaming. A capability for self-training of watchstanders and watch teams in the safe control of routinely encountered casualties must also be evident, e.g., proficient engineering casualty control teams (ECCTT). Propulsion plant drills are not required as part of this examination. However, simple evaluations, such as boiler- and feedwater, or fuel sampling and analysis (as applicable), and casualty control walk-through drills may be conducted at the discretion of the senior member of the examing board.

During an OPPE:

1. Those areas discussed above under the requirements for an LOE will be examined.

2. The PEB will evaluate propulsion plant casualty control drills. The EOSS, where installed, will be the basic guide in evaluating the conduct of equipment light-off/securing and casualty control drills. The inspectors will require demonstration of these capabilities:

   a. The capability of at least two watch sections to support safely underway steaming.

   b. The capability of self-training, i.e., proficiency of ECCTT and of watchstanders and watch teams in the control of routinely encountered casualties.

   c. The capability to combat effectively a major fire in a main propulsion space.

3. Boiler flexibility tests (automatic boiler control (ABC) configured plants) on those boilers normally on the line to support the examination will be conducted to evaluate the ability of the plant to respond to changing power demands.

4. The board may, if examination circumstances warrant, witness and evaluate a high power demonstration.

PEB findings consist of general observations, a list of deficiencies, and a grade of either satisfactory or unsatisfactory.

The board will make an unsatisfactory assessment if they find a material deficiency precluding safe light-off or operation, an administrative deficiency so bad as to preclude safe light-off or operation, if fewer than two watch sections are sufficiently proficient, if there is no capability for self-training (OPPE only), or if the ship is judged unable to combat a major fire in the main propulsion spaces.

A ship graded UNSAT is prohibited from lighting off or operating until its deficiencies are corrected.

Details of the conduct of these two inspections are contained in the respective fleet commander's instructions. An LOE usually takes a day, and an OPPE from two to four days, depending on the size and type of ship.

Prepare for these examinations as the instructions direct. Drill often and prepare well and you should have no trouble. Fail to do so and the board will find you out.

Board of Inspection and Survey. The Board of Inspection and Survey (INSURV) is given basic duties in Article 0321, *Navy Regulations*. In this article the president of the board, assisted by the other members and by permanent and semipermanent sub-boards as designated by the Secretary of the Navy, is required to:

1. Conduct acceptance trials and inspections of all ships and service craft prior to acceptance for service.
2. Conduct acceptance trials on one or more aircraft of each type or model prior to acceptance for service.
3. At least once every three years, if practicable, inspect each naval ship to determine its material condition and, if found unfit for continued service, report this to higher authority.
4. Perform such other inspections and trials as directed by the CNO.

Higher authority schedules INSURV inspections without the knowledge or consent of the commanding officer. Article 0738, *Navy Regulations*, provides one other means of scheduling an INSURV inspection. If you feel that the condition of your ship, or any department therein, is such as to require an inspection by INSURV, you may request it through official channels. This does not occur very frequently.

The three-year INSURV inspection requirement is translated, where possible, into once each training cycle. The best time for an INSURV is four to six months before the commencement of your next yard overhaul. This gives you time to translate those deficiencies either found by the board or confirmed by them into yard work requests. An INSURV-confirmed deficiency gets top attention from all the intermediate authorities who act on or make recommendations regarding your requests.

Preparations for INSURV are discussed in the *Naval Sea Service Command Technical Manual.*

The primary aim of the INSURV inspection is to determine the condition of your machinery and equipment, and then to recommend steps necessary to correct deficiencies and return unsatisfactory items to a satisfactory condition. This means it will be necessary to inspect the inside and all working parts of boilers, pumps, turbines, and other pieces of machinery. The president of the board will tell you in advance which machinery is to be opened. If the carrying out of these instructions leaves you without propulsion or auxiliary power you must make arrangements with your type commander or other administrative authority to have your ship placed in a safe mooring condition and furnished with necessary services while it is undergoing inspection.

Your engineering records will also be an important item of the inspection. Make sure your 3-M system is up to date and that all records are complete and accurate.

Finally, most members of the board feel that a good indication of the condition of the engineering plant and its past maintenance is the cleanliness and preservation evident to the eye. This does not mean that your *spaces* must be spotless. It means that *working machinery* must be clean, lubricated, and immaculate.

Appendix XIII contains a check list to follow in preparing for a material inspection of any kind, including the INSURV inspection.

Material Inspections. There are many types of inspections of material. We have discussed the most important ones. In years past, before the advent of the PEB, the ORSE, the NTPI, and other inspections of a material nature, an inspection called the "material inspection" was usually conducted annually. Some type and administrative commanders still conduct an inspection of this kind, usually an expanded lower decks inspection, using a checkoff list much like Appendix XIII. They may require that certain machinery be opened, but the inspection of major units is usually reserved for INSURV. Regardless of the title or scope of such an inspection, Appendix XIII will give you the information necessary for preparation. If you comply with its requirements you can pass any inspection.

Propulsion Examination (Nuclear) Board. A propulsion examination board for nuclear-powered ships is established by *OPNAV-INST 3540.3c*. The boards, one in each fleet, are maintained within the organizations of the fleet commanders-in-chief, and assist them in ensuring that naval nuclear-powered ships are operated by qualified personnel in accordance with approved procedures. The Commander, Naval Sea Systems Command, and the Director, Naval Reactors, Department of Energy, provide technical assistance to the commanders-in-chief and to the boards.

Each board has a senior member (captain) who has served as CO of a naval nuclear-powered ship, and usually also as an engineering officer. Deputy senior members have the same qualifications, and other members are nuclear-power qualified. Normally four members constitute an inspection team.

The responsibilities of the board are:

1. Examine personnel assigned responsibility for supervision, operation, and maintenance of the propulsion plant to determine their state of training.
2. Witness and evaluate the conduct of propulsion plant drills.
3. Inspect the material condition of the plant to ascertain its readiness, preservation, and cleanliness.
4. Review and evaluate the engineering (reactor) department administration, and the completeness and accuracy of all records relating to the propulsion plant.

The board gives the following types of examinations:

1. *Pre-Critical Reactor Safeguards Examination* of nuclear-powered ships prior to initial criticality of a newly installed reactor core, including new construction ships and ships completing refueling.
2. *Post-Overhaul Reactor Safeguards Examination* (PORSE), prior to initial reactor operation after an overhaul without refueling, but lasting more than six months. The board will ascertain the state of training of the propulsion plant crew, the adequacy of administrative procedures, and the material readiness of the propulsion plant and spaces as they affect impending reactor

operations and propulsion plant power range operations. Appropriate evolutions and casualty drills may be conducted as part of this examination.

3. *Operational Reactor Safeguards Examination* (ORSE) of ships in an operational status. These are conducted no more than one year after the last pre-critical or post-overhaul examination, and thereafter at intervals of approximately one year, as close to the anniversary as practicable. Approval of the Chief of Naval Operations and Director, Division of Naval Reactors, is required to extend the interval between examinations beyond 15 months.

4. *Radiological Control Practices Evaluation* (RCPE) of those reactor support facilities in tenders authorized to handle radioactivity associated with naval nuclear plants. This evaluation is conducted at intervals not exceeding a year. For tenders in overhaul, if the yearly interval will be exceeded during overhaul, an evaluation will be conducted before the end of the overhaul, after work in the nuclear support facility is essentially completed.

An ORSE is conducted on each nuclear-powered ship (and each of the crews of a fleet ballistic missile submarine) at approximately one year intervals, and more frequently if the fleet commander-in-chief or the Director, Division of Naval Reactors so desires.

Following examination, the board submits a written report to the appropriate commander-in-chief, with copies to interested commands. It submits reports of corrective action in the same way. If the board finds the ship unsatisfactory, it submits its findings by immediate precedence message. The ship is then returned to port and shut down. The sequence of actions following such a finding is quite involved and will not be described here. Briefly, though, the crew is re-trained until all discrepancies have been corrected. The ship is then re-examined, and if satisfactory, the restrictions are lifted. Obviously failure has personal consequences for the commanding officer.

Naval Technical Proficiency Program. All ships carrying nuclear munitions receive annual inspections under the Naval Technical Proficiency Program (NTPI). The acronym applies to the inspection rather than to the program. The basic instructions describing the NTPI are classified, and therefore we can describe the inspection only generally. You and your crew, however, should be thoroughly familiar with them.

Like the ORSE, the NTPI should be prepared for by continuous instruction in, and review of, safety precautions and proper handling procedures. Follow this with appropriate casualty drills, frequently repeated. Record establishment and keeping, maintenance, cleanliness, preservation, and frequent inspection are all important to preparation. The most important aspect of the NTPI is demonstrating that you and your crew are knowledgeable, well trained and instructed, and capable of safely handling all aspects of nuclear weapon receipt, preparation, stowage, and firing.

The inspection team is composed of experts from the fleet weapons training groups, augmented by personnel from your parent unit command. Your unit commander is usually the chief inspector. In addition to inspecting the foregoing areas, the team will review your personnel reliability and security programs.

The NTPI, like the ORI, the PEB, and the ORSE, is a formidable inspection. Prepare for it as you would for battle and you will pass.

Annual Competition

In peacetime, annual competitions are a means of attaining and maintaining battle and administrative readiness by using the stimulation of competition. All men do better when they compete with others, and ship's crews are no exception.

The intratype competition was established in 1953 by the Secretary of the Navy's *Instruction 3590.1*. It provided for payment of prize money to enlisted members of the crew from the Marjorie Sterrett Battleship Award Fund for attaining certain scores in battle practices. Qualifying crewmen wore E's on their jumpers, and ships attaining certain scores displayed E's on gun and director mounts. In later years, the competition was expanded to an Intratype Battle Competition conducted in accordance with *OPNAVINST 3590.4A*.

Present regulations authorize type commanders to make awards to ships, submarines, and aircraft for attainment of certain standard scores in overall battle exercise competition. The awards start with individual gun, missile, and department crews, including departments such as communications and minesweeping, and culminate in ship awards. E's of various colors are authorized for display on ships, weapons, and assault boats, and the Efficiency "E" ribbon is worn on the uniform.

The Admiral Arleigh Burke Fleet Trophy was established in 1961 for the ship or aircraft squadron in each fleet achieving the greatest improvement as measured by the criteria of the Battle Efficiency Competition.

Other annual competitions include the Ney award for the best general mess.

In many past years the annual competition has been suspended because of the demands of various crises. However, when it is in effect you will find it a powerful stimulus to your crew. The display of an E ribbon on the uniform, or the E on gun, sail, bridge, or stack is highly prized in the fleet.

Preparation for Deployment

Following completion of refresher training, you will most likely have to begin preparing for deployment. Your preparation may be short in the event of crisis, or may take several months, if scheduling permits. The period of preparation will normally be from 30 to 45 days, and will be listed in the annual employment schedule as Preparation for Overseas Movement (POM).

Written Requirements. Usually the ship you will replace will forward you a "turnover letter" sometime during POM. This should give you an insight into the small day-to-day matters of preparation. The larger areas will be taken care of by your type commander's check list and by the large packages of operation plans and orders you will receive from your future chain of command. Between the turnover letter, the POM check list, and the operation plans and orders, you should have all the written guidance you'll need. The rest of your preparation is making sure you have achieved the necessary training and qualifications, personnel, material, and supplies, and are in a state of readiness adequate to carry out the tasks set forth in the written requirements. To do this you will need to carry out the following detailed preparations.

POM Check List. Obtain a POM Check list from your type commander as early as possible. When you can answer all its questions satisfactorily, you are ready to deploy; and just as importantly, you will be able to pass the POM inspection. The chances are that you will have to carry out many of the following tasks before being able to pass the inspection.

Equipment Calibration. Have all of your equipment which requires calibration checked as completely as possible. This includes magnetic and gyrocompass systems, sonar equipment, communications equipment, radars, ECM equipment, and missile and gun battery alignment.

Combat Systems Readiness Review. If you command a modern ship, with complicated combat systems, you will be scheduled for a Combat Systems Readiness Review (CSRR). This inspection will test all aspects of the readiness of your combat systems. Prerequisites for the CSRR are proper alignment and calibration, presence of full spare parts allowance, and presence of the specially trained personnel required.

Logistics. Obviously you should be at one hundred percent of allowance in all areas. Top off all your consumables before sailing. Make sure the key items in your allowance are *sighted* by responsible officers or petty officers.

Advanced Training. If you are just coming out of refresher training, your type commander will schedule you for advanced training. Additional advanced training is usually possible during transit to the forward areas. The type commander will work closely with the fleet commander responsible for assisting in your preparation. You can expect to participate in exercises appropriate to your type. Cruisers, destroyers, and carriers will take part in air attack-air defense exercises and submarine-antisubmarine exercises. If time permits, they will also take part in an amphibious exercise. Submarines will be worked up by their type commanders and will participate in advanced hunter-killer exercises where possible. The goal, of course, is to prepare your ship or submarine for forward deployment with the Sixth or Seventh Fleets or for independent missions.

POM Reports. Some type commanders require weekly progress reports on POM readiness. You may consider this just so much paperwork and further encroachment on your already eroded authority, but if you look at it objectively you will find that the report will be a help to you as well as to the type commander in monitoring your progress.

Crew Briefings. You will need to schedule many briefings for various groups of your officers and men and some for all hands. These will range all the way from review of operations orders for officers to cultural and drug abuse briefings for the entire crew. Working out this schedule without interfering with other preparations can be challenging for your executive officer.

POM Inspection. Most type commanders schedule POM inspections so as to give you as much time as possible to prepare, and yet allow some time for correction of deficiencies. Passing your POM inspection means that you will be, and feel, ready for deployment. Fail it and you and your crew will be in for some night work. We have no specific good advice; just try to remedy each discrepancy as soon as you can.

If you have planned well, worked hard, and been fortunate in finding a recently returned ship to brief you, you should be reasonably ready. You should also be able to avoid the frantic urgency displayed aboard some ships in the last few days prior to departure. Make sure that you and your crew will spend these last few days at home, and not in line at the supply depot.

Between Deployments

At times, an employment schedule will provide a few months between advanced training and deployment, or between post-deployment and workup for a second deployment. This time is usually spent in type training, in providing services to other types, and in short cruises and port visits. The type commander, who controls your general scheduling, and your unit commander will coordinate those periods given to you for individual ship exercises and upkeep. While you might prefer independence in these matters, you will find it a help to have the arrangements made for operating areas, target services, and other assistance.

During periods between deployments, you can expect rapid personnel turnover. This will require you to go back to basics in your training program to insure that your weapon and other teams are adequately manned and trained and that your ship can continue to operate safely while still trying to improve its advanced training. During these periods, the value of a shipboard training program and adequate records and qualification check lists will be evident to you.

One employment which may be assigned to you during this interim period is taking aboard midshipmen from the Naval Academy or from a university NROTC unit for summer cruising. This may seem like a headache, but it can be rewarding. Your officers and men should realize that they are contributing to the future of the Navy by inspiring these young officer candidates. Usually, the unit boarding you will bring instructors and curricula with it, but sometimes only a few midshipmen will be allocated to each ship. If this happens you may need to provide the instruction. Temporary crowding and a little extra work is a small price to pay for the good you can do.

You may be also chosen to "cruise" or provide underway experience to reserve units. Give this task your attention also. In time of crisis or war the reserve officers and men you take to sea with you will only be as good as you help to make them now.

Operational Chain of Command

One important aspect of joining the fleet is your relationship with your operational commanders. Prior to joining, your contacts will primarily have been with your type commander and the commander of the training command. You will now leave the training command behind, except for some inspections. Your type commander and his staff, however, will always be with you to some extent, and your relationships with them must be fostered and maintained, no matter what demands are placed upon you by operational commanders.

In fact, you will now be beginning a period of divided attention, if not divided loyalty, for you will be trying to please two demanding masters, your administrative commander and your operational commander. You must render prompt and accurate reports up both chains. The surest way to disaster is to fail to notify either of them of some important change in your status, operations, or other critical area. In this day of almost instant communications and worldwide unrest, what appears to be a small incident to you as a busy and harried CO of a small ship can be a crisis to higher authority. Don't bombard either chain of command with trivia, but exercise calm judgment in estimating what you would like to know if you were in their place. One of the best ways to *succeed* to high command is to learn at an early age to *think* like a senior commander. Start with a review of Article 0606 of *Navy Regulations*. This gives a basic outline of reports which must be made to seniors, but it is not all-inclusive.

You can expect to be shifted around from one operational command to another, particularly during your workup period prior to deployment. Remember that each will report on your fitness as a commanding officer. Submit the required fitness report forms promptly, and try to communicate with your operational commander as much as you can without seeming pushy. He needs to see you personally to "get your gauge," and you need to hear from him directly to learn what he wants. In the end, a well-organized, well-commanded ship will stand out. You need only command well to succeed.

Relationships with an Embarked Commander and His Staff

Now that your ship is off and running there still may be a small cloud on your horizon: you may be, or become, a flagship. Many commanding officers and crews regard this with dismay, but a better approach is to look at it as an opportunity. Being a flagship has its compensations; for example, you can expect a preferred berth and an easy station in formation.

You should also consider it an opportunity to associate closely with the unit commander and his staff. Their knowledge and experience can help you, your officers, and your men, if you approach them correctly and assure congenial relationships. Assuming that you intend to take a positive attitude toward this situation, you should examine carefully the legal and regulatory relationships between you, your crew, and the unit commander and his staff. *Navy Regulations* is very general on the subject, and Article 0602–4 declares only that a commander shall hold the same relationship to his flagship with regard to internal administration and discipline as to any other ship of his command. The *SORN*, however, goes into great detail, and you should study it carefully. It covers all phases of the relationship between a commanding officer and an embarked flag officer. These regulations must be carried out exactly. A flagship which does so with good spirit and grace can be a happy one.

When all is said and done, the relationship depends upon the personalities of two people, the flag officer and the flag captain. The commodore or admiral who is arrogant, thoughtless, and devoid of any compensating abilities or graces can cause great dissension, while the officer who takes time to curb himself and his staff, to criticize or correct flagship personnel only when absolutely necessary, and who conducts himself with understanding and good humor can stimulate his flag captain and flagship to produce outstanding performance and support. The flag captain also can make a difference. One who looks for trouble under the guise of maintaining his independence, and who fails to compromise in inconsequential matters not involving principle, will only irritate his flag officer and staff. The captain who remembers that his paramount duty, after assuring the safety of his ship, is to support his flag officer, who takes the side of his officers and crew in their differences with flag personnel, but who still fosters a spirit of cooperation, will create an atmosphere of mutual respect and harmony. Regardless of the kind of flag officer fate assigns you, strive to be a good flag captain and to command a good flagship.

There will be days when it doesn't work out. The flag chief signalman has just criticized your leading signalman, your gig has been preempted, and your flag officer is half an hour late for the movie. While you are sitting in the wardroom waiting for him, remember the words of Confucius. He wrote in his *Analects* that "the relations between superiors and inferiors is like that between the wind and the grass. The grass must bend when the wind blows over it." Bend gracefully, and determine to do better when your turn comes to be a flag officer. This sage advice may not be much practical help, but thinking about it will at least make the half hour pass faster.

Welcome to the Fleet!

12

Active Duty
with the Fleet

The role of world leadership has not been easy. In fact, it has both its pluses and its minuses. The pluses include a singular strength, prominence, power to exert our own will, and the dissemination of our gospel of freedom. The minuses include huge responsibilities, close and constant scrutiny of our actions and inactions, and the application by others, and indeed by ourselves, of the most demanding standards of conduct and ethics.

—Former Secretary of the Navy Edward Hidalgo

At this point, we will assume that you and your ship are trained, inspected, and prepared to join the fleet. You will find that you are sorely needed. The Navy never has enough ships to carry out its tasks, and our country is constantly finding new needs for naval power. You will find your presence of great assistance to our Navy and to our foreign policy; people overseas as well as at home will look to you and your ship with a mingling of pride, respect, and affection. To be deserving of it—this is the challenge.

In the previous chapter, we mentioned your annual cycle, with its two deployments in normal times and the lengthy single deployment in war or extended crisis. In this chapter we will cover your period of active duty with the fleet in greater detail. This will include time with the Second and Third Fleets in preparation for, and in transit to, forward areas, and duty with the Sixth Fleet, Seventh Fleet, Middle East Force, and South Atlantic Force. We will also cover special operations for submarines (as far as security will allow), the annual competition in more detail than in Chapter 1, some cautions on preparing for port visits, forward homeporting, and some miscellaneous "housekeeping subjects."

Type Commander's Requirements

As you leave San Diego or Long Beach enroute to the Seventh Fleet, or Norfolk, New London, or Jacksonville enroute to the Sixth, or your SSBN homeport enroute to your operating area, you may think you have left your type commander behind at last. Not so. You will be hearing from him by mail and dispatch daily. Much of this communication will be welcome, for it will concern personnel replacement, spare part shipment, or other assistance; but there will also be news of detachments and other unpleasantries. You must keep in mind that while you are deployed you must give your all to your operational commander and the tasks he sets for you, but you still belong to your type commander for administration. You will also find a type commander's representative in each fleet. He will probably be a unit commander of your type and will also have an operational task. He will, however, be ready to assist you, and his legal, medical, supply, and other staff members will be available for advice and service.

Annual Competition

In times of peace, if directed by the Chief of Naval Operations, the annual competition will continue while you are deployed. Some target and other services will be available in the Sixth and Seventh Fleet areas, and you can carry out some competitive exercises. Your unit commander can also schedule mutual services. If, however, it is not possible for you to complete all of your exercises, you may be excused from certain of them, or in extreme cases from the entire competition. If you feel that you can do well in the competition, though, a little forward planning will keep you in the running. For example, you can complete exercises requiring services not available in the forward area before or after deployment.

In time of war or prolonged crisis, of course, the competition is cancelled.

Personnel Preparation

In Chapter 2, we briefly discussed the beginning of your preparations for deployment. Now, as it becomes imminent, and your training for it draws to an end, you should concentrate on personnel preparation.

Complete all medical and dental work. Although there will be dental facilities in the forward areas, time and opportunity to use them will be limited. The same is true for elective surgery. Consequently, have your crew complete all such work before deployment. Start your inoculation program early. There will always be absentees, but an early start will ensure that all are ready.

Have your division officers examine each man's situation to ensure that he has made adequate preparations to take care of his dependents. No family should have to depend on mailed paychecks. Counsel your men to allot pay to their wives or to joint accounts so that sudden, long interruptions of mail service will not strand their families financially. In 1980, the Military Personnel and Compensation Amendments expanded the authority for advance pay ("dead horse") to include an advance of allotment to dependents. If a person is less than sixty days away from deployment, he can now register an allotment for his dependents and have the first month's check deducted from pay over a period of up to six months, commencing with the month in which the first payment takes place.

Make sure your men know their overseas mail address and that they pass this on to their families.

There are several more things you can do to keep family ties secure over deployment. One is the establishment of a "call-up" list, to allow the wives to pass along information on movements and ship's activities (in peacetime most ship's movements are unclassified). Consider a commanding officer's newsletter for families. Consider chartering dependents' flights, to meet the ship for one of your port visits. Let the fleet commander in on this, so that he can keep this part of the operating schedule constant. Make advance plans for these visits, if you hold them, and publicize them to all hands.

Make sure your men know, and pass to their dependents, how to find and use the nearest Navy Relief office and the nearest Red Cross facility. Encourage them to update their wills and to provide their wives with powers of attorney. The nearest naval base will have legal officers to help if private attorneys are not available or cost too much.

Having each man make these arrangements before you deploy will save you the headache later of trying to straighten out his family problems by mail or dispatch. You can't *make* them do so, of course; but you can apply pressure by other and still legal means. A man who fails to heed your advice and whose family then gets in trouble can expect lowered marks in forehandedness and willingness to take advice.

Shiphandling and Independent Maneuvering

This may seem rather late in the book to talk about individual shiphandling, but it seemed best to concentrate as much of the discussion of shiphandling in one place as possible. We will therefore discuss here and in the succeeding section some aspects of individual shiphandling, maneuvering singly, and maneuvering in formation or in close proximity to other ships. Other aspects are treated in the sections on safety at sea and independent operations, particularly maneuvering in heavy weather and recovering a man overboard.

Basic shiphandling starts with study of all the forces of which a shiphandler can take advantage—engines, rudder, lines and anchors, tug assistance—and an understanding of what the ship will do as a result of these forces. It also includes study of the environment in which the ship will operate; various kinds of water, its depth, its currents and tides; the atmosphere which surrounds it, in all its forms, fog, ice, wind, and rain.

The best textbook in print today is *Naval Shiphandling*, published by the Naval Institute Press. This book starts with a thorough dis-

Figure 12-1. The USS *Elliot* (DD 967) is powered by gas turbines. This new form of propulsion gives the commanding officer many advantages such as quick warm up, rapid acceleration, and easy engine replacement.

cussion of all the factors that influence a ship. It then sets forth the general principles of handling any type of vessel, single or multiple screw. This includes simple, single ship evolutions at sea and in restricted waters, anchoring, mooring to piers, and mooring to buoys or to other ships. You will need this knowledge early in your command tour as you bring your ship out of its building yard or get it underway for the first time, particularly if you are commanding a type with which you are unfamiliar.

Nomenclature. While we are discussing elementary subjects, it is wise to review your seagoing vocabulary before you begin to give orders regarding engines, linehandling, and mooring and anchoring equipment. Your deck crew will then know exactly what you want done, and will have greater respect for your knowledge of seamanship.

There are some very common errors made in naval shiphandling terminology. Demonstrating early that you are not going to make them will give you an "early up." First, you don't "tie up" a ship; you *moor* it. A horse is "tied up." Second, a *dock* is not something you lay over to, stand on, or moor to. A dock is the open water between piers (or, alternatively, the dry space in a graving or dry dock). You moor to a pier, wharf, or bulkhead. *Pier* and *wharf* are alternate names for the wooden or concrete structure built out from the shore so that ships can moor to it. A *bulkhead* is a system of piles and other building materials along the face of a shore. Some bulkheads are for erosion control; others have deep water alongside and can be used for mooring.

Learn these simple distinctions and you will attain standing in the eyes of a good chief boatswain's mate; but don't be too surprised if yours does not know correct terminology. They don't make them *all* like they used to.

Independent Maneuvers. Naval Shiphandling is very good as far as advice on handling ships independently. It covers all types of ships from carriers to MSOs and hydrofoils. There is no point in repeating this information here. There are, however, two weak points in the book. The advice on standard maneuvers to recover a man overboard is too brief. The *Anderson* turn is incorrectly described, and other standard and well-known maneuvers are not covered. The *Watch Officer's Guide*, published by the Naval Institute Press, is somewhat better on this subject, but also incorrectly describes the *Anderson* turn. The section on man overboard in the chapter on independent operations in this book correctly describes the *Anderson* turn and is better on this subject than the other references.

Secondly, Crenshaw's advice on bringing a destroyer alongside for replenishment is too limited, and therefore we will expand upon it in the next section.

If you now feel secure in your ability to get your ship underway, handle it in restricted waters, and bring it back to port and its moorings safely, it is time to turn to the problems of handling it in close proximity to other ships.

Shiphandling in Formation or in Proximity to Other Ships

As you steam to join your first formation, your first task will be to take your place in formation. Your station, and the safety and maneuvering rules you will use to get there, are set forth in *ATP-1*, *Allied Maritime Tactical Instructions and Procedures*. Your task force commander and unit commander may also have issued standing orders directing the speeds you will make, prohibiting you from crossing ahead of a major vessel, and related matters. Make sure you and your OODs are familiar with them.

In this day of radar, the bridge team depends heavily on the combat information center to provide course and speed recommendations and other information. Many COs like to use a small, hand-held maneuvering board to check CIC's recommendations. Even the best-regulated CIC will occasionally give you a reciprocal course, or one which leads through another vessel. Check on CIC, either with maneuvering boards or plotting directly on the face of a radar repeater; but *never* make the mistake of getting so involved in the process that you lose the "picture." The captain's main function in maneuvering is to look out for the safety of his ship, and the eyeball is his most important piece of equipment. At night you must never reduce its effectiveness by plotting in too much light, or by staying too long in an enclosed bridge behind reflective glass. Be *fast*, if you can; but be *safe* until you and your watch officers are sure you can be *fast safely*.

Stationkeeping. After taking your place in formation, the next task is maintaining it. Only experience will tell you what the task group commander or your screen commander, if you are assigned as a screening unit, wants. There are two schools of thought in stationkeeping. One is the "accuracy above all" type, who has his staff watch officer on the circuit continuously correcting wanderers, no matter how slight the discrepancy. His rationale is that you should do everything right, that the formation is designed to give maximum protection only if maintained without gap, no matter how small, and that you have nothing better to do than keep station. The other and, fortunately, most prevalent type, is the commander who feels that small errors in stationkeeping are not that important and that you, your bridge crew, and your CIC crew should be concentrating on other, more important matters (such as detecting enemy ships, submarines, and aircraft). You will have to figure this one out as evidence develops and then act accordingly.

You will, of course, be called upon to change station from time to time. For large ships this is a relatively easy maneuver, performed by CIC or maneuvering board plot in accordance with the rules of maneuver of *ATP-1* and type instructions. Screening ships will employ more vigorous movements. By now you will know what stationing speeds your task group and screen commander want. Give them initial movement in a hurry, and then refine your course and speed after you are on your way in the general direction of your new station and CIC has had time to calculate. Comply with the same safety rules as when joining formation.

Naval Shiphandling also describes other task group operations peculiar to various types, including carrier air operations, amphibious beaching and retraction, service as rescue destroyer for air operations, and replenishment. These fundamentals will get you through the initial exposure to advanced operations. You will soon become an expert as you observe the "veterans" and gain experience.

Replenishment. After your initial operations you will inevitably need to replenish. For the larger ships providing, this usually means holding an accurate course and speed, although changes in course and speed are often called for to avoid merchantmen or accommodate to changing weather. This is best done by changing a few rpm of speed and a few degrees of course at a time, first communicating the change to the ship alongside by telephone; steadying up; and then making another small change. Approach and stationkeeping by large ships is adequately covered in *Naval Shiphandling*. This is a relatively simple evolution for them, although often lengthy because of the time necessary to transfer large amounts of fuel and ammunition. Larger ships are relatively stable and unaffected both by regular swells and errant seas.

Smaller ships, however, can expect a livelier time. For them, *Naval Shiphandling* describes two basic methods of approach, the "coast in" and the "back down." The "coast in" method is relatively simple, safe, and easily taught to conning officers. Briefly, make your approach at five knots over replenishment speed (usually twelve to fifteen knots) and slow to replenishment speed when about two hundred yards astern. The ship should then "coast" to its proper position. The back down, or high-speed approach, is made at twenty-five knots, with the engines backed two-thirds when the

Figure 12-2. Twenty-five-knot approaches during replenishment are spectacular, but usually counter-productive. After this destroyer has steadied alongside, her deck force and their equipment will be wet and less efficient.

bridge is about one hundred yards astern of the desired position. Judgment and experience are needed to pick the exact moment to shift the engines ahead to replenishment speed. Obviously, this method is more difficult to learn and to teach to others. *Naval Shiphandling* claims that if throttlemen fail to back both engines at the same time little yaw results. This may be true, but experience has shown that this "little yaw," when combined with above normal wind and sea, will result in collision in about one out of one hundred such approaches. The small amount of time saved from several such approaches may be squandered in one repair period. It is true that the first ship approaching may come in at high speed, and can profitably continue at 25 knots into the backdown position. This ship might save one or two minutes. However, subsequent ships will start from standby position three to five hundred yards astern. If they are alert to increase speed to twenty knots as soon as the preceding ship breaks away they will be alongside just as quickly as if they accelerated to twenty-five. The time "saved" will be negligible, and may even turn into a delay if the ship fails to settle down promptly.

The two opposite approach philosophies are well illustrated by one encounter between a Sixth Fleet carrier CO acting as a task group commander and a newly joined destroyer squadron commander. After their first replenishment, during which all the DDs coasted in, the carrier captain called the squadron commander over and informed him that he wanted all destroyers to approach at twenty-five knots in order to save UNREP time. The latter officer paused a moment, and then replied that all of his ships were well versed in the high speed approach, liked to do it, and would in the future comply, provided the carrier commander was willing to accept a one in one hundred chance of damage. Since about one hundred replenishments would take place in the operation, this would mean that one destroyer might be absent for part of that period. While the carrier commander was digesting this, the squadron commander added, as an afterthought, that he noticed that the carrier's pilots were landing at 140 knots. Couldn't they, also, save time, say by landing at 180 knots?

They soon agreed that the destroyers would continue to use the coast-in method, with an occasional high speed approach for practice, and that the carrier pilots would continue to land at 140 knots.

There are many other evolutions which call for skilled maneuvering, for all types of ships, such as minelaying and sweeping, submarine maneuvers in close proximity submerged, surface ship coordinated attacks, and combined destroyer-helicopter operations in ASW. The exact techniques used are classified. Appropriate NWP, NWIP, ATP, and FXP publications describe them in detail.

Preparation with the Second Fleet

Surface units of the Atlantic Fleet are prepared for deployment by the Commander, Second Fleet, who is normally embarked in a flagship at Norfolk, Virginia. Commander Second Fleet schedules fre-

Figure 12-3. Vieques Island in the Atlantic is a site often used for amphibious training.

quent advanced exercises in the Atlantic and Caribbean areas. Where possible, these exercises include all aspects of naval warfare, including carrier air attack, air defense, submarine attack, anti-submarine defense, amphibious operations, and underway replenishment. Ships and submarines of all types, based in New London, Newport, and Jacksonville, join in these exercises. Minor amphibious exercises and naval gunfire and air support firings take place at Vieques Island. SSBNs prepare at Charleston and deploy directly from there, with practice missile firings at Cape Canaveral. If opportunity permits, each ship is exercised in all of its individual capabilities and all of its interactions with other types. The advanced exercises provided during this period should prepare your ship for any requirement of the Sixth Fleet.

In the last few days before getting underway, double-check your chart allowance and corrections. Remember that surface ships will need Indian Ocean charts. You will be given a Prepare for Overseas Movement (POM) inspection to check most of the routine preparation. If you are up-to-date on all publications; up to allowance on spare parts, communication equipment crystals, and cryptographic

Figure 12-4. San Clemente Island is used for amphibious gunfire support exercises for ships preparing for Pacific deployment.

publications; and are loaded to capacity with fuel and provisions, you should now be ready for your transit to the Mediterranean.

Preparation with the Third Fleet

Surface units of the Third Fleet are prepared for deployment by the Commander, Third Fleet, with his headquarters and flagship (when embarked) in Pearl Harbor. Because of his advanced location, he delegates some responsibilities to his subordinate commanders on the west coast. Advanced exercises are scheduled and held off the San Diego-Long Beach area, as well as off Hawaii, for ships home-ported there. Amphibious exercises are held over the beaches at Camp Pendleton. Naval gunfire and air support firings are conducted at San Clemente Island and Kahoolawe Island. SSBNs will prepare at Bremerton and deploy from there, sometimes stopping at Pearl Harbor. Again, as in the Atlantic, each ship exercises all of its capabilities and interacts with all other types as time and opportunity allow.

Before leaving, remember the following details. Your crew will need uniforms for all climates, from tropical in Singapore to near-arctic in northern Japan. Your heating and air-conditioning systems should be in top condition, and of course your medical department should have completed inoculations for all areas you might possibly visit, including the Middle East. Your chart allowance must include all of the Pacific area and the Indian Ocean. As in the Atlantic, upon satisfactory completion of a POM inspection and logistical preparation you will be ready to transit to your forward area.

Transit to Forward Areas

Fleet commanders make every effort to send relieving ships to forward areas in groups, both for mutual support and so they can continue advanced exercises while enroute. The fleet commander involved will write the transit operation order for your movement, and the senior officer in the unit will act as officer in tactical command. Determine early any requirements you may have for services or assistance and submit them, by hand if practicable; you will then be in a position to do a little personal bargaining. Take advantage of the transit to make sure that you arrive in the forward area trained and ready.

Transit to the Seventh Fleet. The transit group to Westpac will usually stop at Pearl Harbor for advanced exercises for one or two weeks. Commander, Third Fleet will arrange these exercises. Commander-in-Chief, Pacific (CINCPAC), and the Commander-in-Chief, U. S. Pacific Fleet (CINCPACFLT) are also located in Pearl. Your transit group commander will usually arrange for the commanding officers of the group to call on all these flag officers. If this is not, or cannot, be done, you should make informal visits to the assistant chiefs of staffs for operations and administration of CINCPACFLT. You will then have some personal "feel" for the direction and information you will be getting from them as your tour progresses. Remember that *both* CINCPAC and CINCPACFLT will be in your chain of command.

After completion of this visit, you will resume transit to the Western Pacific, reporting to the Commander, Seventh Fleet as you pass the longitude separating the responsibilities of the Third and Seventh

Fleet Commanders. At that time you will change operational command (CHOP). The Seventh Fleet Commander maintains a quarterly operational schedule, which should give you a clue to your first orders. Normally you will be allowed some post-voyage repair and recreational time. "Normal," however, is seldom the state in the Western Pacific, so you may be sent anywhere. Be prepared for big changes in employment schedules and sudden evaporation of port and upkeep periods.

Sixth Fleet. In transiting to the Mediterranean, distances are much shorter than in the Pacific, and there probably will be no intermediate stops. You may, however, put in briefly at Bermuda, the Azores, or Rota. You will probably be part of a transit group, although single transits are more common than in the Pacific. You will CHOP at Gibraltar and probably fuel there. There is no set pattern to the transit and relieving system in the Sixth Fleet. Nuclear-powered ships sometimes round South Africa in time of crisis and non-nuclear-powered ships have stopped at Capetown for fueling.

Operations with the Sixth Fleet

The Commander, Sixth Fleet, is normally embarked, but he has public quarters ashore not far from Naples. Some of his supporting elements are located near Naples, as are many of the dependents of his staff and flagship. When you are first in company with the flagship you should arrange to call on him, though sometimes your unit commander will arrange a group call. He, or his chief of staff, will return your call. Do not hesitate to ask permission to call on other unit commanders of the Sixth Fleet.

COMSIXTHFLT provides your deployment schedule on a quarterly basis, but it may change at any time. Currently, destroyers can expect a transit of the Suez Canal and a month of temporary duty with the Middle East Forces. Carriers, cruisers, and amphibious types seldom leave the Med except in time of major trouble in the Middle East. Submarines spend all of their tours in the Mediterranean. Normal operations call for one to two weeks of underway exercises as a fleet, followed by port visits of five to seven days.

Units alternate between the eastern and western Mediterranean.

Port visits are a rewarding change of pace during deployments. Prepare for them with tour arrangements and crew briefings. Briefings should emphasize the cultures and religions of the countries to be visited. It is particularly important that *all* of your crew understand Moslem, Jewish, and Catholic sensitivities of the countries they visit (the next section, "Operations with the Seventh Fleet," covers religions and problems they may engender in more detail). Some cultures, for example, demand that women be treated quite differently from American custom. Liberty parties should go ashore forewarned of situations which might become international incidents. Our enlisted men will respond well if they are clearly told what they must and must not do.

You will find that the hard work and drill you put in have prepared you well for your deployment. The red-starred aircraft overhead and the Soviet ships shadowing your movements will be new, but you can cope with them if you remember the tenets of international law and if you obey the instructions provided by the fleet commander. Perhaps the most hair-raising challenge will be the "chicken" tactics of the Soviet Navy. In this "game" they will try to force you to give way when you are in formation, or when situations are so close as to permit doubt as to their interpretation. Be sure you are legally right, and then don't be "chicken." Your fleet commander will support you if a little metal-bending results. Many commanding officers maintain still and movie cameras on the bridge so that they can photograph any potential incident.

Amphibious operations are held about once a year, but the available landing areas are poor and do not yield much in the way of training ashore.

Transit through the Suez Canal is an event to profit from if you are scheduled for it. The pilots now are mostly Egyptian, and are reasonably competent, though unused to the power and maneuvering capabilities of destroyers. Be careful until yours gets used to your ship. Make arrangements for your crew to be free to be topside as much as possible during the transit. Much of the scenery is sand, but there will be stretches of great interest. The pilots, most of whom speak good English, can tell you when interesting sights are about to come into view.

A tour with the Sixth Fleet can be rewarding, if international conditions allow you good port visits, but it can also be boring if crises require you to steam in circles for weeks awaiting more peaceful conditions. Even at its worst, though, it will be bearable, unless your tour is extended too long. The last few weeks will go by rapidly as you arrange post-deployment leave parties and anticipate a rapid transit home.

Operations with the Seventh Fleet

Commander, Seventh Fleet is embarked in a flagship based in Yokosuka, Japan. He has public quarters ashore there, as do most of his staff and flagship personnel. When he is at sea a small element of his staff stays at the naval base. As with the Sixth Fleet, your transit commander or unit commander will arrange a group call on him at the first opportunity. If this is not feasible, you should arrange your own call.

The staff and components of the U. S. Naval Force, Japan (also located in Yokosuka) furnish much of the support to Seventh Fleet units, both those on rotation and those homeported there. There is a small support facility in southern Japan, at Sasebo, but this group varies in size and capability with the need for it and the state of U.S.-Japanese politics. Mine warfare units and some SSBNs are based in Guam. Carriers, cruisers, and destroyers homeported in Japan are based at Yokosuka, but sometimes overhaul and resupply at Subic Bay, in the Philippines. Occasionally repairs will be scheduled at Singapore or Hong Kong. Okinawa has patrol aircraft facilities at Naha Airfield and shore facilities for the Marine component of the Fleet, and is sometimes visited for minor assistance by surface units. Units of the amphibious force operate from Okinawa. The commander of the service group is homeported in Sasebo, and the Commander, Carrier Striking Force is homeported in Subic, although his flagship is usually elsewhere. All of these arrangements are subject to change as crises in the Far and Middle East ebb and flow.

Figure 12-5. The Navy has taken on new responsibilities in the Middle East. Here, the Seventh Fleet, augmented by Atlantic Fleet units, gathers in the Indian Ocean during the Iranian hostage incident.

The Seventh Fleet usually consists of two carriers, two cruisers, a command ship, three squadrons of destroyers, an augmented amphibious squadron, a Marine division (plus or minus), a service squadron, a submarine squadron, a mine squadron, and a patrol aircraft squadron. It may be somewhat smaller at times, but can be augmented quickly. In the latter stages of the Vietnam War it operated seven carriers, five cruisers, thirty-five destroyers, two amphibious squadrons with embarked Marines, and a host of service force additions, including merchant ships. In terms of ability to deliver sustained bombing and gunfire this fleet was stronger than the Third and Fifth Fleet combination of World War II. At one point, eight-inch barrels were being sent to Subic by air as the intensity of cruiser shore bombardment wore them out in less than a week.

The majority of the Seventh Fleet, like the Sixth Fleet, is provided on a rotation basis, with a few ships homeported forward. (We will cover forward homeporting in a separate section.)

Your operations with the Seventh Fleet will range from short port visits to prolonged assignment to the Middle East Force. When a crisis occurs, the small permanent force of one LSD and two destroyers in the Persian Gulf is augmented by Seventh Fleet forces, usually built around the carrier division commander permanently stationed in the Pacific. Other ships are added as the crisis requires to form a balanced and mutually supporting force. If the crisis is big enough, as in the Iranian hostage incident and the Iran-Iraq war, forces from the Sixth Fleet are added as well.

Submarine operations range from fleet exercises to forward area patrol operations. SSN and SSBN operations will be discussed separately, in a later section of this chapter.

Port Visits. Port visits are one of the most pleasant features of Seventh Fleet duty. They may range all the way from Northern Japan to Australia, including Yokosuka, Sasebo, Pusan, Inchon, Guam, Subic Bay, Hong Kong, Bangkok, Singapore, Kuala Lumpur, and many smaller ports. Nuclear-powered ships are somewhat restricted as to port visits, and you will be provided with probable areas you can visit before you leave the United States. Opposition to nuclear-powered ship visits is decreasing steadily as their safety record convinces host countries that they present little danger.

Once each cruise, arrangements may be made to fly dependents out by chartered aircraft to meet the ship in port. This is a worthwhile endeavor. Chartering assures a reasonably low air fare, and special rates can be obtained for hotel stays. Such a break in a long tour can do wonders for the morale of your crew and their families.

It is a good idea to prepare your crew carefully for each port visit. The Naval Military Personnel Command and Commander, Seventh Fleet provide brochures describing the people, their cultures and religions, and problems which might be encountered while visiting.

It is especially important to understand the religions of each host country. Confucianism, Shintoism, and Buddhism are the three main religions of Japan. Hong Kong and Taiwan are more eclectic, but most Chinese are Buddhists. Singapore is mainly Chinese. Subic Bay and the northern Philippines are predominantly Catholic, but the southern Philippines are Malay, with their own variation of the Moslem religion. As you travel south and west to the Indian Ocean area Mohammedanism becomes predominant, co-existing on a shaky basis with Hinduism in India, Pakistan, and Sri Lanka. Moving further west, variations of the Moslem religion appear. The two major sects are the Shi'ites and the Sunnis, who feel that the teachings of Mohammed were handed down via different prophets; they are bitter enemies. In and near Israel the conflict between the Jews and the Moslems of the surrounding countries is strong. In all of these countries, from Japan to Lebanon, there are scattered groups of Christians and many smaller sects of various kinds.

A thorough knowledge of all these religions is not necessary, but mastery of the fundamentals of the major ones is not difficult; every naval officer should make the effort. The following summary will help you and your crew if no other information is readily available.

Summary of Religions. The ancient and official religion of Japan was Shintoism. This recognizes two kinds of gods, nature-gods and man-gods. Shinto morality is basically compliance with custom. Publicly, this means obeying the will of the sovereign, and therefore the rule of the Emperor in World War II was absolute. In 1946 Shintoism was abolished as the state religion, and its importance has since decreased. Certain elements still remain, such as ancestor worship and respect for such natural phenomena as flowers and trees. Shinto temples of state size are still found in Japan. There are also smaller, roadside temples near views or areas of natural beauty. These must be recognized and respected by your crew.

Buddhism is now the predominant religion in Japan, although most Japanese retain elements of Shintoism. Gautama, the Buddha, was an Indian wise man (many Indians are Buddhists) living in the fifth century B.C. His followers have no authentic written record of his teachings, but use many oral versions of his philosophy in different areas and languages. This is why the practice of Buddhism varies from country to country. Buddhism has no God, but statues of Buddha can be found in every Buddhist country, either standing separately or as the central feature of temples. The moral teachings of Buddha are quite similar to those of Jesus, but seem somewhat more pessimistic to us. Buddhists do not conduct formal group worship. Instead communicants can be found praying at the temple at any hour of the day or night. Buddhist temples are quite elaborate and are sightseeing attractions, so your crew must be warned to conduct themselves quietly and decorously when visiting. Flash cameras must be used guardedly.

There are offshoots of standard Buddhism which your crew should know about. Most of your crew will be familiar with Zen, a cult which spread to the United States in the 1960s. Zen is a passive religion and its practitioners should present no problems to your crew. A more militant movement is called Soka Gokkai, and it is growing daily in Japan. Soka Gokkai means "Society for the Creation of Values." It attempts to meld Buddhism with western utilitarianism, and is much more materialistic than its ancestor. Its members believe themselves to be part of something "new" and "big." "Third World Power" is their watchword. They will attempt to convert westerners, such as your crew, and they have had some success. Caution your men to be polite in refusing their literature and approaches.

Confucianism is mainly found in China, with offshoots in Taiwan and Hong Kong. Confucianism is really a philosophy rather than a religion. Followers of Confucius are usually reserved and tolerant. There are no outward indications of Confucianism such as temples, and therefore there are few, if any, special ways to offend a Confucianist.

The Catholic religion, as practiced in the northern Philippines, is very conservative. Filipinos are a proud people and are conscious of slights of any kind. Your crew should already know the principles of Catholicism. All that is necessary is to treat the Filipinos as one would treat the members of one's family. Be quiet and respectful in their churches. Many Filipinos have church-connected names such as Jesus and Concepcion. Be prepared for this and do not make any comment.

The Moslem religion is practiced by a majority of the people of the Far and Middle East. It is essential that each officer and man know the fundamental tenets of the Mohammedan religion.

Moslems, also known as Muslims, are followers of Mohammed. Many of them are named after him. Be careful not to joke with these persons about their name or to be derogatory toward them. Your attitude may be misinterpreted as insulting the prophet Mohammed. The Moslems believe that there is one God, the same one as in other major religions, and that Mohammed was one of his prophets. Mohammed did not promulgate a new creed or dogma and always said he was presenting the same beliefs as were held by Jesus and Abraham. A Moslem is thus prohibited from uttering blasphemous words against Jesus or Moses.

The Koran is the Moslem equivalent of the Bible. It contains the teachings of Mohammed. In addition to Christian and Jewish-style ethics and morals there are unique provisions regarding the afterlife. A Moslem believes that dying in defense of his beliefs is the surest way to heaven. Moslem temples, called mosques, may not be entered without invitation. Moslems pray several times a day at prayer call, kneeling in groups facing toward their holy city, Mecca. This custom must not be interfered with. Pork and alcohol are forbidden to Moslems and should never be offered to them or consumed in their presence. The month-long fast of Ramadan is another widely observed custom. Moslems fast during daylight, and like any hungry people, they can become irritable as the day progresses.

Hindus worship numerous gods, including Shiva, the God of the universe. Their religious epic is known as the Ramayana, and their gospel as the Bhagavad Gita. Most westerners are familiar with the word "karma," which is defined as the working out of God's justice in every moment of existence. The closest English translation is "fate." There are millions of Hindus, mostly living in India. Hindus and Moslems tend to be enemies, so avoid getting between them in any way, either physically or philosophically. It is difficult to offend a good Hindu, except by seeming to support a Moslem unjustly.

With the knowledge of what religions to expect, and with these fundamentals in mind, you and your crew should be able to visit with pleasure and confidence and without giving offense.

A few other cultural cautions and bits of information may be helpful. Japan, China, and Korea are family-oriented. Generally their streets and residential areas are safe because local areas police themselves and will protect Americans. However, known red light and bar areas do not have this control and can be dangerous. The northern Philippines range from the strictness (particularly with their daughters) of Catholic families in residential districts to the all-out licentiousness found in the poorer areas and the bar areas. Warn your liberty party to be sure of the identity of any women they approach. "Proper" women will be offended, and their male protectors are fast and proficient with the knife. Prostitutes are almost universally infected. In the southern Philippines Moslems go on "holy war" jags without provocation and look for the nearest non-Moslem to machete. Make sure your liberty party stays in groups in Jolo, Zamboanga, and other southern ports. Thailand has some local customs which should not be violated. Showing the sole of your foot or shoe to a Thai is insulting, as is stepping on the jamb when passing through a door. Guam is Americanized and should present no problems.

Thorough briefing of your liberty parties will prevent international incidents, and will keep you from being called to foreign police stations in the middle of the night to bail out members of your crew who "just didn't know." Unfortunately, international incidents, unlike national incidents, don't stop in the local court, but find their way up the chain of command via the reports you are required to make.

In summary, with command attention, careful preparation, and a bit of luck, your tour with the Seventh Fleet will be a rich and rewarding experience, both for you and your crew.

Operations with the Middle East Force

The Commander, Middle East Force, is embarked in an LSD specially configured for tropical operations and homeported in Bahrein, a large island in the northern sector of the Persian Gulf. He has public quarters ashore. In normal times his flagship is augmented by two destroyer types on thirty-day assignments from the Sixth Fleet. Transit to the Middle East area is via the Suez Canal.

This is a very interesting tour of duty. Climate in the Persian Gulf and the Red Sea ranges from cool in the wintertime to very hot (125 degrees) in the summer. Sand storms are frequent even at sea and should be prepared for by making sure all closures are in good working order. Sand in equipment is devastating and can make for long hours for the maintenance gangs. Close up early and tight when sand comes your way. Bahrein is British-influenced, and, unlike other Moslem countries, tolerates alcohol. The restrictions on women are also relaxed. Other liberty opportunities will be limited, other than a fueling stop at Massaua, Ethiopia, coming and going. One or two ports on the Persian Gulf may be visited. Remember that, unlike Bahrein, strict Moslem customs must be observed there. There may also be occasional visits to Karachi and other ports.

In time of crisis, the Middle East Force is augmented by ships of the Seventh Fleet. In large crises the Commander, Carrier Striking Force of the Seventh Fleet assumes tactical command. Forces from the Sixth Fleet may be added via the Suez Canal or directly from the Atlantic via Africa.

When the Middle East Force is operating in an augmented mode our base at Diego Garcia becomes very important. This base is growing in capability every year. Its airfield can handle the largest aircraft and its harbor is adequate for most ships. Diego Garcia is not a complete base in any sense, and its physical limitations will prevent it from becoming one; but we are negotiating for other bases in countries bordering the Indian Ocean, and someday operations in this vast area will be easier.

Duty in time of crisis is interesting if it is acute and your ship is actively involved, but many crises are deadly dull. Prolonged tour lengths, slow mail delivery, and lack of adequate liberty ports will sap the morale of your crew if you do not take positive action to avert it. Keep them informed of the problem, and make every effort to copy or to obtain press news from bigger ships. On-board entertainment, no matter how amateurish, will help. Concentrate on onboard training and education. Keep your crew busy with occupations that are as meaningful as you can make them.

Operations with the South Atlantic Force

When conditions permit, a South Atlantic Force may be activated. A flag officer is assigned as a permanent commander, but when he is not available the senior unit commander takes command. This force is periodically augmented by antisubmarine warfare ships, land-based patrol aircraft, and one or two submarines. A cruise is planned in such a manner that the force visits a succession of Central and South American countries having naval forces. Those countries who wish to do so receive the visit of the ships, submarines, and aircraft of the force, and either before or after the visit detail some of their own air and naval forces to conduct joint exercises with it. Usually the force will complete a circuit of South America and then transit the Panama Canal back to its Atlantic base.

These cruises are infrequent, but they offer a superb opportunity for participants to visit the major countries of Central and South America and to make acquaintances with members of the various navies that can last a lifetime. As for other areas, you will need to prepare thoroughly for the South Atlantic. The Commander, South Atlantic Force will furnish you with cultural information which you can use for crew instruction. Remember that in most Central and South American cultures, being Spanish and Portuguese in origin, most women occupy an inviolate position (at least as far as outsiders are concerned). The point is that your men must carefully ascertain the status of the woman in question before getting into trouble of various sorts. The knife is a potent and frequently-used weapon on this continent and it is resorted to with little provocation.

Forward Area Homeporting

In the 1970s, the Navy began experimenting with increased forward homeporting. This was not a new concept, but the extent of the action was. It is a piece of luck to be ordered to a ship so assigned; you will have the privilege of commanding at sea in the forward area, combined with the opportunity for you and your family to learn the culture and the language of a host country, as well as to travel to points of interest in nearby lands.

As of this writing, forward homeporting is available in the Pacific Fleet in destroyers, a command ship, and a carrier in Yokosuka, Japan; in selected service force types in Sasebo, Japan; and in mine-craft and SSBNs, in Guam.

Such assignments in the Atlantic include Rota, Spain, for SSBNs, and Italy and Greece for cruisers and destroyers. Fleet staffs and some unit staffs are homeported in both the Sixth and Seventh Fleet areas. Finally, the flagship LSD for the Commander, Middle East Force is homeported in Bahrein.

Special Operations for SS, SSN, and SSBNs

So far we have said little about submarine operations. The more conventional operations which can be described here are exercises with parts of the Sixth and Seventh Fleets in submarine-antisubmarine exercises. These are much the same as in rear areas, but with the added hazards of Soviet observation and occasional interference by ships, aircraft, and other submarines. There is the occasional added thrill of discovering a real live Soviet submarine in the "net" during the exercises. These "free services" are invaluable!

Other operations involve reconnaissance in certain advanced areas and cannot be discussed for security reasons. These operations are usually controlled by CINCPACFLT and CINCLANTFLT and monitored by the Commanders of the Sixth and Seventh Fleets.

You may be involved either as the rescued or rescuer in Search and Rescue (SAR) operations for submarines. In either case, be familiar with *NWP 37*, *NWP 37–1*, and those annexes of CINC-PACFLT, CINCLANTFLT, Commander Seventh Fleet, and Commander Sixth Fleet operation orders having to do with SAR. We will cover search and rescue operations in greater detail, both from the point of view of the submarine and that of the rescue vessel, in the chapter on independent operations.

Visits to Foreign Ports with Fleets

About half of your visits to foreign ports will be as part of a group of ships from your fleet. The rest will be as a single ship, and we will cover this in greater detail in the chapter on independent operations.

As part of a visiting group, you can expect the senior officer to arrange pratique, berthing, calls, shore patrol, and shore leave for all ships. Your particular responsibility will be to see that your ship carries out its part of these arrangements.

The senior officer will arrange calls as required on U. S. governmental officials ashore (usually the ambassador or consul), on foreign civilian officials (the mayor, governor, or other appropriate official), and on officers of foreign navies, both ashore and afloat. You will attend these calls and be present on the flagship (if summoned) when they are returned.

After all calls and courtesies are completed, you may then be tasked with arranging wardroom calls on foreign naval vessels present and arranging calls ashore to extend privileges to your officers.

You will be fortunate to have a senior officer make these arrangements. If you visit singly, these and other duties will devolve upon you.

Transit Home and Arrival Home Port

After completing your deployment, you will transit home, usually as part of a group, but sometimes singly. Enroute you will be arranging post-deployment leave plans, a most enjoyable task. Thirty to sixty days is the customary post-deployment leave period. When you have finished arranging your leave schedule, remember to organize fire parties for each remaining section so your ship will stay safe during this happy but disruptive period.

As you approach home, give some thought to pratique and customs. Your medical officer will know whether or not your ship has visited any areas of communicable disease. In any event, your transit period should be long enough to assure that any quarantinable disease will be evident by the day of your return.

Customs. There are two problems associated with customs. The first is the relatively simple one of providing declaration forms to your crew, explaining how to fill them out, and persuading your men not to try to evade the system. There always seems to be at least one "smart" sailor who hides declarable items in such obvious places as the chain locker, though. Usually he is found out because he brags about it to some alleged friend, who then writes an anonymous letter to the customs officials. This causes him considerable trouble and you some embarrassment.

Article 0764, *Navy Regulations*, requires that you facilitate any examination it may be the duty of the customs officer to make. Cargo-carrying naval vessels must follow the same rules as cargo-carrying merchantmen. The regulations require that you furnish customs with a list of all dutiable articles purchased by each man. A compilation of the forms previously filled out in lieu of a list is sufficient. Customs officers don't usually search naval vessels, except when tipped off by the friend of our previously mentioned sailor. Foreign customs officers are prohibited from searching U. S. naval vessels.

In the unlikely event that you have a civilian passenger or passengers aboard, you are required to notify the Immigration and Naturalization Service and to await their instructions.

Narcotics. Narcotics are the second major problem of return to home port. Both Sixth and Seventh Fleet ports of visit are located in areas where drugs are plentiful, cheap, and readily available. Article 0731 of *Navy Regulations* lays specific responsibilities on the commanding officer with regard to drug abuse. You must conduct a rigorous program to prevent the introduction, transfer, or possession of marijuana, narcotics, or other controlled substances. Further, you must publicize the physical dangers involved in drug abuse and the federal, state, and local criminal liabilities. There are certain military punitive measures, including discharge under other than honorable conditions, which you also must explain. The final exhortation of the article is that you must exercise the utmost diligence in preventing importation of marijuana, narcotics, or other controlled substances on board. (In case you are wondering what "controlled substances" are, this catchall legal phrase permits flexibility in determining what drug-like substances are harmful. As soon as one harmful substance is found by the drug community, recognized by enforcement authorities, and controlled, the drug community discovers something else.)

Given the current civilian climate concerning drugs, this is a tall order. Your crew will associate with both Americans and foreigners who openly buy, sell, and use drugs, and they will tend to bring their tolerant attitudes back aboard. You will have a never-ending task of explaining why they must leave both the attitude and the substances ashore.

In spite of diligent post-liberty inspections and a thorough educational program, however, some drugs will always find their way on board. You will then have to find them. Surprise inspections and vigilance on the part of your master-at-arms force will produce some results, but in the end, finding small packages in a large ship is very difficult. If you feel sure that a large amount of drugs is aboard, send a message to the naval authority at or near the home port you are returning to and ask his assistance in arranging to have Naval Investigative Service agents visit your ship on arrival. They are experts in detecting hiding places, and can even bring search dogs aboard if required.

Alcohol is a much easier substance to control because alcohol containers are much larger than drug packets. Also, the profit to be made from bringing it in is insignificant compared with the high resale value of drugs.

Fleet Operations after Deployment

After completing your leave program, you will find that the type commander has been at work on your crew. You can expect many detachments and an influx of untrained men. This means going back to basics on your training plan as you begin long-range plans for the next deployment.

Operationally, you can expect some time now for type training to permit you to begin your workup, some for services to other types, and some for upkeep and limited availability to repair and refit. Later, you will work into advanced exercises again.

You will find fleet operations the most interesting part of your tour. This, of course, is what the Navy is all about. You will look back on deployment with great satisfaction, for you will have trained and molded a ship and crew into a single, effective entity, able to meet all the demands of the forward area. This is the most demanding requirement the Navy has, short of combat.

As you reflect upon your success, though, remember that it does not endure. You will be required to demonstrate it all over again in a few months' time.

In the words of former Secretary of the Navy Edward Hidalgo, "Leadership is acquired slowly, but it can weaken and vanish with frightening speed." With this advice in mind you can never rest on your laurels, no matter how gloriously they have been won.

13

Independent Operations

Let us not wait for other people to come to us and call upon us for great deeds. Let us instead be the first to summon the rest to the path of honor.

—Xenophon, *The Anabasis*

U. S. Navy Regulations, 1973, covers the responsibilities of a ship operating singly by directing that her commander conform to the applicable regulations for the senior officer present (covered by the *Regulations* in Chapter 9). You would do well to study them. The range of responsibilities set forth might seem so broad as to make you want to find a more senior officer to turn them over to. However, all of the duties mentioned will not fall upon you, at least not at once. We will discuss those most likely to occur in this chapter. The others, God willing, may never happen.

Two seemingly simple actions will keep you out of most trouble no matter what type of problem you must deal with. First, *understand your orders*; and second, *make all required reports promptly and accurately.* Having done both, stop "looking behind you," in accordance with the advice of the immortal Satchell Paige, and look forward to independent duty as a privilege and an opportunity. For once you will stand or fall on your own actions and decisions, a condition sought by every aggressive, confident man.

The Changing Nature of Requirements to Keep Seniors Informed

In Chapter 1, we discussed the encroachments by the chain of command during the last decade on the ability of the individual CO to command independently. In line with this, in all of the independent operations about to be discussed, one principle is all-important: *keep the chain of command informed.*

In *Navy Regulations* prior to 1973, reporting to seniors by a commanding officer was covered in detail. A senior officer present was to make to his commander in chief or to the Chief of Naval Operations a detailed report of any important circumstances in connection with, or duty performed by, the forces under him. The 1973 version, strangely enough, no longer contains such a paragraph, mentioning reports in any detail only in Article 0940, which covers granting of asylum and temporary refuge. These are covered in great detail, probably reflecting the preoccupation of authorities with incidents which occurred just before the drafting of the 1973 edition.

Nevertheless, you will find specific requirements for reporting in *NWP 7, Operational Reports*, which summarizes the reports required by the Chief of Naval Operations, fleet commanders, and other operational commanders. Part II of *NWP 7* promulgates movement report requirements for reporting locations and movements of Navy ships and aircraft, Marine ground units, and VIP personnel. Details include preparation of forms and reports and responsibilities of movement report centers and officers.

Amplifying orders to *NWP 7* will also be issued by administrative and operational commanders above you.

All of this will turn out to be a sometimes bewildering array of requirements, but the aggregate demand is to *keep them informed.* Unless your ship is very small you will have the communications equipment to reach your seniors, and they in turn will be in instant contact with superiors all the way to the White House. In these days of critical international situations, a single ship halfway around the world may find herself involved in search and rescue, asylum, collision, or other events of interest to the chain of command. You will find sometimes that *what* you are doing is not nearly as important as how you *describe* it. Indicate the *what, when, where, how,* and *why* of what is happening. If you can predict the next event, do so. Tell them when you will report next. Try to include everything you might want to know if you were a senior commander.

If you feel that an incident or an expected confrontation is of potential international significance, *NWP 7* instructs you to establish direct communications with the Chief of Naval Operations. You are further instructed, if in port, to call the Duty Captain at the Navy Department, Washington, D.C. The Duty Captain is located in, and is in charge of, a naval command center in the Pentagon, and has instant communication with all Washington-based authorities, including the Joint Chiefs of Staff and the President. Establishment of such communication, however, does not excuse you from the responsibility of informing your intermediate seniors. You will hardly want the Duty Captain to call your type commander asking for advice or information regarding the incident you have just reported and find him completely in the dark about it. This tends to produce a very unhappy type commander and subsequently an equally unhappy you.

The Chain of Command

The old days of truly independent operations, when naval vessels disappeared into the South Seas for a year or so without being heard from, are gone. Even the pre-World War II shakedown cruise to foreign ports is no more. Today a ship on independent operations, and even SSBNs sixty days submerged, are firmly a part of the chain of command.

NWP 2, Organization of the United States Navy, describes the basic command organization, the chain of command of the shore organization, and the dual lines of authority to the operating forces. You should master this publication. Note that the CNO, as such, has no operational authority. His operational control comes through his position as a member of the Joint Chiefs. He is, however, in the administrative chain of command. If you are discussing a developing asylum case with his Duty Captain you will have to keep these distinctions straight. Fortunately, the Duty Captain will have a good grasp of them. *NWP 8, Command and Control*, is a simplified discussion of command and control matters and should be of great assistance to you.

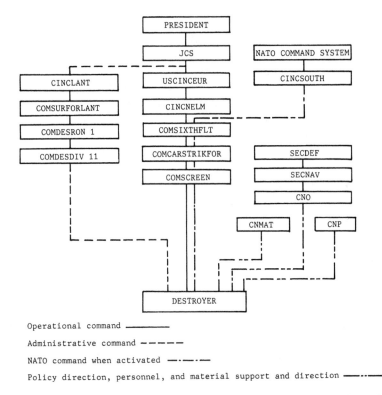

Figure 13-1. Multiple chains of command, direction, and support from the president, as commander-in-chief, to a destroyer serving in the Mediterranean.

Figure 13–1 illustrates the multiple lines of command, administration, and policy converging on a single destroyer serving in the Mediterranean. They are obviously complex, and demanding, but it is essential that you understand them. In summary, *make sure* you understand the responsibilities of your administrative operational seniors and how you relate to them. Keep their interests in mind, and you will protect your own.

Preparation for Independent Operations

You may, at times, be detached suddenly from your fleet assignment and ordered to proceed on independent ops. If this occurs there is little you can do to prepare. Either you are ready or you aren't. If you are given advance warning, however, or are going on a scheduled cruise, there is much preparation to be done.

If you did not do so before deploying, or if your independent operation begins from the rear area, start with the personnel preparations discussed in the chapter on fleet operations. Be sure you are up to date on inoculations and dental work and that all of your men have taken care of their financial affairs.

If you have the opportunity, top off logistically before departing. This means fuel, ammunition, provisions, and spare parts. It also means many smaller but important items that you have been used to getting from supply sources. Things that gave you little concern before will suddenly loom large on the horizon. U.S. stamps, mail order forms, and other postal supplies cannot be found in Australia. Ship's store items, particularly everyday necessities like razor blades and toothpaste, will be needed for a long period. Scrounge all the movies you can, and try to make them the kind that sailors can watch several times. Your supply officer will need extra cash for several paydays. When you reach port he will also need to know supply procedures for letting provision contracts, if none are in force for that port. You will be fortunate in this regard if your ship is big enough to warrant the assignment of a Supply Corps officer. If a line officer is doing this job he will need help and your patience.

When you have a few minutes, have your executive officer survey the language abilities of your crew. Find out which of your officers and men are qualified to act as interpreters, and which can help with a smattering of a language. You will need their help in SAR operations, contacts with merchant vessels, port visits, and on other occasions.

Special Submarine Preparations

Submarines normally operate independently. This provides exceptional training opportunities for our expanding submarine force. For the fast attack force, independent ops provide training conditions not unlike wartime operations. In both SSBNs and SSNs, deployed operations are as independent as any command today, with the commanding officer given much latitude in his decision-making.

SSN deployed operations are usually announced through the chain of command some nine months prior to deployment. As his surface counterpart does, the submarine CO will review in detail his administrative and logistical requirements prior to the deployment. In addition, the SSN commanding officer will review *NWP 79* in detail, in order to indoctrinate thoroughly his wardroom and crew in tactical procedures to be conducted while on station. As in all operations, in-depth planning is the key to success. During the nine-month preparation period, the SSN commanding officer will also be offered the services of the various training commands and technical agencies. Failure to accept their training offers can result in missed opportunities once deployed.

In these times of reduced manning, training deficiencies must be identified and corrected early in the preparation period. The tactical equipment a submarine carries must be used effectively to carry out its mission. If its personnel cannot support the technology, they must be either trained or replaced. There is too much at stake to deploy to a forward area when mission success probability is lessened by lack of experience or technical ability.

The final process in preparing an SSN for deployment is the deployment workup and certification by the squadron commander. *NWP 79* is your guide in preparing for these events. During the entire workup, stress the importance of the mission to the crew. Conduct all preparations as if the ship were deploying in time of war. If you conduct your training and preparation in this spirit, your ship will be successful during its truly *independent operation*, and every man will relish the experience.

SSBN preparations are similar to the SSN workup, except that the off-crew trains in home port without the ship. The successful SSBN captain will set training goals for the crew and for each individual, and will monitor progress toward these goals throughout the nine-week off-crew training period.

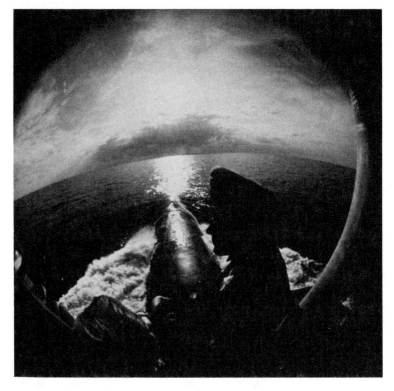

Figure 13-2. Independent duty has its problems, but as you head off on your own, you will enjoy your command independence to the utmost.

Movement Report. Whether in a submarine or a surface ship, the movement report is probably the most important single report you will make on independent ops. The movement report system is responsible for your continuing safety when you are moving alone. If you fail to report, and suffer disaster along your track, help might not reach you for days. The movement report system is designed to provide all necessary authorities with a dead reckoning position for

Figure 13-3. The Navy's mail service is outstanding, but it will only be as good for your ship as your routing instructions.

all units at any time. If because of weather, engineering casualty, or other reason, your progress along your track varies at any time by more than four hours (100 miles for carrier operations; two hours for submarines) you must submit a report of change. Chapters 9, 10, and 11 of *NWP 7*, *Operational Reports*, describe the entire movement report system. Be completely familiar with them.

Mail. A movement report provides information to appropriate naval area postal officials, who then verify the routing information on file. You must still, however, submit separate mail routing instructions to the appropriate fleet commander in accordance with either CINCLANTFLTINST 5110.1 series or COMNAVLOGPACINST 5112.1 series.

Underway Independent Operations

Presumably you are as ready now as foresight and a good foraging group of chief petty officers can make you, and are probably headed for a foreign port visit. During your transit to this port, or just on a simple independent operation, many things can happen to you. When you were part of a task group you could expect the task group commander to take care of each crisis. Now *you* are in charge. To assist you, we will now review some of the most common problems you can expect to face.

Weather. The crisis most likely to strike is heavy weather. Prepare your ship by reviewing your heavy weather plan and making sure all hands know how to implement it. Check your bill against the standard heavy weather bill found in Article 630.7 of the *SORN*. At a minimum, your bill should include all the points the *SORN* includes. If you carry out your bill properly, and ballast correctly, you should be able to handle any heavy weather situation if you maneuver your ship correctly. One exception might be if you command a *very* small ship. Small ships can survive by early avoidance of the dangerous portion of storms, and in some cases are safer than larger vessels.

A *good* ship captain always knows what the weather *is* at any moment. A *very good* one also knows what the weather *will be*. An *outstanding* one also knows what the weather *might* be in the future.

The most important factor in surviving heavy weather is the captain's ability to recognize its existence, its probable movement, and its development.

Your studies of weather should start with the basics of worldwide weather formation, and then proceed to the patterns of your particular area. A good text is *Weather for the Mariner*, published by the Naval Institute Press. The piloting instructions for your area also cover local weather patterns and storm tracks.

These studies will enable you to interpret most weather predictions and weather advisories. The information in these messages will tell you what the weather is now, near you and over a wide area. It will also tell you what the weather *probably* will be, based on past history of weather development and movement, and using the skills of highly trained meteorologists.

This is not enough for your safety. You will remember from your shore duty listening to the evening television weather forecast giving you a forecast of fair weather, and then walking out to the first tee in the rain. Forecasters simply cannot forecast accurately. The movement of weather masses is, at this point in the study of meteorology, not completely predictable even with the finest computer systems. The movement of air masses over the irregularities of land and island chains is particularly unpredictable. Movement over the open seas is somewhat more uniform, and therefore more predictable. The point here is that you cannot place the safety of your ship in the hands of a meteorologist, no matter how skilled he is and how much data he has. In the final analysis he must *guess*, and you must always take this into account. You must learn enough about the science of weather, and, more importantly, the homely, practical knowledge of close-in weather prediction, to know when the forecast you received is wrong or when the weather is refusing to follow it.

Weather for the Mariner is technically correct in as much depth as you will need, and it is written in a readable style. It covers the general theory of weather, the generation of worldwide weather, and the standard patterns of weather to be found throughout the world. It is relatively short, non-mathematical, and its photographs and illustrations will help you make local predictions.

Tropical Cyclones. The most dangerous weather disturbance you will encounter is the tropical cyclone. This type of storm is known as a hurricane in the Atlantic area and as a typhoon in the Pacific. Ships of all sizes are in for trouble during hurricane or typhoon season, which lasts roughly from July to December. There are also tropical cyclones in the southern hemisphere, which rotate clockwise, instead of counter-clockwise as in the northern hemisphere. These storms are given different names, such as the Indian Ocean cyclone, and the Australian willy-willy, but are essentially the same.

To cope with these dangerous and unpredictable disturbances, read the chapter on weather disturbances in *Weather for the Mariner*, par-

Figure 13-4. A hurricane in the Caribbean as seen from a satellite. The eye is in the lower left corner.

ticularly the section on precautions and disengagement. Another good text is *Heavy Weather Guide*, also published by the Naval Institute Press. Also study Appendix XII to this book. It is the well-known letter from Admiral Nimitz regarding typhoon damage, written after the Pacific Fleet had twice encountered severe typhoons. In essence, it reaffirms that you, as commanding officer, are the final authority on the safety of your ship, and as such must know both her capabilities and limitations, and the environment she will travel in—wind, water, and storm. In this age of worldwide satellite weather observation and reporting, you will have advantages that World War II commanders and ship COs never had. You should have ample warning of typhoon and hurricane formation, movement, and prediction.

This said, we will now quickly review our storm precautions.

In essence, a hurricane or typhoon is a large mass of water-laden air, rotating counter-clockwise (in the northern hemisphere) about an eye of low pressure of from twenty to fifty miles in diameter. As one approaches the storm center, air pressure decreases gradually until one enters the eye, when it decreases dramatically, as illustrated in Figure 13–5. The whole mass is hundreds of miles in diameter and moves forward at speeds of up to fifty miles per hour. Occasionally it will remain stationary, though, and may even back up for short periods before resuming forward movement. Rotational wind speeds in the right-hand semicircle (looking along the direction of movement) are added as vectors to the forward speed. Rotational wind speeds in the other semicircle are subtracted from the forward speed. Hence, the right hand semicircle with its higher wind speed is known as the "dangerous semicircle," and the left hand semicircle is known as the "safe semicircle." The direction in which the storm lies from you can be predicted fairly accurately by looking back along the direction from which the swells are coming. The storm center will be within a few degrees of the direction of swells, as indicated in Figure 13–6. Distance away can be predicted roughly by the speed with which the barometer is falling. Sudden falling to very low levels indicates the center is near, as indicated in Figure 13–4.

Wind speeds of over 200 knots have been experienced in hurricanes, and seas can be mountainous. Ships must avoid being caught broadside in the troughs of the seas, particularly destroyers and smaller ships. Hurricanes and typhoons form in tropical latitudes and move west. As they progress they tend to head more northwesterly and finally recurve to the northeast. Predicting the exact track is very difficult.

It is interesting to note that with only primitive prediction services in the period from 1920 to 1940 the ships of the Asiatic Fleet never suffered any serious damage from typhoons. During this period hundreds of typhoons of great violence swept through the Philip-

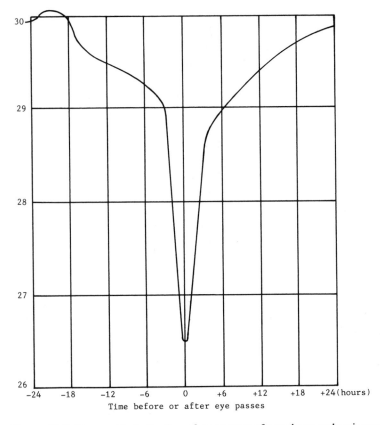

Figure 13-5. Barometric indication of movement of a typhoon or hurricane over a ship or station.

pines area, but never managed to catch any of the thirteen old destroyers of the Asiatic Fleet. The reason was that the commanding officers of these ships soon learned to use some simple rules of typhoon prediction and avoidance that had been handed down from captain to captain. You will want to review the more complete rules in *Weather for the Mariner*, but it is interesting to note how simple they can be made and still be effective. The following rules were

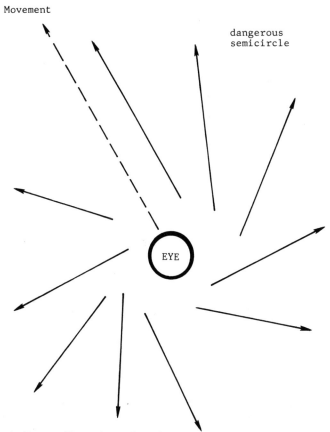

Arrows indicate direction of swell movement, with length of arrows showing relative height of swell. Largest swells are along direction of movement. Swells in dangerous semicircle are highest.

Figure 13-6. Swell directions and heights surrounding a tropical storm.

Direction of movement 320°

Speed of movement 20 knots   Dangerous semicircle

Winds at center 120 knots   Maximum winds 120 + 20 = 140 knots

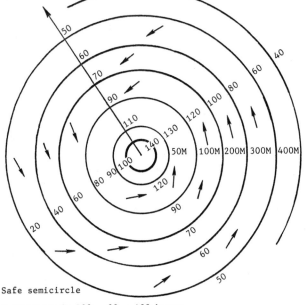

Safe semicircle

Maximum winds 120 - 20 = 100 knots

Figure 13-7. Wind directions and speeds to be expected in a typhoon or hurricane with eye wind speeds of 120 knots and a speed of advance of 20 knots.

taped to the bulkhead of the emergency cabin of the commanding officer of an Asiatic Fleet four-stacker (in this class the emergency cabin was also the charthouse):

1. If the barometer falls below 29.50 inches start worrying.
2. If the barometer falls below 29.35 *really* worry.
3. If you are in port hoist in all boats, move to typhoon anchor-

Figure 13-8. Hurricane winds of 100 knots. Tops of long swells are flattened, but the direction of the swell is still apparent, and helps to locate the center of the storm.

age, put a second anchor down, and be prepared to steam at anchor.

4. If you are at sea watch out for long swells. The direction from which they approach is within 15 degrees of storm center.
5. Observe the direction of the wind. In the northern hemisphere the storm center will be 120 degrees to the right of the direction from which the wind is blowing.
6. Never try to outrun or pass ahead of a typhoon unless you are very close to its path. If you can, avoid the dangerous semicircle (left side looking toward eye.)
7. If the wind shifts clockwise you are in the dangerous semicircle; if it shifts counter-clockwise, you are, if in the northern hemisphere, in the safe semicircle. If the wind direction stays steady and the barometer continues to fall you are directly in the path. Bug out to the west as fast as you can.
8. In the southern Philippines most typhoons are moving in a northwesterly direction. By the time they reach the northern

Figure 13-9. The calm inside the eye of a hurricane.

Figure 13-10. If the typhoon is astern and headed away from you, make best speed and hold divine services.

Philippines, friction of land masses and their natural tendency to curve to the northeast will change their direction of movement to northeast. One in ten will continue northwest to the China coast.

9. If you cannot evade completely take the following actions:
   a. In dangerous semicircle bring wind on starboard bow. Make all speed possible.
   b. In safe semicircle bring wind on starboard quarter. Make all speed possible.
   c. If directly ahead of storm bring wind 160 degrees on starboard side. Make all speed possible, slowing as storm approaches. As eye approaches wind will decrease and then shift to opposite direction as eye passes over you. Keep turning to port to keep sea astern. Do *not* get in troughs.
   d. If behind storm go anywhere you want to go. Hold divine services if you feel sufficiently grateful.

The same instructions taped to the bulkhead of the sea cabin of a more modern destroyer enabled its commanding officer to leave the Third Fleet formation in the second typhoon experienced by Admiral Halsey's fleet and survive easily with no casualties or damage. Others were not as fortunate.

Hurricanes in the Caribbean and the Gulf of Mexico follow similar patterns and can be handled with the same rules of thumb. The island chains of the Caribbean and the large land masses surrounding the Gulf of Mexico influence storm buildup and movement differently from the Western Pacific, but in either area simple principles of physics apply. Water areas add to storm energy and water content; land areas subtract. Storms move more easily over water, and the greater friction of land slows that portion of the storm passing over it. Storms, therefore, veer in the direction of that portion of them passing over land. As they pass over land, rainfall increases, energy lessens, winds decrease, and forward movement slows. The reverse happens if the storm passes out to sea again.

Keep your radars operating. Radar information can define storm center position and will show its movement accurately. This is of great assistance when maneuvering close to the storm's center. Antennas may be damaged by high winds, but you must balance a few hundred dollars' worth of repairs against the safety of your ship.

Frontal Systems. Most of the area of the earth, both sea and seacoast, over which you will operate lies in the northern mid-latitudes. The weather of this area is dominated by frontal systems. You should have a good understanding of what fronts are, how they are formed, travel, interact, and dissipate. They will control ninety percent of your weather. *Weather for the Mariner* has an excellent discussion of this subject, written in an understandable style and accompanied by photographs and diagrams.

There are two principal types of frontal systems, cold fronts and warm. When moving in an orderly fashion and not otherwise influenced, they produce predictable weather. *Weather for the Mariner* contains a set of tables showing weather you can expect at each stage of the approach and passage of both warm and cold fronts. When they are occluded (occlusion occurs when a cold front overtakes a preceding warm front) the occlusion literally lifts up the boundaries of both fronts and weather becomes much more violent and unpredictable. Fronts can also be thrown off their orderly progression from west to east by low and high pressure cells, which can cause them to stall and remain stationary, to change direction, or to speed up. As with hurricanes and typhoons, weather prediction with frontal systems is sometimes educated guesswork. Still, an educated guess is better than an ignorant one. A small investment in the study of frontal weather systems can pay big dividends. A modern naval vessel is not usually vulnerable to frontal storms if properly moored or anchored in port, or well handled at sea, but ship's boats can suffer if not properly secured or hoisted early enough.

Local Storms. Other forms of local storms can be dangerous. The williwaws of the Aleutians, the santa anas of Southern California, and the sandstorms of the Red Sea and the Persian Gulf must be understood and prepared for. The onslaught of local storms is usually sudden and without warning.

Fog is to be expected in various parts of the world at certain seasons. Check piloting instructions and your low visibility bill before entering such areas.

When thoroughly prepared for the vicissitudes of weather, though steaming peacefully under fair skies, you can concentrate on preparing for other emergencies.

Search and Rescue. After heavy weather, the most probable crisis you will encounter will be some form of search and rescue (SAR). Spend a little of your time reviewing your responsibilities in this area. They stem from *Navy Regulations*, and are spelled out in Article 0925: "Assistance to Persons, Ships, and Aircraft in Distress."

You are required, as far as you can do so without serious damage to your ship or injury to your crew, to proceed with all possible speed to the rescue of persons in distress. You must render assistance to any person found in danger at sea and must give all reasonable assistance to distressed ships and aircraft. Should you be so unfortunate as to collide with another ship, you must render assistance to that ship and her crew and passengers. As you would expect, you must report all SAR action to the CNO and to other appropriate superiors in your chain of command as soon as possible.

Article 0925 ends with the reassuring statement that the accounting for rendering assistance and making repairs pursuant to the provisions and directions of the article shall be as prescribed by the Comptroller of the Navy. These instructions are somewhat complicated, but they do provide for your reimbursement. Maintain a good count of blankets, crew's clothing (if you command a small ship and do not have ship's store clothing to use), food, and other equipment and supplies used in rescue operations. Your crew and your ship will be repaid. You are enjoined specifically, however, *not* to effect repairs to a merchant vessel in distress or in collision with you unless in your capacity as senior officer present you feel they are necessary to save life or to prevent the merchant vessel from sinking. If you do make such repairs you must report the cost of labor and materials in your subsequent letter report (again, to the Chief of Naval Operations and appropriate seniors).

Now that you know *what* you are supposed to do, and what *not* to do, a review of *how* you will do it is in order. The *SORN* contains sample bills which, when implemented, will enable you to meet most requirements. Article 630.15.6 provides for the rescue and assistance detail. This bill provides for rescue of survivors of plane crashes, ship sinkings, and other similar accidents. Article 630.16 describes a rescue of survivors bill and provides procedures for rescuing large numbers of survivors from the water. Article 640.2, aircraft crash and rescue bill, is a specific bill for the purpose of rescuing aircraft survivors. There is no specific bill provided for submarine rescue. If you are requested to assist a surfaced submarine treat it like any surface ship in distress. If it requires a tow, the submarine CO will be careful to warn you what underwater portions of the submarine to avoid while passing the line. If it is submerged you will have to try to find it by sonar search. If you are not so equipped, there will be help on the way soon. In the meantime you can search the area for evidence such as smoke flares or a communication buoy. Ships equipped with sonar can communicate with the submarine. The submarine may also have a wire antenna system, which may be usable for radio communication if it is undamaged and the water is shallow enough.

Refugees. The refugee situations in Southeast Asia and the Caribbean presented a problem which may persist to some extent for many years. If you are transiting these areas you may encounter small boats and even fair-sized freighters loaded with refugees. These unfortunate people may have gone for days without food and water and will present all forms of sickness and physical disability. A small ship may be hard pressed to provide the medical care and space that they will require. This kind of contingency has become commonplace in the Seventh Fleet, and there will be annexes to the standard Seventh Fleet operation order telling you exactly what to do, what reports to make, and how to get help. Your standard bills will suffice unless you are overwhelmed by sheer numbers.

Now that you have determined *how* you will handle SAR contingencies, and *what* problems you will be faced with, you should review the various manuals and orders which outline the assistance available to you, the responsibilities of your ship and other forces, and the means of communicating and reporting you will use.

The basic provisions of worldwide search and rescue are set forth in *NWP 37(A)*, titled *National Search and Rescue Manual*. This is a Coast Guard-originated work and it is essentially the same as *Coast Guard Publication CG-308*. You will find that it covers the United States, all of its adjacent maritime regions, and all overseas operating and cruising areas. It sets forth the duties of, and coordination among, all interested agencies. These include the Department of Defense, the Department of Commerce, the Department of the Treasury, the Federal Aviation Agency, the Federal Communications Commission, and the Civil Aeronautics Board. *NWP 37(A)* provides various military and civilian agencies with standard procedures for search and rescue.

The *National Search and Rescue Manual* has an unclassified addendum titled *Submarine Disaster Search and Rescue Operations* which outlines procedures particularly applicable to the search phase of peacetime submarine disaster SAR operations. There is also an unclassified supplement giving maritime SAR procedures which have been approved by the Joint Chiefs of Staff, including command relationships and responsibilities. *NWP 37–1*, titled *Search and Rescue Manual*, is yet to be issued, but it will provide guidance to units assigned SAR responsibilities. This manual will provide standardization of SAR procedures and techniques within the Navy. *ATP 10*, *Search and Rescue*, contains NATO SAR doctrine. An appendix contains Annex 12 to the *Convention of International Civil Aviation*, giving international standards and recommended practices for search and rescue.

The foregoing standard publications are implemented by the Commanders-in-Chief of the Atlantic and Pacific Fleets. They have SAR annexes to their standing operating plans. The Commanders of the numbered fleets also have such annexes. With all of these publications and the fleet plans appropriate to your area and chain of command, you have all the guidance you will need as to what to do. Your bills will tell you how to do it.

The remaining element of SAR is *when* to do it. You may simply run across some one at sea in need of help. If so, your course of action is obvious. However, most SAR incidents in which you will be involved will be initiated by someone else. The communications plan under which you will be operating will require that you guard the international distress frequency. You will hear calls for assistance directly on this frequency. Report these calls up through the chain of command, stating what action you intend to take. You will have to make a judgment as to whether you can reach the scene in time to help and whether your mission will permit you to divert. Usually the chain of command will know the location of other forces available and will quickly take over and decide what to do. You may also get orders directly from a senior, who has received his information by some other means than the distress frequency, such as by aerial sighting. In this case he will know the location of all available forces and will issue appropriate orders.

Man Overboard. One of the most common SAR efforts is a very short-range one: that of recovering a man overboard. If you are part of a formation, finding someone else's man becomes a problem of avoiding other units nearby, maneuvering in accordance with directions from CIC or by visual observation, and bringing the man aboard. Since we are discussing independent operations in this chapter, we will concentrate on the problems of a single ship.

The *SORN*, Article 640.5, contains a bill which covers training, responsibilities, actions, and many other details of man overboard procedure. You should, of course, have a complete man overboard bill patterned after this bill and adapted to your type. CIC and bridge watch personnel should be well qualified and instructed, and exercised frequently at drill.

The one area in which the standard bill is weak is in maneuvering advice, particularly for small ships. Lowering a boat for recovery is feasible less than fifty percent of the time at sea. Thus, the usual method of recovery for small ships is by maneuvering close to the man, throwing a line over the bow or side to him, or, if he is weakened, by sending a strong swimmer over the side with a line attached.

There are many methods of returning your ship to the man's location. The three most widely used methods are the Williamson turn, the *Anderson* turn, and the Y turn. Regardless of the method you use, an immediately established, meticulously kept CIC dead reckoning plot on the 200-yard scale is mandatory. If your special maneuvering method fails, CIC should then be able to assist you.

The Williamson turn is illustrated in Figure 13–11. This maneuver can be used by any type of ship, including carriers, cruisers, destroyers, submarines, amphibious ships, and single-screw vessels. As the diagram shows, it is well-adapted for use when the exact time a man fell overboard is not known, since after making the turn you can continue back along the previous track indefinitely. Its disadvantage is that it takes a long time to execute, and the ship moves so far from the man that sight of him may be lost. Practice making the turn with your ship, for variations in maneuvering characteristics may require some adjustment.

The *Richard B. Anderson* method, illustrated in Figure 13–12, was developed in 1952 by the commanding officer of the *Richard B. Anderson*, then-Commander W. P. Mack. It was promulgated to the destroyers of the Pacific Fleet and tested extensively by them both before and after promulgation. It was designed to be used by twin-screwed destroyers, and it is still widely used by them. Its main purpose is to bring the ship back to the man in a short time in cold weather or reduced visibility. The ship is kept as close as possible to the man, and the maneuver ends with the ship stopped and its bow usually within fifty to one hundred feet of the man. The average time for the turn is three minutes and forty-five seconds, well within survival time in cold water. The *Anderson* turn also provides a simple set of maneuvering instructions readily mastered by inexperienced officers of the deck. After the man is overboard and the initial orders are given to commence the turn (right full rudder, port ahead full, starboard back one third) the officer of the deck has about two minutes to give the necessary orders to make sound signals, pass the word, notify the captain, and otherwise prepare for recovery. The next step is a simple order, given when the ship has swung 240 degrees, to bring the rudder amidships and back all engines one

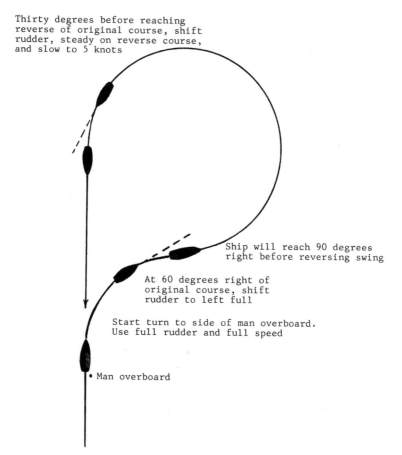

Thirty degrees before reaching
reverse of original course, shift
rudder, steady on reverse course,
and slow to 5 knots

Ship will reach 90 degrees
right before reversing swing

At 60 degrees right of
original course, shift
rudder to left full

Start turn to side of man overboard.
Use full rudder and full speed

• Man overboard

Figure 13-11. The *Williamson turn* can be used with modifications by any type of ship. If a man is overboard to port, reverse the procedure shown.

third. The third equally simple order is to stop all engines when way is off. The ship can then do further maneuvering, if required, but it is not usually necessary. One destroyer, in an actual recovery, sent the boatswains mate of the watch and a messenger to the forecastle.

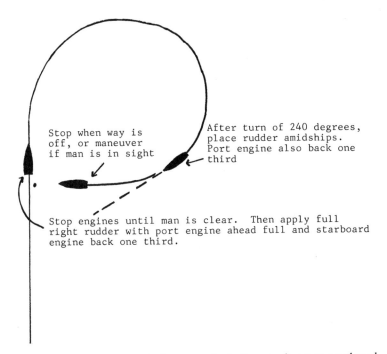

Stop when way is off, or maneuver if man is in sight

After turn of 240 degrees, place rudder amidships. Port engine also back one third

Stop engines until man is clear. Then apply full right rudder with port engine ahead full and starboard engine back one third.

Figure 13-12. *Richard B. Anderson* method of recovering man overboard, designed for use in cold weather, low visibility, or rough weather. Average time to complete the maneuver is three minutes and forty-five seconds.

These two men made the recovery using a line over the bow in three and one half minutes.

The Y turn, illustrated in Figure 13–13, is intended for use by submarines, but may be used by any type. It permits the submarine to stay as close as possible to the man without losing sight of him (this is important because of the submarine's low height of eye). This method is not adapted to low visibility, and for some surface ships, backing into a heavy sea can decrease control. Of all types, the submarine is best able to back into wind and sea because of low freeboard and small sail area.

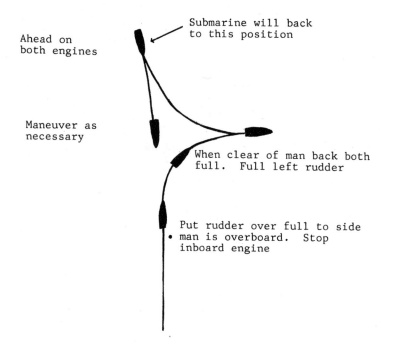

Figure 13-13. Y-backing method of man overboard recovery designed for submarines.

There are other recovery methods in use, notably the racetrack method, described in the *Watch Officer's Guide*, published by the Naval Institute Press. This method is designed for use in column, but in our opinion the *Anderson* turn is superior for this purpose.

Each commanding officer should experiment with his own ship to find out which method is best and to determine what modifications he should make to the standard methods.

Asylum. Every commanding officer who read the newspapers of the 1970s will remember the case of Simas Kudirka, a seaman serving in a Soviet fishing trawler off Martha's Vineyard. A Coast Guard cutter was alongside the trawler conducting a routine search for compliance with fishing regulations when Kudirka came topside, jumped over to the deck of the cutter, and asked for asylum. The trawler captain then asked that he be returned. The Coast Guard captain asked via radio for instructions from higher authority, and was told to allow the return of Kudirka. A party from the trawler was then allowed to board the cutter, bind and gag the man, and return him to the trawler. A subsequent investigation found serious errors in the proceedings and violations of strict standing instructions. Guilt assessed and punishment made is past history, and is relatively unimportant to this discussion. What is important is for each commanding officer to fix the proper asylum procedures in his mind.

As a result of the Kudirka incident, *Navy Regulations* now has much more specific instructions regarding asylum. Article 0940 states that any person requesting asylum on the high seas shall have it granted, and shall not be surrendered except at the personal direction of the Secretary of the Navy or higher authority. When in a foreign port, a request for asylum shall be granted only in extreme humanitarian cases, such as pursuit by a mob. Such protection can be terminated only by the Secretary of the Navy or higher authority. A request by foreign authorities for return of a refugee will be reported to the Chief of Naval Operations by immediate precedence message. However, though they must be protected, the regulations state clearly that persons shall not be *invited* to seek asylum.

The information and direction in Article 0940 should be adequate to handle any situation regarding asylum either ashore or afloat.

Harassment. Harassment by foreign forces may occur in many forms. The most common are direct overflights by Soviet aircraft, Soviet ships coming close aboard or shadowing closely astern, and shadowing by Soviet surveillance ships, either naval ships or trawlers. Harassment occurs most frequently when U. S. or NATO ships or groups of ships are engaged in exercises or other pursuits of technical interest to the Soviets such as missile test firings. They will try to interfere in any way possible. While you are on independent duty

Figure 13-14. The ubiquitous Soviet AGI takes its place in a U.S. Navy formation to shadow, observe, and collect intelligence.

you may be overflown by Soviet long range bombers or reconnaissance aircraft. Take pictures, if possible, and report the incident to the chain of command.

Attempted Boarding or Capture. The title of this section sounds like something out of the nineteenth century, but it is more likely than you may think. We hope that *Pueblo*-style incidents are no longer possible, but they must be considered and planned for.

The *Pueblo* incident in 1968 is well known. There are many opinions regarding the action taken by Cdr. Loyd Bucher, the commanding officer of the *Pueblo*. The official opinion, as expressed by the findings of the Board of Investigation, were, in simplified form, that his actions were incorrect. The final action of the Secretary of the Navy in setting aside these findings is not pertinent, since the rationale for doing so was based on factors extraneous to the principles involved. The opinions expressed as to what action Bucher should have taken range all the way from approval, with the rationale that resistance was useless and fighting the ship to the end would have resulted in the loss of many of the crew and the ultimate capture of any survivors, to the other end of the spectrum, that he should have had his guns ready (and not covered in iced canvas) and should have fought to the end.

The latter is the opinion held by most naval officers. Their reasons are best expressed in Article 0740, *Navy Regulations*, which states straightforwardly and unequivocally that a commanding officer shall not permit a ship under his command to be searched on any pretense whatsoever by any person representing a foreign state, nor shall he permit any of the personnel within the confines of his command to be removed by such person, so long as he has the capacity to repel such act. If force is used in an attempt, he is to resist to the utmost of his power. This leaves no room for doubt. You are to *resist to the utmost*.

Brochures. Descriptive brochures on foreign ports are available from the Naval Military Personnel Command and from the Commanders of the Sixth and Seventh Fleets. Be as forehanded as you can, and ask for a full set the first time you are in company with the flagship. They can provide the basis for comprehensive briefings for the crew as you steam toward your ports of call.

Crossing the Line. Several ceremonies, including crossing the line, may be necessary if operations cause you to cross the equator or the international date line. Again, the Naval Military Personnel Command has certificates which you can stock or order by mail. The crossing the line ceremony can be as elaborate as you and an enterprising and inventive crew want to make it. *Naval Ceremonies, Customs, and Traditions* contains a history of the ceremony and a sample scenario to help you make plans for your own. The ceremony of crossing the international date line is also described, and this too has a special certificate.

Other ceremonies can be held for those visiting the Arctic and the Antarctic, and for those who become golden shellbacks by crossing the intersection of the equator and the international date line.

Visits to a Foreign Port (Single Vessel)

Taking a pilot. As you approach port your next problem will be taking a pilot. *Navy Regulations*, Article 0754, covers your responsibility with regard to pilots. This article states that they are merely advisers. Pilots do not relieve you or your officers of any responsibility for the safe handling of the ship. The one exception is the Panama Canal, where the pilot does have control of the navigation and movement of your vessel (the Suez is *not* an exception). However, there have been at least two occasions in the last fifty years in the Panama Canal when commanding officers of battleships took over from the pilot in the lake and channel sections to avoid grounding, and had their actions subsequently upheld. These were cases where it was necessary to drop an anchor to control the heading of the battleships at sharp angles in the channel, and the pilot did not object. Nevertheless, be sure you are prepared to support your action if you relieve a Panama Canal pilot.

You may allow the pilot to handle your ship much as you would the officer of the deck, but you must maintain your own navigational plot and make sure that your helmsman and engine order telegraph operator are alerted to respond to your order if and when you feel it necessary to take over the conn. You may also simply use the pilot as an adviser and keep the conn yourself. Many pilots do not speak good English, and you will have to stand by to clarify their orders. Also, foreign pilots are accustomed to merchant ships and tend to give orders in their parlance. "Ahead slow" can be interpreted as "ahead one third." Be careful with "ahead full" if you are a destroyer type. The pilot doesn't *really* want twenty knots, so be sure you settle ahead of time as to what he wants when he asks for full. He generally is thinking about ahead standard, or fifteen knots. Orders to the helm may not be familiar to you, but these can be interpreted fairly easily.

The method of paying pilots varies. The *Supply Officer's Manual* will set forth various means. Most pilots and pilot associations will submit bills.

Pratique. Pratique will be your next occupation. Pratique is a French word meaning "the privilege of going ashore." The port health officer will board you either with the pilot or shortly after you are berthed. Remember that you are quarantined until he declares otherwise.

Navy Regulations require that you comply with all quarantine regulations for your port and that you cooperate with the local health authorities, and give them all health information available subject to the requirements of military security. Quarantine will remain in effect, as far as you are concerned, as long as you have doubt as to the sanitary regulations or health conditions of the port; and, from the health officer's point of view, if you have a quarantinable disease aboard or if you came from a port or area under quarantine. You must not conceal such conditions. Assuming that none of these problems exists, you will be granted pratique.

If, during your stay in port, a quarantinable condition arises aboard ship, you must hoist an appropriate signal to notify port authorities and the chain of command.

Boarding Officer's Call. A boarding officer will call on you at the first opportunity. Occasionally he will board with the pilot, or by separate boat as you are proceeding up the channel, but most frequently he will board just after you anchor or moor. In some ports he will have to wait until after pratique is granted. If there is another U. S. ship in port senior to you, he should still send a boarding officer to you with information and instructions. If you are senior, the other ship should send a boarding officer to you to ask when it would be convenient to turn over the SOPA files and duties, and for the commanding officer to call.

The more likely possibility is that you will be the lone U.S. ship in port. If so, the boarding call will come from one of several authorities, perhaps from several. If there is a U. S. naval attache ashore, he will usually call or send someone from his office. If there is no such naval presence, the consul or his representative will call. If there is a naval command of the host country, either ashore or afloat, it will send a representative. Otherwise, the mayor or his representative will call.

In any event, there will be one or more persons who will welcome you and your ship and from whom you can obtain information necessary for the implementation of your responsibilities as SOPA, or for your own ship if you are alone.

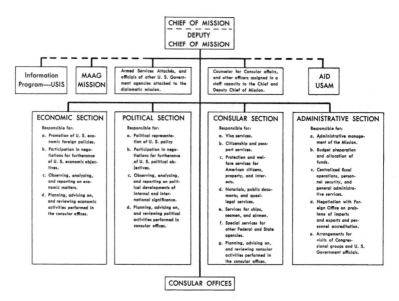

Figure 13-15. Basic organization of a typical United States diplomatic mission.

Relations with U. S. Governmental Officials Ashore

Early in your port visit, and on the occasion of your boarding call, you will make contact with U. S. governmental officials ashore. Figure 13–15 gives you an idea of the organization of a typical U. S. mission in a foreign port. The exact organization and its size will depend on the rank of its head. If the port is the capital of its country, the mission will be headed by an ambassador. This official is appointed by the President and is his personal representative to the head of state. If the port is not the capital, the mission will be called a consular office, and will be headed by a consul. This individual will be a member of the U. S. Foreign Service, if the city is large, and will be seasoned and skilled in his profession. If the port is small, the mission will be headed by a consular agent, appointed by the Secretary of State. He will usually be a local businessman, not necessarily a U. S. citizen, and his primary duties will involve administration of shipping affairs.

Your duties as SOPA will probably require that you visit the mission frequently. A short description of the people you will meet will help you to seek the right persons to solve your problem. The Ambassador, if you are involved with one, may be a political appointee with no previous diplomatic experience. He will, however, be a person of individual achievement and probably will be knowledgeable and communicative.

If not a political appointee, he will be a career member of the Foreign Service. The Foreign Service is the sixth federal service, and is a professional corps of men and women specially selected and trained to carry out the foreign policy of our nation in day-to-day relations with other countries. There are approximately 8,000 members serving abroad in 300 posts in 100 countries. The foreign service officer has a basic designation known as his "class." Class establishes his seniority for internal purposes. He also holds a title, which is his assignment. You will also encounter Foreign Service staff officers and employees who are clerks or typists, and other administrative personnel. Local people will also be employed in supporting roles.

You will enjoy your relations with the embassy or mission personnel. They will be anxious to help, and they in turn will ask for your help in furthering the good image of the United States in the port. This can be done by a people-to-people program, by allowing general visiting, or by personal relations with local governmental and business people. Also, as your career advances, you will meet these same officials later in Washington, or in other ports. The *Naval Officer's Guide*, published by the Naval Institute Press, gives a more detailed explanation of the operations of a U. S. mission in a foreign country.

The Statesmen's Yearbook, published annually by St. Martin's Press of New York, would be a useful addition to your personal library or that of the ship. You can request one from the Naval Military Personnel Command. It is a compendium of information about foreign countries, including descriptions of each, starting with the name of our ambassador and other U. S. governmental officials in that country, and covering the culture, religions, economy, demography, and other aspects. A study of the writeup for each country before you visit will be of great help.

In the absence of such a publication, we include the following short descriptions of the type of governmental officials to be found in the ports you are likely to visit.

Japan. The U. S. Ambassador is located in Tokyo, about thirty miles from Yokosuka (but about two hours by car). You will not need to call on him. The Commander, Naval Forces Japan is located on the naval base at Yokosuka, and you should call on him. He will advise you whether or not the current mayor of Yokosuka desires calls. He will also advise which, if any, calls you should make on commanding officers of ships of the Japanese Maritime Self Defense Force. The SOPA or SOP at Sasebo will advise you concerning calls there. All other Japanese ports have mayors and U. S. consuls. The consul will advise concerning calls. Most Japanese mayors like to meet ships and may be at the pier to greet you. They may also bring a gift. Open it there and admire it. Originally the Japanese did not open gifts until alone, but over the years they have adopted our custom of opening them on receipt. At some later occasion make a return gift. Treat your callers courteously; they can make or break your visit.

Hong Kong. Hong Kong is a British colony with a British governor. The U. S. naval attache will call and advise you. Unless you command a large ship, you probably will not call on the governor or ambassador because of the many U. S. ships calling at the port.

Taiwan. The United States, for political reasons, no longer maintains an embassy at Taiwan. There is an informal trade mission located at Taipei, but it maintains a low profile and will not want to be involved with you. There is a U. S. consul in Taipei who will take care of you.

Guam. Guam is a U. S. Commonwealth under an appointed civilian governor. The senior U. S. naval officer stationed there is the

Commander Naval Forces, Marianas Islands. His staff will advise concerning calls and other matters.

Philippines. The Philippines is a republic, headed by a president. The government and our ambassador are located in the city of Manila, at the head of Manila Bay. If you visit Manila the naval attache will advise you. Your most likely port of call will be Subic Bay (sometimes spelled Subig Bay), which is several miles north of the entrance to Manila Bay. Land transportation between Manila and Subic is impracticable. The Commander, U. S. Naval Forces Philippines is located at Subic Bay Naval Base and his staff will advise you. Your contacts with U. S. and Filipino government officials will be minimal and no calls will be required except upon the Base Commander.

Hawaii. Since Hawaii is a state, no calls are expected on U. S. governmental officials. You will be berthed at Pearl Harbor. Calls upon senior naval officers in the chain of command have been discussed separately. If you are so fortunate as to visit other ports, such as Hilo or Lahaina, calls on local mayors are in order.

Singapore. Singapore is an independent sovereign state. Your port of call will be Singapore City, which is also the capital. The naval attache will call to brief you on necessary calls on state and city officials and on British naval officers in residence.

You may also make port visits in the Pacific to other, more distant ports in Australia, the Malay Barrier, and the Indian Ocean, but space does not permit including them here.

Spain. Rota is the port you are most likely to visit in Spain. You will berth at the U. S. Naval Base and will be advised concerning calls on U. S. naval and Spanish officials.

Gibraltar. Gibraltar is a possession of Great Britain under a governor. It is a free port. The U. S. consul will advise as to calls to be made on local governmental officials and British naval commanders.

Malta. Malta is seldom used now as a port of call because of political sensitivities and difficulties with the past and current heads of state. If you are to visit, Commander Sixth Fleet will undoubtedly brief you as to what you are to do.

France. You will make numerous port visits to the resort ports of the Riviera. French governmental officials are generally somewhat aloof and have gotten used to U. S. port visits. The consul in each port will advise you.

Italy. The larger ports of Italy are also somewhat bored with visiting U. S. ships. The Consul will advise you as to the feeling in his port. If you are fortunate enough to visit the smaller, less blasé ports, you will have a more enjoyable time. If no U. S. consul is present, call on the mayor. Italian hospitality will take care of the rest.

Greece. Piraeus, the port of Athens, can be a difficult visit. Most of the residents are communist or communist-oriented and resent U. S. sailors. Warn your liberty parties about this. The naval attache in Athens will arrange calls there and advise as to the current situation in Piraeus.

Africa. The countries of the north coast of Africa are so diverse in their politics that it is difficult to describe them. If you are sent on a port visit to one, the Commander Sixth Fleet will advise you.

Visits may also be made to Turkish, Egyptian, and Israeli ports when the political situation permits, but politics are so fluid that the Commander Sixth Fleet will advise you on each occasion.

Northern Europe. Port visits to Great Britain, the Netherlands, and Scandinavian countries will be great privileges. In almost all ports here you will be welcomed eagerly and treated well. The calls you will make will depend on local conditions and the size of the port. The U. S. consuls will advise.

Duties as SOPA

Once you have anchored or moored your ship and have received pratique, customs clearance, and your boarding call, you must get on with your duties as SOPA. These are all covered in *Navy Regulations*. You might wish that all you had to do was look out for the safety of your own crew and ship, arrange liberty, and look forward to a pleasant visit, but this is only the beginning. As SOPA, you are the representative of your country and your Navy in that port, and you can be called upon to execute a great many duties.

Security. Your first duty is to look out for the *safety of your ship.*

Ensure that you have a safe mooring, access to weather reports, an assigned typhoon or hurricane mooring if applicable, a method of recalling your crew, and adequate internal security including sentries, watches, locked limited access doors, and proper boat landing and securing facilities, if anchored out. With this done you can turn to your next priority, liberty arrangements.

Leave and Liberty. Article 0921 of *Navy Regulations* requires you as SOPA to regulate leave and liberty in conformance with any orders you may have, such as from a fleet commander or a local U. S. military authority. If you have no specific guidance or authority, issue your own, having due regard to information obtained from local officials as to vice and dangerous areas and local curfews.

Shore Patrol. With the privilege of leave and liberty goes the requirement to establish a shore patrol. Article 0922 of *Navy Regulations* requires that a shore patrol be established whenever liberty is granted to a considerable number of persons, except in an area that can absorb them without danger of disturbance or disorder. The purpose of a patrol of officers, petty officers, and non-commissioned officers, if Marines are embarked, is to maintain order and to suppress unseemly conduct. A lesser but not specifically stated reason is to provide for the safety of your crew ashore. This article goes on to require that the senior shore patrol officer communicate with the chief of police or local officials and make such arrangements as may be practicable to aid the patrol in carrying out its duties. Such duties would include providing assistance to your crew in their relations with police and local courts, including release to your custody.

With regard to the first requirement, which seems to require a patrol only if the liberty area cannot absorb your crew, it is wise to establish a small patrol even though your ship is small and the port is big. Any man getting in trouble usually ends up at the police station, and it is good to have a representative there to look out for him, even though no street patrols are thought necessary.

You must, of course, obtain permission from local authorities to land the patrol, and if permission is denied you must restrict the size of liberty parties accordingly. Overseas the patrol must not be armed, but some countries will permit them to carry nightsticks. Remember to have your executive officer warn the members of the patrol that they may not indulge in intoxicants at any time when assigned to shore patrol.

Provisions and Supplies. Presumably your supply officer will be off attempting to obtain fresh provisions and stock for your ship's store. He should check first with the U. S. military force present or with the embassy or consulate to see if any contracts exist for this purpose. If they do, his paperwork and time spent are very much reduced, and he can get on with his ordering. If not, he will have to go through the time-consuming process of soliciting bids, awarding contracts, and then placing orders. Even these longer processes will be worthwhile, though, for the fresh produce will be welcome and the "exotic" ship's store stock can be sold at sea to produce added profits for recreation funds.

Calls. All of these arrangements sound complicated, but they actually proceed together and do not take too much of your time. Your personal occupation this first day will be to find out from the boarding officer which calls you should make and to get on with arranging them. Since we have assumed that there are no other U. S. ships present, your attention will be ashore first. Article 0911, *Navy Regulations*, requires that the SOPA preserve close relations with the diplomatic and consular representative of the United States. You must consider requests, recommendations, and other communications from such individuals, although the final responsibility for your acts as SOPA is yours. Obviously you should call on the ambassador, if there is one, or the consul at the earliest opportunity.

Article 0912, *Navy Regulations*, requires that you communicate with foreign civil, diplomatic, and consular officials through the local United States diplomatic consular representatives. You are not *required* to communicate or call, but it will be helpful if you have time to do so.

You should make arrangements through the embassy or consulate to call upon senior governmental officials of the host country.

If there are host country military forces present ashore, ask the advice of the embassy or consulate regarding calling.

If there are host country naval forces afloat, arrange a call on their

SOPA. They will probably already have sent a calling officer to see you with the boarding officer.

If there are other foreign naval vessels present use your own judgment about calling. Allied commanding officers will probably receive you enthusiastically. Soviet Bloc commanding officers are unpredictable. When you ask by message to call you may either be ignored or receive a warm invitation. If you are invited, by all means go; you will learn a lot.

You and your officers may receive invitations to use military messes and civilian clubs ashore. If so, arrange to have one or more of your wardroom officers call at the messes and clubs and leave cards. A letter of thanks after departure is also in order. Wardroom-to-wardroom calls are common in the British, Canadian, and Australian Navies. This is a fine custom, and your officers will enjoy it. They can expect a liberal alcoholic welcome anytime after noon. A word to your officers on what to expect would be wise. The Commonwealth officer is long conditioned to handling liquor on board ship. His mess will have an open bar, but if he is observed carefully it will be noted that even though he may drink *often*, he does not drink *much* at a time. He will always be ready for duty. American guests, however, will be plied with strong drinks under the guise of hospitality. Your young officers will do well to follow their hosts' example. *Drink often*, but not *much*, and stick to the soft stuff if possible. British beer is warm but good. Canadian naval messes are somewhat sedate; Australian, just the opposite. The French and Italian naval messes are less outgoing, as is their peoples' nature, but their hospitality will be worth enjoying. The Japanese Navy will be cordial, but formal, and will serve tea rather than strong drinks. All of these nationalities by now are conditioned to making "dry" return calls on your mess. They will always appreciate *fresh* American coffee, and ice cream will be very welcome.

Finally, read Articles 1040 through 1049 of *Navy Regulations*. These cover in great detail your responsibilities regarding calls in a foreign port, and fill in some of the details omitted in the preceding summary of calls.

Honors and Ceremonies. Honors and ceremonies are particularly

Figure 13-16. A ship is evaluated, particularly in foreign ports, by the smartness of its quarterdeck, and the manner in which it renders honors.

important to foreign navies. We tend to play them down, under the theory that sheer power is the most important ingredient of any navy. Foreign navies, lacking in power, depend instead for prestige on the careful and exact carrying out of ceremonies and honors, which they look upon as the true indicators of a respectable navy. We can play in this league, too, and we should. *Navy Regulations*, Chapter 10, sets forth the honors and ceremonies required in foreign ports. Careful study of them and instruction of your quarterdeck crew, boat crews, officers of the deck, and signal gang can ensure that your ship excels.

By now your initial duties will have been completed and your calls will be well on their way. You will also have taken care of all the miscellaneous duties of the SOPA. Try to get ashore for a little personal recreation and sightseeing before the rest of the social routine closes in on you. You will soon be receiving return calls and accepting invitations ashore. These will lead in turn to the possibility of scheduling lunches aboard to return hospitality. Some ships have an open house aboard the last day before leaving port as a convenient way for all hands to return favors.

This is an appropriate time to suggest that you research the *Supply Manual* and appropriate type and fleet directives to find out what source of funds you have to help defray these entertainment costs. A little research and a few message requests will "pay off."

There are many other occasional but important duties that you will fall heir to as SOPA. If there are other ships present you will be responsible for the coordination of all the foregoing actions for all ships. You must also take command if concerted action is necessary for mutual defense or for safety against weather.

Using Military Force. With regard to the use of military force within the territorial waters of another state, Articles 0914, 0915, and 0916 of *Navy Regulations* are very specific. When injury to U. S. citizens is committed or threatened in violation of a treaty or international law, the SOPA must consult with diplomatic or consular representatives if possible, and shall take such action as is demanded by the gravity of the situation. In time of peace, action by United States Navy personnel against any other nation, or against any one within the territories thereof, either an actual use of force or a threat to use force, is illegal unless as an act of self-defense. You are required to exercise sound judgment and to assert this right only as a last resort.

Landing Forces for Exercise. In a more peaceful vein, you may not, in a foreign country, land a force for exercise, target practice, or funeral escort unless permission has been granted. You may not land a force to capture deserters. You may not conduct target practice with guns, torpedoes, rockets, or missiles at any point where these can enter territorial waters.

Medical and Dental Assistance. In a more routine vein, you are required by Article 0924 to render medical and dental assistance to persons not in the naval service when such aid is necessary and demanded by the laws of humanity or the principle of international courtesy.

Marriage Abroad. While you are attempting to relax, you may find the interlude broken by some of your other SOPA duties. One of them will occur when one of your officers or men conducts a romantic campaign ashore and comes to you asking to be married. Fleet regulations will cover the subject; refer first to them. If your ship is big enough to have a legal officer you are in clover. If not, you or one of your officers will have to visit the embassy or consulate to determine the local laws and to help your swain fill out the necessary forms. Hopefully his ardor will cool when he sees the paperwork difficulties and delays he will face, or, if not, he will take charge himself and get them done without involving too much of your time.

Marriage Aboard Ship. If still in the ball game, your man may ask to be married aboard ship. This matter is regulated by Article 0716, *Navy Regulations.* This article is somewhat peculiarly phrased. It starts out by flatly prohibiting you from performing marriage aboard ship. It then, in a rather awkward and negative way, states that you may not *permit* a marriage to be performed aboard ship when outside the territory of the United States, but it then gives certain exceptions. The ceremony must be in accordance with the local laws and the laws of the state, territory, or district in which both parties are domiciled, and must take place only in the presence of a diplomatic or consular official of the United States who has consented to make the certificate and returns required by the consular regulations. From the tenor of the article it can be assumed that the Secretary of the Navy takes a negative view of marriage performed aboard ship. Be very sure you want to do so before going through the bureaucratic necessities involved. Your man will probably be just as happy being married ashore.

In summary, you as commanding officer *cannot* yourself conduct a marriage ceremony aboard ship. A chaplain, if you have one or can borrow one, *can* perform a marriage ceremony aboard if you comply with Article 0716.

SOPA Files. The boarding officer, if he is a U. S. naval or consular person, will probably have delivered to you the SOPA file of previous visitors. It will be of help to you. Update it and return it to the same person or to the senior U. S. commanding officer remaining in port after you depart.

People-to-People Programs. From time to time fleet commanders require that ships conduct people-to-people programs. You may also want to conduct one independently. You will find that your crew will be responsive and even enthusiastic if it is suggested that they visit orphans ashore or invite them aboard ship, donate food to the poor, or take other, more innovative action. Your crew will do best if they are allowed to initiate the kind and amount of response. Be sure that you check any proposed action with embassy or consular officials ashore before carrying it out. You will avoid possible embarrassment to both of you if there is a political situation ashore that only the embassy or consular staff is aware of.

Hopefully, as part of your POM preparation, you will have been told about the White House "Food for Peace" programs set forth in the Executive Order of 24 January, 1961, and supported by *OPNAV-INST 5726.1* series. *OPNAVINST 5726.2* and *5726.3* describe "Project Handclasp," which provides materials and gifts such as toys for unfortunate foreign nationals. The Sixth and Seventh Fleet Commanders will also have souvenirs and materials that will promote the Navy's interests. If you have any of these aboard they can form the nucleus of your people-to-people program. The best material you can have, however, is the enthusiasm and friendliness of the American bluejacket.

Conduct of Officers and Men. Navy Regulations requires you to instruct your enlisted men as to their conduct ashore. They will stand out from the locals in their uniforms and even in their civilian clothes, when they are permitted to wear them, and will bear the brunt of any criticism for misconduct ashore. It is especially important, and many times overlooked, to instruct your junior officers as well. They will all be in civilian clothes and will therefore think

Figure 13-17. The American bluejacket is our country's best ambassador. Prepare him to carry out this role by thorough briefings in the culture of the area to be visited.

themselves less obvious. In fact, because of their neat haircuts, clean clothes, and generally excellent appearance, they will be recognized in every port. Counsel them to use the utmost discretion, particularly in public places, and to conduct themselves as they would in their own home towns. Foreign ports offer every kind of vice known to man. Your officers must lead the way in setting a good example in practicing restraint, if not abstinence.

Article 0917, *Navy Regulations*, enjoins you to uphold the prestige of the United States. Impress upon your officers and men, when in foreign ports, that it is their duty to avoid all possible causes of offense to the inhabitants; that due deference must be shown by them

Figure 13-18. Independent operations will often bring you to such interesting ports as Rio de Janeiro.

to local laws and customs, ceremonies, and regulations; that moderation and courtesy should be displayed in all dealings with foreigners; and that a feeling of good will and mutual respect should be cultivated. Your crew will represent our country well if you have instructed them.

Ship's Boats. Article 0974, *Navy Regulations*, states that ship's boats shall be regarded as part of their ship in all matters concerning the rights, privileges, and comity of nations. In ports where war, insurrection, or armed conflict exists or threatens, you must have an appropriate and competent person in charge of each boat, and take steps to make the nationality of your boats evident at all times. This translates into flying a flag whenever the boat is away from the ship and having a boat officer or competent petty officer assigned. On some occasions the coxswain, if rated and competent in your eyes, may be enough. A deck chief petty officer is appropriate in most circumstances, particularly in small ships with few officers. The rank or rate of your boat officers is purely a matter of your judgment of their competence and the seriousness of the situation ashore and afloat.

Admiralty Claims and Reports. If a U. S. naval or merchant vessel collides with or otherwise damages a foreign vessel or pier in the port where you are SOPA you will have certain responsibilities with regard to processing claims against the United States and rendering consequent reports. Article 0926, *Navy Regulations*, states that you shall process claims in accordance with the procedures set forth in the *Manual of the Judge Advocate General of the Navy*. If you have a legal officer assigned you will be fortunate. If not, you may seek legal assistance from the embassy or consulate. You have limited authority to institute libel proceedings against a foreign vessel in a collision case. However, the *Manual* points out that the matter is within the primary cognizance of the Department of Justice. In view of your limited legal knowledge and experience and short time in port you will do well to heed this advice and leave it to the professionals.

Relations between the SOPA and the SOP. In a few foreign ports, but in many U. S. ports, you will find U. S. military forces ashore.

Τhis brings up the subject of the relations between you, as SOPA, and the SOP ashore. Article 0901, *Navy Regulations*, states that in a locality within an area prescribed by competent authority the senior officer present shall be the senior line officer of the Navy on active duty eligible for command at sea, who is present and in command of any part of the Department of the Navy, except where both Navy and Marine Corps personnel are present on shore and the Marine Corps officer is senior. In such cases the officer of the Marine Corps shall be the senior officer present ashore.

Article 0903 then gives the senior officer present the authority to assume command and to direct the efforts of all persons in the Navy Department present, when, in his judgment, the exercise of authority is necessary. He must exercise his authority in a manner consistent with the full operational command vested in the commanders of unified or specified commands.

The import of these articles is that you must maintain close liaison with the SOP ashore. Commanding officers afloat tend to continue the independence they exercised at sea when they are in port. While you are still independent in certain matters, you must recognize the limitations upon you. Article 0930 specifically states that you must refer all matters affecting the afloat units under you to the Senior Officer Present, either Naval or Marine Corps, ashore. He will not, however, expect literal interpretation of the requirement.

In the event that you as SOPA are senior to the SOP ashore, you must take other considerations into account. Article 0931 describes your general duties and states that as the common superior of all commanders of all naval units in that locality, except such units as may be assigned to shore units by competent authority, you are responsible for matters which collectively affect these commands. You are charged not to concern yourself with administrative matters within other commands, except to the extent necessary to secure uniformity and coordination of effort. You will assume command of all units of the operating forces of the Navy present in case of emergency or enemy attack.

Article 0932 then elaborates on relations with commanders ashore on the level of the Commandant of a Naval District. You are not likely to be senior to such a commander and will not be concerned with this problem.

Powers of Consul. If you are in a foreign port small enough not to have a consul, you may be required to exercise these powers. Article 0935, *Navy Regulations*, states that when upon the high seas, or in any foreign port where there is no resident consul of the United States, the SOPA has the authority to exercise all powers of consul in relation to mariners of the United States.

Article 1144 gives you the authority to issue rations to destitute seamen and airmen. The supply officer making such issue shall do so pursuant to an order in writing from you and shall procure receipts for such supplies in accordance with the *Naval Supply System Command Manual*. Article 0734 permits you to receive distressed seamen on board for rations and passage to the United States provided they agree to abide by *Navy Regulations*. You may also accept merchant seaman prisoners for transport provided that the witnesses against them are also received or adequate means are adopted to ensure the presence of such witnesses at the place where the prisoners are to be detained. Article 0927 states that you may not authorize repairs to a merchant vessel in collision with a Navy ship unless the exigency of war or national defense so requires. You may, however, authorize or perform repairs to save lives or prevent sinking. If you do so you must submit a report of repairs including labor and material costs and a certification as to why repairs were undertaken.

Protection of Commerce. Today, when the mission of the Navy seems to all of us to be the maintenance of the national security of our country, we tend to forget that historically the Navy was created to protect commerce. Article 0920 will remind you that you are required, while acting in conformity with international law and treaty obligations, to protect, insofar as it lies within your power, all commercial craft of the United States and to advance the commercial interests of your country.

International Law and Treaties. Article 1124 requires that in your regulations with foreign nations, and with governments and agents thereof, you shall conform to international law and to the precedents established by the United States in such relations. You are separately enjoined to report to higher authority any violation of international law or treaty both by U. S. citizens and by foreign nationals and their governments. Your reports in these matters should go to the Fleet Commander and the Chief of Naval Operations, and as a matter of courtesy should also be reported to the local ambassador or consul.

NWIP 10–2, Law of Naval Warfare, presents and amplifies international law as related to naval warfare, and legal restrictions on methods and weapons. It provides guidance on the legal status of ships, aircraft, and personnel engaged in naval warfare, and the actions permitted against them under international law. The legal divisions of the sea and air are described, as well as areas in which belligerent naval operations are permitted, and the restrictions on belligerents in neutral jurisdiction. Those treaties which are the principal sources of the laws of naval warfare and the U. S. armed forces code of conduct are presented in appendices to this publication.

Foreign Civil Jurisdiction. The United States Senate, in giving its advice and consent to the NATO Status of Forces Agreement, resolved that safeguards would be provided to protect persons subject to U. S. military jurisdiction who are to be tried by foreign authorities. In implementing the resolution, the Department of Defense directed that in each unified command the commander would designate within each member country a "commanding officer" to ensure that such safeguards are provided. DOD Directive 5525.1 series, SecNav Instruction 5820.3 series, SecNav Instruction 5820.4 series, SecNav Instruction 5820.5 series, and JAG Instruction 5820.1 series apply. Both fleet commanders-in-chief also have issued instructions on this subject. This practice was first started to cover the needs of NATO members, but has now been enlarged to extend the same protection to all U. S. personnel serving abroad, as far as is possible.

Local SOPA regulations should normally cover the basic procedures for dealing with a foreign jurisdictional problem, but in small ports, where such regulations may be sketchy, you will have to take steps on your own. You should first require your officers and those of any other U. S. ship in port to report to you instances where personnel have become subject to foreign jurisdiction. When this occurs you should request a waiver of criminal jurisdiction and release of the person involved. Do so through the standing shore patrol organization, if one exists, or through your own. Notify your next senior in command and other seniors as high as necessary to reach one who has authority to convene a general court-martial. Make sure a U. S. observer attends the trial. This should be one of your own officers if you are still in port. Otherwise, ask the consul to observe and report to you. You should advise and assist the person concerned, helping him to retain counsel, paying his trial expenses, and paying his bail. You may pay for these contingencies. The Act of July 24, 1956 (*10 U. S. Code 1037*) authorizes the Secretary of the Navy to employ counsel and pay counsel fees, court costs, bail, and other expenses required for representation before foreign tribunals and agencies of any person subject to the *Uniform Code of Military Justice*. Where serious incidents are involved (a six-month sentence, the death of a foreign national, poor treatment of prisoners, refusal of permission to visit a prisoner, etc.), message reports up through the chain of command are required, with the Judge Advocate General an information addressee.

U. S. Civil Jurisdiction. Article 0729, *Navy Regulations*, prohibits you from delivering personnel serving under you to U. S. civil authorities except as provided by the *Manual of the Judge Advocate General*. Study it carefully and abide strictly by its provisions. There will probably be a large ship or station nearby where you can seek legal help. This same article authorizes you to permit the serving of a subpoena or other legal process as provided by *Manual of the Judge Advocate General*. There will frequently be occasions where your men will be detained by civil authority ashore. Usually you can seek legal help from other naval sources. Make every effort to see that your men get help. If possible, one of your officers should appear at the jail and in court.

Public Relations. Public relations is a major personal responsibility of every commanding officer. We discuss it in this chapter on independent operations because it is most likely to be a problem when you are operating independently. You will have to deal with

Figure 13-19. These visitors observing flight operations will carry away a good impression of the Navy.

both the positive and negative aspects of public relations in any situation that develops, not only with your own ship, but with regard to any situation involving the Navy or the United States. This translates as follows. If something *bad* happens (negative aspect), you will have to explain what happened and what is being done to correct the situation. Further, if something *good* (positive aspect) *doesn't* happen in the normal course of events, it will be up to you to *create* some positive situation, such as a people-to-people program or a press tour of your ship, so that the U. S. Navy will be seen in a good light.

When you are operating independently this responsibility will devolve upon you. When you are operating under another commander, it will be your responsibility to assist him in the unit's public relations effort, and at the same time to carry out your ship's responsibilities even though you are part of a unit. In other words, public relations is always a problem for, and a responsibility of, every commanding officer at all times.

Your basic guidance for public relations is the *Chief of Information* (CHINFO) *Manual*. Its full title is *U. S. Navy Public Affairs Manual (NAVSO P-1035)*. It covers every aspect of public relations, which, by definition, is the total of your relations with the public, including your relations with the press, public, families, congressmen, and other groups. *Public information* is a limited part of public relations, involving the giving (or withholding) of information to the various media (television, radio, newspapers, and magazines) and to those parts of the public who either want it or, in your judgment, or the view of CHINFO, should be exposed to it. The *Manual* will tell you how to approach the mechanics of public information.

Your public affairs assistant is responsible to you for carrying out the ship's public affairs program. The *SORN*, Article 303.111, outlines his duties, responsibilities, and authority. Subparagraph c., in describing his organizational position, states that he reports to you via the executive officer. This is certainly organizationally correct for all of the other ship's officers, but for the public affairs assistant it is pure poison. Public affairs assistants at all levels, from the White House to the Secretary of the Navy's office to your ship, must have direct and instant access to the commander. Put your PAO in the prescribed organizational box for normal routine, but if you want to avoid disaster, make sure that he and the executive officer both understand his authority to consult with you and to advise you directly at any time of the day or night. He should, of course, fill in the executive officer at the first opportunity after seeing you.

If you understand this, you are now ready to consider a few simple rules which will keep you out of trouble.

First, don't be afraid of reporters. They have a job to do and will ask frank and sometimes embarrassing questions. Treat their questions as opportunities to get across the points that you want to make. You do *not* have to answer every question. You may decline to answer and give a reason for not answering, or you may simply say "no comment." Second, if you have bad news to present, give it all at once and as fully and frankly as you can. If you don't, and it comes out piecemeal, the effect on the media will be to intensify and prolong the negative atmosphere. Third, if you want to tell a positive story about your ship's or crew's activities, carefully prepare a release, give it your personal attention, and make sure your PAO gives it to the press and other local media at a time that allows them to meet their deadlines.

This may seem like a lot of detail to devote to this subject, but we want to underline the increasing importance of telling the Navy's story to the public. The public and the Congress must know what the Navy does and what it needs, and must feel a personal relationship with us. It is your responsibility to produce these results, and you must take part personally and enthusiastically in the public affairs program, afloat, ashore, and overseas.

Asylum. Earlier in this chapter, we outlined the requirements for a commanding officer to grant asylum at sea. The same requirements exist in port and are covered completely in Article 0940, *Navy Regulations.* Be conversant with them. If an incident occurs it will happen quickly and without warning. Your actions should be both informed and automatic.

As your port visit draws to a close you have, we hope, carried out your social responsibilities, fulfilled your duties as SOPA, looked out for the many and varied interests of your navy and your country, bailed your men out of jail, withdrawn your shore patrol, paid all of your ship's bills, and squeezed in a little personal recreation and sightseeing. Now you are more than ready to get underway. Independent duty, and being SOPA, are rewarding experiences, but they are also demanding. Rejoining the fleet or visiting your next port with other, bigger ships will now have a sweeter taste than ever.

The Rewards of Independent Operation

As you steam quietly out of the harbor and set course to rejoin, take time to recall the contingencies you either met or avoided on your independent duty. You can return to your unit secure in the knowledge that you have met the same physical challenges mastered by generations of mariners and some more modern administrative challenges they never dreamed of. The commanding officer of a naval vessel is truly "a man for all seasons." He meets Theodore Roosevelt's description of the man who dares great things. Roosevelt said:

> The credit belongs to the man who is actually in the arena, whose face is marred with sweat and dirt and blood; who strives valiantly; who errs and comes short again and again; who knows the great enthusiasms, the great devotions, and spends himself on a worthy cause; who, if he wins, knows the triumph of high achievement; and who, if he fails, at least fails while daring greatly, so that his place will never be with those cold and timid souls who know neither victory nor defeat.

With the fleet you are, unfortunately, part of the herd. You will have the protection of the herd, but few challenges. Independent duty places upon you, and you alone, the responsibility for meeting challenges with determined, positive action. We hope the accumulated wisdom and information of this volume will help. Accept responsibility; enjoy it; it is what your profession is all about.

LOGREQ. Finally, as you are enjoying the last few days of your independent duty, remember to submit your Logistics Requirement Report. *NWP-7*, page 7–2, outlines its requirements. If you fail to make it, or don't do so promptly or fully, your homecoming will be marred. Make it properly and you will find fuel, food, provisions, mail, pratique, customs clearance, and all those good things you have been dreaming about waiting for you.

Welcome home.

14

Combat Operations

To be born to create, to love, to win at games—is to be born to live in times of peace. But war teaches us to lose everything and become what we were not. It all becomes a question of style.

—Milton, *Comus*

In this chapter we will deal with combat operations.

We will first examine the nature of the most likely of the kinds of wars possible, and then the requirements which these kinds and combinations of wars and confrontations will place upon naval forces. We will then discuss the general preparations each commanding officer should undertake to prepare for these conflicts, and follow this with a few combat "housekeeping" hints. Finally, we will discuss combat attitude and philosophy.

In examining the nature of the next war, we must first recall and analyze past wars and operations, such as World Wars I and II, Vietnam, and Korea. We *may* have a repetition of those styles of combat, and we *must*, therefore, be prepared for all of them; but "the percentages" make us predict that the *next* war will not be like the *last*. We should, then, review *all* of the kinds of warfare a warship might take part in, and then discuss how you should prepare for each.

You will do well at this point to read *Grand Strategy*, by John M. Collins, published by the Naval Institute Press. This is a review of our country's past and present national security policies, and the kinds of threats we will face in the future.

Our government has a plan postulating the kinds of warfare we will most likely face. Each echelon of the Defense Department, starting with the Joint Chiefs, has similar plans designed to implement this national strategy. These plans, as you would expect, are top secret. You will not have access to many of them. You should, however, read *NWP-1, Strategic Concepts of the U.S. Navy*, which provides a basis for the development of naval force requirements to support national security objectives, as well as foreign and domestic policies. Part II of this document establishes a basic system for the employment planning of the Navy's operating forces, on both a long and short term basis, and defines concepts for execution of current operations and for the derivation of the operational planning factors required for program formulation and readiness analysis. This publication will help you understand the problems of upper-level planning, but it will not address your own. You can do that better yourself. We will try to help.

We *cannot* here use any of the foregoing plans or NWP-1 as a basis for discussion, not only because most of them are classified, but because they do not concern themselves with the local problems you will have as a commanding officer.

We *can* summarize the possible kinds of conflicts and combinations of kinds of conflicts from history and our own experience, and by logical deduction from facts and publications in the public domain. The following discussion starts with the most serious type of warfare and concludes with the simplest kind of confrontation. There will undoubtedly be combinations of these kinds of warfare and near-warfare, and we will also discuss these groupings.

Possible Kinds of Warfare

All-Out Strategic Nuclear Exchange. From SALT talk information released to the public we know that both the Western powers and the Soviet Bloc powers have stockpiled large numbers of nuclear weapons and many delivery systems. Even a cursory study of the *Communist Manifesto*, which states that the Communists will use any means to destroy their enemies, should convince you that the Soviets will not hesitate to use nuclear weapons whenever they think it will be in their best interests to do so, and that they will not hesitate to make a preemptive attack if they feel it advantageous. It is the task of our armed forces to deter such attack by demonstrating readiness, strength, and the invulnerability of our nuclear strike forces. Our Navy nuclear forces, composed of Trident and Poseidon submarines and aided by nuclear-capable carrier attack aircraft, are the heart of the American deterrent. We hope that this force will be effective in preventing war, but if it is not, we must be ready to take other steps.

Each bloc is capable of destroying the other many times over. Two factors are important here. The first is the definition of "destroying." Does it mean destroying the enemy's nuclear delivery systems *before* they can launch? Does it mean obliterating a certain percentage of the enemy's cities and population? Does it mean destroying the enemy's governmental functions? Or does it mean all of these together? The answer is important for planning purposes on a high level, but as far as you are concerned, any definition means millions of casualties and the destruction of most of your base facilities. The second factor is timing. If the enemy fires first, do we have the ability to detect it, make a decision, and fire our own weapons before they are destroyed? Again, no matter what happens with regard to timing, you will face the same problems.

It is not our intention here to analyze the position of either side in detail, or to predict what will actually happen, but rather to conclude that *any* strategic nuclear exchange will be devastating ashore and will give you, as commanding officer of any ship from carrier to SSBN, many local problems as a survivor. We will point these out later. First, we will continue to define the various classes of war.

Strategic Nuclear Exchange. This is a total exchange of strategic nuclear weapons by both sides, initiated by either side but probably by the Soviet Union. The initial exchange would be followed by delivery of any remaining strategic weapons, and thereafter war would probably be continued by any means remaining.

Partial Strategic Nuclear Exchange. It is possible, but unlikely, that all-out strategic nuclear exchange could commence and then be arrested as cooler heads prevailed.

Tactical Nuclear Exchange Ashore. If a limited land war were to start in Europe, it is possible that tactical nuclear weapons could be exchanged ashore but that these would be limited in the sense that it would not escalate to a strategic exchange. The war might spread to sea in the same limited way.

Tactical Nuclear Exchange at Sea. Accidental or deliberate sinking of submarines or surface ships might trigger a war at sea. Such a war might not spread ashore, and might be conducted using both conventional weapons and tactical nuclear weapons.

Conventional War at Sea. This is a variation of war at sea in which only conventional weapons are used and there is no active war ashore.

Conventional World War. War might start in Europe and escalate to a widespread conventional war without use of nuclear weapons. Such a war might spread to sea, with the combatants also refraining from use of nuclear weapons there.

Conventional Limited War. Limited war might start in one or more areas other than Europe, such as the Middle East or Africa. The United States and the Soviet Union might be involved in supporting the contending countries. This type of conflict might spread as the superpowers became directly involved in the area of conflict, but decided not to let the war escalate to larger proportions. The United States might also be involved in war with a small country over an incident such as the Iranian seizure of hostages in 1979.

Incident Short of War. The 1979 seizure of hostages produced an incident which was short of a declared war, but which resulted in war-like actions, such as the attempted rescue of the hostages. Other incidents like this may produce stronger reactions by our country.

Confrontation. A confrontation is a show of force which may or may not be accompanied by economic and political measures. We have assembled naval forces in the Indian Ocean on many occasions. We will make shows of force, without actually firing weapons, many times in the future. This is a valuable political technique made possible by a flexible, mobile, strong navy.

Blockade. Blockade, or a blockade-like measure called "quarantine" for purposes of international law, was successful in countering the Soviet introduction of strategic missiles into Cuba. Measures of this nature, whether all-out blockades including war-like actions, or just "paper" blockades, not backed by ships and aircraft, are of great value and may be used in the future.

Cold War Measures. Units of the fleet can be used in measures short of confrontation to influence weaker, reluctant nations. Full confrontation is not always necessary. The mere sight of, and association with, strong naval forces will influence some third world countries to remain neutral or to become committed to the United States.

Harassment. The Soviets may harass our naval and air forces at every opportunity by overflights, by "chicken" tactics with our surface forces, and in keeping surveillance units of all types close to our naval forces. Undoubtedly they will think of more tactics in the years to come.

It is not possible to predict all kinds of armed conflict and military and political action possible short of war. Both major powers are looking for new ways to exert influence. The cleverer, stronger, more persistent power will make gains in the future. We must encourage our country to maintain her strength by pointing out our needs and indicating what we can do to advance her interests.

Whatever we are given, we must use with the utmost skill, for, as Sun Tzu said centuries ago in his *Art of War*: "The skillful fighter puts himself in a position which makes defeat impossible; and does not miss the moment for defeating the enemy."

Requirements of Naval Forces in Future Wars

We have discussed at some length the most probable types of armed and unarmed warfare with which naval forces may be involved in the future. We will now examine what requirements will be laid on them by the various levels of conflict.

All-Out Nuclear Exchange. All-out nuclear exchange will be delivered by many weapons systems on every conceivable target. We must expect the destruction of large ports, and millions of civilian casualties. Your first task, assuming your ship survives, will be to maintain your crew's morale. Obviously they will be thinking about families and friends, and wondering what has happened to them; but you will have no communication with local areas for months or longer, and news broadcasts, if any, will not help.

You thus will have a unique and difficult problem, one never before faced by a nation, a navy, or a commanding officer. There will be no precedent to follow and no external help available. No chaplain can assist you, although strong religious beliefs will be one of the few buttresses your officers and men will have. Your own strong leadership will be called upon; you must be ready to show the strength of character to point the way for your crew, and your example will be all-important. If you can manage this, a mixture of faith, patriotism, and even a desire for revenge will help your ship and crew to surmount the tragedy and carry on through the first difficult days. The American bluejacket's forebears faced somewhat less devastating but nevertheless difficult circumstances in the Revolutionary War and survived. In the case of SSBNs, the requirement to launch missiles almost immediately will help carry the crew through this critical morale period, but after this the letdown may be even more severe than in other ships.

This entire subject must be given more thought, planning, and preparation by higher levels of command. Until this is done, however, you must prepare your ship, your crew, and yourself as best you can.

The second requirement will be the defense of your ship. You and your unit will very likely be attacked either simultaneously with the strategic exchange or soon thereafter. You will be fortunate if it is the latter, for then you will have at least a brief time to make preparations. You may be attacked by air-launched missiles, ship-launched missiles or guns, or submarine-launched missiles or torpedoes, many bearing nuclear warheads. Your reactions and those of your crew must be *automatic*. This will be a time of great mental stress, but you cannot reach for publications; your men must react *automatically* and *instantly*. This is what your months of training have been for. A well-trained team *does* react automatically.

Your ship's defense against incoming weapons is basically a function of the capabilities of its equipment. You may not have the latest, but you can assure that what you have is in top shape. The lives of your crew and the survival of your ship will also depend upon the efficient operation of your detection equipment, the interpretation of information therefrom, your making of quick decisions, and rapid target designation. Destroy the incoming weapons, whether they be aircraft, bombs, missiles, torpedoes, or more exotic carriers, and you will survive to fight on. Fail, and you are gone. If you survive complete destruction, your best hope will then be that you will be able to use the various bills regarding defense against nuclear attack to enable you to decontaminate your ship and to repair damage.

Your first step to prepare for attack now is to understand the basics of nuclear warfare operations. *NWP 28, Nuclear Warfare Operations*, gives the functions, responsibilities, and command relationships in the organization of nuclear warfare. This publication includes information on weapons capabilities, meteorological requirements, and various types of support requirements. Understanding our own system will give you a good insight into that of the Soviets.

You should also review *NWIP 50–3, Shipboard Damage Control*, which describes damage control organization and administration. Review your damage control organization and administration and your damage control bills. Even relatively distant nuclear explosions can cause damage, and controlling it can save your ship.

ATP 25, Nuclear Fallout Forecasting and Warning Organization, gives a good description and survey of nuclear fallout, the organization for reporting nuclear attacks, and the action to be taken by various reporting agencies. Although this is a NATO publication, its information applies in any area of the world.

Finally, you should review all of your nuclear decontamination bills, ship close-up procedures, fallout prediction diagrams, and fallout avoidance maneuvering rules. You will need them in a hurry, and you will be playing for keeps. Use them well and you should be able to defend yourself against all but direct hits and near-misses.

With defense in hand, you must now examine your offensive philosophy. You will have thought about nuclear warheads and even drilled with dummies, but actual use will call for some changes not only in philosophy but in procedures. If you command a carrier, you will have to start with the process of arming aircraft. The safety and security precautions of peacetime should be retained, but you will have to modify them without sacrificing safety to allow *fast* rearming. If you command a cruiser or destroyer you will have to solve the same problem, and in addition will have to be extremely careful when using nuclear weapons for antiaircraft, antimissile, and antisubmarine purposes to avoid damaging your own forces either with blast or fallout. Submarine commanders will have the same problem operating against enemy submarines near friendly forces.

All types must consider rates of weapon and warhead expenditure. There may not be any more supplies of any kind available if the United States and its bases are in ruins. Amphibious types will not be so concerned with offensive weapons problems, but will need to re-cast landing plans to include much greater spread in transport areas and more use of helicopters.

Tactical Nuclear Exchange at Sea Only. The next most serious type of warfare would be a tactical exchange of nuclear weapons at sea without a spread to shore. In planning parlance we call this "nuclear war at sea." In this case morale is not an immediate problem, although there will be apprehension among your crew about the spreading of the conflict ashore. However, the other problems of sharpening your defense and reorienting your offensive policies and precautions will be the same. You will have to economize on weapon use even though supply at the moment will not be a problem. It *may* suddenly become a problem if the war spreads.

Conventional War at Sea. Some of our plans postulate that a war could start by accident or by purposeful use of conventional weapons, and action could then spread to a full conventional war at sea, but would *not* spread to shore. Preparation in the early or anticipatory stages of such a war would start with the same measures as for a nuclear exchange, on the theory that it might soon escalate. Otherwise, preparation should begin with a sharpening of your defense capabilities.

Wars of the future will undoubtedly be fought, in the early stages, by electronics. The proficient use of radar when it *can* be used, and strict discipline when it should *not* be used, will be all-important. Of almost equal importance will be the use of electronic counter-measures (ECM). The range of detection of ECM far exceeds that of radar. The Soviets are experts in its use and employ it extensively. A third factor, evolving in the last few years, is that of satellite sur-veillance. Each side will probably know the type, identity, and lo-cation of all major and many other surface units continuously within fifty miles. The only way to avoid this detection process will be to move between successive satellite passes over home territory or op-erating areas. We will have a small advantage here in that the most probable operating areas in the Atlantic are closer to U.S. than So-viet territory. You can contribute most to electronic readiness by tun-ing and conditioning your radar and ECM equipment and making sure that your operators are trained, skilled, encouraged, and openly appreciated. Your ECM officer and CIC crew must be proficient in recognizing enemy equipment and in relaying the data they derive to you.

In general, confrontations of ships or groups of ships, subma-rines, and aircraft in the future will be characterized by hours of ECM-radar fencing, followed by seconds of lethal weapon ex-change. The ship or unit which excels in the longer first phase will live through the sudden finale. SSBNs and SSNs will be equally dependent on ECM. SSBNs will use it to avoid enemy forces when simple submerged concealment is not enough. SSNs will use it as detection, approach, and even attack information.

After detection, defense will depend on quick and efficient use of conventional weapons. As with all-out nuclear war, survival during conventional war at sea will depend on the excellence of your train-ing program and the performance of your crew. The longer duration of such a war will enable the enemy to deploy more air, submarine, and surface forces against you. The Soviets are experts at coordi-nated attacks, using long-range aircraft and submarines for detec-tion, and then attacking with missiles launched at extreme range from aircraft, submarines, or surface ships. They will try to make several attacks simultaneously at the start of hostilities, and have, in fact, practiced this technique during fleet maneuvers for the last decade. After surprise is lost they will make attacks whenever they can. When coordinated attacks are not possible, you can expect individual attacks by Soviet naval and air forces. As the conventional war at sea proceeds you must be increasingly alert for escalation to nuclear war at sea.

Conventional World War. A world war, probably fought in Europe and limited to conventional weapons, would start for the Navy in a manner similar to that of a conventional war at sea. It would then enter its follow-up phase with the Navy required to convoy troops and supplies to Europe. The Commander-in-Chief of the Atlantic Fleet has publicly stated that attrition of escort forces and transports for such a mission might reach fifty percent. If so, your job as commanding officer of any type of escort, including an SSN, would be demanding; your defenses would have to be in top shape.

There probably would also be an initial conventional exchange with Soviet units in the Pacific area, but this would probably remain a secondary theater, with naval and air action continuing on a holding basis.

Preparation for this type of conflict would be the same as for conventional war at sea, but would include measures for air, surface, and submarine forces to escort U.S. shipping to Europe with as little attrition as possible. Again, your detection equipment, both radar and ECM, will need to operate at peak efficiency, and defensive weapons will be critical. U.S. submarines would play an important role in preventing Soviet forces, both surface and submarine, from entering the Atlantic area and attacking convoys. Finally, amphibious forces would enter the conflict in later stages.

Conventional Limited War. A conventional limited war might take place against a Middle Eastern, African, or South American country which had taken unilateral belligerent action against U.S. citizens or forces, somewhat in the fashion of the 1979 Iranian hostage situation. Naval forces would bear the brunt of such an action by furnishing amphibious forces to transport Marine Corps and eventually Army

Figure 14-1. Ships off Vietnam had to fire gunfire support, dodge enemy shore fire, and still keep track of the Soviet threat in the Gulf of Tonkin with their ECM equipment.

troops and by providing air and gunfire support by carriers, cruisers, destroyers, and smaller ships. All of these types would be required to exercise their detection, communication, gunfire, air support, and amphibious landing capabilities.

The danger of such an operation would not be from shoreward, in the form of strong opposition from the country acted against, but rather from the rear. There is always the possibility that the Soviets might try to interfere. Our force commander, therefore, would have to take precautions against such intervention by establishing seaward surveillance and defense forces. This condition existed during the period from 1971 to the end of the Vietnam war, when U.S. cruisers were concentrating their gun batteries on fire support ashore, but kept the ECM, radar, and missile batteries ready to defend against Soviet ships passing through and gathering occasionally near the mouth of the Tonkin Gulf. Fortunately, no such attack was ever initiated, but the potential was always there, and our defenses were ready. This situation will recur in the future.

Incident Short of War. An incident short of war is one like the 1979 Iranian hostage incident. At that time, belligerent action was taken against us, but no actual war resulted. We attempted a military rescue, and assembled a large naval force in the Indian Ocean, but no fire was exchanged. Similar situations developing in the future will require preparation much like that for a limited war. Operations will require much fuel, equipment, supplies, and a great deal of patience. You will have to face a different kind of morale problem. Your crew will have to be kept interested and motivated over long absences from home port with little but repetitive operations to look forward to.

Blockade. The so-called "Cuban blockade" was actually a variation of a true blockade and is probably best characterized as a quarantine. Either blockades or quarantines are quite likely to be used again. They are flexible weapons and can be effective but bloodless. Their requirements for naval forces are much the same as those of limited war. Ships will have to be ready in all respects for escalation. A blockade, like an incident short of war, may last for a prolonged period, and boredom may become a factor to contend with.

Confrontation. This is a term of growing popularity in planning communities. It really means making a show of force. Since naval and air forces are quite mobile, they are the most likely to be employed in confrontations. You need make no particular preparation except to be familiar with the provisions of international law. You need to know the limits of your ability to exert influence.

Cold War Measures. The possibilities of using naval forces as cold war measures are as varied as a good staff officer or a commanding officer's imagination can produce. You may be sent anywhere on short notice, with or without detailed instructions. On the other hand, you may be deluged with advice. In either event, your unit or ship may be able to exert great influence in a cold war situation.

Combinations. There are many possible combinations and variations of the foregoing forms of warfare, and no one can anticipate them all. If you are always prepared for those discussed, you will be ready to meet any other contingency.

General Preparations for Combat

Engineering Readiness. The first requirement for combat is to be able to get there. This means engineering readiness, both immediate ability to steam at high speeds and to maneuver, and the capability of sustaining this readiness for months on end.

Nuclear-powered ships should have no trouble; they are fueled for the duration and have engineering reliability built into them. They are designed and built with redundant systems in all vital areas. Their safety measures translate into long-term ability to be instantly ready and to maintain this readiness for prolonged periods, such as those they will face in the event of all-out nuclear attack, when bases will either be destroyed or heavily damaged. Further, nuclear-powered ships and submarines will be up to allowance in well-schooled and qualified officers and rated personnel, and will have been well operated and maintained during their previous life. Their condition should be good, having been continuously kept that way by many thorough and demanding inspections.

Non-nuclear powered ships will fare less well. As commanding officer of such a ship, you may have to make up for several years of insufficiently trained officers and rated personnel, lack of spare parts, deficiency of overhaul and repair money, and the running of your ship's engineering plant for long periods when it was not really designed for such abuse.

In the event of combat you will have to maintain your ship for a prolonged period, husbanding your spares, and manufacturing those that you do not have. Life in the engineering spaces will become challenging. Your job will with the passage of time be made somewhat easier by the Navy's recent emphasis on education of senior officers in maintenance problems and techniques, and by the generally increasing emphasis on the training of maintenance personnel.

Damage Control. Assuming that you can *get* your ship to combat, the next challenge will be to *keep* it there. You will find yourself operating in a damage control environment never imagined by a World War II commanding officer.

It is a good idea to study the results of the nuclear explosion damage tests made from 1945 to 1955, but these are only the beginning. Of course you still need simple shoring techniques, electrical casualty cables, and all the other DC measures of the pre-nuclear era. You may still suffer a collision or a hit with a conventional weapon, and these measures will serve for that kind of damage. Your most pressing problem, though, will be coping with close, nearby, or even distant nuclear explosions.

If you command a ship smaller than a carrier, and suffer a direct hit or near-miss with a nuclear weapon, you have nothing to worry about. Your ship will not survive. A submarine will probably survive most air and surface explosions, but will be very vulnerable to underwater bursts. (There is a theory that a large warhead exploded in the sea would cause a tidal wave-like surge that would be very damaging to submarines. This has not, however, been proven.) A carrier, if the warhead is not too big and not too close, may survive, but the ship may not fight again as a carrier. Nuclear blast diagrams and publications will tell you the approximate conditions under which you will survive and have a reasonable chance of putting damage control measures into effect.

With respect to the actual damage you can expect from a nuclear explosion, you will become an instant expert immediately after the first burst near you. Our nuclear explosion damage predictions are all based on tests held in the Pacific in the 1940s and 1950s. These tests were made under closely controlled conditions, with all ships moored, and submarines moored both on the surface and submerged. The locations and aspects of targets were such that blast effect from different directions and of different magnitudes could be measured. This is a scientific way to make a test, but it bears little relation to present-day reality. These were 1940-era ships, submarines, and aircraft. We have made much progress since then in strength of materials, construction techniques, and overall resistance to blast damage. The atmosphere during these tests was clear and tropical, winds negligible, temperature relatively high, and each ship and submarine level and still. In the most likely real-life target area, the Northern Atlantic, things will be quite different. The temperature will be low, the atmosphere will be overcast and probably

Figure 14-2. The Bikini Atoll tests were designed to measure damage to ships and submarines. From these tests effects of other sizes of explosions could be extrapolated. The target array was roughly circular, with similar ships at varying distances from the center. Here the base surge is spreading outward from the center and has enveloped some ships.

moisture-laden, the winds will be medium to high, and the ship's aspect will include some degree of roll.

Roll, for example, can be good or bad. A roll toward the blast at the time the shock wave arrives will increase damage to the superstructure because the off side will be more exposed than if the ship had been level. Low fire control antennas on the off side of a roll toward the blast will suffer more damage, but those on the off side of a roll away from the blast will benefit from the protection of the elevated hull edge. High antenna damage will not be changed by

Figure 14-3. Damage data from the Bikini Atoll tests enabled engineers to estimate damage that would be caused by atomic blasts at various distances. This is the result of the second explosion. The USS *Saratoga*, in the foreground, is sinking slowly. She could not be boarded because of high levels of radio-activity.

Figure 14-4. After the second Bikini Atoll blast, the hull structure of the USS *Independence* was badly damaged, but the ship still floated. Personnel below decks might have survived.

Figure 14-5. The USS *Skate* was on the surface at the time of the first Bikini explosion. She probably would have sunk if she had not been beached for further study.

Figure 14-6. In Operation Sailor Hat, a series of half-kiloton TNT blasts were used to test damage to ships moored a fixed distance away. The USS *Atlanta* was equipped with various antennas and equipment and moored at a known distance from this 17-foot-high pile of TNT.

Figure 14-7. The first of three half-kiloton TNT blasts goes off in Operation Sailor Hat. The shock wave has not yet reached the target ship.

roll. Weapons and other equipment will receive the same extra protection or exposure depending upon the direction of the roll.

Any atmospheric conditions other than high temperature, clear skies, and clear tropical air will reduce blast damage. A combination of all of them might reduce it quite a bit, although the amount is not known and can only be extrapolated from the Pacific tests. Heavy atmosphere and cloud cover will reduce heat damage markedly, but will not affect radiation much. Most days in the North Atlantic, except in the area of the Bermuda high, will be of heavy atmosphere, partial or total cloud cover, and medium to heavy roll-producing seas. Again, our tables predict damage by extrapolating from the Pacific test data, but without taking into account the weather of other areas. The factors just discussed will change these effects, probably in your favor.

In summary, no one, no authority, knows exactly what will happen to you and your ship after a nuclear explosion. You, however, may someday know, and *you* will have to take appropriate action.

Figure 14-8. The damage done here to several antenna arrays and a reproduction of a destroyer bridge area by the half-kiloton blast was used to extrapolate effects of other sizes of weapons at other distances.

Don't be too eager to clear away your damaged equipment topside. So-called "non-repairable" equipment may be all you will have for many months.

You must be as ready as you can be to help others. Your first order of business, after making sure your own ship will not sink and that enemy forces are not present, will be to help other ships which have sustained more damage.

You will, of course, also have to cleanse your ship of nuclear fallout after the blast and before or during damage control measures. *NWIP 50–3, Shipboard Damage Control*, will give you some guidance here. Your refresher training and subsequent training and drills will also guide your actions.

There would seem to be less likelihood of your ship being at-

Figure 14-9. Chemical or biological warfare at sea is a remote possibility. This crew is being exercised in the use of gas masks. Their commanding officer should ensure that they also understand the use of protective clothing.

tacked with weapons bearing chemical or biological agents. The Soviets, however, have this capability, and have been increasing it in recent years. *NWP 36, Armed Forces Doctrine for Chemical and Biological Defense*, contains all the information you will need to cope with this problem.

Detection Systems. You are now in the combat area, and prepared to stay there in spite of damage. Hopefully your vulnerable radar and ECM antennas and equipment will have survived. Your next problem is that of detecting the enemy and, conversely, preventing him from detecting you.

There will be a variety of detection apparatus available to you depending on your ship type and the other ships with you. The best and longest-range will be satellite observation, with surveillance data transmitted to a shore station for analysis and individual contacts of interest to you then being relayed by satellite communications systems. This will not be available to you, however, if the shore stations are destroyed in the initial nuclear exchange. Also, within the next few years both sides will be able to destroy satellites. In other kinds of war, though, satellite observation and communication will remain available.

The next best detection system is aircraft search. It is limited by the number of aircraft available, their range and speed, and the range of their radars and ECM equipment. Shore-based aircraft will suffer from a nuclear exchange. Carrier-based aircraft will be vulnerable to nuclear near-misses, particularly if they are caught on the flight deck or not properly secured below. Those surviving, however, will give your force a great advantage. Surface ship helicopters will give a good search effort in shorter-range situations, but are also quite vulnerable to nuclear blast.

The third best detection system is the submarine. It can observe using passive means, either listening submerged or conducting ECM and visual search at periscope depth.

Surface ships without carriers, submarines, or their own helicopters are limited to ECM, radar, and visual search. ECM range is about twice that of radar. Radar, of course, is limited to line of sight, and has the added disadvantage of revealing your presence to the enemy. Nuclear blast may very well wipe off your radar and ECM antennas and leave you dependent solely upon good old-fashioned visual observation. Sonar-equipped ships can search under water in either active or passive modes. This form of search is relatively invulnerable to nuclear blast damage. All of your electronic methods of search, ECM, radar, and sonar, should be maintained carefully, tuned, and kept at peak performance. Detection ranges can be improved by thirty percent just by careful tuning.

This summary of detection systems may seem oversimplified to the experienced naval officer, but it is useful to re-examine facts that seem obvious in normal times in the light of what might happen after nuclear attack. We may suddenly be forced back to fundamentals. You may have become dependent upon electronic means of detection. Give some thought to shipboard operations as they were in World Wars I and II, prior to the introduction of radar. You may be reduced to that state in a few minutes, or even seconds. If you are,

Figure 14-10. The nuclear-powered guided missile cruiser *Mississippi* (CLG 40) is a new breed of ship, designed for the nuclear age. Her relatively clean topside should survive a nearby nuclear blast with minimal damage to exposed equipment.

binoculars can become very important. Properly trained lookouts, placed high in what is left of your superstructure, can see anything on the surface to the horizon and can see aircraft at amazingly long distances. They will not have these abilities, however, unless you have trained them long before the fatal day.

If you are fortunate enough to avoid nuclear attack, or if war is limited to conventional weapons, your choices come down to whether you want to use radar, and risk revealing your presence to an enemy not using radar but using ECM; or, maintain radar silence, use ECM only, and enjoy the advantage of concealing your presence but do without surface search for periscope detection. If you and the enemy both remain silent, you can both remain undetected, but on the other hand neither can take the offensive unless some other means of detection produces contact. You will have to evaluate your mission and your alternatives and make a choice.

Weapons. Your weapons have an excellent chance of surviving nuclear explosions. Armored gun mounts will do best, and rail-type missile launchers next best. If the blast hits with missiles on the rails, rail damage may result, but this type of repair is relatively easy. Box-type launchers are more vulnerable. Unarmored gun mounts will survive but may need rewiring and other repair before being good for any employment except local control. Aircraft and helicopters topside will not survive. Those belowdecks or in helicopter hangars may survive with moderate damage if properly secured and if the blast is not too close. Exposed ammunition and missiles will be destroyed or rendered useless. Ammunition and missiles in magazines should do well. In submarines, torpedoes and missiles can survive moderate nuclear depth charge damage and close explosions of conventional depth charges and other anti-submarine weapons. Usually, if the submarine survives, you can expect its weapons to survive.

Data on weapon and ammunition survival is sketchy, being mostly extrapolated from tests performed on older ships, submarines, weapons, and munitions.

Enemy Opposition

There is an amazing wealth of information available in the public domain on the types and characteristics of Soviet, Eastern Bloc, and Red Chinese naval forces, aircraft, detection equipment, and weapons. No longer will you have to guess, as we did in World War II, what aircraft and ships the enemy has. In that war, the Japanese were able to use the Zero fighter in initial attacks without our knowledge of anything other than its most general characteristics. Even the building of extremely large battleships and carriers was concealed. Today Soviet and Red Chinese shipbuilding is common knowledge. High level reconnaissance aircraft, such as the U-2 and its successors, and our satellite reconnaissance system permit us to keep track of ship and submarine building, missile testing, and radar and ECM equipment use in detail. Concealment sheds over shipbuilding areas can partially hide details for a time, but when the ship or submarine is launched it is no longer a secret. The Soviets have operated their ships and aircraft within close range of European countries and close to our forces at sea. Consequently, aerial photographs have permitted the best book on the subject, Jane's *Fighting Ships*, to provide an annual updating on the world's navies and aircraft. This book should be in every ship's library and Combat Information Center. A smaller reference published annually by Gerhard Albrecht, *Weyer's Warships of the World*, is available through the Naval Institute Press. It is not as detailed and authoritative as Jane's, but it is smaller, and therefore more suitable for bridge and lookout stations.

The Naval Institute Proceedings, a monthly magazine published by the Naval Institute Press, carries numerous articles and photographs analyzing current Soviet naval and air force ships and aircraft. The December, 1980 issue, for instance, contains a complete description and multiple close-up photographs of the *Kirov*, the newest Soviet nuclear-powered cruiser. In this same issue is a photographic history of the development of Soviet submarine types. This magazine should arrive regularly in every wardroom.

Obviously, the speed and range characteristics Jane's and Weyer's list may not be exactly accurate, because photographs cannot provide this kind of information. Classified sources, however, are available to you which will give them with greater accuracy. These sources will also provide weapon ranges and characteristics and radar and ECM data.

You will find in Jane's and Weyer's data on submarines and long range aircraft, but this is also somewhat suspect as to accuracy. Jane's data will be sufficient for your purpose as to speed and range characteristics, but radar, ECM, and weapons data must come from classified sources.

Finally, note the increasing use of smaller warships by Soviet and Eastern Bloc forces. The Red Chinese Navy will also have an excellent fleet of small ships in the future. These will be troublesome when and if you have to operate near enemy sea coasts or in narrow waters. These smaller ships may also be transferred by the Red Chinese or Soviets to nations which might not otherwise have naval forces. Our Navy has relatively little experience in countering this type of threat, particularly when it is equipped with long-range missiles. A surface-to-surface missile makes a potential giant killer out of a mosquito-sized ship. Learn to counter this threat before it encounters you.

Combat Housekeeping

Lookouts and Recognition. We have already discussed the possibility of nuclear war clearing your topside of radar and ECM antennas. The alternative to these sophisticated means of search is return to the old eyeball and binocular combination.

This means lookouts trained in advance of hostilities. There will always be signs that a good lookout will see, such as water disturbances, flares, low-flying aircraft, rubber rafts, and many other important contacts not seen by radar even in peacetime. Before 1973, you were required by *Navy Regulations*, Article 0789, to ensure that lookouts were properly trained and stationed in peacetime. It then extended your responsibility to combat by requiring that in time of battle lookouts provide timely visual information regarding air, surface, and subsurface contacts. It also required you to select and train them in recognition and to see that they were properly supervised on watch. The article then completed the cycle by requiring that visually obtained information be transmitted expeditiously to appropriate control stations.

This article was discontinued in the 1973 version of *Navy Regulations*, but its requirements are still necessary in peace and in war. The duties of lookouts are now set forth in Articles 439.2 and 439.7 of the *SORN*.

Even in this day of long-range radar and ECM detection, recognition is important. The exact type of enemy aircraft making an approach to you can dictate your defensive maneuvers. The sooner you identify it the quicker you can act. Again, blast damage will return you to the use of the eyeball, day and night. Recognition at night of types of surface ships can be life- and ship-saving, both for your own ship, and for the allied vessel you might be about to shoot at. Visual recognition signals will also be brought back into use if you lose your IFF.

Meals. In wartime, food takes on a special significance. It is the only comfort a man can expect after a long, hard day, a cold watch, or at or after general quarters. Make sure that your battle bill pro-

vides the flexibility needed by commissary personnel and food serv-
ers to prepare and serve adequate meals for all. Certain foods lend
themselves to quick preparation and easy serving. Soup, sand-
wiches, cookies, and fruit are good. Hot coffee is a must. Carriers
have already experimented with twenty-four-hour food service. This
answers the problem of feeding aircraft crews, handlers, maintenance and flight deck personnel, watchstanders, and ship's company,
all of whom will be working long and irregular hours and will be
eating between flight operations. Small ships should try their own
version of this technique. Submarines have long since learned to
feed well and often; they need no help or suggestions!

Articles 82650 and 82652, Volume III, *Supply Systems Command
Manual*, describes feeding problems and solutions in situations of
nuclear, bacteriological, or chemical warfare.

Cleanliness. Even in wartime, your crew must be encouraged to
keep themselves and the ship as clean as possible. In the first days
and hours of combat this will seem impossible, but as a routine is
established, it will be found possible for a few men at a time to
shower and otherwise clean their persons. Sweepdown is possible
even in lulls between action. Even a rapid sweepdown will reduce
the fire hazard caused by trash and expended ammunition debris. A
swept-down ship reduces litter and dirt that might fly up into wounds
when explosions occur. Personal cleanliness also helps to reduce the
possibility of infection from wounds. If your crew knows *why* they
should keep things clean, they will do it without urging.

Keeping the crew informed. Your officers and men will perform
better if they know the ship's mission and objectives. Its mission
will then become theirs. Article 0739, *Navy Regulations*, requires
that the commanding officer, before going into battle or action, communicate to his officers, if possible, his plans for battle or action and
such other information as may be of operational value should any of
them succeed to command. This article was obviously written for
conventional war, but in the nuclear age it is probably even more
important. *All* of your officers must be informed of your mission if
nuclear war is imminent, because few may survive. Further, nuclear

war will be sudden in its onslaught, and you should keep them informed early and continously as conditions change.

During action, do your best to keep personnel belowdecks informed. They will do a better job and display more initiative if they know what they are facing and how they can help. Their morale will also improve, for they will then feel that they are part of a team.

In past wars, ship movements were kept secret. Censorship was imposed on all outgoing mail in an effort to keep the enemy from knowing what ship movements might be forthcoming and what force changes might be in prospect. In future wars this will not serve any purpose. The enemy will know about ship departures and movements within a few hours, by satellite. Therefore, censorship will not be needed, except to guard long range plans, and then only if the war is of long duration. Within the bounds of security and censorship, then, try to give your crew as much information as you can regarding the movements of your ship.

Taking Possession of a Prize. Article 0742, *Navy Regulations*, directs that the commanding officer, on taking possession of a ship, aircraft, installation or other property or equipment, shall keep it from being recaptured, secure or remove enemy personnel, secure and preserve logs, journals, codes and ciphers, charts, maps, orders, instructions, blueprints, plans, diaries, letters, and other documents found, and forward or deliver these to the nearest designated authority at the earliest possible moment. He should also preserve all captured enemy ordnance, fire control, electronic and aviation equipment, and other property of possible intelligence value, unless destruction is necessary to prevent recapture; and make this material promptly available for intelligence evaluation or other authorized use.

Taking possession of a prize in the classic nineteenth-century manner is unlikely in future wars. You might possibly capture or come across a drifting small ship containing equipment of value in a limited or cold war situation. A vessel failing to obey your orders in a blockade situation is also subject to capture. Know the above regulations, re-read your prize crew bill, and then put it back on your bookshelf next to Horatio Hornblower. You will not take many prizes. The *SORN*, Article 630.23, contains a combined Visit and Search, Boarding and Salvage, and Prize Crew Bill. It should provide all the guidance you will need.

Boarding. Boarding, however, might be required in many instances short of actually taking a prize. In war, cold war, or blockade it may be necessary to send a party aboard a merchant vessel acting suspiciously, failing to identify itself, or violating your orders. You should already have canvassed your crew for possible interpreters. Anyone with even a "kitchen" knowledge of a language will help.

Instruct your boarding officer to exercise caution and always to maintain communications with the ship and internally within his party. Booby traps are typical communist weapons and will be quite common in small Far Eastern ships. Certain Middle Eastern countries with predominantly Moslem populations believe that death in defense of their religion and country (the two may not be separable in their minds) is the surest way to heaven. Your men will need to watch such people carefully, and never give them a chance to get to their weapons. Article 630.23 of the *SORN* is a combined bill, one section of which deals with boarding and salvage. Boarding may lead to several subsequent actions, such as salvage, taking the ship as a prize, destroying it, or simply letting it proceed with a warning. This bill will cover most eventualities.

Taking Prisoners of War. Boarding or rescue at sea after ship sinking or aircraft crash would be the most likely sources of prisoners in the future, but there are other possible scenarios. In any event, Article 0741, *Navy Regulations*, states that on taking or receiving prisoners of war the commanding officer shall ensure that such prisoners are treated with humanity. Their personal property must be preserved and protected, they must be allowed the use of such of their effects as may be necessary for health, and they must be supplied with proper rations. They must be properly guarded and deprived of all means of escape and revolt. All provisions of the 1949 Geneva Convention relative to the treatment of prisoners of war must be followed.

Remember the warning about Moslems when boarding merchant

ships. Some sects of Moslem prisoners of war must be watched carefully to prevent suicidal attacks on their guards, both when they are first captured, and later on when they have had a chance to encourage each other. Article 0650.7 of the *SORN* is a prisoner of war bill. Its provisions are quite inclusive, and if you fully implement it you will be sure of carrying out your responsibilities under *Navy Regulations* and the Geneva Convention.

Security. Preparation for war changes normal peacetime use and storage of ammunition, codes, ciphers, and medical supplies, including drugs. You will have to change your internal security measures accordingly. Ammunition will be brought to ready service areas. Magazine access regulations will have to be broadened to give condition watch personnel instant access not only to ready service ammunition but to magazine spaces. This access includes weapons such as missiles and this in turn leads to changes in access to nuclear weapons. You will have to accommodate this without compromising security or endangering your ship.

Decoding will take place around the clock. Additional personnel will have to be qualified to use code, ciphers, and equipment. This will lead to increasing laxity in security if not guarded against. Here again, you will have to temper the loss of security with the need for increased usage and access.

Medical supplies will have to be dispersed to battle stations both for battle and because they should be available throughout the ship in the event of surprise attack. In World War II days we could leave alcohol and morphine widely dispersed with only minimum security measures because they were not abused then as they are now. Now you will have to take greater precautions with your medical supplies. Again, you will have to compromise to maintain security while still making such supplies accessible.

Physical security would not seem to be a problem in wartime. However, there will still be an occasional malcontent who will literally, as well as figuratively, throw a monkey wrench in your gears, and others who will damage equipment for various reasons. You will have to maintain security of equipment and machinery vital to the movement and fighting of your ship, just as you do in peacetime.

Sidearms and other small arms pose the same sort of problems. Make sure they are tightly controlled, but at the same time kept readily available for use.

Security in port is also important. You may not know when war starts just who your enemies may be. Institute sentries, guards, locks, and other appropriate security measures immediately, until the country's internal political situation is clear.

Personnel Casualty Reports. NWP 7 covers personnel casualty reports (PERSCASRPTS). If you are operating as part of a larger unit, make these reports to the task unit or group commander, and these will then be consolidated by the task force commander. If you are operating independently, make your report to your operational commander as soon as possible. You will probably be prohibited from reporting by radio unless you need assistance to care for casualties, or unless losses will leave your ship critically shorthanded.

Death at Sea (Combat). The nature of the action you are engaged in will govern your response to combat deaths at sea. You will have one problem caring for and disposing of the bodies, and another making the required reports.

In general, if your ship's location and its operations will permit, you should return the bodies to port for shipment home. Use your cold storage facilities to preserve them if sufficient space is available, and if there are no qualified personnel available to preserve and prepare bodies.

If this is not possible, a combat burial at sea will then be necessary. Such a ceremony, if it can be held, is described in *Naval Ceremonies, Customs, and Traditions. Navy Regulations*, Article 1089, outlines in detail the requirements for burial at sea. In combat, most of these will not be possible, but a dignified and simple ceremony can be managed. *Navy Regulations* specify that burial should take place between sunrise and sunset, but also state that if it is necessary to conduct ceremonies at night, during combat, such funeral services as are possible shall take place.

The reports required following death at sea are covered in Sections 4210100 through 420140 of the *Naval Military Personnel Command Manual*. During combat you will have to render these reports by mail. These articles cover the methods of notifying next of kin and provide a sample letter. Death certificates (NAVMED-FORM N) are also required. No investigative report is normally required in combat, but in peacetime or cold war short of combat such a report is required. See *JAG Manual*, Section 0803, and the *Manual of the Medical Department*, Chapter 17. If transfer ashore is practicable, the *Decedent Affairs Manual* (BuMed Instruction 5360.1 series) gives instructions for handling the remains.

Towing in Combat Situations. The *SORN*, Article 630.22, contains an emergency towing bill, which you probably will have exercised in refresher training. This bill is detailed and adequate, but the problem in combat is that nothing will work as the bill says it should. The ship towed may not be able to give you much help and perhaps none at all after a nuclear explosion. You may have to decontaminate portions of the ship about to be towed before boarding her to make up her part of the tow rig. The rig itself may have to be a jury one, made up with what is left over after extensive damage. The bill will be an excellent guide, but your crew will have to improvise. Fortunately, you will find that there is no one more ingenious than a good chief boatswains mate faced with a challenge.

Commendation of Personnel. Prompt and adequate recognition of performance beyond the call of duty is a great morale builder. If the recognition is deserved it will raise the morale of the whole crew as well as that of the recipient. If it is *not*, however, it will do more harm than good. Require all of your officers and petty officers to report promptly any commendable action by any person. Your fleet commander will set the requirements for various classes and degrees of awards. His instructions will require complete and adequate documentation. In spite of the work involved at a busy time, the result will be worth the effort.

Material Casualty Reports (CASREPS). We have already discussed CASREPS in general and in peacetime. Before, during, and after combat they will also be important. When made before the battle, they enable your unit commander to adjust his formations, plans, and actions to compensate for deficiencies. When made during the battle, and of course they should be restricted then to major casualties such as drastic reductions in speed or heavy flooding, they enable him to give you help as practicable and to adjust his tactics as necessary. When made after the battle, they help him to plan repairs, assist you as possible, and make plans for the next stage of operations.

You must make CASREPS in battle or in imminent combat with discretion. Decide if your unit commander *needs* and *wants* your report before you clutter up the system with it at a critical time. *Navy Regulations*, Article 0743, requires that immediately after a battle or an action you repair as much damage as possible, exert every effort to prepare your command for further service, and make accurate, explicit, and detailed reports as required. This is a simple requirement. Comply with it as best you can, but hold the detail until your unit commander asks for it.

Battle Station. Regulations do not require that the CO take any particular station in his ship at any time, and specifically not in battle. You should be where you can fight your ship the best, having due regard for weather, visibility, location of friendly forces and their possible interaction with your ship, and the type, location, and probable tactics of the enemy. Obviously you can see *best* from the highest, all-around point of your ship. You will see *least* in CIC.

If you are in close company with your own forces, such as in column, you will have to see to avoid them and to coordinate your actions with theirs. You will have to *see* and see *quickly* and so you should station yourself on the bridge or bridge wing of your ship. Since in this case your own ship's safety is at stake, you will have to delegate weapons control functions to your subordinates.

If your situation is such that you do *not* need to *see* to assure the safety of your ship, you belong in CIC, where you will have instant access to detection, identification, designation, and weapon command systems. This is the ideal location. It is *you* who should make the important decisions involved with combat, and you should be able to make them as quickly as possible. If you are in CIC, you can stay abreast of the situation as it develops, and can receive and evaluate information in a "parallel" flow, rather than a "series" situation with your tactical action officer or CIC watch officer. You can then allow him to reach independent conclusions and recommend action to you, and then you can either implement his recommendation or substitute your own decision.

If at all possible, allow your subordinates to experience the entire decision-making process. If you short circuit them, you will dull their initiative and never find out if they are sound decisionmakers. The whole system will become overly dependent on you.

The carrier commanding officer has a similar decision to make, but he must also put his requirement to observe air operations into the location equation. This is his main battery. In any event, he should be where he thinks the situation most demanding of his attention, personal experience, and wisdom will arise.

The commanding officer of a surfaced submarine usually posts himself in the upper part of the submarine in an exposed sail area where he can see best. During submerged operations he goes where he feels he is most needed. This may range from the control center to the attack center to the sonar room.

During World War II, the executive officer was required to be in a part of the ship removed from the location of the commanding officer, so that one of them would have a good chance of surviving a casualty. This is no longer required, but since damage of the type suffered in World War II may happen in future conventional war, in such a war you should give consideration to dividing your locations accordingly. If nuclear war is near, or has happened, damage will be so widespread that it no longer will make sense to be concerned about separation. You may as well have the counsel and assistance of your most experienced officer by having him near you.

In submarines, the executive officer is usually a key member of the attack team and is therefore required in the attack center. When attack is not imminent he may be anywhere, particularly if he is needed to assess damage.

Heads of departments normally are in their departments or in their communications centers, such as damage control or engineering control.

Educating Your Crew Regarding Duties as a POW. It is your responsibility to educate and inform your officers and men about their obligations and conduct should they become prisoners of war. The treatment they can expect will range all the way from strict compliance with the Geneva Convention to the barbarity of the Vietnamese War. The exact treatment will depend on the country holding them. In general, European countries should tend toward compliance, and Middle and Far Eastern countries will lean toward barbarity. The Soviet Union is an enigma. Treatment of their own people has historically been harsh, and their treatment of our prisoners may be equally bad.

During World War I, prisoners were generally treated with correctness by all the combatants. Since no torture, coercion, or other harsh measures were used on prisoners, there was no problem with their conduct. The Japanese introduced torture in World War II, but not on a widespread basis. Many prisoners were treated fairly well, at least by Oriental standards, and shared the hardships of the average Japanese. Some prisoners were tortured and maltreated to obtain information, but this was done by individual commanders, not as a result of policy. In any event, the information held by the prisoners soon ceased to be timely, and they usually gave up on torture if they didn't break the prisoner promptly.

During the Korean War a new factor was added. Our instructions to POWs were to give name, rank, and serial number, and to resist to the ultimate all attempts to obtain additional information. This was a shortsighted and overly optimistic and idealistic policy. The North Koreans soon proved it unworkable by mentally breaking every American prisoner they held, from major general down to the most junior private.

By the time the war in Vietnam commenced, we had learned something from the Korean experience. We still instructed our personnel to try to hold to giving name, rank or rate, and serial number, but we recognized the impossibility of holding strictly to these instructions. We permitted them to give other information if tortured, but to try to mislead if possible.

As this war progressed we gained still more experience in POW matters. Some escaped, to tell us what the Vietnamese were doing and to give us advice on preparing our men. Many of the prisoners taken were officer pilots of the Navy, Marine Corps, and Air Force. They provided a nucleus of educated, trained, and highly motivated leadership to the POW community. The Vietnamese tried to prevent the exercise of leadership by separation and isolation, but this was not successful. Our POWs found ways to lead and communicate even through the thick walls of prison cells. The wonderful achievements of our POWs, some of whom suffered under conditions of isolation, torture, and hardship for as long as seven and a half years, formed a new set of service traditions.

As a result of the Vietnamese experience, a new and more workable POW policy has been formulated. A POW is still *required* to give only name, rank or rate, and serial number. He is then encouraged to withhold further information until enemy pressure can no longer be withstood. Further revelation is then condoned, although he is encouraged to lie or mislead if possible. On a more positive plane, we require each prisoner to adhere to command structure, in the sense that he must obey military orders of senior and noncommissioned officers of any service. The intention is to preserve military discipline and morale as the way in which prisoners of war can survive and return to society as whole persons.

Article 4620100 of the *Naval Military Personnel Command Manual* describes the Geneva Convention identity card (DD Form 1934) which you are required to issue to all medical and religious personnel who may become prisoners of war. All other personnel will have regular DOD identification cards. In the event of capture, the Geneva Convention requires that these cards be shown to captors, but not surrendered. Obviously, some captors will make their own rules.

Loss of Ship. Finally, if after all your preparations, training, and performance in combat, you lose your ship, there are certain duties and responsibilities you must still carry out. *Navy Regulations*, Article 0744, titled "Loss of a Ship," states that the commanding officer shall remain with her crew as long as is necessary and shall save as much government property as possible. He must make every reasonable effort to save the deck log, personnel diary, and pay records. If it becomes necessary to abandon ship, you should be the last person to leave. This regulation is intended to apply to peacetime, but it should also be complied with in wartime as far as possible. In wartime situations saving records and papers may not be possible. You will be concentrating on saving people, and the abandon ship bill will then be activated.

Article 0745 states that your authority over your crew will continue even after your ship has sunk, until they are regularly reassigned or discharged by competent authority.

Survival Training. Two fine books should form the basis for your efforts to teach your crew how to survive at sea, and then ashore, if they are lucky enough to reach land. *How to Survive on Land and Sea* and the *Bluejackets' Manual*, both published by the Naval Institute Press, cover the subject in great detail, and should form part of your ship's library. If you can salvage any boats, rafts, or floats you should survive for days or weeks. Your foresight in properly equipping them will pay off. If other ships are near you or in company you will not have a problem. If alone, your survival will depend on whether you were able to get off an emergency request for help together with your position, and whether you and your men can stay afloat and alive until help arrives.

Combat Philosophy

This portion of this book is the most important part of our discussion on the art of command at sea. In modern times, we are prone to think that a naval vessel is built and manned for a variety of reasons, ranging from protection and promotion of commerce to carrying out "presence" visits. All of these peacetime occupations are important, but they sometimes obscure the fact that navies exist primarily to protect national security. Even this description of the Navy's mission is not clear, for the phrase "protect national security" is a euphemism, coined to avoid offending the political sensibilities of congressmen and the moral feelings of citizens. The plain, brutally frank truth is that naval vessels exist to *fight*. We must never forget this fact, even though we must always be aware of the other functions and responsibilities we are called upon to carry out.

Effectiveness for Service. This is an unfamiliar and slightly misleading subtitle, but it is the title of Article 0737, *Navy Regulations*, which states that the commanding officer shall exert every effort to maintain his command in a state of maximum effectiveness for war or other service consistent with the degree of readiness prescribed by higher authority. Effectiveness for service is directly related to the state of personnel and material readiness.

Article 0739, titled "Action with the Enemy," is equally low-key. Its first paragraph requires you to communicate to your officers information which might be of value to them should they succeed to command. The next paragraph then gets to the point. It requires you to engage the enemy to the best of your ability during action, and forbids you, without permission, to break off action to assist a disabled ship or to take possession of a captured one.

These are the only words of advice to you in all of *Navy Regulations* regarding your conduct in battle. We can only assume, from the simplicity of the words and the restraint of the rhetoric, that this is deliberate, and that this language must be fleshed out with advice handed down over decades by naval commanders and distilled from the naval tradition of centuries.

U.S. Navy Combat Tradition. The foregoing is a reasonable assumption, and is certainly not contradicted by any written information or directives. Therefore, let us examine the U.S. Navy traditions of the past, and recent additions to them during modern times, from World War I to Vietnam. These traditions are *use of the initiative, boldness and daring, tenacity, courage, aggressiveness, ingenuity,* and the *ability of our young junior officers and enlisted men to carry on and display their own initiative when their seniors are dead or incapacitated.* You, as a commanding officer, may *add* to these traditions or originate others, but you must never *subtract* from them.

The Athenians, no tyros at the naval profession, most prized in their naval officers and men high enthusiasm or spirit, courage, the ability to innovate or solve problems, and the willingness to work long and hard. Our own prized characteristics are, therefore, not new. We have also learned from the British, who have had centuries of a sound naval tradition. The qualities they prized most were courage, aggressiveness, tenacity, and coolness under fire. Note that initiative was not included; in the Royal Navy, junior officers and enlisted men were never trained to exercise initiative, as ours are encouraged to. The British are a stolid race, which may be one reason why the more volatile of the English, Irish, and Scots left their countries years ago and became Americans.

Our own American traditions are outstanding. They have produced the world's finest naval officers, from John Paul Jones to Chester Nimitz. In between came such leaders as David Glasgow Farragut, of whom Admiral Mahan wrote:

> It is in the strength of purpose, in the power of rapid decision, of instant action, and if need be, of strenuous endurance through a period of danger or of responsibility, when the terrifying alternatives of war are vibrating in the balance, that the power of a great captain mainly lies. It is in the courage to apply knowledge under conditions of exceptional danger; not merely to see the true direction for effort to take, but to dare to follow it, accepting all the risks and all the chances inseparable from war, facing all that defeat means in order to secure victory if it may be had. It was upon those inborn moral qualities that reposed the conduct which led Farragut to fame. He had a clear eye for the true key of a military situation, a quick and accurate perception of the right thing to do at a critical moment, a firm grasp upon the leading principles of war; but he might have had all these and yet miserably failed. He was a man of most determined will and character, ready to tread down or fight through any obstacles which stood in the path he sought to follow.

Farragut's other characteristics are well known. He sought responsibility where others shunned it. Above all, he *liked* being a naval officer, as witnessed by his oft-quoted statement, "I have as much pleasure in running into port in a gale of wind as ever a boy did in a feat of skill."

We can learn from those nations who were our predecessors upon the sea, and we can benefit from studying and observing various countries and their cultures and traditions; but in doing so, we must maintain our own established, successful, and honored traditions.

Use of the Initiative. Probably the most distinctively American naval tradition is the use of the initiative, and we will discuss it first.

There is a fine line of distinction between the use of the initiative and the display of boldness, daring, and aggressiveness. Fortunately, the enemy won't know the difference, and he will be at a disadvantage if you display any or all of these characteristics. If all of these fail, remember the advice of that master American tactician, Minnie Pearl: "If you can't beat'em, confuse 'em."

The dictionary states that initiative means to be the "first mover," and to have the ability for original conception and independent action. A commanding officer who takes the initiative is usually also being bold and daring, but not necessarily so. In any event, don't be too concerned about the exact description of what you are about to do. Just do it *first*. Taking the initiative should be a principal part of your combat philosophy.

Boldness and Daring. Charles Lindbergh had a fine feeling for boldness and daring. He said, "What kind of man would live where there is no daring? And is life so dear that we should blame men for dying in adventure? Is there a better way to die?" Still, the ideal is to be bold and daring and *not* to die. Even more ideal is to make sure the *enemy* dies and that *you* survive.

John Paul Jones was the epitome of boldness and daring. He sailed in fast ships and in harm's way, and would not tolerate any captain or subordinate who was not equally bold. Boldness was his legacy to those who would follow in his footsteps.

Modern American naval officers have been equally daring. In the opening weeks of World War II, when the Japanese were overrunning the Philippines and landing large forces in Lingayen Gulf, Lieutenant Commander Wreford "Moon" Chapple took his submarine, the S-38, into the Gulf via a poorly charted and shallow side channel, and for over twenty-four hours did his best to attack Japanese ships. He was harassed and attacked repeatedly by Japanese escorts, and discouraged by the repeated failure of the defective torpedoes he was firing, but he managed to sink and damage some shipping and slow the landing process markedly. His boldness was inspiring to those who were doing their best to hold the Philippines against overpowering odds.

Later, his contemporaries of Destroyer Squadron 29 conducted an equally daring attack on another Japanese landing operation, at Macassar in the Dutch East Indies. Four of these decrepit old four-stackers steamed at 27 knots in the dark of night through a cruiser and destroyer screen into the middle of the Japanese landing area and sank five Japanese landing transports and escorts with torpedo and gunfire. They made repeated passes at high speed until all torpedoes were expended and then retired under cover of darkness and their own gunfire without damage. This was the first such surface action for the United States Navy since the Spanish-American War.

Only boldness and daring made these efforts successful. You will do well to give those characteristics a prominent place in your combat philosophy. They are distinctively American in character.

Tenacity. Tenacity has been a characteristic of our Navy for years. Farragut's order to "Damn the torpedoes; full speed ahead" is a classic example of refusing to fear what *might be*. Don't be put off by small failures; instead drive *tenaciously* forward. You, as commanding officer, will do well to emulate Admiral Farragut. Washington Irving once said, "Great minds have purpose; others have wishes. Little minds are tamed by misfortune; great minds rise above them."

Lest you think tenacity is an old-fashioned quality, remember the advice given in World War II by Commander "Mush" Morton, a superb submarine commanding officer, to Lieutenant Commander Richard O'Kane, who would go on to become an equally famed CO: "*Tenacity*, Dick, you've got to stick with the bastard until he's on the bottom." O'Kane did, repeatedly.

In World War II, other naval officers also continued this tradition of tenacity. Admiral Arleigh Burke's operations repeatedly demonstrated this characteristic. He believed in hitting the enemy hard and fast, delivering repeated blows until his will to resist collapsed. Admiral William Halsey was as tenacious as any officer who ever went to sea.

It can be argued that the Japanese were equally tenacious. They were, but it was a tenacity without purpose, almost a religious belief. They repeatedly lost large numbers of men, aircraft, and ships long after they should have known that a particular battle was a losing strategic or tactical situation. Tenacity of this kind, without the ability to change direction or to modify operations to suit changed conditions, is a losing cause. The Americans probed, jabbed, kept moving forward, but changed the direction of thrust and the magnitude of their efforts to take advantage of uncovered weakness and to avoid strong points. This kind of tenacity is one of our traditions.

"I have not yet begun to fight" is not a failure to hear the starting gun, but a stern statement of tenacity of purpose which has become a part, not only of the traditions of the Navy, but of the personal philosophy of combat of every naval officer. Preserve and use it.

Courage. Courage comes in many varieties, and it has been the mainstay of the combat philosophy of all peoples and services for centuries. It can be wasted, though, as it was in the charge of the Light Brigade at Balaclava, when the Brigade went to certain destruction, knowing that its effort was useless.

American naval officers and men have performed many courageous acts in our relatively short history. Unfortunately for history, the most courageous individual acts are seldom recorded, and are known only to those who performed them. This is the most superb kind of courage: where a man does his duty in the full understanding that no one else will ever know.

There are many kinds of courage, and some in new settings. In Vietnamese prison camps our prisoners of war demonstrated new kinds of courage when they withstood to the death the torture of their captors.

Physical courage will be commonplace in the next war, given the moral upbringing and characteristics of our countrymen. After a partial or complete nuclear exchange many young men will have to meet challenges never before imagined. You, as a commanding officer, will find the personal exercise of physical courage easy. The stimulus of command will make you forget your own personal safety. The more difficult assignment for you will be the proper exercise of moral courage. Situations calling for moral courage will not have the stimulus of combat. It will be necessary when you demand top performance from your officers and men; take steps to correct or punish those who do not perform; make honest reports of your or your ship's failure, should it occur; and when you are completely honest in all of your command relations.

Courage, then, must be part of your combat philosophy, to be expected and required of others, and one which you demonstrate automatically as commanding officer.

Aggressiveness. The dictionary definition of an aggressive person is one who is disposed to vigorous, outgoing activity on behalf of an objective. This is a rather pedantic description of a volatile and intense characteristic. The aggressive commanding officer is one who wants to win so much that he *will* take vigorous action to attain his objective. The key is to determine the right and appropriate action and to pursue it to the utmost, but not to the point of foolhardiness, or of being led into an adverse situation such as an ambush. Normally an aggressive fighter has the advantage, and he will win unless the defender has had the time to arrange his defenses so that attacking becomes a disadvantage.

One key element of aggressiveness is speed of attack. Admiral Arleigh Burke was known for his 31-knot attacks. Burke was usually in the middle of the enemy's formation before he had a chance to retaliate. There were only two adjectives in Admiral Burke's lexicon, *good* and *bad*. He held that the difference between a bad officer and a good officer was about ten seconds. Ten seconds of decision-making by a gunnery, torpedo, missile, or conning officer, translates into three five-inch salvos, the firing of a torpedo spread by either a surface ship or a submarine, a missile firing, a battery-unmasking turn, or the performance of an evasive maneuver. Ten seconds can mean the enemy's destruction or yours.

The same comparison applies to commanding officers. Be *quickly* aggressive if you want to add surprise and confusion of the enemy to your attack plan. By Admiral Burke's standards you are a *good* CO if you take advantage of the time given you by a good gunnery, torpedo, missile, or conning officer by making a quick (but correct) decision. Fritter it away with indecision and you are a *bad* commanding officer who will end up with holes in his ship or a forty-degree list. Speed of decision goes hand in hand with aggressiveness, and aggressiveness has always been one of the hallmarks of our Navy. Make it one of yours.

Ingenuity. Yankee ingenuity produced the fast sailing schooners and clippers of the 18th and 19th Centuries. Their design and speed were incorporated into the ships of our early navy. Further ingenuity put speed and endurance into our steam-powered naval vessels and eventually produced the nuclear-powered ship and submarine, with both speed and unlimited endurance. Industrial ingenuity gave our navy superior armor, excellent major-caliber guns and fire control systems, missiles, computers, solid-state electronics, and a host of other improvements. Bluejacket ingenuity kept them operational in peacetime with shortages of money and spare parts and in wartime in spite of damage and lack of repair facilities. The American naval person, officer or enlisted, is without peer in mechanical ingenuity. Fortunately the same characteristic extends to strategy and tactics. Circular formations for air defense, combined anti-submarine search and attack procedures, amphibious landing techniques, and submarine and aircraft attack tactics are but a few of the ideas pioneered by our navy.

Our tradition of ingenuity is superb, and you can depend upon this characteristic of our officers and men to carry you through many difficult situations. You, as commanding officer, will also be called upon to exercise ingenuity. You will have to improvise tactics, communication plans, personnel reassignments, and emergency repairs of equipment and machinery to meet various contingencies of operations and battle. Ingenuity by a commanding officer can make a superb ship out of a commonplace vessel.

Initiative of Juniors. Our navy has always excelled in using the initiative of our junior officers and enlisted men. Fortunately this process comes naturally to citizens of the United States, where family and cultural atmosphere generally foster initiative. It is a part of our way of life. By contrast, the Japanese discouraged the initiative of juniors before World War II. They suffered accordingly in wartime when seniors were killed or incapacitated. Their juniors were neither trained nor expected to take the initiative, and their ships rapidly lost their efficiency when damaged in battle. Our crews were able to take prompt and heroic measures after damage with little guidance.

We can expect that the Soviet culture will produce the same kind of relationships as in Japan prior to World War II. If so, then their naval personnel will be inferior in this area. It will be up to you to maintain our lead. Add to the natural bent of your officers and men by encouraging them to display initiative in peace. Your efforts will pay for themselves some bleak day when your ship is heavily damaged or has internal communication problems. If you have prepared your crew, you will find the other end of the ship running just as well as if your orders had been received.

Admiral Albert Gleaves, after World War I, said, "To seamen a ship becomes endowed with human virtues and human faults; she ceases to be a mere inanimate thing." This is true, and it is a good thing, but it does not change the fact that *men* fight, not *ships*. Take care of your men, encourage their initiative, and they will take care of the ship whether you are there or not.

Decision Making. Now that you have decided on the elements of your own personal combat philosophy, you should remember that "philosophy" never fired a shot. Only a decision starts the firing process.

The human brain is the finest computer ever made. Like a computer, it stores millions of bits of information. The results of your readings and study are all there; the distillation of your experience; your observations of the experiences of others; the Navy's traditions; your own personal characteristics; and, on a shorter time basis, the input from your senses. This will include the latest information you see, hear, and otherwise observe. With all this information in your memory, and from your current observation, you will have to make your decision.

The proper way to make a decision is to take in all the facts that are available, meld them in your mind with the information already there, and then reach a *tentative* decision. In war, as in life, there is always additional information being developed and brought to your attention. Consider such information and revise your decision accordingly and continuously. Keep your mind open, however, until the moment arrives when a *final* decision is necessary. Then make it, announce it firmly and vigorously, and see that it is carried out instantly.

There are shortsighted persons who think that a commander should make a final decision early and stick to it. They feel that allowing change indicates poor decision making ability. The exact opposite is true. This kind of decision maker is, to speak charitably, an opinionated boob who will end up on a large rock because early on he chose a course heading for it and refused to change his decision.

An example from real life: a U.S. ship, steaming in wartime in an area of patchy fog, detected a radar contact approaching at high speed. A radio challenge produced no response. The decision making process began. The commanding officer decided *tentatively* to take the contact under fire, but he decided to wait until it cleared the fog patches before making a *final* decision. The contact did appear; it was a British destroyer with a defective radio. Had the U.S. ship fired early on a tentative decision, the commanding officer might have, among other penalities, lost his leave and liberty privileges in Great Britain.

Another, slower-paced example from the experience of Admiral Claude Ricketts, an outstanding decision maker, occurred with respect to a mast case. The day before a supposed culprit was to appear at captain's mast, then-Commander Ricketts was asked by his executive officer what punishment he was going to assign the man.

"I don't know," said Commander Ricketts. "I haven't made a final decision yet."

"But, sir," said the executive officer, "we have all the facts, and they indicate he's guilty. Let's get on with it."

The next day a surprise witness appeared, testified that there had been a case of mistaken identity, and the case was dismissed.

As they walked away from the mast area, Ricketts said with his usual compassion to a considerably subdued executive officer, "Don't make a final decision until you have *all* the facts."

A good decision, with all facts included, is vital to success, but *speed* of decision is also important, particularly in time of war. With a *tentative* decision always in your mind, you can produce a *final* decision quickly if circumstances require it. Don't be afraid of a quick decision. If you have done your homework, it will be a good one. If subsequent developments show that it wasn't, remember that even John Paul Jones made a few bad decisions. Also remember that probably no one else could have made a better decision in the same circumstances. You are as good a commanding officer as the navy system produces. It is true that the selection system produced a few Queegs in World War II and the two decades thereafter, but in more recent years the selection system has been tightened and improved to the point where only the very best officers are honored with command. If you are one of these, *humbly* remember that you have been judged to have all the attributes and experience needed to be a superb commanding officer. The rest is up to you.

Losing Your Ship. Now that you have decided that you will have a positive attitude toward your success in combat, it is difficult ever to consider the possibility of the loss of your ship. Nevertheless, thought must be given to it. *Navy Regulations*, as discussed in previous chapters, state positively and without equivocation that you will fight your ship to the end. There can never be a thought about surrendering your ship, allowing boarding, or capture or removal of your crew. The aftermath of the *Pueblo* incident re-affirmed this historical tradition of our navy.

Once your crew is off the ship, you have discharged your responsibilities according to *Navy Regulations*. You are then free to leave, and you are *expected* to do so. Don't be burdened by nineteenth-century stories of captains going down with their ships. Most who did so were badly wounded, and only a few took this final step. The modern Royal Navy and the United States Navy have long discarded any remnants of this tradition. There is no current regulation or tradition which prevents you from leaving your ship after you have discharged your duties, if you are absolutely sure that it is about to sink. You should, of course, remain in the vicinity until it goes under to prevent any enemy from coming on the scene and boarding her. If you have commanded well and fought well the Navy will want to use your experience and talents again.

Summary. Put the thought of losing your ship behind you, and remember only the positive combat philosophy you determine to make your own and to impart to your officers and men. Hope that you do not have to demonstrate it, but decide that if you do, you will be bold, courageous, daring, tenacious, and aggressive, and that you will exercise the initiative with all the ingenuity you can muster. No one could do more.

We have talked much about nuclear war, and the devastation of our world should it occur. This is a necessary but pessimistic task. We must hope for better, and know that the United States is a positive force for peace. We will not be alone in feeling optimistic. In 1842 Lord Tennyson, in *Locksley Hall*, wrote:

> For I dipp'd into the future, far as human eye could see,
> Saw the Vision of the world, and all the wonder that would be;
> Saw the heavens fill with commerce, argosies of magic sails.
> Pilots of the purple twilight, dropping down with costly bales;
> Heard the heavens filled with shouting, and there rain'd a ghastly dew,
> From the nations' airy navies grappling in the central blue.
> Till the war drums throbbed no longer and the battle flags were furled,
> In the Parliament of Man, the Federation of the world.

Perhaps Tennyson was overly optimistic, but whatever happens, we can be sure that the United States Navy will lead the country in peace as in war. You, as the commanding officer of an American man-of-war, will contribute to this vital task.

In Conclusion

We have tried to lead you, as a present or future commanding officer of a United States ship, through the various elements of a commanding officer's career.

We started with the duties of a prospective commanding officer in connection with relieving a previous commanding officer or in commissioning a new ship. We then led you through the logical sequence of forming and reviewing commanding officer's policies; the administration of your ship and its officers and enlisted men; and the logistics, maintenance, and safety of your vessel.

As you passed through refresher training and prepared for active service, we discussed the principal tasks you would have and offered you advice and counsel.

Duty with the fleet and independent operations require advanced training of your crew and your own personal study and thought. We assembled for you the combined insight and wisdom of several generations of successful naval officers.

Finally, we outlined the ultimate task of every commanding officer, preparation for combat, and, if peacekeeping fails, then actual service in combat.

We hope you have learned from your imaginary voyage through this sea of problems and have profited from our advice.

We are sure that you will find your tour as commanding officer of a United States ship interesting, rewarding, and one which, no matter what higher rank you attain or responsibilities you are subsequently given, you will never forget. If you are the type of naval officer who enjoys the mantle of responsibility and the meeting of challenges (and most of you are), you will find your command tour the high point of your life.

Voltaire understood your position when he said:

> The right of commanding is no longer an advantage transmitted by nature; unlike an inheritance, it is the fruit of labors and its price is courage.

Work hard to qualify yourself and be willing to pay the price, and you, like John Paul Jones, will "sail in harm's way." Your Navy and your country depend upon you.

Appendix I

Sample Order for Change of Command Ceremony

USS CONCORD (CVA-78)

1 July 1979

MEMORANDUM

Subject: Change of Command Ceremony

1. At 1000 15 July 1979, a change of command ceremony will take place on this ship at which time I will be relieved by Captain Miles Standish, U.S. Navy. The Executive Officer is responsible for making all arrangements and will act as master of ceremonies.

2. *The Ceremonial Area*. The ceremonial area will be the flight deck adjacent to the superstructure. In the event of inclement weather the ceremonial area will be the after part of the hangar deck. A diagram showing the positioning of those involved and the equipment needed is attached as enclosure 1. In case of inclement weather the diagram will be modified accordingly. The First Lieutenant is responsible for these arrangements.*

3. *Guests*. Invitations will be procured, addressed, and mailed by the Ship's Secretary. Those desiring to invite guests submit names to the Ship's Secretary.

4. *Distinguished Guests*. Distinguished guests will include the Commander, Carrier Division TEN, who will be invited to

Notes: *Ceremonial areas must be modified for smaller ships. Destroyers usually use the after deck. Submarines place guests on adjacent pier or submarine deck.

make a short address. A list of all other distinguished guests will be provided to the Navigator by 0800 15 July 1979.

5. *Honors.* The Navigator will relieve the Officer of the Deck at 0900, 15 July, and will be responsible for all honors to be rendered to distinguished guests. No gun salutes will be fired. Honors will consist of side honors and music. First Division will furnish eight sideboys to report to the Officer of the Deck at 0900 15 July. The band will fall in on the quarterdeck at 0900 and will move to the ceremonial area as directed by the Officer of the Deck.

6. *Uniform.* The uniform for all officers and men of the *Concord* is full dress. The uniform for all military guests is service dress.

7. *Official Party.* Members of the official party will be:
The Division Commander
The Senior Chaplain
Captain John Alden
Captain Miles Standish
Commander Roger Smith

8. *Flags and Pennants.* The Chief Quartermaster will supervise the use of all flags and pennants. The flag of Commander Carrier Division TEN will be broken on his arrival and hauled down on his departure. When Captain Standish states that he relieves Captain Alden, break a new commission pennant and haul down the old one. Fold the old pennant into a neat package for later presentation to Captain Alden.†

9. *Refreshments.* At the conclusion of the ceremony the Executive Officer will announce that refreshments will be served in the Wardroom, the CPO Mess, and the Mess Hall. Caterers and the Supply Officer provide appropriate refreshments.

10. *Program of Events.* The following program of events will be carried out:
0900   Shift to appropriate uniform

---

†Commission pennant is not formally hauled down and then presented as part of ceremony as is done when a Flag Officer relieves. Exchanging commission pennants is carried out by most ships on an informal basis, with the presentation of the pennant at some convenient time after the ceremony.

Navigator relieve the Officer of the Deck

Sideboys and Band report to the Officer of the Deck

0940   Crew assemble

0945   Distinguished guests arrive. Division Commander to be escorted to Captain's Cabin. All other guests to be escorted to ceremonial area.

0955   Band move to ceremonial area.

0958   Official party depart Captain's Cabin

1000

(a) Upon arrival of official party Executive Officer calls crew to attention

(b) Arrival Honors. Ruffles and flourishes and Admiral's March

(c) National Anthem

(d) Master of Ceremonies introduces Senior Chaplain

(e) Invocation

(f) Master of Ceremonies requests all guests be seated

(g) Master of Ceremonies introduces Captain Alden

(h) Remarks and reading of orders by Captain Alden

(i) Captain Alden reports being ready to be relieved

(j) Master of Ceremonies introduces Captain Standish

(k) Captain Standish makes remarks, reads orders, assumes command, and reports to Division Commander

(l) Master of Ceremonies introduces Division Commander

(m) Division Commander makes remarks

(n) Master of Ceremonies asks guests to rise

(o) Benediction

(p) Departure honors for official party

(q) Master of Ceremonies announces conclusion of ceremony and extends invitation to reception in Wardroom, CPO Mess, and Mess Hall.

John Alden
Commanding

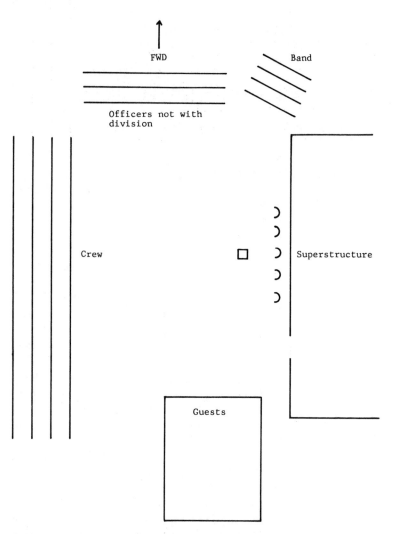

Figure I-1. Ceremonial area for change of command.

Appendix II

Sample Order for Commissioning a Naval Vessel

Commander, Naval Shipyard, Philadelphia
Office of the Prospective Commanding Officer
USS ALTARES (AF-109)

12 September 1978

MEMORANDUM

Subject: Commissioning Ceremony

1. The commissioning ceremony of the USS ALTARES (AF-109) will take place at 1000 25 September 1978. This memorandum covers those portions of the ceremony to be carried out by the precommissioning detail. Those parts of the ceremony which are the responsibility of the Commander, Naval Shipyard, have been arranged separately.

2. Invitations. All members of the detail desiring to invite guests should submit names and addresses to the Ship's Secretary, who will compile a list, and, after its approval, address and mail invitations. Those members of the detail desiring copies of the invitation for souvenir purposes may draw same from the Ship's Secretary.

3. *Guests*. Guests should be cautioned to arrive by 0945. They will

Note: on small ships and on submarines, guests and some of the crew may be placed on an adjacent pier.

be escorted to seats by twenty escorts, to be provided and instructed by the "S" Division.

4. *Distinguished Guests.* Since the ship will not be commissioned upon arrival of distinguished guests, they will be received without honors and escorted to the front seats of the visitors' area. Honors will be rendered upon departure.

5. *Honors.* Honors to be rendered upon departure will consist of music and sideboys. No gun salutes will be fired. Band will be furnished by the Commander, Naval Shipyard. Second Division furnish six sideboys as part of watch to be posted.

6. *Public Relations.* The Ship's Public Affairs Assistant will confer with the Shipyard Public Affairs Officer to assure timely notification of representatives of the media, their invitation, reception, and escort to the ceremony, and their invitation to the various receptions.

7. *Ceremonial Area.* The ceremonial area will be the main deck abaft the Quarterdeck, as provided by enclosure 1. Since an awning will be rigged there will be no need for a foul weather area.

8. *Master of Ceremonies.* The Executive Officer will act as master of ceremonies for that portion of the ceremony which is the responsibility of the Prospective Commanding Officer.

9. *Receptions.* Receptions will be held for guests in the Wardroom, CPO Mess, and the Crew's Mess directly after the ceremony. Outside caterers will provide the refreshments.

10. *Official Party.* The official party will consist of:
Commander, Naval Shipyard
The Prospective Commanding Officer
The Sponsor
Chaplain Blessed
The Prospective Executive Officer
The Aide to the Commander

11. *Program of Events.* The following program of events will be carried out:
(a)   0900   Prepare ceremonial area

(b) 0930   Crew assemble in designated areas
            Band arrive
            First watch assemble as indicated
            Escorts report to quarterdeck
(c) 0950   Commander arrives. Prospective Commanding
            Officer meet and escort Commander and Aide to
            Captain's Cabin
            Sponsor arrives. Prospective Executive Officer
            escort to Captain's Cabin
(d) 0959   Official party departs for ceremonial area
(e)   The first part of the ceremony is under the cogni-
            zance of the Commander, Naval Shipyard, and
            will be as he conducts it. The Prospective Exec-
            utive Officer, however, should call attention when
            the official party arrives. The following events will
            then take place, as directed by the Commander
(f)   Invocation by the Chaplain
(g)   Reading by the Commander of orders for delivery
            of ship
(h)   Commander orders the Prospective Commanding
            Officer to commission the USS *Altares*
(i)   The Prospective Commanding Officer will then
            order the Prospective Executive Officer to com-
            mission the ship
(j)   The Prospective Executive Officer will relay this
            order to the Prospective Navigator, who will be
            the Officer of the Deck
(k)   The Prospective Navigator will then order, "Com-
            mission the USS *Altares*."
(l)   Upon the issuance of this executive order:
            The bugler will sound attention
            The band will play the National Anthem
            The Ensign, Jack, and the Personal Flag of the
            Commander will be broken
(m)   The Prospective Commanding Officer will then

read his orders to command, salute the Commander, and report that he has assumed command of the USS *Altares*

(n)   The Commanding Officer will order, "Set the watch"

(o)   Upon the giving of this order:

The Boatswain and his mates will pipe

The Officer of the Deck will proceed to the quarterdeck and assume the watch

The watch will proceed at double time to their watch stations

(p)   The Executive Officer in his capacity as Master of Ceremonies will then introduce the Commander

(q)   Remarks by the Commander

(r)   The Master of Ceremonies will then introduce the Commanding Officer

(s)   Remarks by the Commanding Officer

(t)   The Master of Ceremonies will then introduce the Sponsor, who will make a presentation of a gift to the ship

(u)   Acceptance by Commanding Officer and remarks

(v)   Benediction

(w)   Departure of the official party

(x)   Announcement of receptions

JOHN SMITH
Prospective Commanding Officer

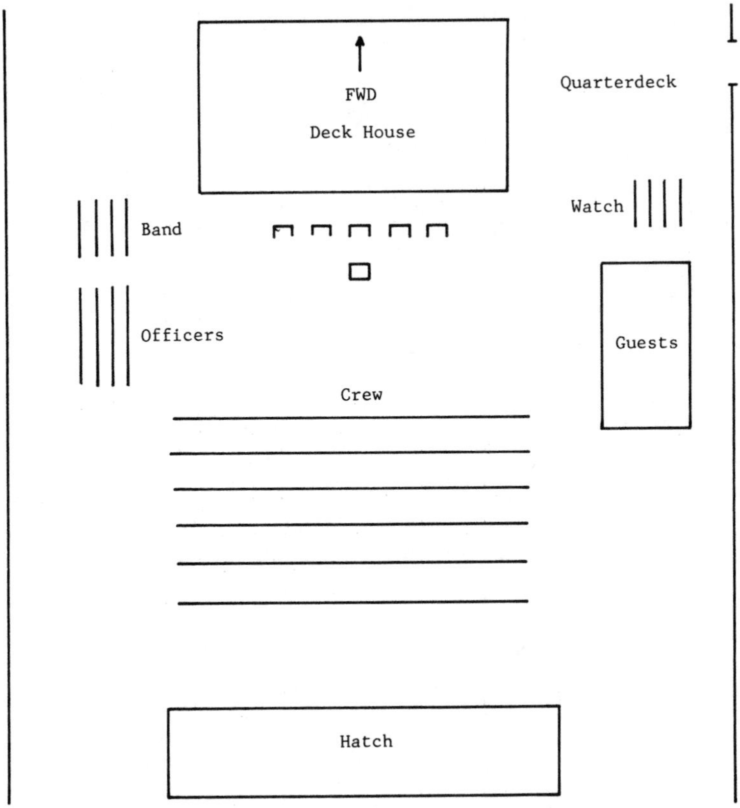

Figure II-1. Ceremonial area for commissioning.

Appendix III

Sample Standing Night Orders for a Destroyer or Other Small Ship

The following is a sample set of standing night orders designed for a destroyer. Other larger or smaller ships may adapt them for their use. Nuclear-powered ships and submarines will have to add sections to cover nuclear matters. These orders should be properly promulgated and then placed in a notebook in such a manner that individual pages cannot be removed. Other pages should be included on which watch officers can indicate by initialling that they have read the orders at least monthly. The Watch Officer's Guide, published by the Naval Institute Press, has a set of sample standing night orders which you may want to combine with this sample.

USS SHIP INSTRUCTION 3120.13

Subj: Standing (Night) Orders

Ref: (a) Navy Regulations, 1973
  (b) USS SHIPINST 3120. _____ (OPNAVINST 3120.32), Ships Organization and Regulations Manual (SORM)
  (c) CG-169, Rules of the Road–International-Inland
  (d) ATP-1(A) Vol. I
  (e) Watch Officers Guide, Tenth ed.

Encl: (1) Duties, Responsibilities and Authority of the Officer of the Deck (SORM, Art. 433) (Note: not included in this Appendix)

1. *Purpose*. To promulgate the Commanding Officer's Standing (Night) Orders.
2. *Cancellation*. USS SHIPINST _____ is cancelled and superseded.
3. *Discussion*.
   a. The time-honored tradition of ultimate responsibility and accountability of the commanding officer of a seagoing vessel is codified in reference (a), and needs no amplification. Your duties, responsibilities and authority as officer of the deck are generally delineated in Chapter 4 of reference (b), Article 433, a copy of which is attached as enclosure (1) for ready reference and frequent re-familiarization.
   b. Reference (b) also requires maintenance of a night order book, part of the ship's official records, which contains special precautions and other night orders for the officer of the deck. This instruction, along with the supplemented night orders, will constitute the night order book and will be carried out whenever I am absent from the bridge.
   c. These orders highlight my particular desires as to standard procedures to be followed in SHIP. I realize that I cannot catalogue specific responses to every conceivable hazardous situation, nor do I desire to reproduce verbatim rules of the road, maneuvering instructions, or watch-standing procedures contained in references (c) through (e). I expect you to have a thorough working knowledge of those publications and applicable operation plans/orders which, coupled with these orders and the initiative and mature judgment you have already demonstrated to become designated as officer of the deck, will serve as a basis for your performance.
   d. I expect these orders to be used as operational standards for all ship control stations, and as guidelines for all watch supervisors in training their successors.
4. *Standing Orders*.
   a. CALL ME IF IN DOUBT.
   b. Understand and comply with applicable portions of SORM, rules of the road, allied naval maneuvering instructions, per-

tinent ship, type, and fleet regulations, and operation plans/ orders.

c. Do not change course or speed without my permission (which may be given in supplemental night orders) except in circumstances which require, in your best judgment, immediate action, such as emergency action to avoid collision or grounding, "immediate executive" tactical signal, maneuvers to maintain sonar contact, or as directed by the tactical action officer (TAO). When so required, *act first*, then call me.

d. Be forehanded. Rehearse emergency situations in your mind, and organize and train your watch team to respond rapidly and effectively with minimum prompting. A quiet, well-organized bridge is a prerequisite to competent teamwork.

e. Be vigilant. You are your own best lookout. Use mechanical and electronic sensors and navigation aids, but do not become solely dependent on them. LOOK where you are going, step onto the open bridge wing toward which you are about to turn (or, if conning alongside or otherwise kept on the opposite wing, have another officer LOOK to ensure the new course is clear). Learn to recognize aspects and determine approximate ranges with binoculars, particularly at night.

f. Be thoroughly familiar with the tactical situation before relieving. Get briefed by the CICWO or TAO on your way to the bridge. If there is a doubt of *anything* amiss, call me at once.

g. Do not relieve the OOD until the rest of the watch section has been relieved and is settled down, normally on the hour.

h. When operating with CVs, stay out of a moving envelope 3000 yards ahead, 2000 yards abeam, and 1000 yards astern. *Never turn toward* a CV during maneuvers. If in doubt about his aspect or course during maneuvers, turn away to open range and call me immediately.

i. Call me (and be *certain* I understand):

    (1)   Prior to executing maneuvers to a new station (including rotation of axis).

(2)   For any surface contact with a CPA less than 10,000 yards, giving: present position (relative), target angle, approximate course and speed, CPA and time of CPA, and recommended course/speed change if required. Do *not* delay required action for want of information, for example if a small boat should suddenly be first detected visually close aboard ahead.

(3)   For all tactical signals. Do not acknowledge a tactical signal until you understand it. Request repeat if not understood.

(4)   Prior to base course and speed changes, unless directed in the supplemental night orders.

(5)   Navigational sightings (positively identify using a stop watch), or non-sightings (if not sighted within 15 minutes or 10 degrees of expected bearing), similarly for radar landfall (or if not made within 10% of expected range).

(6)   Any unusual phenomena.

(7)   Changes in vital equipment status.

(8)   Significant changes in weather (reduced visibility, .04 inches per hour change in barometric pressure, marked change in wind or sea condition). In case of reduced visibility, station fog lookouts, slow, and commence sounding fog signals when visibility is less than two miles.

(9)   Any hostile or potentially hostile contact (to include sonar contact classified possible or above).

(10)   When in formation, and units join or are detached.

(11)   IF IN DOUBT. If you question whether or not to call me—CALL.

j.   Ensure that the ship's position is fixed at sufficiently short intervals to indicate whether or not the ship is standing into danger, or is experiencing significant set and drift. These intervals will normally be included in the supplemental night orders.

k.   When in Condition III, the tactical action officer (TAO) will direct employment of combat systems. You will follow his directions unless such directions or maneuvers will cause imminent danger to the ship. Call me immediately in either case.

l. The executive officer (or navigator) is authorized and expected to relieve you if, in his opinion, you are taking insufficient or inappropriate action to avoid danger.

m. Close liaison is directed between the OOD, CICWO, and the EOOW. Keep each other informed as to the current situation and intentions to permit timely preparation for expected evolutions.

n. The EOOW is to be notified when the ship is about to enter a restricted maneuvering status (alongside, narrow channel, etc.). In this status, the EOOW will *not* automatically secure main propulsion in case of a major casualty, but will obtain CO/OOD permission first.

o. When keeping station, unless otherwise directed, stay within 10% of range or three degrees of bearing. DO NOT close a CV within ranges specified in subparagraph (h) above.

p. Remain in charge until properly relieved, and do not engage in any activity that might divert your attention. THE SAFETY OF THE SHIP AND ITS CREW (PRESENTLY IN YOUR CHARGE) IS *PARAMOUNT*.

q. As captain, I am completely and inescapably responsible for this ship, its equipment, and the lives of all personnel on board. I depend upon and trust you to assist me in this function by informing me promptly and fully of any event or occurrence which bears on the safety and fighting ability of this ship, and taking emergency action when necessary.

C. O. SIGNATURE

Distribution:
All Underway Watch Officers
Captain's Night Order Book
Officer of the Deck Folder

Appendix IV

Sample Night Order Form for a Small Surface Ship

CAPTAIN'S NIGHT ORDERS

Ship _____ Time zone _____ Date _____
Area _____
Enroute _____ From _____ Operating with _____
OTC _____ Flagship _____ In Station _____

FORMATION DATA

In formation _____ Axis _____ Guide _____
In station _____
Guide bears _____ Distance _____
Formation speed _____
Base course _____ T. _____ Mag. _____
PStgC. _____ Variation _____
Lighting condition _____ Emcon condition _____
Readiness cond. _____

SCREEN DATA

Screen type and no. _____ Screen axis _____ Circle ___
Number stations _____ number ships _____
Unassigned stations _____
Screen Comdr. _____ in _____ Own station _____
Patrolling _____ Zigzag plan _____

OWN SHIP DATA

Engines in use _____ Boilers in use _____
Generators on _____

Major Equipment not in use _____

Whaleboat condition _____ Watch condition _____

Radars in use _____ ECM Equipment in use _____

WEATHER

Sunset _____ Sunrise _____ Moonrise _____

Moonset _____

Weather expected _____

NAVIGATION

Navigational instructions _____

_____

Night intentions _____

_____

_____

1. Carry out Standing Night Orders. Return orders to me at 0800
2. Call me when in doubt and at _____
3. _____

_____

Commanding

_____

Executive Officer

_____

Navigator

Watch	OOD	JOOD	JOOW
20–24			
00–04			
04–08			

Watch remarks _____

_____

_____

_____

Appendix V

Sample Standing Orders for the Duty Officer in Port for a Nuclear Submarine

The following standing orders are designed for a nuclear submarine. They may be used in modified form by nuclear-powered surface ships. They are very extensive because of the stringent requirements for safety and security in nuclear-powered submarines. Surface ships with conventional power plants can use a simplified version.

USS SHIP INSTRUCTION 1601.4

Subj: Standing Orders for the Duty Officer in Port

Ref: (a) SHIP INST 5400.1 (SHIP Organization and Regulation Manual)

       (b) SHIP INST 5330.1 (SHIP Daily Routine)

1. *Purpose*. To promulgate the standing orders of the commanding officer for the guidance of ship's duty officers when moored alongside in port or when at anchor.

2. *Discussion*.

    a. These orders are directive in nature, and serve to amplify the general guidance for duty officers contained in reference (a). These orders are not intended to conflict with the basic reference, nor with other pertinent instructions received from higher authority. Any such conflict should be brought promptly to the attention of the executive officer for resolution. Additional amplifying instructions may from time to time be promulgated in the form of night orders or other special directives, and shall have the same force as these standing orders.

b. Nothing in these orders shall be construed as limiting the initiative of the duty officer. No references or standing instructions can envision all possible circumstances. These standing orders are provided to assist the duty officer in some of the more common cases which may be encountered.

3. *General.*

a. *Authority and Responsibility.*

The authority and responsibility of the duty officer are defined in reference (a), Article 2301. The duty officer is responsible to the commanding officer for the security of the ship when moored or at anchor. He is further responsible for the conduct of the ship's in-port routine, for the coordination of conflicting evolutions, and for the supervision of all ship's activities. The duty officer has authority over all personnel on board who are subject to the orders of the commanding officer, except the executive officer. These responsibilities shall not be taken lightly. While the officer of the deck underway has the commanding officer and other ship's officers immediately available if he needs assistance, the duty officer may be the only officer on board in port. He must not become lulled by the apparent security of the ship when shutdown and moored alongside. When in port abnormal conditions are more likely to exist because of maintenance. Fewer men are on board to combat casualties. The weather is a constant hazard to topside safety and shore service lines. It is very important that the duty officer have clearly in mind the potential hazards of any evolution authorized. A careful assessment must be made of possible additional hazards resulting from the simultaneous performance of two operations or maintenance evolutions, either of which might be safe if performed alone. Without full attention devoted to his watchstanding duties such considerations may escape the duty officer's notice. The responsibilities of the watch take precedence over departmental duties for the duty officer.

b. *Relationship of the Engineering Duty Officer.*
The relationship of the engineering duty officer to the ship's duty officer is the same as that of the engineering officer of the watch to the officer of the deck when underway. Occasions may arise when an officer lineally senior to the duty officer is assigned as engineering duty officer. Regardless of relative seniority, the engineering duty officer reports to the ship's duty officer for all matters pertaining to the watch. Maturity and good judgment on the part of both officers will alleviate any difficulty resulting from this complex relationship. In the unlikely event it becomes necessary to get the ship underway in the absence of both the commanding officer and executive officer, the senior line officer attached and on board shall temporarily succeed to command in accordance with Navy Regulations.

c. *Relationship of the Duty Chief Petty Officer.*
The duty chief petty officer is the principal assistant to the duty officer. Like the duty officer, his watchstanding duties take precedence over any departmental requirements. The duty officer shall ensure that the duty chief petty officer is closely involved in all aspects of the in-port watch. In particular, the duty chief petty officer is responsible to the duty officer for:

(1) Carrying out the normal in-port routine.
(2) Supervising the performance of all non-propulsion plant watchstanders.
(3) Mustering and supervising the training of all personnel delinquent in ship's and watch qualification.
(4) Mustering restricted men. Supervising all extra duty men in the absence of the chief of the boat.
(5) Cleanliness and orderliness of topside and adjacent pier areas, and all compartments, heads, access ladders and hatchways, forward of frame 57.
(6) Clean, neat appearance of cooks and mess cooks. Clean-

liness of the crew's mess and galley, and proper disposal of trash and garbage.

(7) Proper stowage of personal effects and neatness of bedding.

(8) Review and submission for approval and removal of all equipment tag-outs associated with the Ship's Tag-Out Log.

d. *Duty Section.* Duty section watch and manning requirements are detailed in reference (a) and the Engineering Department Manual. In view of the fact that some duty assignments may occasionally be doubled up in the person of a single individual, a minimum duty section strength of 15 men exclusive of duty officers and DCPO/EDPO is hereby established to ensure sufficient personnel in an off-watch status to handle ordinary emergencies. In reviewing the section watch bill, the duty officer shall ensure that it provides for all watches required by the above references plus any special watches required by separate instructions. No man may be assigned a watch whose name does not appear in the list of duly qualified watchstanders in the Watch Qualification Book. To permit an orderly assumption of duty by the on-coming watch section, the duty officer shall require that section leaders submit duty section watch bills for approval by noon on the previous working day. The approved watch bill should be posted prior to liberty call on the day before it takes effect. Once approved, the duty section watch bill shall not be changed without the duty officer's concurrence.

4. *Action.* All duty officers shall familiarize themselves with the contents of the pertinent sections of reference (a) and these standing orders. A thorough knowledge of the duties prescribed is essential for the proper execution of the functions of the duty officer in port.

a. *Honors, Ceremonies, and Smartness.*

(1) *Colors.* The duty officer normally shall attend morning and evening colors, arriving topside in sufficient time to

ensure all is in readiness. He will observe that these ceremonies are conducted with proper military smartness, and that anchor and topside lights are switched on/off precisely at sunset/sunrise. It should be noted that any unit commendation pennants or battle efficiency pennants are displayed only from sunrise to sunset, and thus should be hoisted/hauled down coincident with those events. The commissioning pennant is displayed 24 hours a day.

(2) *Tending the Side*. The duty officer shall tend the side on the arrival and departure of the commanding officer and distinguished visitors. To avoid embarrassment he should ensure the petty officer of the deck remains alert to the approach of such personages, and passes the word in sufficient time for the duty officer to meet the commanding officer or visitor at the brow. In the event the duty officer is unavoidably detained, the duty CPO shall tend the side in his stead, and be prepared to brief the captain as would the duty officer. (To do this the duty CPO must proceed toward the brow until he is sure the duty officer has preceded him.) Except on formal occasions the duty officer need not tend the side for the commanding officer during his routine comings and goings in the course of the day. The duty officer should be prepared to brief the commanding officer on the significant events of his watch and important changes in equipment status during his absence upon arrival.

(3) *Honors*. The duty officer should ensure that required honors are rendered punctiliously in accordance with applicable sections of Navy Regulations, DNC-27, and the Watch Officers' Guide. In particular, he should verify with the navigator whether a senior officer's flag or command pennant is to be broken when he comes aboard, and if so, ensure it is done smartly and on time. Note that the commissioning pennant and a command pennant or flag are never flown simultaneously.

(4) *Smartness*. The duty officer shall ensure that the highest standards of smartness are meticulously observed topside and belowdecks. It is noted that by reference (a) the duty CPO is charged with the smart appearance of the ship and its crew and precision in the execution of the plan of the day. The duty officer shall ensure that these duties are carried out with diligence and good effect. Items such as those listed below contribute significantly to a ship's reputation for smartness:

(a)   Appearance, bearing, and performance of the petty officer of the deck.

(b)   Masts and other appurtenances housed when not in use.

(c)   Clean, two-blocked colors and pennants.

(d)   Set of the mooring lines and night riders.

(e)   Orderliness, absence of "irish pennants," and cleanliness topside and pier alongside.

(f)   Cleanliness and preservation of access hatches, trunks, and passageways into the ship.

(g)   Manner of observance of sunrise, colors, etc.

(5) *Inspections*. The routine periodic inspection requirements for duty officers and duty petty officers are set forth in reference (a), Articles 2301–2304. These inspections should be timed such that those of the ship's duty officer, engineering duty officer, DCPO and EDPO occur in alternation in such a manner as to provide optimum coverage during the entire 24-hour period of duty. Each of these individuals is personally responsible for ensuring that he makes a tour of inspection at intervals not greater than every four hours. Trainees should conduct inspections together with their instructor or independently, depending on their state of training. Inspections by trainees shall be in addition to, not in lieu of, the inspections required of duty officers and duty petty officers by reference (a). To the maximum extent possible the inspec-

tions should occur without consistent pattern, and without prior notice to watchstanders whose performance is being observed. In making these rounds the duty officer/ duty petty officer shall enter physically the lower levels of each compartment inspected in order that nothing be overlooked. The inspections must not lapse into perfunctory walkthroughs. Most casualties are preceded by warning signs such as unusual noises or smells, fluids dripping, motors or bearings hot to the touch, changes in operating parameters, etc. During each inspection ship's duty officer and duty chief petty officer shall carefully examine the logs of the below decks watch and petty officer of the deck and initial same. The example set by the duty officers and duty petty officers will be reflected in the performance of their watchstanders.

(6) *Permission*. Except in an emergency, the permission of the commanding officer shall be obtained prior to conducting the following evolutions:

   (a) Loading and unloading of weapons, ammunition or pyrotechnics.

   (b) Impairment of the ship's ability to combat emergencies.

   (c) Charging the main storage battery.

   (d) Breaking or bypassing any interlocks.

   (e) Firing water slugs.

   (f) Discharge, transfer or disposal of radioactive effluent, liquid or solid waste, or transfer of radioactive equipment.

   (g) Opening the shielded volume of the reactor compartment.

   (h) Running any nuclear accident, propulsion plant, or ship's casualty drills.

   (i) Making any changes resulting in a shift from propulsion plant condition 1 to condition 2.

   (j) Energizing CRDMs. Conducting reactor startup

(except fast scram recovery) or shutdown.

(k) Conducting propulsion plant tests or special evolutions.

(l) Leaving prescribed watch stations unmanned, or combining duties of certain watchstanders.

(m) Changing propulsion plant watch requirements from condition 2 to condition 1.

(n) Placing out of commission any equipment or systems affecting our operational capability.

(o) Admitting any non-U.S. citizen below decks.

(p) Any exceptions to prescribed barrier criteria in maintenance of mechanical systems, or any work on or dangerously near energized electrical circuits.

(q) Conducting evolutions which involve the operation of primary plant boundary valves tagged in accordance with Article 304 of NAVSEA 389–0153.

b. *Reports.*

(1) *Morning Reports.* At 0800 each morning in port the duty officer shall ensure the following reports are on my desk for perusal:

(a) Morning message boards.

(b) Daily fuel, water, and chemistry report for the previous day.

(c) Duty officer and duty petty officer monitor reports for previous day.

(2) *Situation Reports.* While in port the following specific reports are desired. If I am off the ship those reports indicated by an asterisk (*) in general may be deferred until my return on board. All others listed should be made promptly whether I am on board or at home. The good judgment of the duty officer is relied upon to determine whether the degree of urgency requires I be contacted immediately if at a public function or social gathering. Similarly, the list below is not necessarily all-inclusive,

and the duty officer may find additional circumstances in which other reports are warranted.

(a)   Any failure to carry out my orders.

(b)   Relief of duty officer/engineering duty officer.

(c)   Significant delay in completing any evolutions for which I have granted permission.

(d)   Casualties to equipment or components affecting our operational capability. Unanticipated delays in repair of such equipment. Completion of repairs and placing back in service major out-of-commission equipment.

(e)   Any failure of our moorings or dragging of the anchor.

(f)   Any emergency on board such as fire, flooding, or collision.

(g)   Storm warnings or changes in hurricane conditions.

(h)   Change in DEFCON condition.

(i)   Initial opening and final closure of the reactor compartment.

(j)   Attainment of reactor criticality, and reactor shutdowns, scrams, or cutbacks.

(k)   Discharge of reactor coolant or oil into the harbor.

(l)   Loss of shore power or failure of the diesel generator if the alternate source is not immediately available.

(m)   Loss of all shore phones for longer than 2 hours.

*(n)   Movement of or casualties to other ships at our pier, in our ship, or at nearby anchorages.

*(o)   Absentees, shore patrol reports, or civil arrests of personnel attached.

*(p)   Significant injuries to personnel on board or attached.

*(q)   Any untoward incident relating to visitors.

*(r)   Family emergencies of concern to crew members.

*(s) Significant changes in the weather without hazards.

*(t) Visits of AEC and squadron monitors.

*(u) Completion of any items for which I have granted permission.

c. *Training.* The duty officer shall be alert to exploit all opportunities for training of personnel in the duty section. In particular he shall carry out the training schedule for the duty section promulgated by the executive officer unless overriding circumstances prohibit, in which case the executive officer shall be so informed by written memorandum. On completion of scheduled duty section drills conduct a drill critique with all participants and promptly forward a drill critique sheet to the executive officer.

d. *Visitors.* The ship's procedures and policies with respect to visitors are clearly and explicitly stated in the Visitors Bill (SSORM Art. 3106) and the Ship's Policy Document. The duty officer shall ensure the strict observance of the guidance provided therein. Visitors shall always be treated with courtesy and respect. The duty officer should ensure the petty officer of the deck understands the difference in procedures to be followed for casual visitors unfamiliar with our rules, for unauthorized visitors who aggressively try to board or otherwise interfere (SOP 3220), or for boarders who present a potential threat to the security of the ship or its personnel (SOP 3127).

e. *Safety.* One of the principal responsibilities of the duty officer is to ensure by his frequent rounds of inspection the safety of the ship and its crew. The dangers of fire, flooding, and collision are readily apparent and will not be elaborated on. Several safety-related aspects of the watch do require mention because of frequent abuses or casualties experienced:

(1) *Topside Watch.* The safety of the topside watch (POOD, sentry, etc.) shall be a matter of personal and continuing concern to the duty officer. The rounded hull of a modern SSN is treacherous, particularly when wet or icy. Top-

side watchstanders are frequently young and careless crew members who may not fully appreciate the dangers inherent in their watch. No compromise in the safety requirements for topside watchstanders, including trainees, shall be permitted. In periods of rough weather when water is washing over the ship all deck hatches should be shut and the POOD should be stationed on the bridge with access to the ship by jacob's ladder and the bridge access trunk.

(2) *Sail.* During upkeep periods the sail is a potentially dangerous area, both for personnel and for equipment. The hydraulically operated masts have sufficient force to crush a man. Tools, etc., left in the sail in the course of work can foul cable sheaves and cause expensive damage. Welding or grinding operations conducted without thorough protective measures can lead to serious damage to hydrophones, radomes, periscope optics, hydraulic cylinders, and mast barrels. Even careless painting which splatters head windows or mast hoists can cause significant damage. Consequently it is incumbent upon the duty officer to ensure the work area has been carefully inspected by competent and responsible personnel before granting permission to undertake work in the sail or cycle a mast. For extensive work he should himself make this inspection. Before a mast is moved when sail plates are off or work is known to have been in progress in or on top of the sail a visual inspection shall have been made through all sail plate openings and a man shall be sent to the bridge to inspect the top of the sail and verify it clear before movement of the mast by the operator at the BCP.

(3) *Divers.* Diving operations are by nature potentially hazardous. The duty officer shall concern himself personally with the safety of diving operations and ensure he knows where the divers will be working. In addition to tagging out underwater appurtenances and refraining from blowing tanks, etc. while divers are in the water, the duty

officer is responsible for ensuring the requirements of the Radiological Controls Manual concerning diving operations in way of the reactor are scrupulously complied with, regardless to what organization the divers belong. In order to ensure safe standoff distances are maintained it may prove necessary to suspend weighted lines over the side to define boundaries for the divers. Divers should also be briefed as to the locations of radioactive discharge openings and cautioned not to touch these openings or sea growth surrounding them to avoid contamination. If such contamination is possible the divers should be monitored on leaving the water.

(4) *Reactor Containment.* Requirements for reactor containment extend further than the boundaries of the reactor compartment itself. When advised by the EDO of the necessity for setting reactor containment, the duty officer needs to be aware of the requirement to be prepared to seal compartments adjoining the reactor compartment with gastight barriers (low pressure). In order to do this the watch must be aware of all openings in these compartments and have necessary materials ready at hand to form the sealing barriers. Not only must WT doors and hatches be considered, especially so if fouled by lines or hoses, but also temporary openings resulting from upkeep work such as a periscope removed, a cable penetration or salvage valve under repair, etc.

(5) *Dry Dock.* With the ship in dry dock a false sense of security may tend to exist. With the disruptions of normal systems and hull integrity due to repair work, the time spent in dry dock is particularly hazardous. Not only must the duty officer be particularly alert for fire hazards within the ship, he must also be alert to those hazards in the ship's tanks and beneath the ship in the dock itself. His routine inspections must include both these areas. Strange as it may seem, serious flooding accidents have

occurred to ships in dry dock, not because the dock was flooded down, but because of a breakdown in work controls or tagouts involving lines containing water or oil under pressure. An additional danger exists in loose gear topside which may accidentally fall into the dock and injure someone standing below. In dry dock the duty officer shall be vigilant and demanding in requiring both repair personnel and ship's force to adhere to high housekeeping and work control standards.

f. *Propulsion Plant Readiness.* The duty officer shall keep himself informed of the state of readiness of the propulsion plant, and of the length of time required to be self-sustaining on at least one SSTG. Normally the reactor plant will not be cooled down unless reliable shore power and the diesel generator are both available. In the event of loss of either of these sources of auxiliary power steps should be taken to make at least one steam side operable and conduct daily checks of plant instrumentation to reduce the preparatory time in the event startup of the reactor plant becomes necessary. In the event both shore power and the diesel generator are lost or unavailable, immediate preparations for reactor startup must begin, as the ship's battery has but limited capacity. If shore power or the diesel has not been regained before startup preparations are complete, the EOOW should be directed to commence reactor startup and continue until self-sustaining.

g. *Relief.* The ship's duty officer shall be relieved at 0800 (0900 on weekends and holidays) or as soon thereafter as practical. In some cases, where a single ship's duty officer is to be relieved by an oncoming engineering duty officer as well as the ship's duty officer, the EDO will be requested to relieve at 0600. The offgoing duty officer shall prepare a Duty Officer Status Sheet using the form of enclosure (2) to this instruction. On completion of the relief, the oncoming duty officer will announce his relief on the 1MC.

h. *Procedures at Anchor.* At anchor all normal in port requirements for the duty officer remain in effect. In addition to these, a number of further requirements ensue because of the change in circumstances. At anchor the duty officer shall ensure that:

(1) The duty section comprises sufficient numbers of men with necessary qualifications to set a full underway watch. When boating is threatened by the weather at least one half the crew shall be retained aboard.

(2) An anchor watch is stationed and systems are kept lined up which will permit:

    (a) Answering bells on the EPM with 5 minutes notice in an emergency.

    (b) Heaving in or veering additional anchor chain on 15 minutes notice.

    (c) Lowering (water depth permitting) and maneuvering on the SPM on 15 minutes notice.

    (d) Getting underway on the diesel/EPM on 15 minutes notice.

    (e) Plotting the ship's position by visual/radar bearings and ranges at intervals not to exceed one half hour, the results of each fix being reported to the duty officer/duty CPO.

    (f) Detecting evidence of dragging of the anchor. (In addition to the evidence provided by the fixes, dragging of the anchor may be revealed by surging of the anchor chain, causing a repetitive thumping heard near the anchor windlass station.)

(3) Either the duty officer or the CPO is up and about at all times supervising the anchor watch. If the duty officer is not absolutely certain of the ship's position, or if wind, seas or current appear to be combining to put a heavy strain on the anchor chain, the duty officer shall station himself in control or on the bridge where he can best supervise the plotting of the ship's position and preparations for getting underway.

(4) The functions of duty officer and engineering duty officer shall not be combined when at anchor.

(5) Either the duty officer or duty CPO shall attend the arrival and departure of all boats, ensuring they are not overloaded in light of existing weather and sea conditions, that sufficient safety equipment is readily available in the boat, that the boat is in good operating condition and equipped with a satisfactory compass, charts, and lights, that the senior man in the boat has been identified, and that good discipline prevails. When appropriate, boating shall be restricted on the duty officer's authority.

(6) The reactor plant normally will be maintained in condition such that reactor startup could be commenced on 15 minutes notice in event of failure of the diesel engine or deterioration of the weather. The battery shall be kept fully charged.

James D. Alden

Appendix VI

Sample At-Anchor Duty Officer Status Sheet

The following status sheet is designed specifically for a nuclear attack submarine. Surface ships can easily design a similar form modified to suit their type, weapons, and power plant.

DUTY OFFICER STATUS SHEET

Rx status: _____ Able to startup in _____ hr, self-sustaining in _____ hrs.

Electric Plant Line-up: _____ Battery Gravity: _____ Amp-hrs out: _____.

Nav bus power supply _____.

Ventilation lineup _____ O_2 pressure: #1 _____ #2 ___

% potable water on hand _____.

Torpedo Tube status: 7. Weapons load status:

#1 LOADED–MK ____ EMPTY/FLOODED/DRY
#2 LOADED–MK ____ EMPTY/FLOODED/DRY
#3 LOADED–MK ____ EMPTY/FLOODED/DRY
#4 LOADED–MK ____ EMPTY/FLOODED/DRY

SINS mode _____ MK 19 gyro _____ MK 27 gyro ___

DEFCON _____. Notional number _____.

COMM guard _____.

SOPA _____ CO at _____. XO at _____.

HERO/Divers/Sonar restrictions _____.

Stores status: Frozen _____, Chill _____,

Dry _____

Critical spares: _____

Logs reviewed: (RDO initial) Watchbill _____

Below Decks _____

OOC List _____ Tagout Log _____

Phones: CO _____ Wardroom _____

Activity Space _____

Deviations from Rig for Surface _____

MBT vent covers installed/not installed (except) _____

Absentees: _____

Restricted men: _____

Training completed: _____

Training for today: _____

Unexecuted orders/major repairs/remarks: _____

_____

_____

_____

_____

_____

_____

Deck Log written _____ . CO morning reports submitted ____

Pre-relief inspection: (RDO initial)

a. DCPO relief tour with off-going DCPO completed. Permission granted to relieve Duty Section: _____

b. DCPO topside inspection completed per topside check off list: __

c. Duty Officer relief tour with offgoing Duty Officer: _____

Duty Officer properly relieved at time: _____

_____   _____

Relieving Duty Officer (RDO)   Offgoing Duty Officer (ODO)

Appendix VII

Admiral Arleigh Burke, on the Occasion of his Retirement:

Letter written by Admiral Arleigh Burke, U.S. Navy, to the officers and men of the United States Navy upon the occasion of his retirement.

10 July, 1961

TO THE OFFICERS AND MEN OF THE UNITED STATES NAVY:

There comes a time in every man's life when he must attempt to evaluate what he has done to better his country, his service, his family, and his group. This review can very well comprise the legacy a man bequeaths to his successors.

I have now—with more than a twinge of reluctance—reached this stage, and in retrospect I find it impossible to single out any one item which I can truthfully say was exclusively and inalienably mine. This is a truism which most men recognize eventually because they learn that major achievements can be achieved only with the cooperation of friends and shipmates.

In forty-two years of naval service I have had a unique opportunity to serve my country which I deeply appreciate. I have also been blessed with the loyalty, support and friendship of the most dedicated people I have ever known, not least of whom is my devoted wife.

Experience has brought me a full appreciation of the prize cargo a man can hoist aboard. To this beloved Navy I do commend:

Love of country, overshadowing all other loves, including service, family, and sea.

Individual desire to excel, not for aggrandizement of self, but to increase the excellence of the Navy.

Devotion—perhaps consecration—to personal integrity in oneself, in one's service, in one's country.

Courage to stand for principle, regardless of efforts to dilute this courage through compromise or evasion.

My service life has been rich and rewarding, and no man can ask for more. May you, too, find satisfaction, and throughout your careers experience fair winds and following seas.

ARLEIGH BURKE

Appendix VIII

Admiral Rickover's Thoughts on Leadership

In a speech titled "Thoughts on Man's Purpose in Life," delivered to the San Diego Rotary Club on February 10th, 1977, Admiral Hyman G. Rickover talked in part on the subjects of responsibility, perseverance, excellence, and courage. This is what he said.

Among these principles of existence, responsibility is the one which forces man to become involved. Acceptance of responsibility means that the individual takes upon himself an obligation. Responsibility is broad and continuous. None of us are ever free of it, even if our work is unsuccessful.

Responsibility implies a commitment to self which many are not willing to make; they are strongly attracted to accepting a course of action or direction for their lives imposed by an external source. Such a relationship absolves the individual from the personal decision-making process. He wraps himself in the security blanket of inevitability or dogma, and need not invest the enormous amounts of time, effort and, above all, the thought required to make creative decisions and meaningfully participate in the governance of life.

Responsibility also implies a commitment to others, or as Confucius taught, each of us is meant to rescue the world. It is the business of little minds to shrink from this task or to go about it without enthusiasm. Neither art, nor science, nor any of the great works of humanity would ever come into being without enthusiasm.

The sense of responsibility for doing a job right seems to be declining. In fact, the phrase "I am not responsible" has become a standard response in our society to complaints on a job poorly done. This response is a semantic error. Generally what a person means is: "I cannot be held legally liable." Yet, from a moral or ethical point of view, the person who disclaims responsibility is correct: by taking this way out he is truly not responsible; he is irresponsible.

The unwillingness to act and to accept responsibility is a symptom of America's growing self-satisfaction with the status quo. The result is a paralysis of the spirit, entirely uncharacteristic of Americans during the previous stages of our history. Even complaints about high taxes and high prices are illusory. Behind them is hidden the reality that the majority, in terms of sheer creature comfort, never had it so good. Those who are still on the outside looking in are not strong or numerous enough to make a political difference.

The task of finding a purpose in life also calls for perseverance. I have seen many young men who rush out into the world with their messages, and when they find out how deaf the world is, they withdraw to wait and save their strength. They believe that after a while they will be able to get up on some little peak from which they can make themselves heard. Each thinks that in a few years he will have gained a standing, and then he can use his power for good. Finally the time comes, and with it a strange discovery: he has lost his horizon of thought. Without perseverance, ambition and a sense of responsibility have evaporated.

Another important principle of existence which gives purpose and meaning to life is excellence. Because the conviction to strive for excellence is an intensely personal one, the attainment of excellence is personally satisfying. Happiness comes from the full use of one's power to achieve excellence. Life is potentially an empty hole, and there are few more satisfying ways of filling it than by achieving and exercising excellence.

This principle of excellence is one which Americans seem to

be losing, and at a time when the Nation stands in need of it. A lack of excellence implies mediocrity. And in a society that is willing to accept a standard of mediocrity, the opportunities for personal failure are boundless. Mediocrity can destroy us just as surely as perils far more famous.

It is important that we distinguish between what it means to fail at a task and what it means to be mediocre. There is all the difference in the world between the life lived with dignity and style which ends in failure, and one which achieves power and glory, yet is dull, unoriginal, unreflective, and mediocre. In a real sense, what matters is not so much whether we make a lot of money or hold a prestigious job; what matters is that we seek out others with knowledge and enthusiasm—that we become people who can enjoy our own company.

In the end, avoiding mediocrity gives us the chance to discover that success comes in making ourselves into educated individuals, able to recognize that there is a difference between living with excellence and living with mediocrity. Sherlock Holmes once told Dr. Watson, "Watson, mediocrity knows nothing higher than itself. It takes talent to recognize genius." To which he could have added, it takes talent to know that what counts is condemning mediocrity not in others but in ourselves.

We should honor excellence, but not necessarily with material rewards alone. The Japanese have a custom which I believe it would be well for us to emulate. Instead of honoring their artists with peerages or knighthoods, they give them the respectful title, "National Human Treasure."

Creativity is another of the basic principles of existence which I believe help to give purpose in life. The deepest joy in life is to be creative. To find an undeveloped situation, to see the possibilities, to decide upon a course of action, and then devote the whole of one's resources to carry it out, even if it means battling against the stream of contemporary opinion, is a satisfaction in comparison with which superficial pleasures are trivial.

To create you must care. You must have the courage to speak

out. The world's advances always have depended on the courage of its leaders. A certain measure of courage in the private citizen also is necessary to the good conduct of the State. Otherwise men who have power through riches, intrigue, or office will administer the State at will, and ultimately to their private advantage. For the citizen, this courage means a frank exposition of a problem and a decrying of the excesses of power. It takes courage to do this because in our polite society frank speech is discouraged. But when this attitude relates to questions involving the welfare or survival of the Nation, it is singularly unfitting to remain evasive. It is not only possible, but in fact a duty of everyone to state precisely what his knowledge and conscience compel him to say. Many of today's problems can be brought forward only by complete candor and frankness; deep respect for the facts, however unpleasant and uncomfortable; great efforts to know them where they are not readily available; and drawing conclusions guided only by rigorous logic.

To have courage means to pursue your goals, or to satisfy your responsibilities, even though others stand in the way and success seems like a dream. It takes courage to stand and fight for what you believe is right. And the fight never ends. You have to start it over again each morning as the sun rises. Sir Thomas More wrote: "If evil persons cannot be quite rooted out, and if you cannot correct habitual attitudes as you wish, you must not therefore abandon the commonwealth. You must strive to guide policy indirectly, so that you make the best of things, and what you cannot turn to good, you can at least make less bad."

These principles of existence—responsibility, perseverance, excellence, creativity, courage—must be wedded with intellectual growth and development if we are to find meaning and purpose in our lives. It is a device of the devil to let sloth into the world. By the age of twenty, some of us already have adopted a granite-like attitude which we maintain throughout life. Intellectually, we must never stop growing. Our conscience should never release us from concern for the problems of the day. Our minds must be forever skeptical, yet questioning. We must strive to be singularly free from that failing so common to man, deplored by Pascal in the "Pensees," of filling our leisure with meaningless distractions so as to preclude the necessity of thought. To be an intellectual in the fullest sense, one's mind must be in constant movement.

Appendix IX

Admiral Gorshkov on the Training Task of the Ship Commander

Excerpt from an article by Fleet Admiral S. Gorshkov, Soviet Union, Commander-in-Chief of the Navy, translated from Morsky Sbornik No. 1 of January 1979

We have begun 1979, a new training year in combat and political training. Improving combat readiness was and remains paramount and decisive in carrying out combat training missions.

Combat readiness—this is the condition which determines the degree of preparedness of a ship for accomplishing the combat missions which it has been assigned. It includes a whole series of components which, like the links in a single chain, are closely interconnected and objectively depend upon one another. It has to do with keeping at full strength the availability of the necessary material, maintaining the ship, weapons, and equipment in good working order, a high level for the combat and political training of the seaman, petty officers, and officers, their teamwork in combat, the CO's training and that of the staff, and firm military discipline.

If we were to sum up the diversity of these elements and to define their principal purpose, we might say that combat readiness denotes the capacity, in any circumstance, to engage the enemy in a disciplined manner, to repulse his attack, to enter into combat against him and to inflict a crushing defeat on him. . .

The tactical skill of the officers and the training of the entire crew depend chiefly upon the personal knowledge of the CO, his persistence, purposefulness, and his organizational abilities. He is personally responsible for preparing and conducting all tactical measures aboard ship, of creating, as part of them, the conditions which correspond to modern combat, and for teaching the men under him to operate under complex circumstances against a powerful, experienced enemy, who has initiative. The training must proceed under conditions of increased complexity which will force the trainees to make decisions and to operate under actual circumstances.

We can no longer overlook instances where individual COs turn over the development of tactical measures to officers with insufficient training, and where the content of group exercises and short tactical exercises is reduced to elementary questions and answers.

We cannot content ourselves only with the satisfactory evaluations of the COs' tactical training. Such evaluations attest to the deficient, not to mention poor, knowledge of the ways and means to employ a ship, weapons, and equipment in combat.

We cannot allow that sometimes tactical manuals, guidelines, and instructions developed aboard ship or in the force are not tested and mastered at sea, but lie about in offices like unnecessary cargo and are not opened except when the ship is checked and inspected.

It is not enough for the CO of a ship today to know only his own ship, her weapons and equipment, and the methods of combat employment. He cannot find the most effective alternative of his own fire and movement, if he has not studied in detail the fighting capabilities of the enemy, his strong and weak points, and does not know how to pick out the main feature which will most influence the outcome of the battle.

Knowing the enemy is one of the most important elements of a CO's tactical training. Not only are the quantitative data, the distribution and the tactical and technical elements of the forces to be kept in mind; the main thing is the knowledge of operational tactics, maneuverability, and employment of weapons, in order to counter the enemy's skill and ability. It is necessary to have done with, once and for all, cases where, during the study of the probable enemy, some officers in charge are restricted to the academic questioning of subordinates, while they evaluate the level of their knowledge from memorized numbers and names. This does not lead to know-how, is of no use, and does not work toward combat readiness.

Appendix X

The Belknap-Kennedy Collision

The Chief of Naval Operations memorandum issued after the completion of the administrative and judicial processes incident to the Belknap-Kennedy collision.

2 October 1976

MEMORANDUM FOR ALL FLAG OFFICERS AND OFFICERS IN COMMAND

Subj: BELKNAP/KENNEDY Collision

Encl: (1)   Summary of Circumstances of Collision and Related Administrative and Judicial Processes

1. On 22 November 1975, USS BELKNAP (CG 26) was severely damaged in a collision at sea with USS JOHN F. KENNEDY (CV 67) which cost the lives of eight Navy personnel and injured forty-eight others. A formal investigation held the Commanding Officer and the Officer of the Deck of BELKNAP accountable for the tragic incident. The Commanding Officer was subsequently referred to trial by general court-martial which resulted in disposition tantamount to acquittal on all charges and specifications. The Officer of the Deck was also tried by general court-martial and, although convicted of three separate charges, was sentenced to no punishment. There has been some outspoken criticism of the outcome of the BELKNAP courts-martial. Much of that criticism reflects concern that the principle of command responsibility may have been imperiled as a result of the BELKNAP cases. I want to here address that concern, and to assure each of you that resolu-

tion of the BELKNAP cases will not in any way jeopardize the concepts of command responsibility, authority and accountability.

2. There has always been a fundamental principle of maritime law and life which has been consistently observed over the centuries by seafarers of all nations: The responsibility of the master, captain or commanding officer on board his ship is absolute. That principle is as valid in this technical era of nuclear propulsion and advanced weapons systems as it was when our Navy was founded two hundred years ago. This responsibility, and its corollaries of authority and accountability, have been the foundation of safe navigation at sea and the cornerstone of naval efficiency and effectiveness throughout our history. The essence of this concept is reflected in Article 0702.1 of Navy Regulations, 1973, which provides in pertinent part that: "The responsibility of the commanding officer for his command is absolute, except when, and to the extent, relieved therefrom by competent authority, or as provided otherwise in these regulations."

3. To understand fully this essential principle, it must first be recognized that it is not a test for measuring the *criminal* responsibility of a commanding officer. Under our system of criminal justice, in both civilian and military forums, in order that a man's life, liberty and property may be placed at hazard, it is not enough to show simply that he was the commanding officer of a Navy ship involved in a collision and that he failed to execute to perfection his awesome and wide ranging command responsibilities. Rather, it must be established by legally admissible evidence and beyond a reasonable doubt that he personally violated carefully delineated and specifically charged provisions of the criminal code enacted by the Congress to govern the armed forces—the Uniform Code of Military Justice—before a commanding officer can be found criminally responsible for his conduct. Military courts-martial are federal courts and the rules of evidence and procedure applicable therein are essentially the same as those which pertain

in any other federal criminal court and the rights of an accused, whether seaman or commanding officer, are closely analogous to those enjoyed by any federal criminal court defendant. The determination of criminal responsibility is therefore properly the province of our system of military justice. The acquittal of a commanding officer by a duly constituted court-martial absolves him of *criminal* responsibility for the offenses charged. It does *not*, however, absolve him of his responsibility as a commanding officer as delineated in U.S. Navy Regulations.

4. When the results of the BELKNAP cases were reported in the press, many assumed that the Commanding Officer and the Officer of the Deck of BELKNAP had been absolved of all responsibility for the collision by the military judges that presided over their respective courts-martial and that the principle of command responsibility had thereby been imperiled. Soon thereafter I began to receive letters from concerned members of both the retired and active naval community. Much of this reaction was critical of the results of the two courts-martial and revealed a serious misunderstanding of the role of military justice in the naval service.

5. The responsibility of a commanding officer for his command is established by long tradition and is clearly stated in U.S. Navy Regulations. In the case of the BELKNAP-KENNEDY incident, the JAG MANUAL investigating officer determined that both the Commanding Officer and the Officer of the Deck of BELKNAP were personally responsible for the collision. CINCUSNAVEUR, the convening authority of the investigation, approved that finding on review, as did I, when I took action on the investigative report as CNO. BELKNAP's Commanding Officer and Officer of the Deck were thereby held to be accountable for that tragic accident.

6. Responsibility having been officially and unequivocally established, it then remained to determine what sanctions, if any, were to be taken against the two officers concerned. It goes without

saying that documented professional shortcomings are appropriately noted in reports of fitness and that errors in judgment thus detailed are taken into account before the individual concerned is considered for assignment or promotion or entrusted with command. However, in this instance, it was determined that further official action was warranted. Accordingly, CINCUSNAVEUR issued a letter of reprimand to the Commanding Officer and recommended that the Officer of the Deck by tried by general court-martial. CINCLANTFLT subsequently referred criminal charges against both the Commanding Officer and the Officer of the Deck to trial by general court-martial. As previously noted, the trial of the Commanding Officer resulted in disposition equivalent to acquittal and the trial of the Officer of the Deck resulted in his conviction. (Enclosure (1) is a summary of these administrative and judicial processes as well as a brief description of the circumstances of the collision itself.)

7. The imposition of the punitive letter of reprimand as nonjudicial punishment constituted a formal sanction against the Commanding Officer. The subsequent judicial resolution of his general court-martial in a manner tantamount to acquittal could not and did not vitiate the established fact of his accountability. It simply determined that the evidence of record was not legally sufficient to find him guilty of the criminal charges for which he had not previously been punished. In the case of the Officer of the Deck of BELKNAP, the court determined that the evidence of record was legally sufficient to find him guilty beyond reasonable doubt of all but one of the criminal offenses charged.

8. In summary, the Commander's responsibility for his command is absolute and he must and will be held accountable for its safety, well-being and efficiency. That is the very foundation of our maritime heritage, the cornerstone of naval efficiency and effectiveness and the key to victory in combat. This is the essence of the special trust and confidence placed in an officer's patriotism, valor, fidelity and abilities. Every day in command tests the strength of

character, judgment and professional abilities of those in command. In some cases, Commanders will be called upon to answer for their conduct in a court of law. In all cases, they will be professionally judged by seagoing officers—a far more stringent accountability in the eyes of those who follow the sea. We in the Navy would have it no other way, for the richest reward of command is the personal satisfaction of having measured up to this responsibility and accountability. The loss of life, personal injuries, and material damages sustained in the collision of USS BELKNAP and USS JOHN F. KENNEDY serve as a tragic reminder of the necessity and immutability of the principle of command responsibility. The Commanding Officer and the Officer of the Deck of BELKNAP have been held accountable for that terrible loss of men and equipment. The concept of command responsibility has not been eroded.

9. The JAG MANUAL investigating officer's report of the collision included a number of lessons learned and specific recommendations designed to ensure that corrective action is taken. I have directed that those recommendations be implemented expeditiously and some of you are now personally involved in that task.

J. L. HOLLOWAY III

Summary of Circumstances Relating to the Belknap-Kennedy Collision and the Administrative and Judicial Processes Emanating Therefrom

The following is a brief description of the circumstances of the collision and of the administrative and judicial processes which should help you understand why the principle of command responsibility in the Navy has not been eroded by the BELKNAP cases.

Collision

On the evening of 22 November 1975, elements of Task Group 60.1, including USS JOHN F. KENNEDY (CV 67) and USS BELKNAP

(CG 26), were operating in the Ionian Sea. At 2130 BELKNAP and KENNEDY were in a line of bearing formation on course 200°, speed 10 kts, with the screen operating independently. BELKNAP was maintaining a station on a relative bearing of 200°, 4000 yards from KENNEDY. At approximately 2145 KENNEDY began preparations for the last recovery of aircraft, scheduled for 2200, and was displaying flight deck lighting for aircraft operations. KENNEDY transmitted her intentions to turn into the wind with a "CORPEN J PORT 025–12" signal. The signal was acknowledged in BELKNAP and KENNEDY's execute signal followed very closely thereafter. The OOD in BELKNAP planned to slow, allow KENNEDY to complete her turn in front, and then bring BELKNAP around to port to the new course and maneuver into station. The CO of BELKNAP was not on the bridge at the time this maneuver was commenced and it is not clear whether he was apprised of the signal before the OOD executed his plan of action. The OOD and CO had discussed two previous CORPEN J STARBOARD maneuvers and the CO had concurred in the OOD's intention to "slow and follow the carrier around" in both prior instances. However, a course of action in the event of a possible CORPEN J PORT maneuver had not been discussed.

At about 2148 BELKNAP began to slow and ease to port as KENNEDY increased speed and came left toward the new course of 025T. Shortly thereafter the OOD in BELKNAP began to evidence first doubts as to the target angle of KENNEDY. CIC, realizing that the CPA would be close, recommended that BELKNAP come right. That recommendation, however, was not acknowledged by the bridge. The OOD, becoming less and less sure of KENNEDY's target angle, summoned the CO to the bridge at 2156. Immediately prior to the CO's arrival, the OOD ordered left full rudder causing BELKNAP's head to swing left and prompting KENNEDY to signal "Interrogative your intentions" followed by "come right full rudder now." CO, BELKNAP, now on the bridge, recognized that his ship was in extremis, and ordered right full rudder, all engines back emergency. KENNEDY had also applied right full rudder and all engines back full and BELKNAP passed down KENNEDY's port side close aboard on an approximately opposing course (see attached diagram). However, KENNEDY's flight deck extension collided with BELKNAP's bridge, sheared off a large portion of BELKNAP's superstructure and knocked over the macks. Fire fed by aviation fuel from KENNEDY engulfed BELKNAP. A total of eight crewmen were killed and forty-eight injured in the two ships as a direct result of the collision. Damages exceeded $100,000,000.00.

JAG Manual Investigation

RADM Donald D. Engen, USN, was appointed by CINCUSNAVEUR to conduct a formal one officer investigation of the collision and to "fix individual responsibilities for the incident." The commanding officers and officers of the deck of both BELKNAP and KENNEDY were designated as parties to the investigation. The investigation was begun on 23 November 1975 and was completed on 31 December. The investigating officer determined that BELKNAP's Commanding Officer and Officer of the Deck were responsible for the collision and the ensuing personnel casualties and material damages.

The investigating officer recommended, among other things, that the Commanding Officer of BELKNAP be awarded a punitive letter of reprimand for his failure to ensure the safety, well-being, and efficiency of his command, as evidenced by his "failure to be present on the bridge . . . during the initial maneuvers in a new station in close proximity . . . to KENNEDY and his failure to assure the proper training of . . . bridge team members." The convening authority, CINCUSNAVEUR, also determined that the Commanding Officer was responsible for the collision and approved the investigating officer's recommendation that a punitive letter of reprimand be issued. A punitive letter of reprimand was awarded to the Commanding Officer by CINCUSNAVEUR on 2 January 1976 for failing to secure a clear description of the Officer of the Deck's plan for the maneuver prior to its execution, for failure to assure himself that the Officer of the Deck understood the maneuvering requirements which should have been anticipated, and for failing to ensure that only adequately trained and competent personnel were permitted to assume positions of responsibility on BELKNAP's bridge team.

The investigating officer recommended that BELKNAP's Officer of the Deck be referred for trial by general court-martial for his failure to keep himself informed of the tactical situation, his failure to take appropriate action to avoid collision in accordance with the International Rules of the Road and accepted Navy doctrine, and his failure to make required reports to the Commanding Officer. CINCUSNAVEUR approved that recommendation and forwarded a charge sheet to COMNAVSURFLANT alleging violations of Article 92, UCMJ (disobedience of OPNAV Instructions and BELKNAP Standing Orders), Article 108, UCMJ (suffering the two ships to be damaged through neglect), Article 110, UCMJ (suffering the two ships to be hazarded through neglect) and Article 119, UCMJ (manslaughter).

Court-Martial of Belknap's Commanding Officer

Notwithstanding the prior imposition of a punitive letter of reprimand on the Commanding Officer of BELKNAP as non-judicial punishment by CINCUSNAVEUR, COMNAVSURFLANT caused an Article 32, UCMJ, pretrial investigation to be conducted to inquire into the Commanding Officer's role in the collision. The pretrial investigating officer recommended that the Commanding Officer be tried by general court-martial on two specifications of violation of Navy Regulations and three specifications of dereliction of duty, all in violation of Article 92, UCMJ; one specification of suffering damage to BELKNAP and KENNEDY through neglect, in violation of Article 108, UCMJ, and one specification of suffering the two ships to be hazarded through neglect, in violation of Article 110, UCMJ.

COMNAVSURFLANT concurred in that recommendation and forwarded the sworn charges to CINCLANTFLT for consideration. On 12 March 1976, CINCLANTFLT referred the charges to trial by general court-martial.

At his request, the accused, Commanding Officer, USS BELKNAP, was tried by military judge alone. During the course of the trial that ensued, the two specifications alleging violation of Article 0702, U.S. Navy Regulations, were dismissed by the military judge on the ground that Article 0702 constitutes a guideline for performance and not an order to be enforced with criminal sanctions. Two specifications alleging that the Commanding Officer was derelict in his duty by failing to ascertain the specific maneuvers contemplated by the Officer of the Deck and by failing to ensure that only adequately trained personnel were permitted to assume responsible positions on the bridge watch were dismissed by the military judge on the ground that the Commanding Officer had previously been punished for those offenses by virtue of the punitive letter of reprimand imposed upon him by CINCUSNAVEUR. One specification alleging that the Commanding Officer was derelict in his duty in that he failed personally to supervise the Officer of the Deck during BELKNAP's maneuvering in close proximity to KENNEDY was dismissed by the military judge on the ground that it involved the same misconduct alleged under the charge of suffering the hazarding of the two vessels through neglect, and was therefore an undue multiplication of the charges.

As a result, the Commanding Officer was arraigned on one specification alleging that through neglect he suffered the two ships to be damaged by failing to personally supervise and instruct his OOD and JOOD and by failing to post a fully qualified bridge watch section, in violation of Article 108, UCMJ, and one specification of negligently suffering the two ships to be hazarded, also by his failure to provide personal supervision and training to his OOD and JOOD and by his failure to post a fully qualified bridge watch section. The Commanding Officer entered pleas of Not Guilty to these remaining charges and specifications. On 12 May 1976, following two days of testimony from eighteen Government witnesses, the military judge granted a defense motion for findings of Not Guilty as to both charges and their specifications on the ground that testimony of the witnesses failed to establish that the bridge watch was improperly qualified or that the Commanding Officer was negligent in not personally supervising and instructing his OOD and JOOD, and, therefore, that the evidence of record failed to establish a prima facie case that the Commanding Officer was criminally negligent as alleged.

Court-Martial of Belknap's Officer of the Deck

Pursuant to the recommendations of the JAG MANUAL investigating officer, of CINCUSNAVEUR and of COMNAVSURFLANT, CINCLANTFLT referred the charges against the Officer of the Deck of BELKNAP to trial by general court-martial on one specification of failure to obey OPNAV Instruction 3120.32 by failing to keep fully informed of the tactical situation and to take appropriate action to avoid the collision, failing to issue necessary orders to the BELKNAP's helm and main engine control to avoid danger, and failing to make required reports to the Commanding Officer, and one specification of failure to obey BELKNAP Standing Orders to notify the Commanding Officer of a major course change order by the Officer in Tactical Command, both in violation of Article 92, UCMJ; one specification of suffering damage to the two ships through neglect, in violation of Article 108, UCMJ; and one specification of suffering the two ships to be hazarded through neglect, in violation of Article 110, UCMJ. At his request, the Officer of the Deck was also tried by military judge alone and entered pleas of Not Guilty to the offenses charged. The military judge found the accused Not Guilty of the specification alleging failure to obey BELKNAP's Standing Orders but found him Guilty of the remaining charges and specifications. Subsequent to presentation of matters in mitigation and extenuation, the military judge elected not to impose punishment on the accused on the ground that, under the circumstances, the conviction by general court-martial itself constituted an adequate and appropriate punishment.

Trial by Military Judge Alone

An additional misunderstanding of military justice which came to light in the aftermath of the BELKNAP courts-martial involves the concept of trial by military judge alone. As you are undoubtedly aware, every accused in a non-capital case tried by general court-martial or by a special court-martial presided over by a military judge has the unqualified right to request trial by judge alone. The military judge's ruling on such a request is final. This provision for trial by military judge alone is modeled after Rule 23(a) of the Federal Rules of Criminal Procedure. Unlike the Federal Rule, however, Article 16 of the UCMJ makes the accused's right to waive trial by court members independent of the consent of the Government. The Senate Report on the proposed legislation which ultimately became the Military Justice Act of 1968, makes it clear that this difference was generated by Congressional concern over the spectre of unlawful command influence. Consequently, the election of the accused in the BELKNAP cases to exercise their right to trial by military judge alone and the granting of that request by the military judges in those two cases, was entirely proper under the law.

In any event, it would be well to remember that the concept of an independent judiciary is as essential to the administration of military justice as is the concept of command responsibility to fleet operations. Moreover, these two concepts are as compatible as they are essential. Strict adherence to one does no violence to the other.

Appendix XI

Sample Internal Supply Management Report

An example of a supply management report designed to present to the commanding officer a summary of the ship's supply status. This form can be modified to suit the individual characteristics and needs of each ship.

INTERNAL SUPPLY MANAGEMENT REPORT

MEMORANDUM

From: Supply Officer
To: Commanding Officer
Via: Executive Officer
Subj: Supply Data Report for the period _____ through ___

Encl: (1) List of Outstanding IG One Requisitions and Outstanding "Hot List" Requisitions
       (2) Weekly Medical Department Representative (MDR) Sanitation Inspection Report

PART I STORES DIVISION

1. Supply effectiveness.

	#this period	#this FY	%this FY	TYCOM GOAL
a. Repair Part Demands	___	___	N/A	N/A
b. SIM Issues	___	___	___	___

c. Not _____ _____ _____ _____
   Carried
   Demands
d. Not in _____ _____ _____ _____
   Stock
   Demands
e. SIM Not _____ _____ _____ _____
   in Stock
   Demands

2. Number of uncompleted COSAL maintenance action items. __
Explanation: _____

3. Number of defective MTR carcasses awaiting turn-in (Exclusive of Advise Code 5S Requirements): _____
Explanation: _____

4. Number of allowance items with zero balance.
    SIM _____ USAGE _____ Q-COSAL _____
OTHER _____
Explanation: _____

5. Additional information on outstanding IG One and/or "Hot List" requisitions in enclosure (1): _____
_____

6. Requisition Control.
    a. Number of outstanding requisitions: _____
    b. Number of outstanding requisitions over 90 days old: _____
    c. Number of unordered stock deficiencies: _____
    d. Requisition Priority Breakdown.

	#this period	%this period	#this FY	*%this FY
IG One	_____	_____	_____	_____
IG Two	_____	_____	_____	_____
IG Three	_____	_____	_____	_____

7. Financial Control.
   a. Total OPTAR granted this period/fiscal year:$_____ /
      $_____
   b. Obligations:
      (1) Total dollar value obligated to date: $_____ /
      (2) % OPTAR obligated: _____ %
      (3) Repair Part Obligations: $_____   OPTAR Target
          $/%: $_____ / _____ %
      (4) Consumable Obligations: $_____   OPTAR Target
          $/%: $_____ / _____ %
      (5) OPTAR balance: $_____
   c. Date of latest reconciliation with accounting activity
   (Report 21): _____
8. Additional remarks: _____
_____
_____
_____

PART II FOOD SERVICE DIVISION
1. Value over/under issue in Enlisted Dining Facility: _____
2. Rations allowed/fed: _____
3. Date of last inventory: _____
4. Date of last "spot" inventory: _____
5. Endurance load (days) on board: _____
6. Date of last Food Service Returns Submission/Next
   Returns due: _____ / _____
7. Date of last Food Service Officer sanitation inspection:_____

                              _____
                              Supply Officer

Appendix XII

Admiral Nimitz on Storm Damage

Excerpts from Fleet Admiral C. W. Nimitz's letter on typhoon damage.

13 February 1945

From: Commander in Chief, U.S. Pacific Fleet
To: Pacific Fleet and Naval Shore Activities, Pacific Ocean Areas
Subj: Damage in Typhoon; Lessons of

1. On 18 December 1944, vessels of the Pacific Fleet, operating in support of the invasion of the Philippines in an area about 300 miles east of Luzon, were caught near the center of a typhoon of extreme violence. Three destroyers, the HULL, MONAGHAN, and SPENCE, capsized and went down with practically all hands; serious damage was sustained by the CL MIAMI, the CVL'S MONTEREY, COWPENS, and SAN JACINTO, the CVE'S CAPE ESPERANCE and ALTAMAHA, and the DD'S AYLWIN, DEWEY, and HICKOX. Lesser damage was sustained by at least 19 other vessels from CA's down to DE's. Fires occurred on three carriers when planes were smashed in their hangars, and some 146 planes on various ships were lost or damaged beyond economical repair by the fires, by being smashed up, or by being swept overboard. About 790 officers and men were lost or killed, and 80 were injured. Several surviving destroyers reported rolling 70° or more, and we can only surmise how close this was to capsizing completely for some of them. It was the greatest loss that we have

taken in the Pacific without compensatory return since the First Battle of Savo.

2. In the light of hindsight it is easy to see how any of several measures might have prevented this catastrophe, but it was far less easy a problem at the time for the men who were out there under the heaviest of conflicting responsibilities. The important thing is for it never to happen again, and hence, while it is impracticable herein to go into all the factors involved and the experiences undergone, some of the outstanding lessons will be discussed.

3. Possibly, too much reliance was placed on the analysis broadcast from the Fleet Weather Central, Pearl Harbor. Weather data were lacking from an area some 240 to 300 miles in diameter (where the storm was actually centered); and the immediate signs of it in the operating area were not heeded early enough. Groups of the Third Fleet tried to avoid the storm center, but neither radically enough nor to best advantage, since their information as to its location and path was meager. Fleet damage and losses were accentuated by the efforts of vessels and subordinate commanders to maintain fleet courses, speeds, and formations during the storm. Commanding officers failed to realize sufficiently in advance of the fact that it was necessary for them to give up the attempt, and give all their attention to saving their ships. There was a lack of appreciation by subordinate commanders and commanding officers that really dangerous weather conditions existed, until it was too late to make the preparations for security that might have been helpful.

4. The following conditions were typical during the typhoon:

    a. Visibility zero to a thousand yards.

    b. Ships not merely rolling, but heeled far over continually by the force of the wind, thus leaving them very little margin for further rolling to leeward.

    c. Water being taken in quantity through ventilators, blower intakes, and every topside opening.

    d. Switchboards and electrical machinery of all kinds shorted and drowned out, with fires from short circuits. Main distribution board in engine room shorted by steam moisture when topside openings were closed to keep out water.

e. Free water up to two or three feet over engines or fireroom floor plates, and in many other compartments. It apparently all came in from above; there is no evidence of ships' seams parting.

f. Loss of steering control, failure of power and lighting and stoppage of main propulsion plant. Loss of radar and of all ability to communicate.

g. Planes on carriers going adrift, crashing into each other and starting fires.

h. Wind velocities and seas that carried away masts, stacks, boats, davits, and deck structures generally, and made it impossible for men to secure gear that had gone adrift, or to jettison or strike below topside weights when necessity had become apparent. Men could not even stay up where they would have a chance of getting clear of the ship.

i. Maneuvering up to the time of sinking, in the attempt to maintain station, by all ships that were lost. DEWEY, saved by apparently a narrow margin, had given up the attempt.

j. The storm "taking charge" and making impossible various evasive and security measures which might have been effective at an earlier stage.

k. Testimony that the ships lost took a long roll to leeward, varying from 50° to 80°, hung there a little while, and then went completely over, floating a short time before going down.

. . .

7. Various weaknesses were brought to light in our forecasting and dissemination of weather information, in structural details which permitted flooding with consequent loss of power, short circuiting, etc. and in the stability of some of our destroyers. Measures to correct these faults are being taken as far as possible. Yet the Commander in Chief, Pacific Fleet wishes to emphasize that to insure safety at sea, the best that science can devise and that naval organization can provide must be regarded only as an aid, and never as a substitute for good seamanship, self-reliance and sense of ultimate

Note: Paragraphs 5, 6, 16, 17 omitted.

responsibility which are the first requisites in a seaman and naval officer.

8. A hundred years ago, a ship's survival depended almost solely on the competence of her master and on his constant alertness to every hint of change in the weather. To be taken aback or caught with full sail by even a passing squall might mean the loss of spars or canvas; and to come close to the center of a genuine hurricane or typhoon was synonymous with disaster. While to be taken by surprise was thus serious, the facilities for avoiding it were meager. Each master was dependent wholly on himself for detecting the first symptoms of bad weather, for predicting its seriousness and movement, and for taking appropriate measures to evade, if possible, and to battle through it if it passed near to him. There was no radio by which weather data could be collected from over all the oceans and the resulting forecasts by expert aerologists broadcast to him and to all afloat. There was no one to tell him that the time had come to strike his light sails and spars, and snug her down under close reefs or storm trysails. His own barometer, the force and direction of the wind, and the appearance of sea and sky were all that he had for information. Ceaseless vigilance in watching and interpreting signs, plus a philosophy of taking no risk in which there was little to gain and much to be lost, was what enabled him to survive.

9. Seamen of the present day should be better at forecasting weather at sea, independently of the radio, than were their predecessors. The general laws of storms and the weather expectancy for all months of the year in all parts of the world are now more thoroughly understood, more completely catalogued, and more readily available in various publications. An intensive study of typhoon and Western Pacific weather was made over a period of many years by Father Depperman at the Manila observatory, and his conclusions have been embodied in the material available to all aerologists. What Knight and Bowditch have to say on the subject is exactly as true during this war as it was in time of peace or before the days of radio. Familiarity with these authorities is something no captain or navigator can do without. The monthly pilot charts, issued to all ships, give

excellent information as to the probable incidence and movement of typhoons. Stress on the foregoing is no belittlement of our aerological centers and weather broadcasts. But just as a navigator is held culpable if he neglects "Log, Lead, and Lookout" through blind faith in his radio fixes, so is the seaman culpable who regards personal weather estimates as obsolete and assumes that if no radio storm warning has been received, then all is well, and no local weather sign need cause him concern.

10. It is possible that too much reliance is being placed on outside sources for warnings of dangerous weather, and on the ability of our splendid ships to come through anything that wind and wave can do. If this be so, there is need for a revival of the age-old habits of self-reliance and caution in regard to the hazards from storms, and for officers in all echelons of command to take their personal responsibilities in this respect more seriously.

11. The most difficult part of the whole heavy-weather problem is, of course, the conflict between the military necessity for carrying out an operation as scheduled, and the possibility of damage or loss to our ships in doing so. For this no possible rule can be laid down. The decision must be a matter of "calculated risk" either way. It should be kept in mind, however, that a ship which founders or is badly damaged is a dead loss not only to the current operation but to future ones, that the weather which hinders us may be hindering the enemy equally, and the ships which, to prevent probable damage and possible loss, are allowed to drop behind, or to maneuver independently, may by the very measure be able to rejoin later and be of use in the operation.

12. The safety of a ship against perils from storm, as well as from those of navigation and maneuvering, is always the primary responsibility of her commanding officer; but this responsibility is also shared by his immediate superiors in operational command since by the very fact of such command the individual commanding officer is not free to do at any time what his own judgment might indicate. Obviously no rational captain will permit his ship to be lost fruitlessly through blind obedience to plan or order, since by no chance could that be the intention of his superior. But the degree of a ship's danger

is progressive and at the same time indefinite. It is one thing for a commanding officer, acting independently in time of peace, to pick a course and speed which may save him a beating from the weather, and quite another for him, in time of war, to disregard his mission and his orders and leave his station and duty.

13. It is here that the responsibility rests on unit, group, and force commanders, and that their judgment and authority must be exercised. They are, of course, the ones best qualified to weigh the situation and the relative urgency of safety measures versus carrying on with the job in hand. They frequently guard circuits or possess weather codes not available to all ships; and it goes without saying that any storm warnings or important weather information which they are not sure everybody has received should be transmitted as far as practicable. More than this, they must be conscious of the relative inexperience in seamanship, and particularly hurricane seamanship, of many of their commanding officers, despite their superb fighting qualities. One division commander reports that his captains averaged eight years or less out of the Naval Academy and this is probably typical.

14. It is most definitely part of the senior officer's responsibility to think in terms of the smallest ship and most inexperienced commanding officer under him. He cannot take them for granted, give them tasks and stations, and assume either that they will be able to keep up and come through any weather that his own big ship can, or that they will be wise enough to gauge the exact moment when their task must be abandoned in order for them to keep afloat. The order for ships to be handled and navigated wholly for their own preservation should be originated early enough by the seniors, and not necessarily be withheld until the juniors request it. The very gallantry and determination of our young commanding officers need to be taken into account here as a danger factor, since their urge to keep on, to keep up, to keep station, and to carry out their mission in the face of any difficulty, may deter them from doing what is actually wisest and most profitable in the long run.

15. Yet, if the OTC is to be held responsible for his smaller vessels, he must be kept aware of their conditions, and the onus of this rests

on the commanding officers themselves. Each of them must not only do whatever he is free and able to do for his ship's safety but must also keep his superiors in the chain of command fully informed as to his situation. If there is anything in his ship's particular condition or in the way she is taking the weather that worries him, he should not hesitate to pass the information to his seniors. To let this be regarded as a sign of faintheartedness is to invite disaster, and seniors should indoctrinate their commanding officers accordingly. Going still further, it has been shown that at sea the severity of the weather may develop to a point where, regardless of combat commitments of the high command, the situation will require independent action by a junior without reference to his senior. This becomes mandatory if grave doubts arise in the mind of the junior as to the safety of his vessel, the lives of crew, and the loss of valuable government property and equipment.

. . .

18. In conclusion, both seniors and juniors must realize that in bad weather, as in most other situations, safety and fatal hazards are not separated by any sharp boundary line, but shade gradually one into the other. There is no little red light which is going to flash on and inform commanding officers or higher commanders that from then on there is extreme danger from the weather, and that measures for ship's safety must now take precedence over further efforts to keep up with the formation or to execute the assigned task. This time will always be a matter of personal judgment. Naturally, no commander is going to cut thin the margin between staying afloat and foundering, but he may, nevertheless, unwittingly pass the danger point even though no ship is yet *in extremis*. Ships that keep on going as long as the severity of wind and sea has not yet come close to capsizing them or breaking them in two, may nevertheless become helpless to avoid these catastrophes later if things get worse. By then they may be unable to steer any heading but in the trough of the sea, or may have their steering control, lighting, communications, and main propulsion disabled, or may be helpless to secure things on deck or to jettison topside weights. The time for taking all measures for a ship's

safety is while still able to do so. Nothing is more dangerous than for a seaman to be grudging in taking precautions lest they turn out to have been unnecessary. Safety at sea for a thousand years has depended on exactly the opposite philosophy.

Signed C. W. NIMITZ

Appendix XIII

Sample Listing of Items to Look for When Inspecting

a. Mechanical Joints
 (1) Check for corrosion deposits.
 (2) Check for damaged threads.
 (3) Loose connections? Check all connections and bolts for tightness.
 (4) Are there any bent or unevenly loaded studs?
 (5) Do all gaskets appear to be properly sized?
 (6) Are any leaks apparent? Use a mirror or other shiny surface to check for steam leaks around packing glands.
 (7) Are there any seals broken, lock wires broken?
 (8) Are tags installed, labeled properly, readable to the watchstander?
 (9) Do bolts on flanges have the proper number of threads showing?
 (10) Are locking devices properly engaged?
 (11) Are closure bolts installed (especially door and drawer bolts on captive bolts as applicable).
 (12) Are valve caps installed and spare "O" rings available as required?
 (13) Are valve handwheels proper size, shape, style, color, and correctly attached?
 (14) Are valves installed in correct orientation in accordance with and as denoted by bridge wall markings?

    (15) Are correct style lock washers installed where required; lock devices such as pant leg washers used only where authorized by plan or technical manual and properly made up?

    (16) Are the chains attached to caps where required; special tool holders installed, such as for spanner wrenches on hose connections?

    (17) Are mechanical indicators visible and operation correct?

    (18) Are all required valve locks installed properly, labeled correctly, and functional?

    (19) Are orifice diameters identifiable without disassembly?

b. *Piping*

    (1) Is any of the piping arrangement such that a sound short exists? (Note especially piping that by-passes sound mounts.)

    (2) Is piping covered to protect against damage as applicable?

    (3) Are there any loose hangers?

    (4) Are hangers mounted with rubber inserts as required?

    (5) Are there enough hangers?

    (6) Is correct material installed (e.g., seawater systems must have non-corrosive material for piping, studs, and nuts)? (Brass, aluminum, and bronze not permitted.)

    (7) Is proper termination of drains slightly above funnels, no siphon connections, screens installed in funnels, funnel lines checked clear to bilge?

    (8) Is piping free of weld arc strikes (especially important on high pressure systems because arc strikes are stress raisers which could cause local failure of the pipe)?

    (9) Is piping clean with no tape, adhesives, or unauthorized paint?

c. *Cleanliness*

    (1) Are open pipes and hoses capped and taped shut?

    (2) Are funnels clean and covered?

    (3) Are funnel covers removable?

    (4) Are electrical panels clean and free of loose material?

    (5) Are all fuse holders covered over, or fused?

(6) Are pump and motor shafts clean?

(7) Is any component excessively dirty?

(8) Check for external and internal equipment cleanliness.

(9) Are sound mounts clean, no nicks or abrasions or paint?

(10) Are packing glands clean, free of paint, properly bolted down (proper bolts), square with valve bonnet and the valve stems clean, free of paint, packing installed?

(11) Are sight glasses clean and of proper material?

(12) Are hatches and watertight doors clean; gear mechanism clean and lubricated?

(13) Are out of the way areas such as under switchboards, panels and under piping clean? (A flashlight and getting on hands and knees is necessary to perform this adequately.)

d. *Preservation and Maintenance*

(1) Are damaged and loose parts apparent?

(2) Are there any broken units or parts in the system? Check all gage lines, connections, meter faces, meter dials, panel switches, hinges, universal joints, gage glasses, sight glasses, wire leads, etc.

(3) Are sound mounts clean of oil or paint?

(4) Have meters and gages been calibrated?

(5) Is there any damaged or wetted lagging?

(6) Are there any loose joints or fittings?

(7) Are drains clear of obstructions? Do drains lead to funnels? Are drains properly labeled?

(8) Are tags readable?

(9) Are there any unevenly loaded sound mounts?

(10) Are hoses unstressed and straight?

(11) Are there any fire hazards in the system?

(12) Is there any indication that units have been greased as necessary?

(13) Is rotating machinery free to rotate? Check all shafts by hand.

(14) Are panels shut and tight?

(15) Are any loose wires noted?

(16) Do electrical units have ground straps attached where required?

(17) Are all color codes correct?

(18) Check stowage and labeling of special equipment (e.g. cross-connect hoses, sea chest blow hoses, etc.).

(19) Are valve labels correct?

(20) Are gages and indicating devices properly calibrated and current sticker affixed?

(21) Are grease lines connected as labeled? Have they been checked for proper operation by one man greasing labeled joint and second man on phones verifying grease out at correct joint?

e. *Operational Aspects of a System*

(1) Are relief valves properly set? Check your print and the information stamped on the nameplate.

(2) Are all valves labeled properly and according to diagram print? Tags attached securely?

(3) Are all fuses in the system the proper size as called for in the prints?

(4) Are all name plates installed? Do all temperature indicators have tags?

(5) Is the system tagged out in accordance with the operational status?

(6) Are gages calibrated as required? (Check calibration sticker dates.)

(7) Are there proper clearances for sound mounted equipment (usually at least ¾″ clearance for equipment sound mounted with snubbers, at least 1″ clearance for equipment sound mounted without snubbers)?

(8) Is there proper lighting to provide for adequate and safe operation of equipment?

(9) Are required labels, safety precaution signs, etc., installed in accordance with the plan and legible (e.g., valves, controllers, flow arrows, system marking on pipe or pipe lagging)?

(10) Are proper radiation markers installed?

(11) Is equipment located behind panels or recessed in lockers accessible, with locker or panel correctly labeled for item inside or behind?

(12) Are personnel protective guards installed (metal screens at blowdown stations, blowdown pots, etc.)?

(13) Are safety precautions posted as appropriate and as called for by plan?

(14) Do all deck hatches have grab rails, safety chains, or safety guard rails?

(15) Is there unobstructed ventilation flow to equipment?

f. *Cabling*

(1) Is cabling properly hung and strapped?

(2) Are there any frays or breaks in the armor?

(3) Are cables marked properly?

(4) Are ground straps installed when required?

(5) Are electrical switchboards properly drip proofed (gaskets properly installed)?

(6) Are stuffing tubes made up properly, correct size and material, armor cut back from stuffing tube as required?

(7) Is wire marking correct?

(8) Are ground straps installed and with length sufficient not to break under maximum movement of equipment by shock? Is ground strap of proper material (braided or solid) as required by plan?

(9) Is cable armor intact, no evidence of cable being burned or overheated, no in-line splices of cables? Are cables properly labeled with bands?

Bibliography

Ageton, A.A., and Mack, W.P. *The Naval Officer's Guide*, 8th ed. Annapolis: Naval Institute Press, 1970.

Albrecht, A. *Weyer's Warships of the World*. Annapolis: Naval Institute Press, 1980.

Buell, Thomas B. *Master of Sea Power*. Boston: Little Brown and Co., and Annapolis: Naval Institute Press, 1980.

Buell, Thomas B. *The Quiet Warrior*. Boston-Toronto: Little Brown and Co., and Annapolis: Naval Institute Press, 1974.

Churchill, Winston. *The Second World War*. Boston: Houghton Mifflin, 1953.

Collins, J.M. *Grand Strategy*. Annapolis: Naval Institute Press, 1973.

Couhat, J.L., *Combat Fleets of the World*. Annapolis: Naval Institute Press. Bi-annual.

Crenshaw, R.S., Jr. *Naval Shiphandling*, 4th ed. Annapolis: Naval Institute Press, 1975.

Deutermann, P.T. *The Ops Officer's Manual*. Annapolis: Naval Institute Press, 1980.

Felger, D.G. *Engineering for the Officer of the Deck*. Annapolis: Naval Institute Press, 1979.

Hart, Lidell. *Thoughts of War*. London: Faber and Faber, Ltd., 1944.

Hunter, W.J. *Challenge; a Professional Anthology*. Annapolis: Naval Institute Press, 1970.

Jane, F.T., *Jane's Fighting Ships*. New York: Arco Publishing House and London: Paulton House. Annual.

Joliff, J.V., and Robertson, H.E. *Naval Engineer's Guide*. Annapolis: Naval Institute Press, 1972.

Kotsch, W.J. *Heavy Weather Guide*. Annapolis: Naval Institute Press, 1965.

Kotsch, W.J. *Weather for the Mariner*, 2nd ed. Annapolis: Naval Institute Press, 1977.

Lewis, C.L. *David Glasgow Farragut*. Annapolis: Naval Institute Press, 1941.

Mack, W.P., and Connell, R. *Naval Ceremonies, Customs, and Traditions*, 5th ed. Annapolis: Naval Institute Press, 1980.

Moran, Lord. *The Anatomy of Courage*. London: Constable, 1945.

Noel, J.V., Jr. *Division Officer's Guide*, 8th ed. Annapolis: Naval Institute Press, 1982.

Potter, E.B. *Nimitz*. Annapolis: Naval Institute Press, 1976.

Roskill, R.N. *The Art of Leadership*. London: Collins, 1964.

Winters, D.D. *The Boat Officer's Handbook*. Annapolis: Naval Institue Press, 1981.

Wolfe, M. et al. *Naval Leadership*. Annapolis: Naval Institute Press, 1959.

U.S. Government Publications.

U.S. Navy Regulations, 1973.

Bureau of Naval Personnel Manual.

Standard Organization and Regulations of the U.S. Navy.

Standard Submarine Organization and Regulations Manual, U.S. Atlantic Fleet.

The Judge Advocate's Manual.

Manual of the Medical Department.

Decedent Affairs Manual.

Naval Warfare Publications Guide, NWP 0

Strategic Concepts of the U.S. Navy, NWP 1

Organization of the U.S. Navy, NWP 2

Operational Reports, NWP 7

Law of Naval Warfare, NWP 10–2

Replenishment at Sea, NWP 14

Striking Force Operations, NWP 20

Doctrine for Amphibious Operations, NWP 22

Submarine Missions, NWP 23–1

Mining Operations, NWP 26

Nuclear Warfare Operations, NWP 28

Fast Patrol Boat Operations, NWIP 29–2

Electronic Warfare, NWP 33

Armed Forces Doctrine for Chemical Warfare and Biological Defense, NWP 36

National Search and Rescue Manual, NWP 37

Index